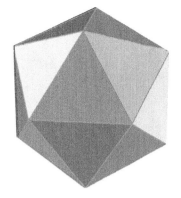

ADVANCED ACT MATH

Developed by
Joseph Hammerman

Table of contents

1. Introduction

It is recommended that students who are not at top score levels start with the Common Problems section, which is relatively easy, but extremely important to success on the exam. The Study Guide section is also more accessible to a wide range of students. The main part of the book, with problems by topic, focuses on the most difficult types are problems which may appear on the exam, so it should be more challenging.

As a tutor, I found that there was a lack of good materials for students looking for top scores on standardized exams. Most books try to imitate real exams. There are books that are a little more difficult than real exams. However, when working with students going for good scores, I had to assign a large amount of problems and often just the last parts of several tests to get enough missed problems to go over in a lesson.

Most ACT and SAT books are very similar. Those books contain imitation exams, which are generally not as useful as real exams, and they explain the basics of the material on the exam. What this book does is very different. It contains problems designed to be more challenging than real problems and more helpful in preparing the student to get a top score.

There were 3 books that contained are really difficult problems for the old pre–2016 SAT. I worked through all of those books and used them with students. However, to my knowledge no one has attempted to produce anything similar for the current version of the SAT or the ACT. Particularly for the math ACT, there are to my knowledge no competing advanced workbooks available.

This book concentrates on the hardest material on the exam. I also made problems similar to those on the exam, but made them harder in various ways. This is designed to ensure the student has the skills for similar problems and is prepared for any more difficult problems on future exams.

While this book does not try to imitate real exams in difficulty, it tries to keep the material as realistic as possible. Every problem is designed to test skills needed for the exam.

This book is fairly long and comprehensive. The math ACT includes a wider variety of topics than other standardized exams. Almost every topic and type of problem that might be on the exam is included. The cover says "a must have", and this book should give you a major advantage if you are going for a top score.

My first book, published in September 2020, is the "Ultimate Advanced Guide to the Math SAT 2 Subject Test". Unfortunately, subject tests have been discontinued effective immediately. The subject test book had generally more difficult problems than this book and emphasized more multiple solutions to the same problem, as was appropriate to the nature of that exam. This book includes a wider variety of topics, as almost anything in high school math excluding calculus can be on the ACT.

Not many high school students will be able to work through this book without missing many problems. However, this book is more practical than the super challenging books for the old math SAT.

While the emphasis is strongly on what is likely to be on the test, this book has value purely as a math book, containing fairly difficult problems covering most of high school math.

Although I would have preferred consistency, I changed the title of this book from the SAT 2 book to be more accurately reflect its contents. There are lots of books called ultimate etc. The emphasis is now on "advanced", and this book concentrates on advanced topics much more than any other.

The problems in this book are generally more difficult than real problems, so these problems should not be used to determine your projected score. These problems should also not be worked timed. However, you should take some real or realistic practice tests timed.

While this book can be used to make major improvements, and students have gotten perfect scores using my previous book and my tutoring, this book does not promise to help to improve to your score or to improve to any particular score.

This book is in the range that a student at just an above average level can learn from and may be better for some students at that level than other books. However, this book is not recommended for students with a current math ACT score of 23 or below. It concentrates on the most challenging material, and there are many books available that explain the basics.

The emphasis in this book is on the mathematics. However, this book also discusses test taking techniques such of plugging in answers, substituting a made up number for a variable and graphing with a calculator.

2. ACT Math Formula Sheet

Percentages

To find 23% of 70, take $.23 \times 70$. 23 is what percent of 70? $\dfrac{23}{70} \times 100$.

23 is 70% of what? $23 = .7x$, $\quad \dfrac{23}{.7} = x$.

A 10% increase followed by a 20% increase is $\big((1.1 \times 1.2) - 1\big) \times 100 = 32\%$.

Miscellaneous

distance $=$ rate $*$ time

Contrapositive: "All tables are flat" is the same as "If it is not a flat, it is not a table".

Switch them and make them both not, and it is the same thing. Triangle inequality: if two sides have length a and b, the other side c is in a range such that $|a - b| < c < a + b$.

A $30 - 60 - 90$ triangle has side lengths $1 - \sqrt{3} - 2$.

A $45 - 45 - 90$ triangle has side lengths $1 - 1 - \sqrt{2}$.

Lines and Slope

Midpoint formula: $\left(\dfrac{x_1 + x_2}{2}, \dfrac{y_1 + y_2}{2} \right)$.

Slope formula: $\dfrac{y_1 - y_2}{x_1 - x_2}$.

Distance formula: $\sqrt{(x_1 - x_2)^2 + (y_1 - y_2)^2}$;

If two lines are perpendicular, their slopes are negative reciprocals.

Given a point (x_1, y_1) and a slope m, the equation of the line is $y - y_1 = m(x - x_1)$.

Alternatively, you can use $y_1 = mx_1 + b$, and solve for b.

Slope of line in form $ax + by = c$ is $-\dfrac{a}{b}$.

In slope intercept form:

$$by = -ax + c \rightarrow y = \left(-\dfrac{a}{b}\right)x + \dfrac{c}{b}$$

Area and Volume

Volume of a box: lwh.   Volume of a cube: s^3.

Surface area of a box: $2(lw + lh + wh)$.

Surface area of a cube: $6s^2$.

Diagonal of a box: $\sqrt{l^2 + w^2 + h^2}$.

Diagonal of a cube: s^3.

If a cube is inscribed in a sphere, the diagonal of the cube $=$ the diameter of the sphere.

Volume of a cone: $\dfrac{\pi r^2 h}{3}$.

Volume of a sphere: $\dfrac{4\pi r^3}{3}$.

Surface area of a sphere: $4\pi r^2$.

Surface area of a cylinder: $2\pi r^2 + 2\pi r h$.

Area of an equilateral triangle: $\dfrac{\sqrt{3}s^2}{4}$.

Area of a parallelogram: bh.

Area of a trapezoid: $\dfrac{(b_1 + b_2)h}{2}$.

The diagonals of a rhombus are perpendicular.

Perimeter of a rectangle $2l + 2w$.

Circumference of circle $2\pi r$.

Area of a circle πr^2.

Volume of cylinder $\pi r^2 h$.

Surface area of cylinder $2\pi r^2 + 2\pi r h$.

Rhombus area formula $\dfrac{d_1 d_2}{2}$.

Sum of interior angles of polygon $180°(n - 2)$.

15

Algebra

The sum of the roots of a quadratic: $-\dfrac{b}{a}$.

The quadratic formula $\dfrac{-b \pm \sqrt{b^2 - 4ac}}{2a}$.

x-coordinate of the vertex of a parabola $\dfrac{-b}{2a}$.

$y = (x - a)^2 + b$ is a parabola in vertex form. Its vertex is (a, b).

To find the equation of a quadratic given x-intercepts a and b, take $y = (x - a)(x - b)$ and FOIL it out.

Sum and difference of cubes formulas:
$a^3 + b^3 = (a + b)(a^2 - ab + b^2)$,
$a^3 - b^3 = (a - b)(a^2 + ab + b^2)$

Trigonometry

$\cot = \dfrac{1}{\tan}, \quad \csc = \dfrac{1}{\sin}, \quad \sec = \dfrac{1}{\cos}$,

$\sin = \dfrac{\text{opp}}{\text{hyp}}, \quad \cos = \dfrac{\text{adj}}{\text{hyp}}, \quad \tan = \dfrac{\text{opp}}{\text{adj}}$

Radians to degrees: $\dfrac{180°}{\pi}$;

degrees to radians: $\dfrac{\pi}{180°}$.

law of sines: $\dfrac{\sin A}{a} = \dfrac{\sin B}{b} = \dfrac{\sin C}{c}$

law of cosines: $c^2 = a^2 + b^2 - 2ab \cos C$

or $\cos C = \dfrac{a^2 + b^2 - c^2}{2ab}$.

$\sin^2 x + \cos^2 x = 1, \quad \sin^2 x = 1 - \cos^2 x$,

$\cos^2 x = 1 - \sin^2 x. \quad \tan^2 x + 1 = \sec^2 x$,

$1 + \csc^2 x = \cot^2 x, \quad \sec^2 x - \tan^2 x = 1$.

$\sin 2x = 2 \sin x \cos x$

$\cos 2x = \cos^2 x - \sin^2 x = 2 \cos^2 x - 1 = 1 - 2 \sin^2 x$.

$\sin 30° = \cos 60° = \dfrac{1}{2}, \quad \sin 60° = \cos 30° = \sqrt{3}/2$,

and $\sin 45° = \cos 45° = \dfrac{\sqrt{2}}{2}$,

$\tan 30° = \sqrt{3}/3 \quad$ and $\quad \tan 60° = \sqrt{3}$.

The trigonometric area formula is

$\text{area} = \dfrac{bc \sin A}{2}$

In the function $y = a \sin bx$, $|a|$ is the amplitude and $\dfrac{2\pi}{b}$ is the period.

Logarithms and Circles

$\log ab = \log a + \log b, \quad \log \dfrac{a}{b} = \log a - \log b,$

$\log a^b = b \log a$

$\text{arc length} = 2\pi r \dfrac{\theta}{360}, \quad \text{area of pie slice} = \pi r^2 \dfrac{\theta}{360}.$

Circle with center (x_1, y_1) and radius r is
$(x - x_1)^2 + (y - y_1)^2 = r^2.$

Combinations and Permutations / Sequences and Series

Factorial: $n! = n(n-1)(n-2)\ldots 1$.

Combinations: pick k of n: $\dfrac{n!}{k!(n-k)!}$.

Permutations: $\dfrac{n!}{(n-k)!}$.

The number of permutations of the letters in `MISSISSIPPI` is $\dfrac{11!}{(4! * 4! * 2!)}$.

A sum of arithmetic series formula is

$a_1 + a_2 + \cdots + a_n$ equals $\dfrac{(a_1 + a_n) \times n}{2}$.

The sum of an infinite geometric series:

$a_1 + a_2 + \cdots = \dfrac{a_1}{(1 - r)}.$

Interest and Depreciation

for depreciation, $A = P(1 - r)^t$;

for interest compounded annually, use $A = P(1 + r)^t$;

for interest compounded more frequently than annually, use $A = P\left(1 + \dfrac{r}{n}\right)^{nt}$;

for continuous interest, use $A = Pe^{rt}$;

Reflections and Rotations

Rotating $90°$ clockwise, $(a, b) \to (-b, a)$,

Rotating $90°$ counterclockwise, $(a, b) \to (b, -a)$,

rotating $180°$ $(a, b) \to (-b, -a)$.

Reflecting about the x-axis, $(a, b) \to (a, -b)$, about the y-axis, $(a, b) \to (-a, b)$.

If $y = x^2$ is moved 3 up and 5 to the right, the new equation is $y = (x - 5)^2 + 3$.

Similarly if the circle $x^2 + y^2 = 36$ is moved 3 up and 5 to the right,

the new equation is $(x - 5)^2 + (y - 3)^2 = 36$.

3. Factoring and Multiples

3.1. Prime Factorization

You can factor the numbers with a factoring tree. First, apply the following rules. Any even number is divisible by 2 and any number ending in 5 or 0 is divisible by 5. If the sum of the digits is divisible by 3, then the number is divisible by 3. Then check if the number is divisible by larger primes in increasing order: 7, 11, 13, 17, 19, etc. If the number remaining is less than the square of the smallest prime that has not been checked, that remaining number should be prime, and you do not need to continue the process. For the problems given here, it is possible to backsolve and multiply out the expressions in the answer choice, but you should also know how to solve the problems directly.

Factoring Tree

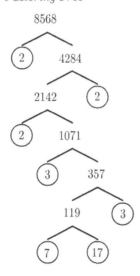

1. What is the prime factorization of 126? ②
   A. $2 \cdot 3 \cdot 7$
   B. $2 \cdot 3^2 \cdot 7$
   C. $2^2 \cdot 3^2 \cdot 7$
   D. $2 \cdot 3^4$
   E. $2 \cdot 3^3$

2. Which of these is the prime factorization of 63000? ②
   A. $2^4 \cdot 3^2 \cdot 5^3 \cdot 7$
   B. $2^4 \cdot 3^2 \cdot 5^2 \cdot 7$
   C. $2^3 \cdot 3^2 \cdot 5^3 \cdot 7$
   D. $2^5 \cdot 3^2 \cdot 5^2 \cdot 7$
   E. $2^3 \cdot 3^2 \cdot 5^2 \cdot 7^2$

3. Which of these is the prime factorization of 3564? ②
   A. $2^2 \cdot 3^4 \cdot 11$
   B. $2^3 \cdot 3^4 \cdot 11$
   C. $2^2 \cdot 3^2 \cdot 11^2$
   D. $2^4 \cdot 3^3 \cdot 11$
   E. $2^2 \cdot 3^3 \cdot 11$

17

3.2. Least Common Multiple

For least common multiple, take every factor that is in either, but do not count them more than once. You may be asked to find the least common denominator, which is basically the same problem.

For example, you could be asked to find the LCM of $60x^3y^2$ and $96xy^5$. Factored, those two expressions are $2^2 \cdot 3 \cdot 5x^3y^2$ and $2^5 \cdot 3xy^5$. Taking the highest power in either, the LCM is $2^5 \cdot 3 \cdot 5 \cdot x^3y^5 = 480x^3y^5$.

LCM problems may be asked in terms of how often 2 events occur simultaneously. For example, sign A flashes every 30 seconds and sign B flashes every 42 seconds. If the signs flash at the same time, how many seconds before they flash simultaneously again? Take the least common multiple, $30 = 2 \cdot 3 \cdot 5$ and $42 = 2 \cdot 3 \cdot 7$. Taking all factors in either, $2 \cdot 3 \cdot 5 \cdot 7 = 210$. Therefore, the answer is 210 seconds.

4. What is the least common multiple of 6 and 28? ③
   A. 42
   B. 84
   C. 2
   D. 126
   E. 168

5. Which of these is the least common multiple of 100, 110, and 120? ③
   A. 2200
   B. 3300
   C. 5500
   D. 6600
   E. 13200

6. What is the least common multiple of the numbers 1, 2, 3, 4, 5, 6, 7, and 8? ④
   A. 420
   B. 840
   C. 1260
   D. 1680
   E. 3360

7. What is the least common multiple of $2^3 \cdot 3^2 \cdot 5$, $2 \cdot 3^3 \cdot 11$, and $5^2 \cdot 13 \cdot 17$? ③
   A. $2^3 \cdot 3^3 \cdot 5 \cdot 11 \cdot 13 \cdot 17$
   B. $2^4 \cdot 3^4 \cdot 5^2 \cdot 11 \cdot 13 \cdot 17$
   C. $2^3 \cdot 3^3 \cdot 5^2 \cdot 11 \cdot 13 \cdot 17$
   D. $2^5 \cdot 3^3 \cdot 5^2 \cdot 11 \cdot 13 \cdot 17$
   E. $2^4 \cdot 3^3 \cdot 5^2 \cdot 11 \cdot 13 \cdot 17$

8. What is the least common multiple of 360 and 432? ④
   A. 1080
   B. 2160
   C. 3240
   D. 4320
   E. 8640

3.3. Greatest Common Divisor

Find the GCD of $60x^3y^2$ and $96xy^5$. Factored, those expressions are $2^2 \cdot 3 \cdot 5x^3y^2$ and $2^5 \cdot 3xy^5$. Taking the highest factors that are in both, $2^2 \cdot 3xy^2 = 12xy^2$.

9. For 12 and 21, what is the least common multiple divided by the greatest common divisor? ④
   A. 7
   B. 14
   C. 21
   D. 28
   E. 56

1B 2C, 3A, 4B, 5D, 6B, 7C, 8B, 9D

3.4. Solutions

1. (B) $2 \cdot 63 = 2 \cdot 3 \cdot 21 = 2 \cdot 3 \cdot 3 \cdot 7 = 2 \cdot 3^2 \cdot 7$.

2. (C) The number ends in 0s, so first take out factors of 10. $63 \cdot 1000 = 3^2 \cdot 7 \cdot 2^3 \cdot 5^3 = 2^3 \cdot 3^2 \cdot 5^3 \cdot 7$.

3. (A) Since the number is even, you can take out factors of 2. Since the digits add up to a multiple of 3, you can also take out factors of 3. $2 \cdot 1782 = 2^2 \cdot 891 = 2^2 \cdot 3^2 \cdot 99 = 2^2 \cdot 3^4 \cdot 11$.

4. (B) Prime factorization of 6 is $2 \cdot 3$; Prime factorization of 28 is $2 \cdot 2 \cdot 7$; Least common multiple is $2 \cdot 2 \cdot 3 \cdot 7 = 84$.

5. (D) Factor each of the numbers, and then take the greatest number of each factor in any. $100 = 2^2 \cdot 5^2$, $110 = 2 \cdot 5 \cdot 11$ and $120 = 2^3 \cdot 3 \cdot 5$. Finding the LCM, $2^3 \cdot 3 \cdot 5^2 \cdot 11 = 6600$.

6. (B) Prime factoring each number: $2, 3, 2^2, 5, 2 \cdot 3, 7, 2^3$. Taking every prime factor in any of the numbers, $2^3 \cdot 3 \cdot 5 \cdot 7 = 840$.

7. (C) Take every prime factor that is in any of the given expressions, taking the highest power in any.

8. (B) Prime factoring both numbers: $2^3 \cdot 3^2 \cdot 5$ and $2^4 \cdot 3^3$. Taking every prime factor in either number, $2^4 \cdot 3^3 \cdot 5 = 2160$.

9. (D) $12 = 2^2 \cdot 3$ and $21 = 3 \cdot 7$, so the GCD (everything that is in both multiplied) = 3 and LCM (everything that is in either multiplied) $= 2^2 \cdot 3 \cdot 7 = 84$; now we take LCM / GCD to get the answer: $\dfrac{84}{3} = 28$.

4. Averages

This chapter covers several types of interesting and challenging problems who might appear on the exam. You should get familiar with the basic and more difficult "what do you need on a test" problems, including those with variable expressions. It is also important to be able to find both the mean as a weighted average and the median from a frequency distribution.

4.1. Finding an Average

To find an average, apply the average formula, which means add up all the elements and divide by the number of elements. For example, what is the average of the squares of the first 4 positive integers?

$$\frac{1+4+9+16}{4} = \frac{30}{4} = \frac{15}{2}.$$

Some of the more difficult problems of this type involving taking the average of fractions. These can be accomplished by taking the least common denominator and adding the fractions as in elementary school. It is also possible to add with your calculator and compare with the decimal values corresponding to the answer choices.

1. What is the average of 8, 11, and 17? ②
   A. 11
   B. 11.3
   C. 11.7
   D. 12
   E. 12.3

2. What rational number is halfway between $\frac{3}{7}$ and $\frac{4}{5}$? ③
   A. $\frac{22}{35}$
   B. $\frac{2}{3}$
   C. $\frac{43}{70}$
   D. $\frac{41}{70}$
   E. $\frac{4}{7}$

3. What is the average of $\frac{1}{4}$, $\frac{1}{3}$, and $\frac{1}{2}$? ③
   A. $\frac{13}{36}$
   B. $\frac{10}{27}$
   C. $\frac{2}{5}$
   D. $\frac{25}{72}$
   E. $\frac{7}{24}$

4.2. What Do You Need on a Test?

You need to master basic "what do you need on the test" problems in order to handle the more difficult ones which may appear on the exam. The basic question states if you have an average of 77 on 4 tests, what do you need to score on the 5th test to get an average of 80 for all 5 tests? Take 77×4 to find your total score on the 4 tests. Then add that to the unknown score x to get the total score on all 5 tests. Then divide by 5 for the 5 tests and set that equal to the desired percentage. Total scores / number of tests = overall score.

$$\frac{77 \cdot 4 + x}{5} = 80 \implies 308 + x = 400 \implies x = 92.$$

There could be problems similar to that one on the exam, but more difficult and involving variable expressions: those are covered in the problems. You should be able to work these problems with either numerical or variable test scores. The problems with variable expressions can be fairly challenging, and you should practice those.

The basic equation for equally weighted tests takes

$$\frac{(\text{total points})}{(\text{number of tests})} = \text{average grade}.$$

The unknown could be a score on an additional test being taken or a low test score being dropped. However, the unknown can also be the final grade.

A more difficult question is Wilbert has a 67 average on n tests. What does he need on the $(n+1)^{th}$ test to average 70 for all $n + 1$ tests. His total score on the n tests is the average times the number of tests, $67n$ Taking total scores over total tests,

$$\frac{67n + x}{n + 1} = 70 \quad \text{(multiplying)}$$
$$67n + x = 70n + 70 \implies x = 70n + 70 - 67n,$$
$$x = 3n + 70.$$

4. Octavius has an average of 76 on 3 Latin tests. If all tests are equally weighted, what does he need to score on the 4th test to average 80 for all 4? ③
   A. 88
   B. 89
   C. 90
   D. 91
   E. 92

5. Anabel's average on 5 equally weighted BC Calculus tests is 87. If Mr. Smith drops her lowest score of 75, what will her average on the remaining 4 tests be? ③
   A. 89
   B. 90
   C. 91
   D. 92
   E. 93

6. Candice has a 76 average in AP Physics C going into the final, and that final counts for 40% of the course grade. What must she score on the final to get an 80 in the class? ③
   A. 84
   B. 85
   C. 86
   D. 87
   E. 88

7. There are 7 equally weighted tests in Kevin's Financial Mathematics class. If he has a 77 average on the first 5 tests, what must he average on the last 2 tests to get exactly an 80 in the class? ③
   A. 86.5
   B. 87
   C. 87.5
   D. 88
   E. 88.5

8. If Diego has an average of x on 3 equally weighted Organic Chemistry tests, what does he need to score on the fourth test to

raise his average to $x + 5$ on the 4 tests combined?

A. $x + 20$

B. $x + 15$

C. $x + 25$

D. $x + 30$

E. $x + 40$

9. Assuming that all tests are equally weighted, Bert's average for 6 Precalculus tests is q, and after taking a 7th test, his average for all 7 is r, what did he score on the 7th test? ④

A. $6r - 5q$

B. $6r - 6q$

C. $8r - 7q$

D. $6r - 7q$

E. $7r - 6q$

10. If the final counted for 30% of her Calculus grade, her grade going into the final was q and her grade for the class was r, what did Cassandra score on the final in terms of q and r? ④

A. $\dfrac{9r - 7q}{3}$

B. $\dfrac{7r - 7q}{3}$

C. $\dfrac{10r - 7q}{3}$

D. $\dfrac{8r - 7q}{3}$

E. $\dfrac{6r - 7q}{3}$

4.3. Weighted Average

To find the weighted average, multiply the values by their frequencies, add them up, and divide by the total number of elements. This is basically the same as adding all the elements and dividing by the number of elements, but you are adding some elements in groups. For example, if 5 people got a 7 on a Multivariable Calculus quiz, 3 people got an 8 and 2 people got a 9, the

average score would be:

$$\frac{5 \cdot 7 + 3 \cdot 8 + 2 \cdot 9}{5 + 3 + 2} = \frac{35 + 24 + 18}{10} = 7.7$$

11. If 2 students averaged 90 and 3 students averaged 70, what is the average for all 5 students? ③

A. 77

B. 78

C. 79

D. 80

E. 82

12. The average score of 10 students on a Statistics test was 88 and the average score of another 14 students was 80. Which of these was closest to the average score of all 24 students? ③

A. 83.0

B. 83.3

C. 83.5

D. 83.8

E. 84.3

13. If 2 customers gave the Better Than Fast Food Cafe a rating of 1, 5 customers a rating of 2, 11 customers a rating of 3 and 22 customers a rating of 4, what was the mean rating of all the customers? ③

A. 3.1

B. 3.2

C. 3.3

D. 3.4

E. 3.5

14. If 12 students averaged 90 on a calculus test and the average for the whole class of 20 students was 80, what was the average of the other 8 students? ④

A. 65

B. 66

C. 67

D. 68

E. 69

15. The scores on a Latin quiz are as follows:

Score	Frequency
10	3
9	8
8	10
7	4
6	3
5	1
4	1

What is the mean score on the test? ④

A. 7.8

B. 7.9

C. 8.0

D. 8.1

E. 8.2

16. If x students averaged a on a Differential Equations test and y students averaged b, what is an expression for the average for all $x + y$ students? ④

A. $\dfrac{a + b}{x + y}$

B. $\dfrac{ax + by}{2x + 2y}$

C. $\dfrac{ax + by}{2xy}$

D. $\dfrac{ax + by}{x + y}$

E. $\dfrac{ax + by}{xy}$

4.4. Median

The median is the middle element when the elements are sorted in order. If there is an even number of elements, the median is the average of the two middle elements. To find the median given a frequency distribution, add up the elements from either direction. The value of the section where the middle element appears is the median.

You may need to sort the elements first before finding the median. For example, what is the median of the set $\{15, 24, 11, 43, 2, 34, 48, 4\}$. First sort the data: $\{2, 4, 11, 15, 24, 34, 43, 48\}$. Since there are an even number of elements, now take the average of the two middle elements:
$$\frac{15 + 24}{2} = 19.5.$$

17. What is the median of the dataset 25, 17, 28, 10, 36, and 42? ③

A. 10

B. 19

C. 25

D. 26.5

E. 28

18. If 2 customers gave the Blue Moon Juice Bar a rating of 1, 5 customers a rating of 2, 11 customers a rating of 3 and 22 customers a rating of 4, what was the median rating? ④

A. 3

B. 3.5

C. 3.8

D. 4

E. 4.5

19. What is the product of the mean and median of the first 7 prime numbers? ④

  A. 56
  B. 58
  C. 60
  D. 63
  E. 65

20. What is the absolute value of the difference between the mean and median of the set of numbers $\{1, 2, 3, 5, 8, 13, 21, 34\}$? ④

  A. 3.8
  B. 4.0
  C. 4.2
  D. 4.4
  E. 4.6

21. What is the difference between the mean and median of $\{1, 4, 9, 16\}$? ④

  A. 0
  B. 0.3
  C. 0.5
  D. 1
  E. 1.2

22. The scores on a Latin quiz are as follows:

Score	Frequency
10	3
9	8
8	10
7	4
6	3
5	1
4	1

What is the median score on the quiz? ④

  A. 6.5
  B. 7
  C. 7.5
  D. 8
  E. 8.5

4.5. Other Statistics

23. Which data set has the greatest standard deviation? ③

  A. 2, 2, 7, 7
  B. 2, 3, 4, 5
  C. 2, 3, 5, 6
  D. 3, 3, 4, 4
  E. 3, 3, 5, 7

24. What is the difference between the median and the interquartile range of the box plot shown? ③

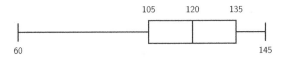

  A. 5
  B. 30
  C. 85
  D. 90
  E. 115

— ANSWER KEY

1D 2C, 3A, 4E 5B, 6C, 7C, 8A, 9E, 10C, 11B 12B, 13C, 14A, 15B, 16D,17D 18D, 19B, 20D, 21D, 22D, 23A, 24D

4.6. Solutions

1. (D) $\dfrac{8+11+17}{3} = \dfrac{36}{3} = 12.$

2. (C) Find the least common denominator, add fractions, and divide by the number of elements.

$$\dfrac{\dfrac{3}{7} + \dfrac{4}{5}}{2} = \dfrac{\dfrac{15+28}{35}}{2} = \dfrac{43}{70}.$$

   You could also add the decimal representations using a calculator and compare them with the decimal representations of the answer choices.

3. (A) Find the least common denominator, add fractions, and divide by the number of elements.

$$\dfrac{\dfrac{4}{12} + \dfrac{3}{12} + \dfrac{6}{12}}{3} = \dfrac{\dfrac{13}{12}}{3} = \dfrac{13}{36}.$$

4. (E) $\dfrac{76 \cdot 3 + x}{4} = 80 \longrightarrow 228 + x = 320 \longrightarrow x = 92.$

5. (B) Find the total scores of the 5 tests, subtract the score on the test being removed and divide by $5 - 1 = 4$ tests.
$$\dfrac{5 \cdot 87 - 75}{4} = x = \dfrac{435 - 75}{4} = \dfrac{360}{4} = 90.$$

6. (C) Set up a weighted average equation and then solve for the score on the final.

$$76 \cdot 0.6 + 0.4x = 80 \implies 45.6 + 0.4x = 80 \implies 0.4x = 34.4 \implies x = 86.$$

7. (C) Set up an equation with total scores over total tests and then solve for the total on the last 2 tests. Then divide by 2 to get the average score on those 2 tests. $\dfrac{77 \cdot 5 + 2x}{7} = 80$ (multiplying) $385 + 2x = 560 \implies 2x = 175 \implies x = 87.5.$

8. (A) Let y be his grade on the fourth test, $3x$ because we multiply the average by the number of tests to get the total; $x + 5$ because the average needs to go up by 5.
$\dfrac{3x + y}{4} = x + 5 \implies 3x + y = 4x + 20 \implies y = x + 20.$

9. (E) Let x be his grade on the 7th test, $\dfrac{6q + x}{7} = r \implies 6q + x = 7r \implies x = 7r - 6q.$

10. (C) Let x be her score on the final. Based on 30% for the final, the rest must be 70%, so

$$0.7q + 0.3x = r \implies 0.3x = r - 0.7q \implies x = \frac{10r - 7q}{3}.$$

11. (B) $\dfrac{2 \cdot 90 + 3 \cdot 70}{2 + 3} = \dfrac{180 + 210}{5} = 78.$

12. (B) Applying the weighted average formula, taking the sum of frequencies multiplied by values divided by the sum of frequencies,

$$\frac{10 \cdot 88 + 14 \cdot 80}{10 + 14} = \frac{880 + 1120}{24} = \frac{2000}{24} = \frac{250}{3} = 83.3$$

13. (C) Applying the weighted average formula, taking the sum of frequencies multiplied by values divided by the sum of frequencies,

$$\frac{2 \cdot 1 + 5 \cdot 2 + 11 \cdot 3 + 22 \cdot 4}{40} = \frac{2 + 10 + 33 + 88}{40} = \frac{133}{40} = 3.33$$

14. (A) Applying the weighted average formula taking the sum of frequencies multiplied by values divided by the sum of frequencies, and solving for the unknown score,

$$\frac{12 \cdot 90 + 8x}{20} = 80 \quad \text{(multiplying)} \quad 1080 + 8x = 1600 \implies 8x = 520 \implies x = 65.$$

15. (B) Applying the weighted average formula, taking the sum of frequencies multiplied by values divided by the sum of frequencies, using multiple values from the table,

$$\frac{10 \cdot 3 + 9 \cdot 8 + 8 \cdot 10 + 7 \cdot 4 + 6 \cdot 3 + 5 \cdot 1 + 4 \cdot 1}{30} = \frac{237}{30} = 7.9.$$

16. (D) Taking the total scores over the total number of students, multiply the frequency by the score, add those and divide by sum of the frequencies. $\dfrac{ax + by}{x + y}.$

17. (D) Sort the elements in order and then average the two middle elements. $\dfrac{25 + 28}{2} = 26.5.$

18. (D) There were 40 ratings. So the median is the average of the 20th and 21th rating with the ratings in order, which occurs in 4.

19. (B) The first 7 prime numbers in order are 2, 3, 5, 7, 11, 13, 17.
The median is the middle element, 7. The mean is $\dfrac{\text{sum}}{\text{number of elements}} = \dfrac{58}{7}.$
Their product is $7 \cdot \dfrac{58}{7} = 58.$

20. (D) Averaging the two middle elements when the data is sorted, the median$= \dfrac{5 + 8}{2} = 6.5$ and
the mean is the sum of the elements divided by the number of elements: mean$= \dfrac{87}{8} = 10.875.$
Therefore,

$$\text{mean} - \text{median} = 10.875 - 6.5 = 4.375.$$

21. (D) Mean is the sum of the elements divided by the number of elements: mean $=$ $\dfrac{1+4+9+16}{4} = \dfrac{15}{2}$ and since there are an even number of elements, average the two middle elements with the data sorted: the median $= \dfrac{4+9}{2} = \dfrac{13}{2}$.

$$\text{mean} - \text{median} = \frac{15}{2} - \frac{13}{2} = 1.$$

22. (D) There are 30 elements, so the median is between the 15th and 16th element. That is contained in 8, so the answer is 8.

23. (A) The more spread out the data is, the higher the standard deviation, Actually calculating the standard deviations of each data set in a time trap.

24. (D) Median is 120, the middle vertical line. Interquartile range is the difference between the beginning and end of the box, $135 - 105 = 30$. $120 - 30 = 90$.

5. Percentages

5.1. Finding a Percentage

To find the percentage of a quantity, take $0.01\times$ the percentage $\times$ what you are taking the percentage of. Multiply by 0.01 or divide by 100 to convert from percentage to decimal. This section includes problems as difficult as possible, but these types are problems are most frequently seen as basic low numbered problems. For example, 8% of \$1,500 is $0.08 \cdot 1,500 = \$120$.

1. What is 12% of 400? ①
   A. 4.8
   B. 33.3
   C. 48
   D. 480
   E. 4800

2. What is 0.052% of 8×10^6? ④
   A. 3,400
   B. 4,000
   C. 4,080
   D. 4,160
   E. 4,200

3. What is 0.2% of 93×10^6? ④
   A. 86,000
   B. 86,500
   C. 106,000
   D. 180,600
   E. 186,000

4. The sum of 200% of 3 and 400% of 2 has the same value as which of these? ③

   A. 300% of 4
   B. 600% of 2
   C. 200% of 7
   D. 500% of 3
   E. 800% of 2

5. What is $\dfrac{2}{11}$% of $\dfrac{3}{4}$? ④
   A. $\dfrac{3}{1,100}$
   B. $\dfrac{3}{2,200}$
   C. $\dfrac{3}{4,400}$
   D. $\dfrac{7}{3,300}$
   E. $\dfrac{11}{3,300}$

6. What is 5% of 0.14% of 9.3×10^7? ④
   A. 6,110
   B. 6,210
   C. 6,310
   D. 6,410
   E. 6,510

7. What is a% of b? ③
   A. $\dfrac{ab}{100}$
   B. $\dfrac{ab}{50}$
   C. $100ab$
   D. ab

29

E. $\dfrac{a}{100b}$

5.2. What Percent?

To find a percentage increase or decrease, take the change divided by the original value and multiply by 100 to convert from decimal to a percentage.

To find the percent increase from 124 to 128, take 128 minus 124 and find that the increase is 4. Then take

$$\frac{4}{124} \cdot 100 = 3.2\%.$$

The increase from 7 to 8 is greater than the decrease from 8 to 7 because in that case you divide the change by the original value. Therefore, if you increase the price by 20% and then decrease it by 20%, the final price is less than the original value.

Percentages are decimal values which are multiplied by 100 so that they are in a form that is easier to understand. When taking a percentage of a value, divide the percentage by 100 to convert it to a decimal and then multiply. When finding a percentage, divide the 2 quantities, and then multiply the resulting decimal value by 100.

8. If sales at Angel's Cafe increased from $1,100 on Tuesday to $1,400 on Wednesday, what was the percentage increase? ③

   A. 22%
   B. 25%
   C. 27%
   D. 28%
   E. 30%

9. If a water sample taken by a representative of a regulatory agency near a chemical factory contains 47 parts per million of a toxin, what percent of the water is that toxin? ③
   A. 0.47%
   B. 0.047%
   C. 0.0047%
   D. 0.00047%
   E. 0.000047%

10. If a is 40% of b, what percent of a is b? ④
   A. 80%
   B. 125%
   C. 200%
   D. 250%
   E. 500%

11. $a \times 10^3$ is what percent of $b \times 10^4$? ④
   A. $\dfrac{10a}{b}\%$
   B. $\dfrac{a}{10b}\%$
   C. $\dfrac{100a}{b}\%$
   D. $\dfrac{1000a}{b}\%$
   E. $\dfrac{50a}{b}\%$

12. If the distance from the earth to the sun is 9.3×10^7 miles and the distance from Neptune to the sun is 2.8×10^9 miles, the distance from the earth to the sun is what percent of the distance from Neptune to the sun? ③
   A. 2.7%
   B. 2.8%
   C. 2.9%
   D. 3.1%
   E. 3.3%

13. a is what percent of b? ③
   A. $\dfrac{100a}{b}\%$

B. $\dfrac{10a}{b}\%$

C. $\dfrac{1000a}{b}\%$

D. $\dfrac{50a}{b}\%$

E. $\dfrac{200a}{b}\%$

5.3. Percent of What?

These problems are more difficult, and result in dividing by the decimal version of the percentage. Suppose the 3% of the people in a certain country who have graduate degrees total 600,000 people. How many people are in the country?

$$600,000 = .03x \implies \frac{600,000}{0.03} = x$$
$$\implies 20,000,000 = x.$$

Similarly if there is a 7% sales tax and you have the after tax price, you divide by $1 + 0.07 = 1.07$ to find the pretax price. Furthermore, if you have the price before a 20% discount and want to find the original price, you divide by $1 - 0.2 = 0.8$.

14. 12 is 4% of what? ③
  A. 30
  B. 48
  C. 300
  D. 480
  E. 3000

15. 17 is 13% of what? ③
  A. 131
  B. 132
  C. 133
  D. 134
  E. 135

16. If a bicycle is selling for $250 at 30% off, what was the original price? ③
  A. $315
  B. $320
  C. $344
  D. $347
  E. $357

17. 11 is 5% of 4% of what? ④
  A. 4,400
  B. 4,950
  C. 5,500
  D. 6,050
  E. 6,600

18. If Carson paid $440 for a bicycle including a 7% sales tax, what was the before tax price of the bicycle to the nearest dollar? ④
  A. $409
  B. $411
  C. $412
  D. $413
  E. $415

5.4. Pie Charts

A pie chart is constructed using degrees between 0 and 360. Therefore, to convert percentages to degrees, multiply by 3.6; and to convert from pie chart degrees to a percentage, divide by 3.6.

This section explains the basic principles. On the exam, there is likely to be data from a table or a pie chart to convert.

19. A 15% share of the total expenses of a corporation would be represented by a how many degree angle on a pie chart? ③
   A. 24°
   B. 36°
   C. 40°
   D. 48°
   E. 54°

20. How many degrees would 1% of the school districts budget be represented as in a pie chart? ③
   A. 1.8°
   B. 2.4°
   C. 3.0°
   D. 3.6°
   E. 4.0°

21. A 1° angle in a pie chart represents what percent of the total to the nearest hundredth percent? ③
   A. 0.28%
   B. 0.32%
   C. 0.37%
   D. 0.41%
   E. 0.56%

5.5. Compound Percentages

Convert the percentages to decimals. Then add or subtract the result from 1 depending on whether it is a percent increase or decrease, and then multiply the results. Finally, subtract 1 from the result and multiply by 100 to convert back to a percentage. If the result is positive, it is a percent increase; if it is negative, it is a percent decrease.

The following is a type of problem that you should know and which could appear with variations. If the length of a rectangle is increased by 10% and the width is increased by 20%, by what percentage is the area increased? $1.1 \cdot 1.2 = 1.32$. $(1.32 - 1) \cdot 100 = 32\%$.

This topic is similar to interest and depreciation, which are covered under Exponential Equations. In this section we are mostly multiplying quantities. In that section, we would take them to a power.

22. Alfi plays a game in which she increases a number by 80%, and then decreases the resulting number by 80%. What percent is the new number of the original number? ④
   A. 36%
   B. 40%
   C. 42%
   D. 45%
   E. 50%

23. Jim bought a drone for 15% off the $60 list price and paid 7% sales tax on the discounted price. How much did he pay? ③
   A. $51.00
   B. $54.57
   C. $54.84
   D. $55.20
   E. $64.20

24. For a larger size of ground coffee, radius of a cylinder is increased by 20% and its height is increased by 30%, by what percent is the volume increased? ④
   A. 85%
   B. 87%
   C. 88%
   D. 89%
   E. 90%

25. If the side length of a cube is increased by 20%, what is the percent increase in its volume? ④
   A. 73%
   B. 75%
   C. 77%
   D. 79%
   E. 81%

26. If the value of a start up social media company increased by 40% per year for 5 years, what is the percentage increase in its value over the 5 years? ④

    A. 40%

    B. 200%

    C. 338%

    D. 438%

    E. 538%

① Easiest

⑤ Most Difficult

1C, 2D, 3E, 4C, 5B, 6E, 7A, 8C, 9C, 10D, 11A, 12E, 13A, 14C, 15A, 16E, 17C, 18B, 19E, 20D, 21A, 22A, 23B, 24B, 25A, 26D.

5.6. Solutions

1. (C) $0.12 \cdot 400 = 48$.

2. (D) Divide percentages by 100 to convert them to decimals and then multiply by what you are taking the percentage of. That applies to all problems in this section.

$$0.00052 \cdot 8,000,000 = 4,160.$$

3. (E) Divide by 100 to convert to decimal and then multiply, $0.002 \cdot 93,000,000 = 186,000$.

4. (C) 200% of $3 + 400\%$ of $2 = 6 + 8 = 14$. 200% of $7 = 14$.

5. (B) Divide by 100 to convert from percentage to fraction and multiply out:

$$\frac{2}{11} \times \frac{1}{100} \times \frac{3}{4} = \frac{3}{2,200}.$$

6. (E) Divide each percentage by 100 and then multiply by what you are taking a percentage of. $9.3 \times 10^7 \cdot 0.0014 \cdot 0.05 \approx 6,510$.

7. (A) To take the percentage of, multiply the quantities and divide by 100: $\frac{a}{100} \times b = \frac{ab}{100}$.

8. (C) $\frac{1,400}{1,100} = 1.2727$, to find the percentage, take $(1.27 - 1) \cdot 100 = 27\%$.

9. (C) Multiply by 100 to convert to a percentage, $\frac{47}{1,000,000} \cdot 100 = 0.0047\%$.

10. (D) $a = 0.4b$ (solving for b) $b = 2.5a$, now multiply by 100 to convert to a percentage: $2.5 \cdot 100 = 250\%$.

11. (A) Divide a/b and multiply by 100 to convert to a percentage. $a \times 10^3 \cdot \frac{100}{b \times 10^4} = \frac{10a}{b}$.

12. (C) $12 = 0.04x \longrightarrow x = \frac{12}{0.04} \to x = 300$.

13. (E) First take Earth's distance divided by Neptune's distance: $\frac{9.3 \times 10^7}{2.8 \times 10^9} = 0.0332$, converting to percentages, 3.3%.

14. (A) Dividing a by b and multiplying the result by 100 to convert to a percentage, $\frac{100a}{b}$.

15. (A) Convert to decimal, and divide by decimal to get the larger number.

$$17 = 0.13x \implies \frac{17}{0.13} = x \implies 130.8 = x.$$

16. (E) 30% is 0.3, $1 - 0.3 = 0.7$. $x \cdot 0.7 = 250 \implies x = \frac{250}{0.7} \approx 357.$

17. (C) Multiply the percentages and divide by the result.

$$11 = 0.04 \cdot 0.05x, \quad \frac{11}{0.04 \cdot 0.05} = x \implies x = 5500.$$

18. (B) 1 is for the price $+ 0.07$ for the sales tax. Divide by 1.07 to get the answer.

$$1.07x = 440 \implies x = \frac{440}{1.07} \approx 411.$$

19. (E) Multiply by 360 degrees and divide by 100 percent: $15 \cdot \frac{360}{100} = \frac{5400}{100} = 54°.$

20. (D) Multiply by 360 degrees and divide by 100 percent: $1 \cdot \frac{360}{100} == 3,6°.$

21. (A) Multiply by 100 percent and divide by 360 degrees: $1 \cdot \frac{100}{360} = 0.28\%.$

22. (A) The result is not the same as the initial amount at all.

$$(1 + 0.8)(1 - .8) = 1.8 \cdot 0.2 = 0.36; \quad 0.36 \cdot 100 = 36\%.$$

23. (B) $0.85 \cdot 60 = 51$. $51 \cdot 1.07 = \$54.57$

24. (B) Convert percentages to decimals, substitute into the volume of cylinder formula to find the volume. Note, you do not have to use the whole formula with π because you are working with ratios and π would cancel out. $1.2^2 \cdot 1.3 \approx 1.87$. $(1.87 - 1) \cdot 100 = 87\%.$

25. (A) Convert to a decimal, cube the result, and then convert back to percentages.
$1.2^3 = 1.728$ (now find the percentage increase)
$(1.728 - 1) \cdot 100 = 72.8\%.$

26. (D) Take the increase per year to the 5th power, since there are 5 years, and then convert back to percentages. $(1.4^5 - 1) \cdot 100 \approx 438\%.$

6. Midpoint and Distance Formulas

6.1. Midpoint Formula

A common low numbered problem on the exam just gives two points and asks for the midpoint. That type of problem is not emphasized in this book, which concentrates on advanced material. However, it is important to know, memorize, or be able to derive the midpoint formula. It is also possible to reason out answers without the formula. It is important to understand the concepts, because some problems just require the formula whereas for some more complex problems, you cannot apply the formula directly.

The midpoint formula is $\left(\dfrac{x_1 + x_2}{2}, \dfrac{y_1 + y_2}{2}\right)$. Note that the midpoint is a point, so it includes both an x and a y-value. Also note that we are adding, since we are taking the average, unlike many formulas in which we subtract to find the distance. To find the midpoint, substitute the $x-$ and y-values into the formula.

A less common problem is given one endpoint and the midpoint, find the other endpoint. There are various approaches, and you can do it intuitively or by reasoning, but the standard one is to substitute the midpoint and one endpoint into the midpoint formula and then solve for the other endpoint. Both types of questions are covered in the problems below.

An easy problem would be find the midpoint M of $A(1,2)$ and $B(7,13)$. By the midpoint formula, the midpoint is $((1+7)/2, (2+13)/2) = 4, 15/2)$.

A more difficult problem would be to find a point which is twice as far from A as from B assuming

$A(1,2)$ and $B(7,13)$. Set twice the distance from B equal to the distance from A. An algebraic solution is as follows:

$x - 1 = 2(7 - x) \implies x - 1 = 14 - 2x$, $3x = 15$, $x = 5$;
$y - 2 = 2(13 - y)$, $y - 2 = 28 - 2y$, $3y = 28$, $y = \dfrac{28}{3}$.

Therefore, x is $\left(5, \dfrac{28}{3}\right)$.

If the ratio was 3:5, you would multiply the the distance from the closer point by 5 and the further point by 3, and set the results equal and solve.

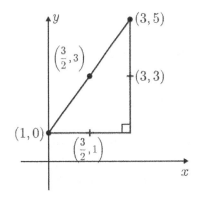

1. What is the midpoint between $(3,5)$ and $(1,11)$? ②
   A. $(2,8)$
   B. $(8,2)$
   C. $(-1,3)$
   D. $(3,7)$
   E. $(1,3)$

2. If $f(x) = x^2$, what is the midpoint between $(2, f(2))$ and $(6, f(6))$? ③
   A. $(4,18)$
   B. $(4,21)$
   C. $(4,20)$
   D. $(5,20)$
   E. $(5,25)$

3. M is the midpoint between A and B. If A is $(-11,-2)$ and M is $(1,-8)$, what are the coordinates of B? ③
   A. $(10,-14)$
   B. $(13,-14)$
   C. $(11,-14)$
   D. $(12,-14)$
   E. $(13,-15)$

6.2. Pythagorean Theorem

The Pythagorean Theorem is $a^2 + b^2 = c^2$, where a and b are the legs of a right triangle and c is the hypotenuse.

You substitute into that formula and solve for the unknown side. It is an error and falling into a trap to assume the unknown side is the hypotenuse c.

The sides of an isosceles right triangle are in the ratio of $1 - 1 - \sqrt{2}$.

4. Which of these is the exact value of the perimeter of an isosceles right triangle with legs of length $2\sqrt{10}$? ③
   A. $\sqrt{5} + \sqrt{10}$
   B. $2(\sqrt{5} + \sqrt{10})$
   C. $4(\sqrt{5} + \sqrt{10})$
   D. $4(2\sqrt{5} + \sqrt{10})$
   E. $3(\sqrt{5} + \sqrt{10})$

5. One leg of a right triangle is 5 and the hypotenuse is 6. What is the other leg of the right triangle? ③
   A. 1
   B. 2
   C. 3
   D. $\sqrt{11}$
   E. $\sqrt{17}$

6. What is the perimeter of an isosceles right triangle with hypotenuse x? ③
   A. $(1 + \sqrt{2})x$
   B. $(2 + \sqrt{2})x$
   C. $(2 + 2\sqrt{2})x$
   D. $\sqrt{2}x$
   E. $2\sqrt{2}x$

7. If the hypotenuse of a right triangle is 7 meters and one leg is 6 meters, what is the length of the other leg to the nearest centimeter? ③
   A. 383
   B. 361
   C. 401
   D. 432
   E. 461

8. If a right triangle has legs $5a$ and $8a$, what is the length of the hypotenuse? ③

   A. $\sqrt{39}\,a$

   B. $\sqrt{73}\,a$

   C. $\sqrt{85}\,a$

   D. $\sqrt{83}\,a$

   E. $\sqrt{89}\,a$

9. If a right triangle has sides 2 and 3, what could be the length of the other side? ③

   A. $\sqrt{5}$

   B. $\sqrt{5}$ or $\sqrt{13}$

   C. $\sqrt{13}$

   D. $\sqrt{5}$ or $\sqrt{11}$

   E. $\sqrt{5}$ or $\sqrt{14}$

10. If a rhombus has perimeter of 30 and one diagonal is 10, what is the length of the other diagonal? ④

   A. $\sqrt{5}$

   B. $10\sqrt{5}$

   C. $10\sqrt{2}$

   D. $8\sqrt{3}$

   E. $5\sqrt{5}$

6.3. Distance Formula

The distance formula states that the distance between (x_1, y_1) and (x_2, y_2) is

$$\sqrt{(x_2 - x_1)^2 + (y_2 - y_1)^2}.$$

That formula can be derived from the Pythagorean Theorem, $a^2 + b^2 = c^2 \implies \sqrt{a^2 + b^2} = c$, and then substituting $x_2 - x_1$ for a and $y_2 - y_1$ for b.

For example, the distance between $(11, 20)$ and $(27, 7)$ is

$$\sqrt{(7 - 20)^2 + (27 - 11)^2} = \sqrt{(-13)^2 + 16^2}$$
$$= \sqrt{169 + 256} = \sqrt{425} \approx 20.6.$$

A more difficult problem is if the distance between $(a, 2a + 3)$ and $(5, a)$ equals 4, what could a be? Apply the distance formula, substituting in variable expressions, and then set the result equal to 4.

$$\sqrt{(5 - a)^2 + (a - (2a + 3))^2} = 4,$$
$$\sqrt{(5 - a)^2 + (3 - a)^2} = 4,$$
$$\sqrt{25 - 10a + a^2 + 9 - 6a + a^2} = 4,$$
$$\sqrt{2a^2 - 16a + 34} = 4 \quad \text{(squaring)}$$

$2a^2 - 16a + 34 = 16$ (bringing the terms to one side and dividing) $a^2 - 8a + 9 = 0$. Applying the quadratic formula,

$$\frac{8 \pm \sqrt{(-8)^2 - 4 \cdot 9}}{2} = \frac{8 \pm \sqrt{28}}{2}$$
$$= \frac{8 \pm 2\sqrt{7}}{2} = 4 \pm \sqrt{7} \approx 1.4 \quad \text{or} \quad 6.6.$$

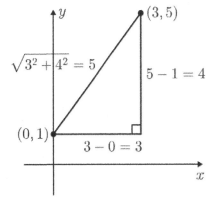

11. What is the distance between $(3, 5)$ and $(1, 11)$? ③

  A. $\sqrt{10}$

  B. $2\sqrt{10}$

  C. $2\sqrt{5}$

  D. $2\sqrt{11}$

  E. $\sqrt{42}$

12. In the standard (x, y) plane, what is the distance in coordinate units between $(-37, 11)$ and $(-5, -10)$? ③

  A. 35

  B. 36

  C. 37

  D. 38

  E. 39

13. In the standard (x, y) plane, what is the distance in coordinate units between the x and y-intercepts of $y = 3x + 2$? ③

  A. 2.1

  B. 2.4

  C. 2.7

  D. 3.0

  E. 3.3

14. If city A is at $(2, 11)$ and city B at $(4, 2)$ on a map where coordinates are in inches and each inch represents 75 miles, how far apart are the cities to the nearest ten miles? ③

  A. 650

  B. 660

  C. 670

  D. 680

  E. 690

① Easiest

⑤ Most Difficult

6.4. Solutions

1. (A) $\left(\dfrac{x_1+x_2}{2}, \dfrac{y_1+y_2}{2}\right) \longrightarrow \left(\dfrac{3+1}{2}, \dfrac{5+11}{2}\right) \longrightarrow (2,8)$.

2. (C) $f(2)=4$ and $f(6)=36$. Applying the midpoint formula,

$$\left(\frac{2+6}{2}, \frac{4+36}{2}\right) = (4,20).$$

3. (B) Substituting into the midpoint formula the coordinates of M as the answer and solving for x and y, the coordinates of B, $\dfrac{-11+x}{2} = 1$ and $\dfrac{-2+y}{2} = -8$ (first find the x-value) $x - 11 = 2 \implies x = 13$ (now find the y-value) $y - 2 = -16 \implies y = -14$. So the coordinates of B are $(13,-14)$.

4. (C) The ratios are $1-1-\sqrt{2}$ for an isosceles right right angle. You can also apply the Pythagorean theorem or trigonometry. Therefore,the hypotenuse $= 2\sqrt{10} \cdot \sqrt{2} = 4\sqrt{5}$, so

$$\text{the perimeter} = 4\sqrt{5} + 2(2\sqrt{10}) = 4(\sqrt{5} + \sqrt{10}).$$

5. (D) $x^2 + 5^2 = 6^2 \implies x^2 + 25 = 36 \implies x^2 = 11 \implies x = \sqrt{11}$.

6. (A) The legs are both $\dfrac{x}{\sqrt{2}}$. The perimeter is $x + 2 \cdot \dfrac{x}{\sqrt{2}} = x + \sqrt{2}x$.

7. (B) Setting one leg to x and solving for x: $x^2 + 6^2 = 7^2$ (simplifying and taking the square root) $x = \sqrt{13} = 3.61$. Converting from meters to centimeters, $3.61 \cdot 100 = 361$.

8. (E) By the Pythagorean theorem, the hypotenuse is

$$\sqrt{(5a)^2 + (8a)^2} = \sqrt{25a^2 + 64a^2} = \sqrt{89a^2} = \sqrt{89}a.$$

9. (B) Find both possible right triangles, one with 3 as a leg and the other with 3 as the hypotenuse:

$$\sqrt{2^2 + 3^2} = \sqrt{13}; \quad \sqrt{3^2 - 2^2} = \sqrt{5}.$$

10. (E) The sides are 7.5 and half the diagonal is 5. The diagonals of a rhombus are perpendicular and the diagonals bisect each other, so $5^2 + x^2 = \left(\dfrac{15}{2}\right)^2$ (squaring) $25 + x^2 = \dfrac{225}{4}$ (isolating x) $x^2 = \dfrac{125}{4}$ (taking the square root of both sides) $x = 5\dfrac{\sqrt{5}}{2}$. The other diagonal is twice that, $5\sqrt{5}$.

11. (B) Distance $= \sqrt{(x_1 - x_2)^2 + (y_1 - y_2)^2} = \sqrt{(1-3)^2 + (11-5)^2} = \sqrt{4 + 36} = \sqrt{40} = 2\sqrt{10}$.

12. (D) Apply the distance formula.

$$\sqrt{(-37-(-5))^2 + (11-(-10))^2} = \sqrt{(-32)^2 + 21^2} = \sqrt{1024 + 441} = \sqrt{1465} \approx 38.3.$$

13. (A) First, find the intercepts, which are $(0, 2)$ and $\left(\dfrac{-2}{3}, 0\right)$; then apply the distance formula,

$$\sqrt{(2-0)^2 + \left(0 - \left(\dfrac{-2}{3}\right)\right)^2} = \sqrt{4 + \dfrac{4}{9}} = \sqrt{\dfrac{40}{9}} = \dfrac{2\sqrt{10}}{3} \approx 2.1.$$

Since in both cases, one of the coordinates is 0, this problem could also be solved by applying the Pythagorean theorem directly.

14. (E) Distance on the map $= \sqrt{(2-4)^2 + (11-2)^2} = \sqrt{4 + 81} = \sqrt{85}$ (now multiply by the scale factor to get the actual distance) actual distance between the cities $= \sqrt{85} \cdot 75 \approx 691.46 \approx 691$.

7. Fractions and Rational Expressions

7.1. Basic Fractions

Questions may be asked in ways that require adding fractions as in elementary school and make it difficult to use a calculator. You can still work the problems with decimal representations of fractions using a calculator, and compare your answer with the decimal versions of the answer choices. You may also be able to get some calculators to add fractions.

1. If $\frac{1}{5}+\frac{1}{6}+\frac{1}{2}$ is computed and reduced to lowest terms, what is the numerator? ②

   A. 4
   B. 5
   C. 11
   D. 13
   E. 19

2. If $x+\frac{1}{8}=\frac{7}{12}$, then x equals what? ②

   A. $\frac{5}{12}$
   B. $\frac{11}{24}$
   C. $\frac{1}{2}$
   D. $\frac{13}{24}$
   E. $\frac{17}{24}$

3. Which of these is equivalent to $\frac{1}{2}\cdot\frac{1}{3}+\frac{1}{4}\cdot\frac{1}{5}$? ②

   A. $\frac{7}{30}$
   B. $\frac{13}{60}$
   C. $\frac{1}{5}$
   D. $\frac{1}{4}$
   E. $\frac{11}{60}$

4. $2\frac{1}{5}$ is what fraction of $3\frac{1}{3}$? ③

   A. $\frac{33}{50}$
   B. $\frac{31}{50}$
   C. $\frac{16}{15}$
   D. $\frac{27}{50}$
   E. $\frac{29}{50}$

45

5. What is $\dfrac{3! + 4!}{5! + 6!}$ in simplified form? ③

    A. $\dfrac{1}{28}$

    B. $\dfrac{1}{12}$

    C. $\dfrac{1}{30}$

    D. $\dfrac{1}{24}$

    E. $\dfrac{1}{14}$

7.2. Complex Fractions

Simplify starting with the most enclosed fraction.

With Numbers

6. What is $\dfrac{1}{1 + \dfrac{1}{1 + \dfrac{1}{3}}}$ in simplified form? ③

    A. $\dfrac{7}{4}$

    B. $\dfrac{4}{3}$

    C. $\dfrac{7}{11}$

    D. $\dfrac{4}{7}$

    E. $\dfrac{4}{9}$

7. Which of these is $\dfrac{1}{1 + \dfrac{1}{1 + \dfrac{3}{8}}}$ in simplified form? ③

    A. $\dfrac{11}{19}$

    B. $\dfrac{8}{11}$

    C. $\dfrac{19}{11}$

    D. $\dfrac{11}{8}$

    E. $\dfrac{19}{30}$

With Variables

Combine the fractions in stages. Most of these problems can also be solved by making up numbers. However, some of the problems here and on the exam ask for the numerator or whatever, which makes them difficult to solve except algebraically.

8. Which of the following equals $\dfrac{\dfrac{x}{5} + \dfrac{1}{3}}{\dfrac{3}{4} - \dfrac{1}{3}}$? ④

    A. $\dfrac{3x + 4}{5}$

    B. $\dfrac{3x + 5}{5}$

    C. $\dfrac{3x + 5}{6}$

    D. $\dfrac{4(3x + 4)}{25}$

    E. $\dfrac{4(3x + 5)}{25}$

9. Which of these is the numerator of $\dfrac{1}{\dfrac{1}{x} + \dfrac{1}{x+3}}$ in simplified form? ④

   A. $x^2 + 4x + 2$

   B. $x^2 + 4x + 5$

   C. $x^2 + 4x + 3$

   D. $x^2 + 3x$

   E. $x^2 + 4x + 1$

10. Which of these is $\dfrac{c}{d} + \dfrac{d}{c}$ as one fraction? ③

    A. $\dfrac{c^2 + d^2}{c + d}$

    B. $\dfrac{c^2 + d^2}{cd}$

    C. $\dfrac{c + d}{cd}$

    D. $\dfrac{c^2 + d^2}{c^2 d^2}$

    E. $c^2 + d^2$

11. $\dfrac{1}{x+y} + \dfrac{1}{x-y} = ?$ ③

    A. $\dfrac{x + 1}{x^2 - y^2}$

    B. $\dfrac{2x + 1}{x^2 - y^2}$

    C. $\dfrac{x}{x^2 - y^2}$

    D. $\dfrac{2x + y}{x^2 - y^2}$

    E. $\dfrac{2x}{x^2 - y^2}$

12. Which of these is $\dfrac{2 + \dfrac{1}{x}}{5 + \dfrac{1}{x}}$ in simplified form?

    ④

    A. $\dfrac{3x + 1}{5x + 1}$

    B. $\dfrac{x + 1}{5x + 1}$

    C. $\dfrac{2x + 1}{5x + 1}$

    D. $\dfrac{2x + 3}{5x + 1}$

    E. $\dfrac{4x + 3}{5x + 1}$

13. If $f(x) = \dfrac{x + 3}{x}$, what is $f\left(\dfrac{1}{x}\right)$? ④

    A. $\dfrac{1 + 3x}{x}$

    B. $\dfrac{1 + 4x}{x}$

    C. $1 + 4x$

    D. $1 + 3x$

    E. $2 + 3x$

14. Which of these is the numerator of the simplified form of $\dfrac{\dfrac{1}{2} + \dfrac{x}{3}}{\dfrac{1}{4} + \dfrac{x}{5}}$? ④

    A. $20x + 30$

    B. $2x + 3$

    C. $4x + 6$

    D. $20x + 32$

    E. $20x + 36$

15. Which of these is $\dfrac{\dfrac{1}{x}-\dfrac{1}{y}}{\dfrac{1}{x}+\dfrac{1}{y}}$ in simplified form?

③

A. $\dfrac{x-y}{y+x}$

B. $\dfrac{y}{y+x}$

C. $\dfrac{x}{y+x}$

D. $\dfrac{y-x}{y+x}$

E. $\dfrac{3y-x}{y+x}$

7.3. Adding Rational Expressions

These involving adding fractions with the least common denominator, as in 5th grade or so, but with variable expressions. In some cases you need to factor the denominators of both addends, and there may be common factors between the denominators.

The following is an example of a relatively difficult problem for which you need to factor both denominators and find their least common denominator:

$$\frac{1}{x^2+6x+8}+\frac{1}{x^2-4}$$
$$=\frac{1}{(x+2)(x+4)}+\frac{1}{(x+2)(x-2)}$$
$$=\frac{(x-2)+(x+4)}{(x+2)(x-2)(x+4)}=\frac{2x+2}{(x+2)(x-2)(x+4)}.$$

16. What is $\dfrac{x+3}{5}+\dfrac{x-2}{8}$? ②

A. $\dfrac{14x+14}{40}$

B. $\dfrac{15x+14}{40}$

C. $\dfrac{13x+12}{40}$

D. $\dfrac{13x+15}{40}$

E. $\dfrac{13x+14}{40}$

17. Which of these is the numerator of the simplified form of $\dfrac{1}{x^2}+\dfrac{1}{x^2+5}$? ④

A. $2x^2+6$

B. $2x^2+4$

C. $2x^2+3$

D. $2x^2+5$

E. $2x^2+2$

18. Which of these is the numerator of the simplified form of $\dfrac{2}{x^2-4}+\dfrac{3}{x^2+6x+8}$? ④

A. $5x+2$

B. $3x+2$

C. $3x-4$

D. $5x+4$

E. $5x+3$

7.4. Adding with Exponential Expressions in the Denominator

These problems may appear intimidating, but they can be solved by finding the least common denominator. For example, what is $\frac{1}{3^{27}} + \frac{5}{3^{29}}$? The least common denominator is 3^{29}, so

$$\frac{9}{3^{29}} + \frac{5}{3^{29}} = \frac{14}{3^{29}}.$$

These problems force you to add fractions like in elementary school, as they are not easy to do with a calculator, which is probably partly why they are on the exam.

It is assumed the student has a basic knowledge of exponents, which are covered later in the book.

19. What fraction is equal to $\frac{1}{3^{20}} + \frac{1}{3^{21}}$? ④

    A. $\dfrac{2}{3^{21}}$

    B. $\dfrac{4}{3^{21}}$

    C. $\dfrac{1}{3^{21}}$

    D. $\dfrac{5}{3^{21}}$

    E. $\dfrac{8}{3^{21}}$

20. Which of these is $\frac{1}{7^{20}} - \frac{1}{7^{21}}$ as a single fraction? ④

    A. $\dfrac{4}{7^{21}}$

    B. $\dfrac{5}{7^{21}}$

    C. $\dfrac{6}{7^{21}}$

    D. $\dfrac{8}{7^{21}}$

    E. $\dfrac{5}{7^{22}}$

21. Which of these is the average of $\frac{1}{2^{30}}$ and $\frac{1}{2^{32}}$? ⑤

    A. $\dfrac{5}{2^{32}}$

    B. $\dfrac{3}{2^{32}}$

    C. $\dfrac{5}{2^{31}}$

    D. $\dfrac{7}{2^{33}}$

    E. $\dfrac{5}{2^{33}}$

1D, 2B 3B, 3A, 5A, 6D, 7A, 8E 9D, 10B, 11E, 12C, 13D, 14A, 15E, 16D, 17E, 18D, 19A, 20B, 21C, 22E

7.5. Solutions

1. (D) Taking the least common denominator, adding, and simplifying:

$$\frac{1}{5} + \frac{1}{6} + \frac{1}{2} = \frac{6}{30} + \frac{5}{30} + \frac{15}{30} = \frac{26}{30} = \frac{13}{15}.$$

2. (B) $x = \frac{7}{12} - \frac{1}{8} = \frac{14}{24} - \frac{3}{24} = \frac{11}{24}.$

3. (B) Multiplying, then taking the least common denominator, adding, and simplifying,

$$\frac{1}{2} \cdot \frac{1}{3} + \frac{1}{4} \cdot \frac{1}{5} = \frac{1}{6} + \frac{1}{20} = \frac{10}{60} + \frac{3}{60} = \frac{13}{60}.$$

4. (A) Convert to improper fractions and then divide. $\dfrac{\frac{11}{5}}{\frac{10}{3}} = \frac{11 \cdot 3}{5 \cdot 10} = \frac{33}{50}.$

5. (A) Compute the factorial value, add, and then simplify. $\dfrac{3! + 4!}{5! + 6!} = \dfrac{6 + 24}{120 + 720} = \dfrac{30}{840} = \dfrac{1}{28}.$

6. (D) $\dfrac{1}{1 + \dfrac{1}{\frac{4}{3}}} = \dfrac{1}{1 + \frac{3}{4}} = \dfrac{1}{\frac{7}{4}} = \dfrac{4}{7}.$

7. (A) $\dfrac{1}{1 + \dfrac{1}{\frac{11}{8}}} = \dfrac{1}{1 + \frac{8}{11}} = \dfrac{1}{\frac{19}{11}} = \dfrac{11}{19}.$

8. (E) $\dfrac{\frac{3x+5}{15}}{\frac{9-4}{12}} = \dfrac{\frac{3x+5}{15}}{\frac{5}{12}} = \dfrac{(3x+5) \cdot 12}{15 \cdot 5} = \dfrac{4(3x+5)}{25}.$

9. (D) $\dfrac{1}{\frac{1}{x} + \frac{1}{x+3}} = \dfrac{1}{\frac{x+3+x}{x(x+3)}} = \dfrac{x^2 + 3x}{2x+3}.$

10. (B) $\dfrac{c}{d} + \dfrac{d}{c} = \dfrac{c^2 + d^2}{cd}.$

11. (E) $\dfrac{1}{x+y} + \dfrac{1}{x-y} = \dfrac{x-y+x+y}{(x+y)(x-y)} = \dfrac{2x}{x^2 - y^2}.$

12. (C) $\dfrac{2+\dfrac{1}{x}}{5+\dfrac{1}{x}}=\dfrac{\dfrac{2x+1}{x}}{\dfrac{5x+1}{x}}=\dfrac{2x+1}{5x+1}.$

This problem and similar ones can also be solved by making up numbers as follows: let $x=1$ (1 is easiest, as with it we do not need to deal with complex numerical fractions, but has disadvantages in that it can work for incorrect answers). Then the expression in the problem is $(3+1)/(5+1)=3/6=\dfrac{1}{2}$. A is 2/3, B is 1/3, C is 1/2, D is 5/6, and E is 7/6. Therefore, the answer is C.

13. (D) $f(x)=\dfrac{x+3}{x}$, what is $f\left(\dfrac{1}{x}\right)=\dfrac{\dfrac{1}{x}+3}{\dfrac{1}{x}}=\dfrac{\dfrac{1+3x}{x}}{\dfrac{1}{x}}=1+3x.$

14. (A) $\dfrac{\dfrac{1}{2}+\dfrac{x}{3}}{\dfrac{1}{4}+\dfrac{x}{5}}=\dfrac{\dfrac{3+2x}{6}}{\dfrac{5+4x}{20}}=\dfrac{20(3+2x)}{6(4x+5)}=\dfrac{20x+30}{12x+15}.$

15. (E) $\dfrac{\dfrac{3x+5}{15}}{\dfrac{9-4}{12}}=\dfrac{\dfrac{3x+5}{15}}{\dfrac{5}{12}}=\dfrac{(3x+5)\cdot 12}{15\cdot 5}=\dfrac{4(3x+5)}{25}.$

16. (D) $\dfrac{\dfrac{y-x}{xy}}{\dfrac{y+x}{xy}}=\dfrac{y-x}{y+x}.$

Making up numbers, let $x=2$ and $y=3$. Then the expression in the problem is $(1/2-1/3)/(1/2+1/3)=(1/6)/(5/6)=1/5$. For A, we get $(2-3)/(2+3)=-1/5$. For B, we get $3/(3+2)=3/5$. For C, we get $2/(2+3)=2/5$. For D, we get $(3-2)/(3+2)=1/5$. For E, we get $(3\cdot 3-2)/(3+2)=7/5$. Therefore, D is the answer.

17. (E) Find the least common denominator, combine, and then simplify.

$$\dfrac{8\cdot(x+3)+5\cdot(x-2)}{40}=\dfrac{8x+24+5x-10}{40}=\dfrac{13x+14}{40}.$$

18. (D) Find the least common denominator, add, simplify, and then take the numerator as the answer.

$$\dfrac{x^2+5+x^2}{x^4+5x^2}=\dfrac{2x^2+5}{x^4+5x^2}, \quad \text{so the answer is } 2x^2+5.$$

19. (A) Factor the denominators of both expressions. Find the least common denominator of the factors (they have one factor in common). Then take the numerator as requested.

$$\dfrac{2}{(x+2)(x-2)}+\dfrac{3}{(x+2)(x+4)}=\dfrac{2(x+4)+3(x-2)}{(x+2)(x-2)(x+4)}=\dfrac{5x+2}{(x+2)(x-2)(x+4)}.$$

20. (B) This expression may seem complicated, but it is doable if you understand how to add using the least common denominator.

$$\frac{1}{3^{20}} + \frac{1}{3^{21}} = \frac{3}{3^{21}} + \frac{1}{3^{21}} = \frac{4}{3^{21}}$$

21. (C) Find the least common denominator and subtract: $\frac{1}{7^{20}} - \frac{1}{7^{21}} = \frac{7}{7^{21}} - \frac{1}{7^{21}} = \frac{6}{7^{21}}$.

22. (E) Since we are taking the average, add the fractions using the least common denominator and divide by 2.

$$\frac{\frac{1}{2^{30}} + \frac{1}{2^{32}}}{2} = \frac{\frac{4}{2^{32}} + \frac{1}{2^{32}}}{2} = \frac{5}{2^{33}}.$$

8. Fundamental Topics

8.1. Units of Measure

When converting from a larger unit to a smaller unit, multiply by the number of the smaller units in a larger unit. When converting from a smaller unit to a larger unit, divide by the number of the smaller units in a larger unit.

How many cubic inches are there in a cubic foot? $12^3 = 1728$.

1. How many square feet are there in a square yard? (2)
   - **A.** 2
   - **B.** 6
   - **C.** 9
   - **D.** 27
   - **E.** 144

2. If Mr. Magoo's living room is 3 by 5 yards, what is its area in square inches? (4)
   - **A.** 16,740
   - **B.** 18,450
   - **C.** 18,540
   - **D.** 19,440
   - **E.** 19,620

3. How many cubic inches are there in one cubic mile (1 mile $= 5,280$ feet)? (4)
   - **A.** 5.5×10^{12}
   - **B.** 2.5×10^{14}
   - **C.** 5.5×10^{14}
   - **D.** 3.5×10^{14}
   - **E.** 5.5×10^{13}

4. At 186,000 miles per second, about how many miles does a beam of light travel in a week? (4)
   - **A.** 1.7×10^{11}
   - **B.** 3.4×10^{10}
   - **C.** 1.1×10^{10}
   - **D.** 1.1×10^{11}
   - **E.** 1.7×10^{10}

5. If Heloise needs 450 square feet of carpet, how much will she have to pay for that carpet if it costs $28 per square yard? (4)
   - **A.** $1,400
   - **B.** $1,700
   - **C.** $2,100
   - **D.** $2,800
   - **E.** $12,600

6. If Barnabas ran nine 400-meter laps at the St. Clair High School track in 15 minutes, what was his average speed in kilometers per hour? ④

   A. 12.0

   B. 12.6

   C. 13.6

   D. 14.4

   E. 15.0

7. If Liam is traveling at 30 meters per second on his way to a concert, at how many kilometers per hour is he traveling? ④

   A. 96

   B. 100

   C. 104

   D. 108

   E. 112

8. If the distance from the sun to Neptune is 2.78 billion miles and light travels at 186,000 miles per second, how long in hours and minutes would it take a beam of light to travel from the sun to Neptune? ④

   A. 4 hours and 2 minutes

   B. 4 hours and 9 minutes

   C. 4 hours and 23 minutes

   D. 4 hours and 34 minutes

   E. 4 hours and 36 minutes

9. What is the minimum number of 3 by 4 inch tiles needed to cover a 10 by 20 yard room? ④

   A. 5,400

   B. 10,800

   C. 16,200

   D. 21,600

   E. 28,800

10. If there are 7.2×10^{14} nitrogen molecules in $2 \times 2 \times 3$ meter tank, how many nitrogen molecules are there per cubic centimeter? ④

   A. 8×10^7

   B. 7×10^7

   C. 6×10^7

   D. 5×10^7

   E. 9×10^7

8.2. Scientific Notation

Scientific notation is a way of expressing very large or small numbers as the product of a number between 1 and 10 and 10 to a positive or negative exponent.

Often you need to adjust values and powers when multiplying and dividing so that the value will be between 1 and 10. For example, $\frac{3 \times 10^7}{5 \times 10^3} = 0.6 \times 10^4 = 6 \times 10^3$.

11. What is 0.00024 expressed in scientific notation? ②

   A. 2.4×10^{-3}

   B. 2.4×10^{-4}

   C. 2.4×10^{-5}

   D. 2.4×10^4

   E. 2.4×10^3

12. What is 362 million expressed in scientific notation? ②

   A. 3.62×10^7

   B. 3.62×10^6

   C. 3.62×10^9

   D. 3.62×10^8

   E. 3.62×10^{10}

13. What is the weight in pounds expressed in scientific notation of 57 million bricks if each brick weighs 4 pounds? ③

A. 2.28×10^8

B. 1.14×10^9

C. 2.28×10^9 *

D. 4.56×10^9

E. 2.28×10^{10}

14. What is 12% of 2.5×10^{115}? ③

A. 3.0×10^{114}

B. 3.0×10^{115}

C. 3.0×10^{116}

D. 6.0×10^{114}

E. 6.0×10^{115}

15. What is $3 \times 10^7 + 8 \times 10^5$ expressed in scientific notation? ③

A. 3.8×10^7

B. 3.8×10^5

C. 3.08×10^5

D. 3.08×10^7

E. 3.08×10^8

16. If a light-year is 5.9×10^{12} miles, about how many light-years away is a star that is 3.7×10^{15} miles away? ③

A. 63

B. 627

C. 629

D. 6268

E. 6274

17. What value of x makes the following equation true: $2 \times 10^{11} \cdot 4.7 \times 10^{3x+5} = 94,000$? ③

A. -2

B. -3

C. -4

D. -5

E. -6

18. What is $\sqrt{1.6 \times 10^{1301}}$? ③

A. 4×10^{651}

B. 4×10^{1300}

C. 4×10^{649}

D. 4×10^{1299}

E. 4×10^{650}

19. If a water sample taken near a chemical plant has 8 parts per million of a toxin, how many milliliters of the toxin will be in 20,000 liters of the water? ③

A. 16

B. 160

C. 400

D. 1600

E. 4000

20. What is $5 \times 10^{3000} \cdot 7 \times 10^{5000}$ expressed in scientific notation? ③

A. 3.5×10^{8001}

B. 3.5×10^{8000}

C. 3.5×10^{8002}

D. 3.5×10^{7999}

E. 3.5×10^{2000}

8.3. Linear Equations in One Variable

This book assumes you know how to solve easy equations of this type. These problems sometimes involve combining fractions with least common denominators and may also involve isolating the variable to solve. A typical problem asks what must be added to both the numerator and denominator of $\frac{2}{7}$ to get $\frac{3}{4}$?

$\frac{2+x}{7+x} = \frac{3}{4}$ (cross multiplying) $4(2+x) = 3(7+x)$

$\implies 8 + 4x = 21 + 3x \implies x = 13.$

21. What value of x satisfies the equation $-5(3 - 2x) = -2(5 - x)$? ②

   A. $\frac{-25}{8}$

   B. $\frac{5}{8}$

   C. $\frac{5}{6}$

   D. $\frac{25}{12}$

   E. $\frac{25}{8}$

22. If $\frac{x}{3} + \frac{x}{5} = \frac{4}{7}$, what is x? ③

   A. $\frac{14}{15}$

   B. $\frac{15}{14}$

   C. $\frac{12}{11}$

   D. 1

   E. $\frac{7}{6}$

23. If $\frac{1}{x} + \frac{1}{3x} = 5$, what is x? ③

   A. $\frac{2}{15}$

   B. $\frac{8}{25}$

   C. 10

   D. $\frac{4}{15}$

   E. $\frac{15}{8}$

24. If $\frac{2x}{5} + \frac{3x}{11} = \frac{3}{4}$, what is x? ③

   A. $\frac{155}{148}$

   B. $\frac{165}{148}$

   C. $\frac{40}{37}$

   D. $\frac{41}{37}$

   E. $\frac{175}{148}$

25. What number must be added to both the numerator and denominator of $\frac{1}{3}$ to get $\frac{3}{4}$? ④

   A. 4

   B. 5

   C. 6

   D. 7

   E. 8

26. What number must be added to both the numerator and denominator of $\frac{a}{b}$ to get $\frac{3}{4}$? ⑤

   A. $3b - 2a$

   B. $3b + 4a$

   C. $3b - a$

   D. $3b - 4a$

   E. $b - a$

27. Suppose the sum of 4 consecutive integers is a. In terms of a, what is the sum of the largest 2 of those integers? ④

    A. $\dfrac{a}{2} + 3$

    B. $\dfrac{a}{2} + 4$

    C. $\dfrac{a}{3} + 3$

    D. $\dfrac{a}{3} + 5$

    E. $\dfrac{a}{2} + 2$

8.4. Exponents

The problems may look complicated, but are easy to solve by following the laws of exponents, $x^m x^n = x^{m+n}$ and $(x^m)^n = x^{mn}$. For example, $x^3 \cdot x^5 = x^8$, $(x^3)^5 = x^{15}$. It is also necessary to follow rules and approaches for negative exponents and complex fractions.

28. What is $(2x^3)^4$ equal to? ②

    A. $8x^7$

    B. $4x^{12}$

    C. $16x^{12}$

    D. $2x^7$

    E. $32x^7$

29. Which of the following is equivalent to $\left(\dfrac{2a^4 b^5}{3c^7}\right)^5$ if $c \neq 0$? ③

    A. $\dfrac{32a^{20} b^{25}}{81c^{30}}$

    B. $\dfrac{32a^{20} b^{25}}{81c^{35}}$

    C. $\dfrac{32a^{20} b^{25}}{243c^{25}}$

    D. $\dfrac{32a^{20} b^{25}}{243c^{40}}$

    E. $\dfrac{32a^{20} b^{25}}{243c^{35}}$

30. Which of the following is equivalent to $\dfrac{\left(\dfrac{x^{11}}{x^3}\right)^2}{\dfrac{x^5}{x^2}}$ if $x \neq 0$? ②

    A. x^{10}

    B. x^{16}

    C. x^5

    D. x^{13}

    E. x^2

31. Which of the following is equivalent to $\left(\dfrac{4}{3}\right)^{\frac{-5}{2}}$? ④

    A. $\dfrac{9\sqrt{3}}{4}$

    B. $\dfrac{9\sqrt{3}}{32}$

    C. $\dfrac{9\sqrt{3}}{8}$

    D. $\dfrac{9\sqrt{3}}{16}$

    E. $\dfrac{9\sqrt{3}}{64}$

32. What is $(x^3)^5 \cdot (x^4)^6$? ③

    A. x^{41}

    B. x^{21}

    C. x^{360}

    D. x^{39}

    E. x^{51}

33. What is $(2a^{10}\sqrt{b})^4$? ③

    A. $64a^{40} b^2$

    B. $16a^{40} b^2$

    C. $16a^{20} b^2$

    D. $8a^{40} b^2$

    E. $8a^{20} b^2$

8.5. Evaluating Function Values

Just substitute the value in and evaluate. These often involve finding the function of a negative number, which is a trap where students can make calculator errors.

34. If $f(x) = x^2 + 3x + 5$, what is $f(-2)$? ②
   - **A.** -3
   - **B.** 0
   - **C.** 2
   - **D.** 3
   - **E.** 5

35. If $f(x, y) = x^2 + y^2 - 4xy$, what is $f(5, 2)$? ②
   - **A.** 59
   - **B.** 11
   - **C.** -11
   - **D.** -59
   - **E.** -29

36. $t = 23 - .008a$ models the temperature on June 17 in near Denver, where a is the height above sea level in meters. According to that model, what would be the temperature at $3,000$ meters? ③
   - **A.** $-1°$ C
   - **B.** $3°$ C
   - **C.** $5°$ C
   - **D.** $7°$ C
   - **E.** $9°$ C

37. Temperature in degrees Fahrenheit is related to temperature in degrees Centigrade by the formula $F = \dfrac{9}{5}C + 32$. An increase of 10 degrees Fahrenheit is equivalent to an increase in how many degrees Centigrade? ③
   - **A.** $\dfrac{40}{9}$
   - **B.** $\dfrac{50}{9}$
   - **C.** 6
   - **D.** 12
   - **E.** 18

38. If the graph of $f(x) = x^5 + 5x^4$, what is $f(-2)$? ③
   - **A.** 40
   - **B.** 42
   - **C.** 44
   - **D.** 46
   - **E.** 48

39. If $f(x) = 7 \cdot 2^x$, $g(x) = 2 \cdot 3^x$, and $h(x) = f(x) - g(x)$, what is the value of $h(4)$? ③
   - **A.** -50
   - **B.** -20
   - **C.** 10
   - **D.** 20
   - **E.** 50

8.6. Words to Algebra

40. If the rental charge is $100 for the first day and $60 for each subsequent day, which of the following expresses the rental charge y in terms of the number of days rented x? ④

   - **A.** $60x + 100$
   - **B.** $60x + 140$
   - **C.** $60x + 40$
   - **D.** $40x + 60$
   - **E.** $40x + 100$

8.7. Simplifying Algebraic Expressions

41. Simplify $\dfrac{5x^4 + 15x^2}{5x^2}$. ③
   - **A.** $x^2 + 3$
   - **B.** $x^2 + 5$
   - **C.** $2x^2 + 3$
   - **D.** $2x^2 + 3$
   - **E.** $2x^2 + 5$

1C, 2D, 3B, 4D, 5A, 6D, 7D, 8B, 9D, 10C, 11B 12D, 13C, 14A, 15D, 16B, 17C, 18E, 19B, 20A,21B
22B,23D,24B, 25B, 26D, 27E, 28C, 29E, 30D, 31B, 32D, 33B, 34D, 35C, 36A 37B, 38E, 39A,40C
41A

8.8. Solutions

1. (C) 1 yard equals 3 feet. $3 \cdot 3 = 9$.

2. (D) Convert to square inches by multiplying by the number of inches in a yard squared. $3 \cdot 5 \cdot (12 \cdot 3)^2 = 19,440$.

3. (B) Take the cube of the number of inches in a mile. Multiply the number of inches in a foot by the number of feet in a mile to get inches in a mile.
   $(12 \cdot 5280)^3 \approx 2.5 \times 10^{14}$.

4. (D) Multiply by the number of seconds in a week, which is seconds in a minute × minutes in an hour × hours in a day × days in a week, $186,000 \cdot 60 \cdot 60 \cdot 24 \cdot 7 = 1.12 \times 10^{11}$.

5. (A) Divide by 3^2 to convert to square yards, and then multiply by the price per square yard. 450 square feet $= \dfrac{450}{3 \cdot 3} = 50$ square yards. $50 \cdot \$28 = \$1400$. It is a trap the just divide by 3 and not square it.

6. (D) Convert to kilometers and to hours, and then divide.
   9×400 meters $= 3600$ meters $= 3.6$ kilometers. 15 minutes $= 0.25$ hours.

   $\dfrac{3.6 \text{ kilometers}}{0.25 \text{ hours}} = 14.4 \dfrac{\text{km}}{\text{h}}$.

7. (D) Convert to kilometers and to hours. $30 \cdot \dfrac{3600}{1000} = 108$

8. (B) Use the formula: distance = rate × time $\implies$ time $= \dfrac{\text{distance}}{\text{rate}}$. Then convert the time in seconds to hours and minutes. $\dfrac{2.78 \cdot 10^9}{1.86 \cdot 10^5} = 14946$ seconds (converting to minutes) $\dfrac{14946}{60}$ minutes $= 249.1$ minutes ≈ 4 hours and 9 minutes.

9. (D) Find the area in square yards, multiply that by the number of square inches in a square yard, and divide by the number of square inches in each tile. $\dfrac{10 \cdot 20 \cdot 36^2}{3 \cdot 4} = 21,600$.

   Alternate solution: each square yard needs $\dfrac{36}{3} \cdot \dfrac{36}{4} = 108$ tiles. Find the number of square yards, $10 \cdot 20 = 200$ square yards (now multiply by tiles per square yard to get the number of tiles) $200 \cdot 108 = 21,600$ tiles.

10. (C) Convert from cubic meters to cubic centimeters and then divide. Note that there are 100 centimeters in a meter and we need to cube that to find the number of cubic centimeters in a cubic meter. $12 \cdot (10^2)^3 = 1.2 \times 10^7$ cubic centimeters. $\dfrac{7.2 \times 10^{14}}{1.2 \times 10^7} = 6 \times 10^7$ molecules per cubic centimeter.

11. (B) You need to move the 2 over 4 spaces to get it to the left of the decimal point, so 2.4×10^{-4}.

12. (D) One million is 10^6. Put the resulting number between 1 and 10 for scientific notation. $362 \cdot 10^6 = 3.62 \times 10^8$.

13. (C) 1 million is 10^6, so 57 million is $57 \times 10^6 = 5.7 \times 10^7$. $5.7 \cdot 10^7 \cdot 4 = 22.8 \times 10^7 = 2.28 \times 10^8$.

14. (A) $0.12 \cdot 2.5 \times 10^{115} = 0.3 \times 10^{115} = 3.0 \times 10^{114}$ in scientific notation.

15. (D) Convert the second term to the same exponent as the first and add.

$$3 \times 10^7 + 0.08 \times 10^7 = 3.08 \times 10^7.$$

16. (B) Divide the distances, and then convert to an integer. $\dfrac{3.7 \times 10^{15}}{5.9 \times 10^{12}} \approx 0.627 \times 10^3 \approx 627$

17. (C) Since we get 9.4 on the left side, which cancels, we can equate the exponents of the powers of 10: $11 + 3x + 5 = 4 \implies 3x = -12 \implies x = -4$

18. (E) Convert both portions to forms from which it is easy to take the square root.

$$\sqrt{1.6 \times 10} = \sqrt{16} = 4; \ \sqrt{10^{1300}} = 10^{650},$$

so the answer is 4×10^{650}

19. (B) Convert to the form of the portion of toxin, then multiply by the number of liters, and finally convert from liters to milliliters. $\left(\dfrac{8}{1,000,000} \right) \cdot 20,000 = 0.16$ liters; $0.16 \times 1000 = 160$ milliliters.

20. (A) Multiply the terms, and then adjust to get the result into scientific notation form.

$$7 \times 5 = 3.5 \times 10^1; \quad 10^{3000} \cdot 10^{5000} = 10^{8000}; \quad 3.5 \times 10^1 \cdot 10^{8000} = 3.5 \times 10^{8001}.$$

21. (B) $-15 + 10x = -10 + 2x \implies 8x = 5 \implies x = \dfrac{5}{8}$.

22. (B) $\dfrac{x}{3} + \dfrac{x}{5} = \dfrac{4}{7} \implies \dfrac{(5+3)x}{15} = \dfrac{4}{7} \implies \dfrac{8x}{15} = \dfrac{4}{7} \implies x = \dfrac{4}{7} \times \dfrac{15}{8} = \dfrac{15}{14}$.

23. (D) $\dfrac{1}{x} + \dfrac{1}{3x} = 5 \implies \dfrac{3}{3x} + \dfrac{1}{3x} = 5 \implies \dfrac{4}{3x} = 5 \implies 15x = 4 \implies x = \dfrac{4}{15}$.

24. (B) $\dfrac{2x}{5} + \dfrac{3x}{11} = \dfrac{3}{4} \implies \dfrac{22x + 15x}{55} = \dfrac{3}{4} \implies 148x = 165 \implies x = \dfrac{165}{148}$.

25. (B) Convert the word problem into an equation, cross multiply, and then solve. $\dfrac{1+x}{3+x} = \dfrac{3}{4}$ (cross multiplying) $(1+x) \cdot 4 = (3+x) \cdot 3 \implies 4 + 4x = 9 + 3x \implies x = 5$. This problem can also be solved fairly easily by substituting in the answer choices and seeing which work.

26. (D) Convert the word problem into an equation, cross multiply, and then solve. $\dfrac{a+x}{b+x} = \dfrac{3}{4}$ (cross multiplying) $4a + 4x = 3b + 3x \implies x = 3b - 4a$.

27. (E) Let the first integer equal x, so the second one equals $x+1$, etc. $x + x + 1 + x + 2 + x + 3 = a \implies 4x + 6 = a \implies x = \dfrac{a}{4} - \dfrac{3}{2}$

The sum of the larger two integers is $(x+2)+(x+3) = 2x + 5 = 2\left(\dfrac{a}{4} - \dfrac{3}{2}\right) + 5 = \dfrac{a}{2} - 3 + 5 = \dfrac{a}{2} + 2$.

28. (C) $2^4(x^3)^4 = 16x^{12}$.

29. (E) $\dfrac{2^5(a^4)^5(b^5)^5}{3^5(c^7)^5} = \dfrac{32a^{20}b^{25}}{243c^{35}}$.

30. (D) $\dfrac{(x^8)^2}{x^3} = \dfrac{x^{16}}{x^3} = x^{13}$.

31. (B) $\dfrac{(\sqrt{3})^5}{(\sqrt{4})^5} = \dfrac{9\sqrt{3}}{2^5} = \dfrac{9\sqrt{3}}{32}$.

32. (D) $x^{15} \cdot x^{24} = x^{39}$.

33. (B) Take the constant to the power and multiply the exponents: $(2a^{10}\sqrt{b})^4 = 16a^{40}b^2$.

34. (D) $(-2)^2 + 3(-2) + 5 = 4 - 6 + 5 = 3$.

35. (C) $5^2 + 2^2 - 4 \cdot 5 \cdot 2 = 25 + 4 - 40 = -11$.

36. (A) $23 - 0.008 \cdot 3000 = 23 - 24 = -1°$ C.

37. (B) $10 \cdot \dfrac{5}{9} = \dfrac{50}{9}$.

38. (E) $f(x) = x^5 + 5x^4$. Substitute -2 for x. This question tests taking powers of negative numbers, which can be miscalculated with a calculator.

$$f(-2) = (-2)^5 + 5(-2)^4 = -32 + 80 = 48.$$

39. (A) $f(4) = 7 \cdot 2^4 = 112$, $g(4) = 2 \cdot 3^4 = 162$. $112 - 162 = -50$.

40. (C) The easiest approach for most student is to take two points $(1, 100)$ and $(2, 160)$. The slope is $\dfrac{160 - 100}{2 - 1} = 60$. Using $y = mx + b$ and $(1, 100)$, $100 = 60 \cdot 1 + b \implies b = 40$. So $y = 60x + 40$.
It is easier in a way to realize the daily charge is 60 and the initial charge is $100 - 60 = 40$, but the more methodical approach usually works better.

41. (A) $\dfrac{5x^2(x^2+3)}{5x^2} = x^2 + 3.$

9. Number Theory

Number theory is a significant part of this book, although a small part of the exam, because many of the trickiest problems on the exam involve number theory.

The material is this chapter is difficult, although it does not involve advanced high school math, and problems similar to all those here have appeared on the exam.

9.1. Digit in Decimal Representation

If you are asked for the 100th digit after the decimal point in the decimal representation of $\frac{1}{7}$, enter $\frac{1}{7}$ into a calculator and get $0.\overline{142857}$. Notice that the pattern repeats every 6 digits. On the exam, it will usually be a number divided by 7, which repeats every 6 digits. However, sometimes it will be a fraction which repeats more frequently. Sometimes they will give you the repetition, and sometimes you will need to discover it by dividing with your calculator. Take $\frac{100}{6}$ and you get a remainder of 4. You can either divide by hand as in elementary school or divide using a calculator and multiply the decimal part, 0.666666. by 6. You may be able to get a remainder from a calculator. We take the fourth digit to the right of the decimal, which is 8.

1. What is the 17th digit to the right of the decimal point in the decimal expansion of $\frac{7}{11}$? ③

   A. 1
   B. 2
   C. 3
   D. 6
   E. 7

2. What is the 88th digit to the right of the decimal in the decimal representation of $\frac{241}{999}$?
   ④
   A. 1
   B. 2
   C. 3
   D. 4
   E. 5

3. What is the 125th digit after the decimal in the decimal representation of $\frac{6}{7}$? ④

   A. 2
   B. 4
   C. 6
   D. 7
   E. 8

4. What is the product of the 100th and 200th digits in the decimal representation of $\frac{4}{7}$? ⑤

   A. 8
   B. 16
   C. 28
   D. 35
   E. 40

9.2. Units Digit in Number to a Power

These are fairly difficult problems. If asked to find the units digit of 132^{87}, treat it the same as 2^{87} because we are only concerned with the units digit and raising a multiple of 10 to a positive integer power does not affect the units digit. $2^2 = 4$, $2^3 = 8$, $2^4 = 6$ (taking only the units digit) and $2^5 = 2$. Since $2^5 = 2^1$ modulo 10, the pattern repeats every 4. For these units digit problems, the pattern will always repeat every 4, as it will for powers of i, where i is $\sqrt{-1}$. Now, what is 87 modulo 4? If you divide 87 by 4 by hand, you get a remainder of 3. You can also compute $\frac{87}{4}$ using a calculator and get 21.75. Then take $0.75 \cdot 4 = 3$. Now we take $2^{87} = 2^3$, only looking at the units digit. Therefore, the answer is $2^3 = 8$.

5. The digit in the ones place of 8^{127} is 2. What is the digit in the ones place of 8^{130}? ④
   A. 2
   B. 3
   C. 4
   D. 6
   E. 8

6. What is the units digit of 38^{39}? ⑤
   A. 2
   B. 4
   C. 6
   D. 8
   E. 9

7. What is the units digit of 53^{250}? ⑤
   A. 1
   B. 3
   C. 6
   D. 7
   E. 9

9.3. Other Number Theory

This is a topic for which there may be difficult problems designed to test reasoning ability. Therefore, it is impossible to cover here or predict all problems that could appear on the exam.

An example is what is the largest 3-digit number divisible by both 3 and 7? If the number is divisible by 3 and 7, then it must be divisible by their product, 21. With a calculator, take $\frac{1000}{21} \approx 47.61$. Multiply $47 \cdot 21$ to get the answer 987. If you do not remember these steps, check the answer choices from highest to lowest and seeing which is divisible by 21 (or by both 3 and 7). If you get an integer with no decimal or remainder when dividing by 21, the number is divisible by 21.

Another example is what is the product of the 2 largest prime numbers less than 300? First, write down all the numbers between 280 and 300 (we pick 280 because it is likely at least 2 primes are between 280 and 300) that are not divisible by 2, 3, or 5 (a number is divisible by 3 if and only if the sum of its digits is divisible by 3): 281, 283, 287, 289, 293, 299. Then take the next prime, 7. 287 is divisible by 7 and can be eliminated. 299 is divisible by 13 and can be eliminated. 289 is 17^2 and can be eliminated. Since $23^2 > 300$, so we do not consider 23 or any higher primes. So we are left with 281, 283, and 293. The 2 largest are 283 and 293. Their product is 82,919, which is the answer.

8. If j is a positive odd integer and k is a positive even integer, then $(-7)^{jk}$ is which? ③

   A. Negative and even
   B. Negative and odd
   C. Not necessarily an integer
   D. Positive and even
   E. Positive and odd

9. What time is exactly 130 hours after 5 PM? ④

   A. 1 AM
   B. 3 AM
   C. 11 PM
   D. 4 AM
   E. 7 AM

10. A rectangle with area 36 square inches has sides that are integer lengths in inches. Which of the following CANNOT be its perimeter in inches? ④

   A. 24
   B. 26
   C. 30
   D. 36
   E. 40

11. Which of the following has an odd number of distinct positive integer factors? ④

   A. 9
   B. 10
   C. 12
   D. 18
   E. 24

12. If x is an integer, the sum of $2x$ and $3x$ is always divisible by which number? ④

   A. 2
   B. 3
   C. 5
   D. 6
   E. 10

13. Which set lists all the digits that a perfect square cannot end in? ④

   A. $\{2,3,7\}$
   B. $\{2,3,8\}$
   C. $\{2,7,8\}$
   D. $\{2,3,7,8\}$
   E. $\{3,7,8\}$

14. How many 2-digit numbers have a units digit that is twice their tens digit? ④

   A. 2
   B. 3
   C. 4
   D. 5
   E. 6

15. How many prime numbers are between 100 and 130? ④

   A. 5
   B. 6
   C. 7
   D. 8
   E. 9

16. What fraction of the numbers from 10 to 99 inclusive have at least one digit that is a 3? ⑤

    A. $\dfrac{1}{7}$

    B. $\dfrac{1}{5}$

    C. $\dfrac{1}{4}$

    D. $\dfrac{2}{9}$

    E. $\dfrac{3}{10}$

17. What fraction of the numbers from 100 to 999 inclusive have at least one digit that is a 7? ⑤

    A. $\dfrac{1}{3}$

    B. $\dfrac{1}{5}$

    C. $\dfrac{7}{25}$

    D. $\dfrac{2}{7}$

    E. $\dfrac{8}{25}$

18. Which of these could be the last two digits of a perfect square? ⑤

    A. 12

    B. 18

    C. 32

    D. 54

    E. 84

19. Which of these could be the last two digits of a perfect square? ⑤

    A. 15

    B. 19

    C. 32

    D. 41

    E. 48

— ANSWER KEY —————————————————————————————

1D 2B, 3B, 4C, 5A, 6C, 7E 8E, 9B,10D 11C,12A 9D, 10C, 11B, 12B, 13C, 14E, 15D

9.4. Solutions

1. (D) $.\overline{63}$. The odd digits are 6s.

2. (B) $\dfrac{241}{999} = 0.\overline{241}$. The decimal repeats every 3 digits.

   88 mod 3 = 1, so we take the first digit, which is 2.

3. (B) $\dfrac{6}{7} = 0.\overline{857142}$. The decimal repeats every 6 digits.

   You can determine that with a calculator.

   125 mod 6 = 5. The 5th digit is a 4, so the answer is 4.

4. (C) $\dfrac{4}{7}$ is $0.\overline{571428}$. The pattern repeats every 6 digits.

   100 mod 6 = 4 and 200 mod 6 = 2.

   The fourth digit is 4 and the second digit is 7. We take the product of those digits, $4 \cdot 7 = 28$.

5. (A) $8^2 = 4$ mod 10, $8^3 = 2$ mod 10, $8^4 = 6$ mod 10, $8^5 = 8$ mod 10, so the pattern repeats every 4.

   $39 = 3$ mod 4, so 38^{39} mod $10 = 38^3$ mod $10 = 8^3$ mod $10 = 2$ mod 10

6. (C) $2 \cdot 8^{130-127} = 2 \cdot 8^3 = 2 \cdot 512 = 4 (\text{mod } 10)$.

7. (E) Positive and odd. An odd integer times an even integer is an even integer. A negative number raised to an even integer power is positive. An odd number raised to an integer power is odd.

8. (D) $6 \cdot 6$ Perimeter $= 2 \cdot 6 + 2 \cdot 6 = 24$, $9 \cdot 4$ Perimeter $= 2 \cdot 9 + 2 \cdot 4 = 26$, $12 \cdot 3$ Perimeter $= 2 \cdot 12 + 2 \cdot 3 = 30$, $2 \cdot 18$ Perimeter $= 2 \cdot 2 + 2 \cdot 18 = 40$.

9. (E) $3^1 = 3$, $3^2 = 9$, $3^3 = 7$, $3^4 = 1$, looking only at the units digit, so the pattern repeats every 4. 250 mod 4 = 2, so $3^{250} = 3^2$ mod 4. Therefore, $3^2 = 9$

10. (B) 3 AM. $\dfrac{130}{120} = 5$ remainder 10. $5 + 10 = 15$. $15 - 12 = 3$ AM.

11. (C) $2x + 3x = 5x$. $5x$ must be divisible by 5 if x is an integer. (A) 9 has 1, 3, 9. Generally, only perfect squares have an odd number of distinct factors. 10 has 1, 2, 5, 10, so 4 factors. 12 has 1, 2, 3, 4, 6, 12, so 6 factors. 18 has 1,2, 3, 6, 12, 18, so 6 factors. 24 has 1, 2, 3, 4, 6, 8, 12, 24, so 8 factors.

12. (D) We only have to look at the last digit because if, for example, $7^2 = 49$, the perfect square of any number ending in 7 will end in 9. $1^2 = 1$, $2^2 = 4$, $3^2 = 9$, $4^2 = 6$, $5^2 = 5$, $6^2 = 6$, $7^2 = 9$,

$8^2 = 4$, $9^2 = 1$, $0^2 = 0$, so a perfect square must end in 0, 1, 4, 5, 6, or 9. Therefore, a square cannot end in 2, 3, 7, or 8.

13. (C) Taking numbers whose units digit is double their tens digit, we get 12, 24, 36, and 48. There can be no more because twice 5 or greater is not a single digit. Therefore, the answer is 4.

14. (B) Take all the numbers in that range not divisible by 2, 3, or 5.

A number is divisible by 3 if and only if its digits add up to a multiple of 3.

A number is divisible by 5 if and only if it ends in 5 or 0.

Therefore, we have reduced the list of possible primes to 101, 103, 107, 109, 113, 119, 121, 127.

119 is divisible by 7 and 121 is divisible by 11.

We do not need to check the divisibility of primes 13 or higher, since $13^2 = 169 > 130$.

Therefore, the only primes in the range are 101, 103, 107, 109, 113, 127, so there are 6 primes.

15. (B) Take 1 minus the proportion of numbers without a 3 in order to determine the proportion with a 3. 9/10 of units digits do not have a 3. However, 8/9 of tens digits lack a 3 because there are only 9 possible tens digits, 1–9.

$$1 - \frac{8}{9} \cdot \frac{9}{10} = 1 - \frac{8}{10} = \frac{1}{5}.$$

Another approach is to enumerate the numbers with a 3 as follows: 13 23 30-39 43 53 63 73 83 93.

Therefore, there are 18 numbers with 3s, so $\frac{18}{90} = \frac{1}{5}$

16. (C) In this case the most practical approach is to take 1 minus the numbers without a 7 as explained above. There are 10 tens digits and 10 units digits, but only 9 possible hundreds digits for a 3-digit number.

$$1 - \frac{8}{9} \cdot \frac{9}{10} \cdot \frac{9}{10} = 1 - \frac{72}{100} = \frac{28}{100} = \frac{7}{25}.$$

17. (E) Solution 1: The last 2 digits of the first 25 perfect squares are as follows.

After 25^2, the last two digits repeat counting down, that is $24^2 = 26^2$, $19^2 = 31^2$ etc., just looking at the last 2 digits. 01 04 09 16 25 36 49 64 81 00 21 44 69 96 25 56 89 24 61 00 41 84 29 76 25 After 50^2 they repeat the first 50 perfect squares.

Solution 2: Work out the first 25 perfect squares. As that approach is difficult, you can also eliminate choices ending in 2, 3, 7, and 8, which cannot be perfect squares, as shown in problem 2.

Solution 3: According to the solution of the question 2, a perfect square cannot end in 2, 3, 7 or 8, so A, B, and D can be rejected immediately. Notice that the other two answer choices are even numbers, so the numbers are divisible by 2. Every square which is divisible by 2 must also be divisible by 4. Using the criteria for divisibility by 4 (a number is divisible by 4 if and only if the ending 2-digit number is divisible by 4) we can see only 84 works. Therefore, the answer is E.

18. (D) Approach described above.

10. Lines

10.1. Slope

Finding the slope

The slope formula is $\dfrac{y_2 - y_1}{x_2 - x_1}$, which is the change in y divided by the change in x. If a linear equation is in slope-intercept form, that is solved for y ($y = mx + b$), the coefficient of x is the slope.

For example, what is the slope of the line between (2, -3) and (5, 8)? Substituting into the slope formula, $\dfrac{8 - (-3)}{5 - 2} = \dfrac{11}{3}$.

Another simple example, and likely low numbered problem on the exam is what is the slope of the line $4x + 5y = 11$? First get the line into slope-intercept form by solving for y: $5y = -4x + 11 \implies y = \dfrac{-4x}{5} + \dfrac{11}{5}$. The slope is the x−coefficient $\dfrac{-4}{5}$

1. What is the slope in the standard xy-coordinate plane of the line passing through $(3, 5)$ and $(1, 11)$? ②

    A. -4

    B. -3

    C. $\dfrac{-1}{3}$

    D. $\dfrac{1}{3}$

    E. 3

2. What is the slope of the line in the standard xy-coordinate plane passing through the origin and $\left(-\dfrac{5}{7}, -\dfrac{2}{3}\right)$? ③

    A. $\dfrac{15}{14}$

    B. $-\dfrac{15}{14}$

    C. $\dfrac{4}{5}$

    D. $-\dfrac{14}{15}$

    E. $\dfrac{14}{15}$

3. What is the slope of the line in the standard xy-coordinate plane $ax + by = c$? ③

    A. $\dfrac{a}{b}$

    B. $\dfrac{c - a}{b}$

    C. $-\dfrac{b}{a}$

    D. $\dfrac{b}{a}$

    E. $-\dfrac{a}{b}$

73

4. What is the slope of the line in the standard xy-coordinate plane $\dfrac{3x}{5} + \dfrac{2y}{3} = 8$? ③

   A. $\dfrac{10}{9}$

   B. $-\dfrac{10}{9}$

   C. $\dfrac{9}{10}$

   D. $-\dfrac{9}{10}$

   E. -1

5. What is the slope of a line in the standard xy-coordinate plane containing (a, a^2) and (b, b^2)? ③

   A. $a - b$

   B. $a^2 + b$

   C. $a + 2b$

   D. $a + b$

   E. $a + 3b$

Slope of a Line Perpendicular to a Given Line

The slope perpendicular to a given line is the negative reciprocal of the slope of the original line, so the the product of the two slopes equals -1. Therefore, the slope of a line perpendicular to a line with a slope of $\dfrac{3}{4}$ is $-\dfrac{4}{3}$.

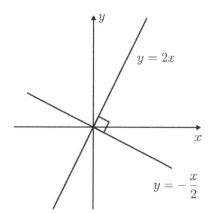

6. What is the slope in the standard xy-coordinate plane of the line perpendicular to the line passing through $(3, 5)$ and $(1, 11)$? ④

   A. $\dfrac{1}{3}$

   B. $\dfrac{-1}{4}$

   C. 3

   D. $\dfrac{1}{4}$

   E. $\dfrac{-1}{3}$

7. What is the slope of a line perpendicular to the line $\dfrac{3y}{5} = \dfrac{2x}{7} + \dfrac{1}{3}$ in the standard xy-coordinate plane? ③

   A. $\dfrac{10}{21}$

   B. $-\dfrac{10}{21}$

   C. $\dfrac{21}{10}$

   D. $-\dfrac{21}{10}$

   E. $\dfrac{1}{2}$

8. Which of these is the slope of a line perpendicular to the line $ax + by = c$ in the standard xy-coordinate plane? ④

   A. $-\dfrac{b}{a}$

   B. $\dfrac{b}{a}$

   C. $\dfrac{a}{b}$

   D. $-\dfrac{a}{b}$

   E. $\dfrac{c}{a}$

Other Slope

In these problems, you are given the slope and asked to solve for one or more coordinates of the points which determine the slope.

9. The slope of a line passing through $(1, a)$ and $(a, 2)$ in the standard xy-coordinate plane is 5. What is a? ④

   A. $\dfrac{6}{7}$

   B. 1

   C. $\dfrac{7}{6}$

   D. $\dfrac{5}{4}$

   E. $\dfrac{9}{8}$

10.2. Equations of Lines

You could be given 2 points and asked to find the equation of the line containing them. First, find the slope of the line containing them using $m = \dfrac{y_2 - y_1}{x_2 - x_1}$. Then find the equation of the line using $y - y_0 = m(x - x_0)$ or $y = mx + b$, where (x_0, y_0) is one of the given points and b is the y-intercept.

10. Which of these is $\dfrac{3x}{5} + \dfrac{2y}{3} = 8$ expressed in standard form? ③
    A. $9x + 10y = 130$
    B. $9x + 10y = 140$
    C. $9x + 10y = 150$
    D. $9x + 10y = 160$
    E. $9x + 10y = 120$

11. What is the equation of the line in the standard xy-coordinate plane of the line passing through $(3, 5)$ and $(1, 11)$? ③
    A. $y = -4x + 5$
    B. $y = -4x + 15$
    C. $y = -3x + 14$
    D. $y = 4x + 7$
    E. $y = -3x + 13$

12. Which of these is the equation of the line in the standard xy-coordinate plane containing $(3, 5)$ with $x-$intercept of 4? ③
    A. $-5x + 4$
    B. $-5x + 16$
    C. $-5x + 20$
    D. $-5x - 20$
    E. $-5x - 4$

13. Which of these is the equation of the line in the standard xy-coordinate plane containing $(100, 300)$ and $(500, 3100)$? ④
    A. $y = 7x - 400$
    B. $y = 7x - 300$
    C. $y = 7x - 500$
    D. $y = 8x - 500$
    E. $y = 8x - 600$

14. If the equation of line p in the standard xy-coordinate plane is $y = mx + b$, which of these could be the equation of line n? ④

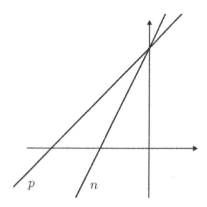

- **A.** $y = mx + 2b$
- **B.** $y = 2mx - b$
- **C.** $y = \dfrac{x}{2} + b$
- **D.** $y = -mx + b$
- **E.** $y = 2mx + b$

15. Which of these is the equation of a line through $\left(\dfrac{1}{3}, \dfrac{1}{2}\right)$ and $\left(\dfrac{1}{4}, \dfrac{1}{5}\right)$ in standard form? ④
- **A.** $36x + 10y = 10$
- **B.** $36x + 10y = 17$
- **C.** $36x + 10y = 19$
- **D.** $36x - 10y = 7$
- **E.** $36x - 10y = 17$

16. Assuming that line l is $y = x$ and $l \parallel m$, what is an equation for line m? ④

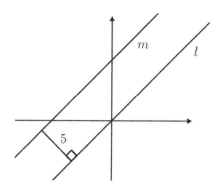

- **A.** $y = \dfrac{x}{2} + 5\sqrt{2}$
- **B.** $y = x + 5$
- **C.** $y = x + \dfrac{5\sqrt{2}}{2}$
- **D.** $y = x + 5\sqrt{2}$
- **E.** $y = x + 10$

17. Which of these is the y-coordinate of the intersection point of the line in the standard xy-coordinate plane containing $(3, -6)$ and $(-4, -2)$ and the line containing $(5, 8)$ and $(3, 4)$? ④
- **A.** $-\dfrac{17}{5}$
- **B.** $-\dfrac{34}{9}$
- **C.** $-\dfrac{19}{5}$
- **D.** $-\dfrac{21}{5}$
- **E.** $-\dfrac{22}{5}$

10.3. Intercepts

If an equation is in slope-intercept form, the y-intercept is the constant term. For example, if $y = 3x + 4$, the y-intercept is $(0, 4)$. To find the

x-intercept, set $y = 0$, $0 = 3x + 4$ (solving for x) $x = -\frac{4}{3}$, so the x−intercept is $\left(-\frac{4}{3}, 0\right)$.

Another example is given $3x - 5y = 10$, find its x and y-intercepts. Set $x = 0$ to find the y-intercept: $3 \cdot 0 - 5y = 10 \implies -5y = 10 \implies y = -2$, so the y-intercept is $(0, -2)$. Set $y = 0$ to find the x-intercept: $3x - 5 \cdot 0 = 10$, $3x = 10$, $x = \frac{10}{3}$, so the x-intercept is $\left(\frac{10}{3}, 0\right)$.

18. Which of these is y-coordinate of the y-intercept of a line in the standard xy-coordinate plane with slope $\frac{5}{8}$ and x-intercept $(-12, 0)$? ④

   A. $-\frac{96}{5}$

   B. $\frac{15}{2}$

   C. $-\frac{17}{2}$

   D. $\frac{17}{2}$

   E. $-\frac{15}{2}$

19. If $f(x) = x^2$ and $g(x)$ is the line in the standard xy-coordinate plane through $(2, f(2))$ and $(3, f(3))$, what is the y-coordinate of the y-intercept of $g(x)$? ④

   A. -7

   B. -6

   C. -5

   D. -4

   E. -3

20. If $y = x^2 - 6x + 8$, what is the equation of the line in the standard xy−coordinate plane containing the y-intercept and the smallest x-intercept? ④

   A. $y = -3x + 8$

   B. $y = -5x + 8$

   C. $y = -4x + 8$

   D. $y = -6x + 8$

   E. $y = -2x + 8$

21. Which of these is the x-intercept of the line $y = ax + b$ in the standard xy-coordinate plane? ③

   A. $-\frac{b}{a}$

   B. $\frac{b}{a}$

   C. ab

   D. $\frac{b^2}{a}$

   E. $\frac{a}{b}$

22. Which of these is the y-intercept of the line $ax + by = c$ in the standard xy-coordinate plane? ③

   A. $-\frac{c}{a}$

   B. $\frac{c}{a}$

   C. $\frac{c}{b}$

   D. $-\frac{c}{b}$

   E. $\frac{a}{c}$

23. Which of these is the equation of a line in the standard xy-coordinate plane with x-intercept of 3 and slope of 10? ③

   A. $y = 3x - 30$

   B. $y = 10x - 30$

   C. $y = 3x - 10$

   D. $y = 10x - 10$

   E. $y = 10x - 3$

24. If $f(x) = x^2$, what is the y-intercept of the line in the standard xy−coordinate plane containing $(2, f(2))$ and $(10, f(10))$? ④

   A. -20

   B. -18

   C. -16

   D. 18

   E. 20

25. Which of these is the equation of a line in the standard xy-coordinate plane with x-intercept $(a, 0)$ and y-intercept $(0, b)$? ④

   A. $y = -\dfrac{bx}{a} + b$

   B. $y = \dfrac{bx}{a}$

   C. $y = bx + a$

   D. $y = -\dfrac{bx}{a}$

   E. $y = -\dfrac{bx}{a} + a$

26. If a line in the standard xy-coordinate plane which has intercepts $(0, 5)$ and $(7, 0)$ is expressed in the form $ax + by = c$, where a, b, and c are integers, what is b? ④

   A. -7

   B. -5

   C. 5

   D. 7

   E. 35

— ANSWER KEY

1B, 2E, 3E, 4D, 5D, 6A, 7D, 8B, 9C, 10E, 11C, 12C, 13A, 14E, 15D, 16D, 17B, 18B, 19B, 20C, 21A, 22C, 23B, 24A, 25A, 26D

10.4. Solutions

1. (B) Slope $= \dfrac{y_2 - y_1}{x_2 - x_1} = \dfrac{11 - 5}{1 - 3} = \dfrac{6}{-2} = -3.$

2. (E) Apply the slope formula and then simplify. $\dfrac{-\frac{2}{3}}{-\frac{5}{7}} = \dfrac{2 \cdot 7}{3 \cdot 5} = \dfrac{14}{15}.$

3. (E) Apply the slope formula and then simplify. $\dfrac{\frac{3}{4} - \frac{1}{3}}{\frac{2}{3} - \frac{1}{2}} = \dfrac{\frac{9}{12} - \frac{4}{12}}{\frac{4}{6} - \frac{3}{6}} = \dfrac{\frac{5}{12}}{\frac{1}{6}} = \dfrac{5}{12} \cdot \dfrac{6}{1} = \dfrac{30}{12} = \dfrac{5}{2}.$

4. (D) Solve for y, write the equation in slope-intercept form, and then the slope is the coefficient of x. $\dfrac{2y}{3} = -\dfrac{3x}{5} + 8$ (simplifying and solving) $y = -\dfrac{9x}{10} + 12$, so the slope is the coefficient of x, $-\dfrac{9}{10}.$

5. (D) $\dfrac{b^2 - a^2}{b - a} = \dfrac{(b + a)(b - a)}{b - a} = b + a.$

6. (A) First determine the slope: $m = \dfrac{y_2 - y_1}{x_2 - x_1} = \dfrac{11 - 5}{1 - 3} = \dfrac{6}{-2} = -3.$ The slope of the line perpendicular is the negative reciprocal. $-\dfrac{1}{-3} = \dfrac{1}{3}.$

7. (D) Convert into slope-intercept form, $y = \dfrac{10x}{21} + \dfrac{5}{9}$, so the slope is $\dfrac{10}{21}$. The slope of a line perpendicular to that one is the negative reciprocal of that $-\dfrac{21}{10}.$

8. (B) $by = c - ax \implies y = \dfrac{c}{b} - \dfrac{ax}{b}$, so the slope of the given line is $-\dfrac{a}{b}$. The slope of a line perpendicular to that given line is its negative reciprocal, $\dfrac{b}{a}.$

9. (C) Set the formula to find the slope equal to the given slope, and then solve for a.

$$\dfrac{2 - a}{a - 1} = 5 \implies 2 - a = 5a - 5 \implies 7 = 6a \implies a = \dfrac{7}{6}.$$

10. (E) Multiplying by 15 to clear the denominator, $9x + 10y = 120$

11. (C) $m = \dfrac{y_2 - y_1}{x_2 - x_1} = \dfrac{11 - 5}{1 - 3} = \dfrac{6}{-2} = -3.$ $y = mx + b,\ m = -3\ (1, 11) \longrightarrow 11 = -3 \cdot 1 + b \longrightarrow b = 14,$
so $y = -3x + 14.$

12. (C) The points are $(3, 5)$ and $(4, 0)$. First find the slope: $m = \dfrac{5 - 0}{3 - 4} = -5.$ Then find the y-intercept: $y = mx + b \longrightarrow 0 = 4 \cdot (-5) + b \longrightarrow b = 20.$ So $y = -5x + 20.$

13. (A) Find the slope, then find the equation of the line, and finally simplify.
Slope $= \dfrac{3100 - 300}{500 - 100} = 7$ (finding the equation of the line)

$$y - 300 = 7(x - 100) \implies y - 300 = 7x - 700 \implies y = 7x - 400.$$

14. (E) Line n also has its y-intercept at b, but has a higher slope, so $y = 2mx + b$ is the only choice consistent with the graph.

15. (D) Slope $= \dfrac{\frac{1}{2} - \frac{1}{5}}{\frac{1}{3} - \frac{1}{4}} = \dfrac{\frac{3}{10}}{\frac{1}{12}} = \dfrac{18}{5}$ Now find the equation of the line using $y - y_0 = m(x - x_0)$ You could also use $y = mx + b$

$$y - \frac{1}{2} = \frac{18}{5}\left(x - \frac{1}{3}\right) \implies y - \frac{1}{2} = \frac{18x}{5} - \frac{6}{5} \implies y = \frac{18x}{5} - \frac{7}{10}$$

(multiplying by 10 to get an equation with integer coefficients in standard form) $10y = 36x - 7$
(getting the line into standard form) $36x - 10y = 7.$

16. (D) Using an isosceles right triangle, the y-intercept of m is $5\sqrt{2}$, so the equation of line m is $y = x + 5\sqrt{2}.$

17. (B) The first line has slope $\dfrac{-2-(-6)}{-4-3} = -\dfrac{4}{7}$.

Therefore, the equation of the first line is

$$y + 6 = \left(-\frac{4}{7}\right)(x - 3) \implies y + 6 = -\frac{4x}{7} + \frac{12}{7} \implies y = -\frac{4x}{7} - \frac{30}{7}.$$

The second line has slope $\dfrac{8-4}{5-3} = 2$.

Therefore, the equation of the second line is

$$y - 4 = 2(x - 3) \implies y - 4 = 2x - 6 \implies y = 2x - 2$$

To find the intersection point, since the lines are both in slope-intercept form, solved for y, set the other portions of the lines equal and solve for x.

$$-\frac{4x}{7} - \frac{30}{7} = 2x - 2 \implies -\frac{16}{7} = \frac{18x}{7} \implies x = -\frac{8}{9}$$

(substituting for x in the equation of the second line) $y = 2\left(-\dfrac{8}{9}\right) - 2 = -\dfrac{34}{9}$.

It is possible to sketch the lines from the points to get an estimate or graph the lines with a graphing calculator after you have the lines and find the intersection point.

18. (B) Find the equation of the line, convert to slope-intercept form, and then the constant term is the y-intercept. $y - 0 = \dfrac{5}{8}(x + 12)$ (solving for y to get slope-intercept form) $y = \dfrac{5x}{8} + \dfrac{15}{2}$; therefore, the y-intercept is $\left(0, \dfrac{15}{2}\right)$.

19. (B) Find the 2 points from the equation, find the slope of the line containing them, then find the equation of the line, and set $x = 0$ to find the y-intercept. From the initial equation, the points are $(2, 4)$ and $(3, 9)$.

Slope $= \dfrac{9-4}{3-2} = 5$. Finding the equation of the line, $y - 4 = 5(x - 2) \implies y - 4 = 5x - 10 \implies$ $y = 5x - 6$. Therefore, the y-intercept is $(0, -6)$.

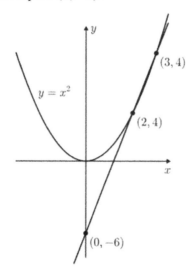

20. (C) The solutions of the quadratic equation in x are 2 and 4, so $(2,0)$ is the smallest x-intercept. Setting $x = 0$ and solving for y, the y-intercept is $(0,8)$. Therefore, the slope $= \dfrac{8-0}{0-2} = -4$. Therefore, the equation of the line is $y = -4x + 8$.

21. (A) Set $y = 0$ to find the x-intercept: $0 = ax + b \implies -b = ax \implies x = -\dfrac{b}{a}$.

22. (C) $by = c - ax \implies y = \dfrac{c}{b} - \dfrac{ax}{b}$. Setting $x = 0$, the y-intercept is $\dfrac{c}{b}$.

23. (B) Use the point and slope given to find the equation of the line. $y - 0 = 10(x - 3)$ (simplifying and converting to slope-intercept form) $y = 10x - 30$.

24. (A) Find the points, then find the slope of the line containing them, and finally find the equation of the line. The points are $(2,4)$ and $(10,100)$, Slope $= \dfrac{100-4}{10-2} = 12.$
The equation of the line is $y - 4 = 12(x - 2) \implies y - 4 = 12x - 24 \implies y = 12x - 20.$

25. (A) Find the slope as a variable expression, and then find the line in terms of variables.
Slope $= \dfrac{b-0}{0-a} = -\dfrac{b}{a}$. So the equation of the line is $y = \dfrac{-bx}{a} + b$

26. (D) Slope $= \dfrac{5-0}{0-7} = -\dfrac{5}{7}$. The y-intercept is given to be 5, so the equation is $y = -\dfrac{5x}{7} + 5$ in slope-intercept form.
Converting to standard form, $7y = -5x + 35 \implies 5x + 7y = 35.$

11. Rates

11.1. Rates Involving Travel

Some of these problems may require converting units, as the following one does. A plane flies 3 miles in 37 seconds, what is its speed in mph?

$$\frac{\text{Distance}}{\text{time}} = \text{rate}$$

(substituting distance and speed into that formula)

$$\frac{3}{(37/3600)} = \frac{10800}{37} \approx 292 \text{ mph}.$$

The basic formula is distance=rate × time. You may need to find any of those from the other two. You also may need to work with times in days, hours and minutes and convert between them.

When converting to a larger unit, divide; when converting to a smaller unit, multiply. For example, divide by 5280 converting feet to miles and multiply by 5280 converting miles to feet. If it is per unit of time, multiply by 3600 converting per second to per hour and divide by 3600 converting per hour to per second. This makes sense, since you will be able to go much further in an hour than a second.

If you have a decimal number of hours, such as 2.7 hours, multiply the 0.7 by 60 to get 42 minutes, so the total would be 2 hours and 42 minutes.

For example, how many minutes is it between 7:42 PM Friday and 3:15 PM the following Wednesday? That is 4 days to 7:42 PM Tuesday plus 12 hours to 7:42 AM Wednesday plus 7 hours to 2:42 PM Wednesday plus 33 minutes to 3:15 PM Wednesday, so the total is $4 \cdot 24 \cdot 60 + 12 \cdot 60 + 7 \cdot 60 + 33 = 5760 + 720 + 420 + 33 = 6,933$ minutes.

1. It used to be the there was no speed limit on many highways in Montana, but they had trouble with German tourists wanting something like the autobahn with less traffice. Therefore, the speed limit on most highways in Montana is 80 mph. Which is closest to that speed in feet per second (1 mile = 5280 feet)?
   A. 101
   B. 105
   C. 109
   D. 113
   E. 117

2. If Gertrude drove 7 miles in 11 minutes on her way to work, what was her average speed to the nearest mile per hour? ③
   A. 37
   B. 38
   C. 39
   D. 40
   E. 42

3. How many minutes would it take for a plane to travel 160 miles at a constant speed of 400 miles per hour?③
   A. 12
   B. 16
   C. 20
   D. 24
   E. 32

4. A fighter plane flies at 1,600 mph. How far will it fly in 18 minutes?③
   A. 300
   B. 360
   C. 400
   D. 480
   E. 540

5. If a bird travelled 2 miles in 50 seconds, what was its average speed in mph? ④
   A. 72
   B. 108
   C. 136
   D. 144
   E. 288

6. If a Norfolk and Western Railway freight train with 73 cars travelled 3000 kilometers between a major city and a railroad town in a 24 hour day, what was its average speed in meters per second? ④
   A. 32.7
   B. 33.1
   C. 33.7
   D. 34.3
   E. 34.7

7. If Sylvester ran 12 laps around a circular track at Wilkinson High School field with radius 200 meters in 37 minutes, what was his average speed in kilometers per hour? ④
   A. 21.5
   B. 22.5
   C. 23.5
   D. 24.5
   E. 25.5

8. Dwayne left at noon, travelled 250 miles, and averaged 57 mph. At what time did he arrive at his destination to the nearest minute? ④
   A. 3:23 PM
   B. 3:43 PM
   C. 4:03 PM
   D. 4:13 PM
   E. 4:23 PM

9. If a train left New York at 2 PM Tuesday and travelled 3000 miles to Seattle at an average speed of 48 mph, on what day and at what time did it arrive, to the nearest 5 minutes? ④
   A. Friday at 1:30 AM
   B. Friday at 2:30 AM
   C. Friday at 3:30 AM
   D. Friday at 4:30 AM
   E. Friday at 5:30 AM

10. If a train left Atlanta at 4:26 PM Monday and arrived at its destination 2300 miles away at 7:11 AM Wednesday, what was its average speed to the nearest mile per hour? ④
    A. 55
    B. 56
    C. 57
    D. 58
    E. 59

11. If Gabriel averaged 30 mph going to the beach in heavy traffic and 60 mph going home, what was his average speed for the round trip? ④

   A. 40 mph

   B. 42 mph

   C. 43 mph

   D. 44 mph

   E. 45 mph

12. Kevin ran a 6 mile cross country course in 31 minutes and Robert took 34 minutes for the same course. To the nearest tenth what was the difference in their speeds in miles per hour? ④

   A. 1.0

   B. 1.1

   C. 1.2

   D. 1.3

   E. 1.4

13. Steve averaged 60 mph for the first 120 miles and 80 mph for the final 240 miles of an important business trip; what was his average speed in mph for the 360 miles trip? ④

   A. 70 mph

   B. 71 mph

   C. 72 mph

   D. 73 mph

   E. 75 mph

14. A tire has a radius of 30 cm. About how many times does it rotate when the vehicle travels 7 km? ④

   A. 3,424

   B. 3,524

   C. 3,624

   D. 3,724

   E. 3,824

11.2. Other Rates

A backyard pool is $10' \times 20' \times 5'$. If the pool is full and starts to be emptied at 2 PM at the rate of 4 cubic feet per minute, when will the pool be empty? $10 \cdot 20 \cdot 5 = 1000$. $\frac{1000}{4} = 250$. 250 minutes=4 hours and 10 minutes, so it will be empty at 6:10 PM.

When finding the area between two geometric figures, take the area of the larger figure minus the area of the smaller figure.

15. Each case of apple juice contains 24 16-ounce bottles. What is the least number of cases needed to serve 500 people 6 ounces each?③

   A. 6

   B. 7

   C. 8

   D. 9

   E. 10

16. A cylindrical pool at a motel with radius 20 meters and height of water when full 2 meters is filled at 2 cubic meters per second. To the nearest minute, how many minutes would it take for the pool to go from empty to full? ⑤

   A. 21

   B. 22

   C. 24

   D. 27

   E. 33

17. A point on the rim of a wheel with a radius of 100 meters travels 70 meters in 1 minute. At how many degrees per second does the wheel rotate? ④

   A. 0.5°

   B. 0.7°

   C. 1.1°

   D. 1.3°

   E. 1.4°

18. A wheel with a radius of 100 meters rotates at 2 degrees per second. How many meters does a point on the wheel the maximum distance from the center travel in 1 minute? ④

A. $\dfrac{230\pi}{3}$

B. $\dfrac{280\pi}{3}$

C. $\dfrac{250\pi}{3}$

D. $\dfrac{220\pi}{3}$

E. $\dfrac{200\pi}{3}$

19. A pool is the area between two concentric circles with radii 5 and 8 feet and is 4 feet deep. If the pool is empty at 1:20 PM and is filled at a rate of 7 cubic feet per minute, at what time to the nearest minute will the pool first become full? ⑤

A. 2:25 PM

B. 2:30 PM

C. 2:35 PM

D. 2:40 PM

E. 2:45 PM

20. If a vehicle's tire with radius 15 inches turns at 1000 revolutions per minute, what is the approximate speed of the vehicle in miles per hour (1 mile = 5,280 feet)? ④

A. 82

B. 84

C. 89

D. 97

E. 104

— ANSWER KEY

1E, 2B,3D 4D 5D, 6E, 7D, 8E, 9D, 10E, 11A,12A 13C, 14D 15C 16A, 17B, 18E, 19B, 20C.

11.3. Solutions

1. (E) $80 \cdot \dfrac{5280}{3600} \approx 117.3 \approx 117$

2. (B) Take miles divided by minutes to get miles per minute. Then multiply miles per minute by 60 to convert to miles per hour: $\dfrac{7}{11} \cdot 60 - \dfrac{420}{11} \approx 38$.

3. (D) $\dfrac{160}{400} \cdot 60 = \dfrac{2}{5} \cdot 60 = 24$ minutes.

4. (D) $1600 \cdot \dfrac{18}{60} = 480$.

5. (D) First take miles divided by seconds. Then multiply miles per second by 3600 seconds in an hour to convert to mph:
$$\frac{2}{50} \cdot 3600 = 144 \text{ mph}.$$

6. (E) Multiply by 1000 to convert from kilometers to meters and divide by $24 \cdot 3600$ to convert from days to seconds. $3000 \cdot \dfrac{1000}{24 \cdot 3600} \approx 34.7$.

7. (D) Determine the distance in meters. Then convert meters per second to kilometers per hour.
$$200 \cdot 2\pi \cdot 12 = 15079.64 \text{ meters} \approx 15.08 \text{ kilometers}; \quad 15.08 \cdot \frac{60}{37} = \frac{15.08 \times 60}{37} \approx 24.5.$$

8. (E) Distance / rate = time: substitute in distance and rate and find time: $\dfrac{250}{57} = 4.386$; now convert the decimal portion of an hour to minutes: $0.386 \cdot 60 \approx 23$, so 4 hours and 23 minutes; therefore, he arrived at 4:23.

9. (D) $\dfrac{3000}{48} = \dfrac{125}{2} = 62.5$ hours. Dividing by 24, we get 2 days and 14.5 hours. $0.5 \times 60 = 30$ minutes, so 2 days, 14 hours, 30 minutes, adding to the initial day and time, we get Friday at 4:30 AM.

10. (E) Find the total time in hours by adding 24 hours for a day to the number of hours to the proportion of an hour the number of minutes represents: hours $= 24 + 14 + \dfrac{3}{4} = \dfrac{155}{4}$ (now take miles divided by hours to get mph) $= \dfrac{2300}{\frac{155}{4}} \approx 59.4$ mph.

11. (A) Assume the trip was 120 miles (this number makes it easier; you could assume a different number or use a variable). Then it took 4 hours going there and 2 hours going back. The total

time is 6 hours and the total distance 240 miles, so the average speed is $\dfrac{240}{6} = 40$ mph. It is a trap to just take the average of the speeds in each direction. You can understand this concept by considering that the average is closer to the slower speed than the faster one because you spend more time travelling at that slower speed.

12. (A) Kevin's speed $= \dfrac{6}{\frac{31}{60}} = \dfrac{360}{31} \approx 11.61$ mph. Robert's speed $= \dfrac{6}{\frac{34}{60}} = \dfrac{360}{34} \approx 10.59$. $11.61 - 10.59 = 1.02 \approx 1.0$.

13. (C) Find the total time there and back, and then take total miles divided by total hours.

2 hours+3 hours=5 hours; $\dfrac{360 \text{ miles}}{5 \text{ hours}} = 72$ mph.

14. (D) 7 km$= 7 \cdot 100 \cdot 1000 = 700,000$ cm. Circumference of tire $= 2\pi r = 2\pi \cdot 30 = 60\pi$ cm. $\dfrac{700,000}{60\pi} \approx 3,724$ rotations.

15. (C) $\dfrac{500 \cdot 6}{24 \cdot 16} = \dfrac{3000}{384} \approx 7.81$. Rounding up, 8 cases are needed.

16. (A) Using the volume of cylinder formula, $\pi r^2 h$, the volume of the pool $= 2 \times 20^2 \times \pi = 800\pi$ cubic meters; therefore, to find the time, divide that volume by the rate, and then convert seconds to minutes:

$\dfrac{800\pi}{2} = 400\pi \approx 1256$ (now convert from seconds to minutes) $\dfrac{1256}{60} \approx 21$ minutes.

17. (B) Find the portion of the circle rotated per minute, and then convert that to degrees.

$\dfrac{70}{100 \cdot 2\pi} = 0.1114$ of a circle per minute (converting to degrees and to second: multiply by 360 to convert to degrees and divide by 60 to convert per minute to per second)

$0.1114 \cdot \dfrac{360}{60} = 0.668 \approx 0.7°$.

18. (E) Find the circumference and convert to minutes. Multiply by the rate and divide by the number of degrees in a circle. $60 \cdot 2 = 120$ degrees per minute. Circumference $= 2\pi r = 200\pi$, find the distance in meters, $200\pi \cdot \dfrac{120}{360} = \dfrac{200\pi}{3}$ meters.

19. (B) The volume of the pool is the area of the larger circle minus the area of the smaller circle, taking the result times the depth, $(8^2\pi - 5^2\pi) \cdot 4 = 156\pi$ (find the time to fill the pool by taking volume divided by rate) $\dfrac{156\pi}{7} = 70.01$. Therefore, filling the pool takes about 70 minutes. 70 minutes after 1:20 PM is 2:30 PM.

20. (C) Multiply by 2π to convert radius to circumference ($C = 2\pi r$), multiply by 60 to convert to hours, and divide by 5280 (you multiply because you go 60 times further in an hour than a minute and divide because you travel many fewer miles than feet) to convert to miles as follows:

$$\dfrac{1000 \cdot 2\pi \cdot 60 \cdot 15}{5280 \cdot 12} \approx 89 \text{ mph.}$$

12. Ratios

12.1. General Ratios

An example of finding a ratio from two other ratios is a:b=2:5, b:c=3:7. What is a:c?

$$\frac{a}{c} = \frac{a}{b} \cdot \frac{b}{c} = \frac{2}{5} \cdot \frac{3}{7} = \frac{6}{35};$$

as a ratio that fraction can be expressed as 6:35.

1. What is the length of AB? ④

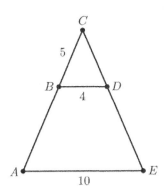

A. 7.5
B. 8
C. 9
D. 10
E. 12.5

2. The ratio of a to b is $5:8$ and b to c is $3:2$. Which of these is the ratio of a to c? ④
   A. $20:3$
   B. $15:16$
   C. $16:15$
   D. $12:5$
   E. $5:12$

3. If a:b=3:2 and b:c=4:1, what is $\dfrac{a+b}{b+c}$? ④

   A. 3
   B. $\dfrac{5}{2}$
   C. 4
   D. 2
   E. $\dfrac{3}{2}$

4. Which ratio is equivalent to 8^5 to 16^3? ③
   A. $8:3$
   B. $16:1$
   C. $16:3$
   D. $8:1$
   E. $4:1$

5. What fraction of an 8-inch pizza contains the same amount of pizza as a slice of a 10-inch pizza cut into 8 equal slices, assuming that all parts of both pizzas have the same thickness? ④

   A. $\dfrac{5}{16}$

   B. $\dfrac{7}{32}$

   C. $\dfrac{25}{128}$

   D. $\dfrac{1}{5}$

   E. $\dfrac{11}{64}$

6. The ratio of $a : b$ is $3 : 2$, what is $\dfrac{2a + 5b}{3a + b}$?
   ④

   A. $11 : 16$

   B. $20 : 11$

   C. $16 : 11$

   D. $21 : 11$

   E. $18 : 11$

12.2. Algebraic

If you are given some rational expression in two variables and asked to find the ratio, say $\dfrac{y}{x}$, cross multiply or multiply by the denominator to clear it, then get all the terms with the same variable on the same side, and finally combine like terms and divide to get the ratio.

For example $\dfrac{x + y}{2x + y} = \dfrac{3}{4}$; what is y/x? Cross multiply: $(x + y) \cdot 4 = (2x + y) \cdot 3 \implies 4x + 4y = 6x + 3y \implies y = 2x \implies y/x = 2$

7. What value of x makes the proportion true $\dfrac{6}{3 + x} = \dfrac{4}{5}$? ③

   A. 1

   B. $\dfrac{3}{2}$

   C. 2

   D. $\dfrac{5}{2}$

   E. $\dfrac{9}{2}$

8. If $\dfrac{x + y}{2x + 5y} = a$, what is $\dfrac{y}{x}$? ④

   A. $\dfrac{1 - 2a}{5a - 1}$

   B. $\dfrac{5a - 2}{1 - 2a}$

   C. $\dfrac{5a - 4}{1 - 2a}$

   D. $\dfrac{5a - 1}{1 - 2a}$

   E. $\dfrac{5a - 3}{1 - 2a}$

9. If $\dfrac{3x + 5y}{5x + 2y} = \dfrac{4}{5}$, what is $\dfrac{y}{x}$? ④

   A. $\dfrac{-5}{11}$

   B. $\dfrac{5}{17}$

   C. $\dfrac{-1}{17}$

   D. $\dfrac{3}{11}$

   E. $\dfrac{-3}{17}$

12.3. Maps and Scale Factors

You need to be able to convert distance on a map to real life distance using a scale factor.

For example, if $\frac{3}{8}$ inch equals 200 miles, 2 inches is $\frac{2 \cdot 200}{(3/8)} = \frac{3200}{3} \approx 1067$ miles.

10. If $\frac{1}{2}$ inch on a map represents 30 miles, what is the distance between towns that are $2\frac{3}{8}$ inches apart on the map? ③

   A. 130 miles

   B. 132.5 miles

   C. 135 miles

   D. 137.5 miles

   E. 142.5 miles

11. If $\frac{1}{4}$ inch on a map represents 75 miles, how far apart on the map in inches are Beta City and Gamma Town that are 400 miles apart? ③

   A. $1\frac{1}{4}$

   B. $1\frac{1}{2}$

   C. $\frac{2}{3}$

   D. $2\frac{1}{3}$

   E. $1\frac{1}{3}$

12. One inch on a map represents 5 miles. What would be the area on the map in square inches of a rectangular park this measures $\frac{1}{2}$ mile by 3 miles? ④

   A. 0.06

   B. 0.12

   C. 0.3

   D. 0.6

   E. 1.2

① Easiest

⑤ Most Difficult

— ANSWER KEY

1A, 2B, 3D, 4D, 5C, 6C, 7E, 8A, 9B, 10E, 11E, 12A

12.4. Solutions

1. (A) $\dfrac{CB}{AC} = \dfrac{BD}{AE}$ by similar triangles

$$\dfrac{5}{AC} = \dfrac{4}{10} \implies AC = 12.5 \text{ (now find } AB) \quad AB = 12.5 - 5 = 7.5.$$

2. (B) $\dfrac{a}{b} = \dfrac{5}{8}$ and $\dfrac{b}{c} = \dfrac{3}{2}$ (multiplying the ratios) $\dfrac{a}{c} = \dfrac{a}{b} \cdot \dfrac{b}{c} = \dfrac{5}{8} \cdot \dfrac{3}{2} = \dfrac{15}{16}.$

3. (D) Find a and c in terms of b. $\dfrac{a}{b} = \dfrac{3}{2} \implies a = \dfrac{3b}{2}$ and $\dfrac{b}{c} = \dfrac{4}{1} \implies c = \dfrac{b}{4}.$

   Now substitute to get the whole expression in terms of b, and then simplify to get the ratio.

   $$\dfrac{\dfrac{3b}{2} + b}{\dfrac{b}{4} + b} = \dfrac{\dfrac{5b}{2}}{\dfrac{5b}{4}} = 2.$$

4. (D) Convert to powers of 2 (because the bases are powers of 2; if the bases were 9 and 27, you would express them as powers of 3) and then simplify the expression in terms powers of 2 using the laws of exponents. Power of power means multiply exponents. Dividing means subtract exponents.

   $$\dfrac{(2^3)^5}{(2^4)^3} = \dfrac{2^{15}}{2^{12}} = 2^3 = 8, \text{ so the ratio is } 8 : 1.$$

5. (C) Find the area of 1/8 of the large pizza and set that equal to the unknown portion of the small pizza. Using the formula for the area of a circle, πr^2,

   $$\dfrac{10^2 \cdot \pi}{8} = 8^2 \cdot \pi x \implies \dfrac{100}{8} = 64x \implies x = \dfrac{100}{512} = \dfrac{25}{128}.$$

6. (C) Solve for a in terms of b. $\dfrac{a}{b} = \dfrac{3}{2} \implies a = \dfrac{3b}{2}$ (now substitute for a in the given rational expression and then simplify to find the ratio)

   $$\dfrac{2\left(\dfrac{3b}{2}\right) + 5b}{3\left(\dfrac{3b}{2}\right) + b} = \dfrac{8b}{\dfrac{11b}{2}} = \dfrac{16}{11}.$$

7. (E) $30 = 12 + 4x \implies 18 = 4x \implies x = \dfrac{9}{2}.$

8. (A) Multiplying both sides by $2x + 5y$ to clear the denominator, we obtain: $x + y = 2ax + 5ay$ (get the y terms on one side and the x terms on the other) $x - 2ax = 5ay - y$ (factoring out x and y) $(1 - 2a)x = (5a - 1)y$ $\left(\text{now divide to get } \dfrac{y}{x}\right)$ $\dfrac{y}{x} = \dfrac{1 - 2a}{5a - 1}$.

9. (B) Cross multiply, get like terms on the same side, combine like terms, and divide to get the required ratio. Cross multiplying, we obtain.

$$(3x + 5y) \cdot 5 = (5x + 2y) \cdot 4 \implies 15x + 25y = 20x + 8y \implies 17y = 5x \implies \frac{y}{x} = \frac{5}{17}.$$

10. (E) We are given 1 inch equals 60 miles; now take that ratio times the distance on map converted to an improper fraction. $60 \cdot \dfrac{19}{8} = \dfrac{285}{2}$.

11. (E) Set up a ratio and solve,

$$\frac{x}{400} = \frac{\frac{1}{4}}{75} \implies x = 400 \cdot \frac{\frac{1}{4}}{75} = \frac{100}{75} = \frac{4}{3} = 1\frac{1}{3} \text{ inches.}$$

Another solution is finding 1 inch is $4 \cdot 75 = 300$ miles. (taking the ratio of given miles to miles corresponding to an inch) $\dfrac{400}{300} = \dfrac{4}{3} = 1\dfrac{1}{3}$ inches.

12. (A) $\dfrac{1}{10}$ inch by $\dfrac{3}{5}$ inches. $\dfrac{1}{10} \cdot \dfrac{3}{5} = \dfrac{3}{50}$ square inches $= 0.06$ square inches. Alternative solution: $\dfrac{\frac{1}{2} \cdot 3}{5^2} = \dfrac{\frac{3}{2}}{25} = \dfrac{3}{50} = 0.06$.

13. Absolute Value Equations

This is another area emphasized in this guide because extremely difficult absolute value problems may appear on the exam.

Absolute value equations and inequalities generally need to be split into 2 equations, because if what is inside the absolute value symbols is negative, you take the negative of it, but do not change it if it is positive.

A typical ACT trap question asks the student to solve $|3x + 7| = -2$. This has no solutions, as absolute value cannot be negative. It is easy to split it up and find 2 solutions, which are incorrect, and which incidentally do not check. $|3x + 7| < -2$ also has no solutions, whereas $|3x + 7| > -2$ is true for all real numbers.

13.1. Evaluating Expressions

1. What is $|3x + 7|$ when $x = -11$? ③
   - **A.** 4
   - **B.** 18
   - **C.** 26
   - **D.** 33
   - **E.** 40

13.2. Linear Equations

To solve $|2x - 3| = 5$, (split the equation into 2 equations) $2x - 3 = 5$ and $2x - 3 = -5$ (and solve both equations) $2x = 8$ or $2x = -2 \implies x = 4$ or $x = -1$.

Solve $|x + 1| = x + 6$ (split the equation) $x + 1 = x + 6$ if $x + 1 \geq 0$ ($x \geq -1$) or $-x - 1 = x + 6$ if $x + 1 < 0$ ($x < -1$) $\implies 1 = 6$ (which is impossible) or $-7 = 2x \implies x = \dfrac{-7}{2}$

2. If $|x - 7| = 18$, what is x? ③
   - **A.** -25
   - **B.** -11 or 25
   - **C.** -11
   - **D.** 11 or 25
   - **E.** 11 or -25

3. Solve $|11x + 4| = 21$. ③
   - **A.** $\dfrac{17}{11}$ or $-\dfrac{25}{11}$
   - **B.** $\dfrac{19}{11}$ or $-\dfrac{25}{11}$
   - **C.** $\dfrac{19}{11}$
   - **D.** $\dfrac{17}{11}$
   - **E.** $-\dfrac{25}{11}$

4. What is the positive difference of the solutions of $|x + 11| = 35$? ③

    A. 35

    B. 50

    C. 60

    D. 70

    E. 140

5. For what range of a-values does $|2x + 5| = a$ have no solution? ④

    A. $\left(-\infty, \dfrac{5}{2}\right)$

    B. $\left(-\dfrac{5}{2}, \dfrac{5}{2}\right)$

    C. $\left(-\infty, -\dfrac{5}{2}\right)$

    D. $(-\infty, 0]$

    E. $(-\infty, 0)$

6. What is the solution set of $|x| = x + 3$? ④

    A. $\dfrac{3}{2}$

    B. No solution

    C. $\left\{-\dfrac{3}{2}, \dfrac{3}{2}\right\}$

    D. $-\dfrac{3}{2}$

    E. $\left\{-\dfrac{3}{2}, 0\right\}$

7. What is the solution set of $|x + 2| = x + 5$? ④

    A. $\left\{-\dfrac{7}{2}, \dfrac{7}{2}\right\}$

    B. $\left\{-\dfrac{7}{2}, -\dfrac{3}{2}\right\}$

    C. $-\dfrac{7}{2}$

    D. $\left\{-\dfrac{7}{2}, \dfrac{3}{2}\right\}$

    E. $\left\{-\dfrac{7}{2}, \dfrac{1}{2}\right\}$

8. What is the solution set of $|x - 5| = x - 5$? ④

    A. $x \geq 5$

    B. $x > 5$

    C. $x = 5$ or $x = -5$

    D. $x = 5$

    E. $x \geq 5$ or $x \leq -5$

13.3. Quadratic Equations

An example of a relatively difficult problem is $|x|^2 - 2|x| - 15 = 0$ (splitting the equation) $x^2 - 2x - 15 = 0$ if $x \geq 0$ or $x^2 + 2x - 15 = 0$ if $x < 0$. For the first equation, 5 and -3 are solutions. For the second equation -5 and 3 are solutions. Only 5 and -5 check because of the above restrictions on x, so the solution set is $\{-5, 5\}$. Usually, in this type of problem, 2 solutions with the same absolute value will be the correct answer. If you do not know how to solve this type of problem algebraically, it may be easier to substitute in answer choices.

In some complicated problems, you need to first split based on the outer construct, whether it be squared or absolute value, and then split based on the inner construct. These problems often have 4 solutions, although some of those may not check.

9. Which of these is the product of all the solutions of $|x^2 - 9| = 4$? ④

    A. -65

    B. -36

    C. 9

    D. 36

    E. 65

10. What are the solutions of $(|x|-7)^2 = 16$? ④

    A. $\{-11, 11\}$

    B. $\{-11, -3, 0, 3, 11\}$

    C. $\{-11, -3, 3, 11\}$

    D. $\{3, 11\}$

    E. $\{-3, 3\}$

11. What are all the solutions of $|x^2| + 4|x| - 21 = 0$? ⑤

    A. $\{3, -3\}$

    B. $\{-7, -3\}$

    C. $\{7, -7\}$

    D. $\{3, -3, 7, -7\}$

    E. $\{3, 7\}$

12. What are the solutions of $x^2 + 5|x| = 14$? ⑤

    A. $\{2\}$

    B. $\{-7, -2, 2, 7\}$

    C. $\{2, -2\}$

    D. $\{2, 7\}$

    E. $\{-2\}$

13. What are the solutions of $|x^2 - 5| = 2$? ⑤

    A. $\pm\sqrt{3}$

    B. $\pm\sqrt{7}$

    C. $\pm\sqrt{3}, \pm\sqrt{7}$

    D. 3 and 7

    E. $\pm\sqrt{3}, \pm\sqrt{2}$

13.4. Inequalities

The following formulas are key and should be memorized and/or understood.

$|x| < a$ is equivalent to $-a < x < a$

$|x| > a$ is equivalent to $x < -a$ or $x > a$.

With absolute value inequalities, the solutions are ranges, and you need to be careful when effectively dividing by a negative. If you are asked to solve $|4x - 5| \geq 7$, then split it into two inequalities $4x - 5 \geq 7$ and $5 - 4x \geq 7 \implies 4x \geq 12$

and $-2 \geq 4x \implies x \geq 3$ or $\dfrac{-1}{2} \geq x$. In interval notation, the solution is $\left(-\infty, \dfrac{-1}{2}\right] \cup [3, \infty)$. You could also have worked the second part of the problem as $4x - 5 \leq -7$ (switching the sign) $4x \leq -2 \implies x \leq \dfrac{-1}{2}$.

14. How would one express that the temperature T in a room needs to be between 70 and 86 degrees Fahrenheit as an absolute value inequality? ③

    A. $|T - 86| \leq 70$

    B. $|T - 78| \leq 16$

    C. $|T - 78| \leq 8$

    D. $|T - 86| \leq 16$

    E. $|T - 78| \leq 4$

15. What is the solution of $|2x - 5| < 3$? ④

    A. $1 < x < 7$

    B. $1 \leq x \leq 4$

    C. $1 < x < 4$

    D. $x < 1$ or $x > 4$

    E. $0 < x < 5$

16. What are the solutions of $|2x - 7| > 5$? ④

    A. $(-\infty, 1)$

    B. $(-\infty, 1) \cup (6, \infty)$

    C. $(6, \infty)$

    D. $(-\infty, 1] \cup [6, \infty)$

    E. $(1, 6)$

17. What is the solution set of $|x^2-3x-7| > -2$? ④

    A. $(-\infty, \infty)$

    B. $\left(-\dfrac{7}{3}, \infty\right)$

    C. $(-\infty, -4) \cup \left(\dfrac{7}{3}, \infty\right)$

    D. $\left(\dfrac{7}{3}, \infty\right)$

    E. $\left(-\infty, -\dfrac{7}{3}\right)$

18. What is the solution set of $|x - 5000| \leq 23$? ③

    A. $[4977, 5023]$

    B. $[0, 5023]$

    C. $[-23, 4977]$

    D. $[23, 4977]$

    E. $(4977, 5023)$

19. For what values is $|x - 3| \geq x$? ④

    A. $x \leq \dfrac{3}{2}$ or $x > 6$

    B. $x < \dfrac{3}{2}$

    C. $x \leq 0$

    D. $x \leq 3$

    E. $x \leq \dfrac{3}{2}$

20. How would one express that a machine part for a turbine must have a radius of 12 cm plus or minus 0.02 cm as an absolute value inequality? ③

    A. $|x - 0.02| \leq 12$

    B. $|x - 12| \leq 0.02$

    C. $|x - 12| \leq 0.04$

    D. $|x - 12| \leq 0.2$

    E. $|x - 12| \geq 0.02$

21. The temperatures T in Fahrenheit recorded in Death Valley are described by $|T - 76| \leq 58$. What is the lowest temperature recorded in Death Valley? ③

    A. $12°$

    B. $14°$

    C. $16°$

    D. $18°$

    E. $20°$

22. Which of these is equivalent to $(|x| + 2)^2 < 25$? ⑤

    A. $-3 < x < 3$

    B. $x < 3$

    C. $-10 < x < 3$

    D. $0 < x < 3$

    E. $-5 < x < 3$

① Easiest

⑤ Most Difficult

xC 1B, 2A, 3D, 4E, 5D, 6C, 7A, 8E, 9C, 10A, 11C, 12C, 13C, 14C, 15B, 16A, 17A, 18E, 19B, 20D, 21A

13.5. Solutions

1. (C) $|3 \cdot (-11) + 7| = |-33 + 7| = |-26| = 26$.

2. (B) $x - 7 = 18 \Rightarrow x = 25$ or $x - 7 = -18 \Rightarrow x = -11$.

3. (A) Split the absolute value equation into 2 equations: $11x + 4 = 21$ or $11x + 4 = -21 \implies 11x = 17$ or $11x = -25$.

    $$\implies x = \frac{17}{11} \quad \text{or} \quad x = -\frac{25}{11}.$$

4. (D) Splitting the equation, $x + 11 = 35$ or $x + 11 = -35 \implies x = 24$ or $x = -46$, so the positive difference of the solutions is $24 - (-46) = 70$. It is possible to figure out the answer without working through the problem.

5. (E) Look only at the range for which $a < 0$ because absolute value cannot be negative.

6. (D) $x = x + 3$ or $-x = x + 3$ The first equation gives $0 = 3$ (which is impossible), but the second equation gives $-3 = 2x \implies \frac{-3}{2} = x$.

7. (C) $x + 2 = x + 5$ or $-x - 2 = x + 5$ the first equation gives $2 = 5$ (which is impossible), but the second one gives $-7 = 2x \implies x = \frac{-7}{2}$.

8. (A) $x - 5 = x - 5$ for $x \geq 5$, which is true for all x, so any $x \geq 5$ is a solution. For $x \leq 5$, $5 - x = x - 5 \implies 10 = 2x \implies x = 5$. Therefore, the solution is $x \geq 5$.

9. (E) First split the absolute value equation and then take the square roots. $x^2 - 9 = 4$ or $x^2 - 9 = -4 \implies x^2 = 13$ or $x^2 = 5 \implies \sqrt{13}$ and $-\sqrt{13}$ or $\sqrt{5}$ and $-\sqrt{5}$ Multiplying the solutions, $\sqrt{13} \cdot (-\sqrt{13}) \cdot \sqrt{5} \cdot (-\sqrt{5}) = 65$.

10. (C) Take the square root first and then split the absolute value equations. Taking the square root of both sides of the given equation, $|x| - 7 = \pm 4 \implies |x| = 11$ or $|x| = 3$ (taking both values that satisfy each absolute value equation) $-11, -3, 3, 11$.

11. (A) $x^2 + 4x - 21 = 0$ (solving the quadratic) $x = 3$ or -7, and $x^2 - 4x - 21 = 0$ (solving the other quadratic) $x = -3$ or 7. Only 3 and -3 check. You can determine that by checking the solutions, but also because they are the only solutions in the ranges for the split problems.

12. (C) $x^2 + 5|x| = 14$ Splitting the equation, $x^2 + 5x - 14 = 0$ and $x^2 - 5x - 14 = 0$. The solutions are $-7, -2, 2$ and 7, but only 2 and -2 check. You can determine that by checking the solutions, but also because they are the only solutions in the ranges for the split equations.

13. (C) Splitting the original equation into 2 equations, $x^2 - 5 = 2 \implies x = \pm\sqrt{7}$ and $5 - x^2 = 2 \implies x = \pm\sqrt{3}$.

14. (C) Take the average of the extremes to determine the center point, and half their difference to determine how far we can move in either direction from the center point.

$$\frac{70 + 86}{2} = 78 \quad \text{and} \quad \frac{86 - 70}{2} = 8.$$

15. (C) Splitting the inequality, $2x - 5 < 3 \implies 2x < 8 \implies x < 4$ or $2x - 5 > -3 \implies 2x > 2 \implies x > 1$, so $1 < x < 4$

16. (B) $2x - 7 > 5$ or $2x - 7 < -5 \implies 2x > 12 \implies x > 6$ or $2x < 2 \implies x < 1$; in interval notation, $(-\infty, 1) \cup (6, \infty)$.

17. (A) Any absolute value expression is greater than or equal to 0, so there are no restrictions on x.

18. (A) $x - 5000 \leq 23$ or $x - 5000 \geq -23 \implies x \leq 5023$ or $x \geq 4977$; in interval notation $[4977, 5023]$.

19. (E) $x - 3 \geq x$ or $3 - x \geq x \implies -3 \geq 0$ (which is impossible) or $3 \geq 2x \implies x \leq \dfrac{3}{2}$.

20. (B) The difference from 12 must be less than or equal to 0.02. $|x - 12| \leq 0.02$.

21. (D) Splitting the absolute value inequality into two inequalities, $T - 76 \leq 58$ and $T - 76 \geq -58$. Therefore, the range of temperatures is $T \leq 134$ and $T \geq 18$. Therefore, the answer is 18.

22. (A) $|x| + 2 < 5$ and $|x| + 2 < -5 \implies |x| < 3$ and $|x| < -7$. The second case is never true, since absolute value cannot be negative, so solutions only need to satisfy the first case: $|x| < 3 \implies x < 3$ and $x > -3$ (combining inequalities) $-3 < x < 3$.

14. Radicals

14.1. Simplifying Radical Expressions

1. Which expression is equivalent to $\sqrt[3]{160}$? ③

    A. $2\sqrt[3]{10}$

    B. $2\sqrt[3]{20}$

    C. $4\sqrt[3]{10}$

    D. $4\sqrt[3]{5}$

    E. $8\sqrt[3]{5}$

2. Which expression is equivalent to $\sqrt{108}$? ③

    A. $6\sqrt{2}$

    B. $6\sqrt{3}$

    C. $9\sqrt{3}$

    D. $12\sqrt{3}$

    E. $9\sqrt{2}$

3. If $x^3 = 300$, and x is real then x is between which of the following integers? ③

    A. 4 and 5

    B. 5 and 6

    C. 6 and 7

    D. 7 and 8

    E. 8 and 9

14.2. Radical Equations

If the problem states $\sqrt{x+3} = 5$, then square both sides, $x + 3 = 25 \implies x = 22$. You are supposed to also check the solution in the original equation. Radical equations for which some of the solutions do not check are common on the SAT, but not on the ACT. Back solving (substituting in the answer choices for the variable and seeing which gives a correct equality) is the preferred method for most SAT radical equations, because multiple choice SAT radical problems generally have solutions which do not check, so you have to substitute in the answers anyway. It can also be used to solve most similar ACT problems.

4. If $\sqrt{x+3} = 5$, what is x? ③

    A. 22 or 28

    B. $\pm\sqrt{5}$

    C. 7

    D. 22

    E. 28

5. If $\sqrt{4 + \sqrt{x}} = 5$, then x equals? ④

    A. 21

    B. 84

    C. 105

    D. 441

    E. 941

6. If $\sqrt[5]{3x + 5} = 2$, what does x equal? ④

    A. $\dfrac{37}{3}$

    B. 9

    C. 1

    D. $\dfrac{11}{3}$

    E. -1

7. If $\sqrt{3x + 2} + 5 = 11$, what is x? ③

    A. $\dfrac{35}{3}$

    B. $\dfrac{31}{3}$

    C. $\dfrac{32}{3}$

    D. 11

    E. $\dfrac{34}{3}$

8. If $\sqrt{2}x = \sqrt{3}$, what does x equals? ③

    A. $2\sqrt{3}$

    B. $\dfrac{\sqrt{6}}{4}$

    C. $\sqrt{6}$

    D. $\dfrac{\sqrt{6}}{2}$

    E. $2\sqrt{6}$

14.3. Radical Expressions Squared or Multiplied

FOIL out the expressions and then simplify.

It is falling into a trap to square the terms individually, which results in missing terms, rather than FOILing out. For examples $12^2 = (10 + 2)^2 = 10^2 + 10\cdot2 + 10\cdot2 + 2^2 = 100 + 20 + 20 + 4 = 144$. It would not be correct to set $(10 + 2)^2 = 10^2 + 2^2 = 100 + 4 = 104$.

FOILing out,

$$\left(a\sqrt{b} + b\sqrt{a}\right)^2$$
$$= a^2b + ab\sqrt{ab} + ab\sqrt{ab} + b^2a$$
$$= a^2b + 2ab\sqrt{ab} + b^2a.$$

9. Which of these is $\left(4\sqrt{a} - 3\sqrt{b}\right)\left(4\sqrt{a} + 3\sqrt{b}\right)$ in simplified form? ④

    A. $256a - 81b$

    B. $4a - 9b$

    C. $16a - 9b$

    D. $64a - 9b$

    E. $16a + 9b$

10. Which of these is $\left(\sqrt{a} + \sqrt{b}\right)^2$ in simplified form? ③

    A. $a + b^2 + 2\sqrt{ab}$

    B. $2a + 2b + 2\sqrt{ab}$

    C. $a + b + \sqrt{ab}$

    D. $a + 2\sqrt{ab}$

    E. $a + b + 2\sqrt{ab}$

11. Which of these is $\left(2a + 3\sqrt{b}\right)\left(5a + 3\sqrt{b}\right)$ in simplified form? ④

   A. $10a^2 + 27a\sqrt{b} + 9b$

   B. $10a^2 + 18a\sqrt{b} + 9b$

   C. $10a^2 + 21a\sqrt{b} + 9b$

   D. $10a^2 + 20a\sqrt{b} + 9b$

   E. $10a^2 + 24a\sqrt{b} + 9b$

14.4. Radical Expressions Added or Divided

First, simplify the radical expression, taking out the real part. Then perform the operation. The problems will generally result in 2 or 3 terms with square root of the same number, such as $7\sqrt{5} + 4\sqrt{5}$.

For example, simplify and then subtract

$$\sqrt{242} - \sqrt{98} = 11\sqrt{2} - 7\sqrt{2} = 4\sqrt{2}$$

12. Which of following is equal to $\sqrt{3} + \sqrt{12}$? ④

   A. 3
   B. 9
   C. $\sqrt{18}$
   D. $\sqrt{27}$
   E. $\sqrt{54}$

13. The expression $\dfrac{24\sqrt{18}}{4\sqrt{2}}$ is equal to which of the following? ③
   A. 12
   B. 18
   C. 24
   D. $12\sqrt{2}$
   E. $9\sqrt{2}$

14. Which of these is equivalent to $\dfrac{\sqrt{108}}{\sqrt{75}}$? ③

   A. $\dfrac{6}{5}$

   B. $\dfrac{12}{5}$

   C. $\dfrac{\sqrt{6}}{2}$

   D. $\dfrac{9}{5}$

   E. $\dfrac{3}{5}$

15. Which of these is equivalent to $\dfrac{\sqrt{12}}{\sqrt{50}}$? ③

   A. $\dfrac{\sqrt{3}}{5}$

   B. $\dfrac{\sqrt{6}}{25}$

   C. $\dfrac{2\sqrt{6}}{5}$

   D. $\dfrac{\sqrt{2}}{5}$

   E. $\dfrac{\sqrt{6}}{5}$

16. Which of these is equivalent to $\sqrt{8} + \sqrt{18}$? ③
   A. $4\sqrt{2}$
   B. $5\sqrt{2}$
   C. $6\sqrt{2}$
   D. $2\sqrt{2}$
   E. $2\sqrt{10}$

14.5. Fractional Exponents and Radical Form

You should be able to convert back and forth between radical and fractional exponent form. You also should be able to perform operations on expressions in exponential form, using the laws of exponents. The basic relationship is $\sqrt[5]{x^8} = x^{\frac{8}{5}}$.

What is $x^{\frac{2}{3}} y^{\frac{4}{5}}$ in simplest radical form? Taking the least common denominator,

$$x^{\frac{10}{15}} y^{\frac{12}{15}} = \sqrt[15]{x^{10} y^{12}}.$$

17. Which of the following equals $x^{-1/2}$? ③

   A. $\dfrac{1}{x^2}$

   B. $\sqrt{x}$

   C. $\dfrac{\sqrt{x}}{x}$

   D. $\dfrac{\sqrt{x}}{x^2}$

   E. $x\sqrt{x}$

18. Which of the following is NOT equivalent to $2^{\frac{2}{3}}$? ③

   A. $\dfrac{\sqrt[3]{2}}{2}$

   B. $\sqrt[3]{4}$

   C. $\left(\sqrt[3]{2}\right)^2$

   D. $\dfrac{2}{\sqrt[3]{2}}$

   E. $\sqrt[6]{16}$

19. What is $x^{4/5}$ is radical form? ③

   A. $\sqrt[5]{x^2}$

   B. $\sqrt[4]{x^5}$

   C. $\sqrt[5]{x^4}$

   D. $\sqrt[5]{x}$

   E. $\sqrt[5]{x^8}$

20. For all positive real numbers x, $\left(\sqrt[4]{x^6}\right)^{1/3}$ equals what? ③

   A. $\sqrt[4]{x}$

   B. $\sqrt{x}$

   C. x

   D. $x\sqrt{x}$

   E. x^2

21. What is $\sqrt[5]{x^2}\,\sqrt[4]{x}$ in radical form? ③

   A. $\sqrt[20]{x}$

   B. $\sqrt[20]{x^9}$

   C. $\sqrt[20]{x^{13}}$

   D. $\sqrt[20]{x^{17}}$

   E. $\sqrt[10]{x^7}$

22. If $\sqrt[3]{\sqrt[4]{x^5}} = x^a$, what is a? ④

   A. $\dfrac{12}{5}$

   B. $\dfrac{7}{12}$

   C. $\dfrac{12}{7}$

   D. $\dfrac{5}{12}$

   E. $\dfrac{11}{12}$

23. Which of these is $\left(x^{\frac{7}{3}}\right)^{\frac{1}{2}}$ in radical form? ④

   A. $\sqrt[5]{x^7}$

   B. $\sqrt[3]{x^7}$

   C. $\sqrt[8]{x^7}$

   D. $\sqrt[6]{x^7}$

   E. $\sqrt[4]{x^7}$

24. Which of these is equivalent to $\sqrt[5]{x^3} \cdot \sqrt[3]{x^2}$? ③

   A. $x^{\frac{23}{15}}$

   B. $x^{\frac{17}{15}}$

   C. $x^{\frac{19}{15}}$

   D. $x^{\frac{13}{15}}$

   E. $x^{\frac{11}{15}}$

25. Which of these is $a^{\frac{1}{3}} a^{\frac{1}{4}}$ in simplest radical form? ④

   A. $\sqrt[12]{a^7}$

   B. $\sqrt[24]{a^7}$

   C. $\sqrt[12]{a^5}$

   D. $\sqrt[8]{a^7}$

   E. $\sqrt[6]{a^7}$

14.6. Rationalizing the Denominator

If there is an expression like $3 + \sqrt{2}$ in the denominator, multiply the numerator and denominator by the conjugate of that denominator, $3 - \sqrt{2}$, in order to eliminate irrational terms in the denominator. For example,

$$\frac{5 + 2\sqrt{3}}{4 + \sqrt{3}} = \frac{(5 + 2\sqrt{3})(4 - \sqrt{3})}{(4 + \sqrt{3})(4 - \sqrt{3})}$$
$$= \frac{20 - 5\sqrt{3} + 8\sqrt{3} - 6}{16 - 3} = \frac{14 + 3\sqrt{3}}{13}.$$

In general, these problems can be solved by rationalizing the denominator, either by multiplying the numerator and denominator by the denominator, when it is a simple radical expression or multiplying by the conjugate of an expression in the denominator with rational and irrational parts.

Solution 2 shows how to find the decimal value of the expression in the problem with your calculator and then compare it to the decimal values of the answer choices. That approach can also be applied to most of these problems, and using it avoids doing complicated math with radicals. However, calculator methods may be harder to implement with problems involving rationalizing complex denominators, which are covered later in this book.

26. Which of these equals $\dfrac{\sqrt{5}}{\sqrt{7}}$ in simplest radical form? ④

   A. $\dfrac{\sqrt{7}}{35}$

   B. $\dfrac{\sqrt{14}}{7}$

   C. $\dfrac{\sqrt{35}}{7}$

   D. $\dfrac{\sqrt{105}}{7}$

   E. $\dfrac{\sqrt{35}}{35}$

27. Which of these equals $\dfrac{1}{5 + \sqrt{2}}$? ③

   A. $\dfrac{5 - \sqrt{2}}{23}$

   B. $\dfrac{5 - \sqrt{2}}{27}$

   C. $\dfrac{5 + \sqrt{2}}{23}$

   D. $\dfrac{5 + \sqrt{2}}{27}$

   E. $\dfrac{5 - \sqrt{2}}{21}$

28. Which of these equals $\dfrac{1}{\sqrt{3}-\sqrt{2}}$ with a rational denominator? ④

A. $\sqrt{3}+\sqrt{2}$

B. $\dfrac{\sqrt{3}+\sqrt{2}}{6}$

C. $\sqrt{3}-\sqrt{2}$

D. $\dfrac{\sqrt{3}+\sqrt{2}}{2}$

E. $\dfrac{\sqrt{3}+\sqrt{2}}{3}$

29. Which of these is equivalent to $\dfrac{3+\sqrt{5}}{4+\sqrt{5}}$ with a rational denominator? ③

A. $\dfrac{7+\sqrt{5}}{12}$

B. $\dfrac{7+\sqrt{5}}{10}$

C. $\dfrac{7+\sqrt{5}}{11}$

D. $\dfrac{7+\sqrt{5}}{13}$

E. $\dfrac{7+\sqrt{5}}{9}$

30. Which of these is equivalent to $\dfrac{\sqrt{2}}{\sqrt{3}}+\dfrac{\sqrt{3}}{\sqrt{2}}$? ④

A. $\dfrac{5\sqrt{6}}{6}$

B. $\dfrac{5\sqrt{3}}{6}$

C. $5\sqrt{6}$

D. $\dfrac{5\sqrt{6}}{10}$

E. $\dfrac{5\sqrt{6}}{2}$

31. Which of these is equivalent to $\dfrac{1}{\sqrt{2}}+\dfrac{1}{\sqrt{5}}$? ④

A. $\dfrac{5\sqrt{2}+2\sqrt{5}}{10}$

B. $\dfrac{5\sqrt{2}+2\sqrt{5}}{20}$

C. $\dfrac{\sqrt{2}+\sqrt{5}}{10}$

D. $\dfrac{5\sqrt{2}+2\sqrt{5}}{5}$

E. $\dfrac{5\sqrt{2}+\sqrt{5}}{20}$

— ANSWER KEY

1B, 2B, 3C, 4D, 5D, 6B, 7E, 8D, 9C, 10E, 11C, 12D, 13B, 14A, 15E, 16B,17C 18A, 19C,20B 21C, 22D, 23D, 24C, 25A, 26C, 27A, 28A, 29C, 30A, 31A

14.7. Solutions

1. (B) $160 = 2 \cdot 80 = 2^2 \cdot 40 = 2^3 \cdot 20 = 2^4 \cdot 10 = 2^5 \cdot 5. Therefore, \sqrt[3]{2^5 \cdot 5} = \sqrt[3]{2^3} \cdot \sqrt[3]{2^2 \cdot 5} = 2\sqrt[3]{20}$.

2. (B) $108 = 54 \cdot 2 = 27 \cdot 2^2 = 9 \cdot 3 \cdot 2^2 = 3^3 \cdot 2^2$. Therefore, $\sqrt{108} = \sqrt{3^3 \cdot 2^2} = \sqrt{3} \cdot \sqrt{3^2 \cdot 2^2} = 6\sqrt{3}$.

3. (C) 6 and 7. With your calculator, $\sqrt[3]{300} = 300^{1/3} \approx 6.693$. Or take third powers, $5^3 = 125$, $6^3 = 216$, $7^3 = 343$.

4. (D) Squaring both sides, $x + 3 = 25 \implies x = 22$

5. (D) There are 2 radicals, so we need to square twice.

$$\sqrt{4 + \sqrt{x}} = 5 \text{ (squaring) } 4 + \sqrt{x} = 25 \implies \sqrt{x} = 21 \text{ (squaring again) } x = 441.$$

The answer checks.

6. (B) $\sqrt[5]{3x + 5} = 2$ (taking both sides to the 5th power) $3x + 5 = 32 \implies 3x = 27 \implies x = 9$. The answer checks.

7. (E) $\sqrt{3x + 2} + 5 = 11 \implies \sqrt{3x + 2} = 6$ (squaring) $3x + 2 = 36 \implies 3x = 34, x = \dfrac{34}{3}$. The answer checks.

8. (D) Divide to isolate x and then rationalize the denominator.

$$\sqrt{2}x = \sqrt{3} \implies x = \frac{\sqrt{3}}{\sqrt{2}} \text{ (rationalizing the denominator) } x = \frac{\sqrt{6}}{2}.$$

The answer checks.

9. (C) $\left(4\sqrt{a} - 3\sqrt{b}\right)\left(4\sqrt{a} + 3\sqrt{b}\right) = 16a + 12\sqrt{ab} - 12\sqrt{ab} - 9b = 16a - 9b$. These are conjugates, so the irrational terms drop out when you FOIL them.

10. (E) $\left(\sqrt{a} + \sqrt{b}\right) \cdot \left(\sqrt{a} + \sqrt{b}\right) = a + b + 2\sqrt{ab}$.

11. (C) $\left(2a + 3\sqrt{b}\right)\left(5a + 3\sqrt{b}\right)$ FOILing, $10a^2 + 6a\sqrt{b} + 15a\sqrt{b} + 9b = 10a^2 + 21a\sqrt{b} + 9b$.

12. (D) $\sqrt{3} + 2\sqrt{3} = 3\sqrt{3} = \sqrt{3^2 \cdot 3} = \sqrt{27}$.

13. (B) $6\sqrt{9} = 6 \cdot 3 = 18$.

14. (A) $\dfrac{\sqrt{108}}{\sqrt{75}} = \dfrac{6\sqrt{3}}{5\sqrt{3}} = \dfrac{6}{5}$.

15. (E) $\dfrac{\sqrt{12}}{\sqrt{50}} = \dfrac{2\sqrt{3}}{5\sqrt{2}}\left(\text{multiplying by} \dfrac{\sqrt{2}}{\sqrt{2}}\right) = \dfrac{2\sqrt{6}}{10} = \dfrac{\sqrt{6}}{5}.$

Alternate solution: dividing the numerator and denominator in the original expression by $\sqrt{2}$,
$\dfrac{\sqrt{6}}{\sqrt{25}} = \dfrac{\sqrt{6}}{5}.$

16. (B) $\sqrt{8} + \sqrt{18} = 2\sqrt{2} + 3\sqrt{2} = 5\sqrt{2}.$

17. (C) $x^{-1/2} = \dfrac{1}{\sqrt{x}} = \dfrac{\sqrt{x}}{x}.$

18. (A) $\sqrt[3]{4} = \sqrt[3]{2^2} = 2^{\frac{2}{3}}.$ $\sqrt[3]{2}^2 = 2^{\frac{2}{3}}.$ $\dfrac{2}{\sqrt[3]{2}} = \dfrac{2^1}{2^{\frac{1}{3}}} = 2^{\frac{2}{3}}.$ $\sqrt[6]{16} = \sqrt[6]{2^4} = 2^{\frac{4}{6}} = 2^{\frac{2}{3}}.$

19. (C) $\sqrt[5]{x^4}.$ The numerator is the power and the denominator is the root.

20. (B) $(x^{6/4})^{1/3} = x^{6/12} = x^{1/2} = \sqrt{x}$

21. (C) $\sqrt[5]{x^2}\sqrt[4]{x} = x^{\frac{2}{5}} \cdot x^{\frac{1}{4}} = x^{\frac{8}{20}+\frac{5}{20}} = x^{\frac{13}{20}} = \sqrt[20]{x^{13}}.$

22. (D) $\sqrt[3]{\sqrt[4]{x^5}} = x^{5 \cdot \frac{1}{4} \cdot \frac{1}{3}} = x^{\frac{5}{12}}.$

23. (D) $\left(x^{\frac{7}{3}}\right)^{\frac{1}{2}}.$ When taking the power of a power, multiply exponents. Then convert to radical form.

$$x^{\frac{7}{3}\cdot\frac{1}{2}} = x^{\frac{7}{6}} = \sqrt[6]{x^7}.$$

24. (C) $\sqrt[5]{x^3} \cdot \sqrt[3]{x^2}$ (convert to fractional exponents, and then add the fractions)

$$x^{\frac{3}{5}} \cdot x^{\frac{2}{3}} = x^{\frac{3}{5}+\frac{2}{3}} = x^{\frac{19}{15}}.$$

25. (A) $a^{\frac{1}{3}}a^{\frac{1}{4}}$ (Add the exponents, and then convert to radical form.)

$$a^{\frac{1}{3}+\frac{1}{4}} = a^{\frac{4}{12}+\frac{3}{12}} = a^{\frac{7}{12}} = \sqrt[12]{a^7}.$$

26. (C) Multiply the numerator and denominator by the denominator to rationalize,

$$\dfrac{\sqrt{5}\cdot\sqrt{7}}{\sqrt{7}\cdot\sqrt{7}} = \dfrac{\sqrt{35}}{7}.$$

27. (A) Multiply the numerator and denominator by the conjugate of the denominator,

$$\dfrac{5-\sqrt{2}}{\left(5+\sqrt{2}\right)\left(5-\sqrt{2}\right)} = \dfrac{5-\sqrt{2}}{25-2} = \dfrac{5-\sqrt{2}}{23}.$$

28. (A) Multiply the numerator and denominator by the conjugate of the denominator,

$$\dfrac{\sqrt{3}+\sqrt{2}}{\left(\sqrt{3}-\sqrt{2}\right)\left(\sqrt{3}+\sqrt{2}\right)} = \sqrt{3}+\sqrt{2}.$$

Alternate Solution: With a calculator, $\sqrt{3} - \sqrt{2} \approx 0.32$, $1/(\sqrt{3} - \sqrt{2}) \approx 3.146$. At this point, you may be able to determine by inspection that the answer is A. With a calculator, A is 3.146, so that is the answer.

29. (C) Multiply the numerator and denominator by the conjugate of the denominator,

$$\frac{(3 + \sqrt{5})(4 - \sqrt{5})}{(4 + \sqrt{5})(4 - \sqrt{5})} = \frac{7 + \sqrt{5}}{11}.$$

30. (A) Add fractions using the least common denominator,

$$\frac{\sqrt{2}}{\sqrt{3}} + \frac{\sqrt{3}}{\sqrt{2}} = \frac{\sqrt{2} \cdot \sqrt{2} + \sqrt{3} \cdot \sqrt{3}}{\sqrt{6}} = \frac{5}{\sqrt{6}} = \frac{5\sqrt{6}}{6}.$$

31. (A) Add fractions using the least common denominator,

$$\frac{1}{\sqrt{2}} + \frac{1}{\sqrt{5}} = \frac{\sqrt{5} + \sqrt{2}}{\sqrt{10}} = \frac{\sqrt{50} + \sqrt{20}}{10} = \frac{5\sqrt{2} + 2\sqrt{5}}{10}.$$

Alternate solution: rationalize the denominators of each expression first, and then add using an integer common denominator.

$$\frac{\sqrt{2}}{2} + \frac{\sqrt{5}}{5} = \frac{5\sqrt{2} + 2\sqrt{5}}{10}.$$

15. Systems of Equations

It is important to understand how to solve systems of equations by substitution and elimination. This book assumes you know that and does not try to teach the basics. I believe there are calculator programs which will solve systems of equations, and do similar math. I do not agree that programmable calculators should be allowed, but I am letting you know what is available. It is also best to understand how to solve problems on your own, as you can get confused in various ways using programs.

Often it is possible to solve systems by graphing with a calculator and finding the intersection point. However, you need to enter the equations in the right way for that to work.

15.1. Linear Systems

The following are examples of typical problems, one involving linear combinations and the other where you need to find a system of equations from a word problem.

1. If $\dfrac{4}{x} = 5$ and $\dfrac{y}{x} = 3$, what is y? ③
   A. $\dfrac{4}{5}$
   B. $\dfrac{12}{5}$
   C. $\dfrac{15}{4}$
   D. $\dfrac{36}{5}$
   E. $\dfrac{15}{2}$

2. If $y = 3x - 1$ and $y = x + 4$, what is x? ③
   A. $\dfrac{3}{4}$
   B. $\dfrac{5}{4}$
   C. $\dfrac{3}{2}$
   D. $\dfrac{7}{4}$
   E. $\dfrac{5}{2}$

3. If $2x + 5y = 10$ and $4x + 3y = 5$, what is $x + y$? ③
   A. $\dfrac{23}{14}$
   B. $\dfrac{27}{14}$
   C. $\dfrac{13}{7}$
   D. $\dfrac{25}{14}$
   E. $\dfrac{12}{7}$

4. At a food stand at the state fair, 10 hamburgers and 5 fries cost $95 and 6 hamburgers and 7 fries cost $69. How much does one hamburger cost? ③
   A. $7
   B. $7.25
   C. $7.50
   D. $7.75
   E. $8

15.2. Nonlinear Equations

In some cases the problem is easy to solve using algebraic relationships. For example, suppose you are given $x + y = 11$ and $x - y = 7$, and are asked to find $x^2 - y^2$? Observe that $(x+y)(x-y) = x^2 - y^2$, so $x^2 - y^2 = 11 \cdot 7 = 77$. You could also solve the system of equations and square the results, but that would be slower.

You should be prepared to solve systems of equations that include or result in a quadratic equation.

A difficult problem would be to find x and y that satisfy $x + y = 10$ and $xy = 17$. The easiest approach is to solve the left equation and substitute into the right equation. $y = 10 - x$ (substituting) $x(10-x) = 17$, so we have a quadratic to solve. Distributing, $10x - x^2 = 17$ (getting all the terms on one side) $x^2 - 10x + 17 = 0$. Applying the quadratic formula,

$$x = \frac{10 \pm \sqrt{100 - 68}}{2} = \frac{10 \pm \sqrt{32}}{2}$$

$$= \frac{10 \pm 4\sqrt{2}}{2} = 5 \pm 2\sqrt{2} \approx 7.8 \text{ and } 2.2.$$

Alternatively, you could solve the second equation for either variable and substitute into the first one.

$$y = \frac{17}{x} \text{ (substituting) } x + \frac{17}{x} = 10$$

(multiplying by x, which technically could introduce an extraneous solution, but is OK here)

$$x^2 + 17 = 10x \implies x^2 - 10x + 17 = 0,$$

which is the same equation as above.

5. Suppose $\dfrac{x^2}{4} + \dfrac{y^2}{25} = 1$. If $y = 2$, what is a positive value of x? ③
   A. $\dfrac{2\sqrt{22}}{5}$
   B. $\dfrac{2\sqrt{23}}{5}$
   C. $\dfrac{2\sqrt{21}}{5}$
   D. $\dfrac{2\sqrt{17}}{5}$
   E. $\dfrac{2\sqrt{19}}{5}$

6. If $a^2 - b^2 = 28$ and $a + b = 4$, what does a equal? ③
   A. $\dfrac{13}{2}$
   B. $\dfrac{9}{2}$
   C. $\dfrac{15}{2}$
   D. $\dfrac{17}{2}$
   E. $\dfrac{11}{2}$

7. If $m - n = 4$ and $mn = 10$, what is $m^2 + n^2$? ④
   A. 30
   B. 32
   C. 33
   D. 36
   E. 40

8. If $c + d = 8$ and $\dfrac{c}{d} = \dfrac{2}{3}$, what is $d - c$? ④

- **A.** $\dfrac{7}{5}$
- **B.** $\dfrac{11}{5}$
- **C.** $\dfrac{9}{5}$
- **D.** $\dfrac{13}{5}$
- **E.** $\dfrac{8}{5}$

9. Which of these is the largest x-value of the intersection points of $y = x^2$ and $y = 2x + 1$? ④

- **A.** 2.4
- **B.** 2.6
- **C.** 2.8
- **D.** 3.0
- **E.** 3.2

10. The sum of two positive numbers is 5 and their product is 3. Which of these is closest to the larger of those two numbers? ④

- **A.** 3.5
- **B.** 3.7
- **C.** 3.9
- **D.** 4.1
- **E.** 4.3

15.3. More Variables than Equations

If you are given more variables than equations, it is generally not possible to solve that problem completely and get numeric values for all the variables. All you can do with 2 equations and 3 variables is to eliminate one variable and get the second variable in terms of the third.

For example, $x - y = a$ and $2x + 3y = 5a$. What is x in terms of a? Solving the first equation for y, $y = x - a$. Now substitute that for y in

the second equation, $2x + 3(x - a) = 5a \implies 2x + 3x - 3a = 5a \implies 5x = 8a \implies x = \dfrac{8a}{5}$.

11. If $x + y = a$ and $x - y = b$, what is $x^2 - y^2$? ④

- **A.** ab^2
- **B.** $2ab$
- **C.** $\dfrac{a}{b}$
- **D.** $a^2 b$
- **E.** ab

12. If $2x + 3y = a$ and $5x + 2y = 2a$, what is x in terms of a? ④

- **A.** $\dfrac{5a}{13}$
- **B.** $\dfrac{6a}{13}$
- **C.** $\dfrac{4a}{13}$
- **D.** $\dfrac{3a}{13}$
- **E.** $\dfrac{4a}{11}$

15.4. Systems of Equations in Exponential Form

Use the laws of exponents (taking the logarithm of both sides or equating exponents in an exponential equation) to obtain 2 linear equations in 2 variables and then solve the resulting system of linear equations. Usually, you want to express both sides of the exponential equation in term of a common base, such as 2 or 3.

13. If $5^a \cdot 5^b = 125$ and $\dfrac{2^a}{2^b} = 32$, what is the value of a? ③

    A. 2

    B. 3

    C. 4

    D. 5

    E. 8

14. If $4^a = 8$ and $27^{a+b} = 9$, what is b? ④

    A. $\dfrac{1}{6}$

    B. $\dfrac{1}{5}$

    C. $\dfrac{-5}{6}$

    D. $\dfrac{-5}{2}$

    E. $\dfrac{1}{9}$

15. If $\left(\sqrt{2}\right)^a = 32^b$ and $8^a \cdot 4^b = 1024$, what is a? ④

    A. $\dfrac{49}{16}$

    B. $\dfrac{27}{8}$

    C. 3

    D. $\dfrac{7}{2}$

    E. $\dfrac{25}{8}$

① Easiest

⑤ Most Difficult

— ANSWER KEY

15.5. Solutions

1. **(B)** $x = \dfrac{4}{5}$. Substituting, $\dfrac{y}{\frac{4}{5}} = 3 \implies y = 3 \cdot \dfrac{4}{5} \implies y = \dfrac{12}{5}$. .

2. **(E)** Since both equations are equal to y, set the x parts equal to each other. $3x - 1 = x + 4 \longrightarrow$ $2x = 5 \implies x = \dfrac{5}{2}$

3. **(D)** Multiplying the second equation by 3 and adding it to the first one (you know to multiply by 3 because the difference between the x- and y-coefficients in the first equation is 3 times the difference between the coefficients in the second equation). We get:

$$12x + 9y + 2x + 5y = 15 + 10 \implies 14x + 14y = 25 \text{ (dividing by 14) } x + y = \dfrac{25}{14}.$$

A more time consuming approach is to solve for x and y individually, multiplying the first equation by -2 and adding it to the second one:

$$-4x - 10y + 4x + 3y = -20 + 5 \implies -7y = -15 \implies y = \dfrac{15}{7}.$$

Substituting that value into the first equation,

$$2x + 5\left(\dfrac{15}{7}\right) = 10 \implies 2x + \dfrac{75}{7} = 10 \text{ (isolating } x) \; 2x = \dfrac{-5}{7}$$
$$\implies x = \dfrac{-5}{14} \text{ (now add } x \text{ and } y) \; x + y = \dfrac{15}{7} + \dfrac{-5}{14} = \dfrac{25}{14}.$$

4. **(E)** Let $h = $ the cost of a hamburger and $f = $ the cost of an order of fries. Set up equations based on each combination of hamburgers and fries.

   $10h + 5f = 95$ and $6h + 7f = 69$. Dividing the first equation by 5 yields $2h + f = 19$. Solve that equation for f so that we can substitute for f into the second equation, $f = 19 - 2h$. Substituting for f, $6h + 7(19 - 2h) = 69 \implies 6h + 133 - 14h = 69 \implies 64 = 8h \implies 8 = h$. You could also use linear combinations or various matrix methods to solve the system of 2 equations in 2 variables. It may be possible to solve the equations with programs on your calculator once you have set them up correctly.

5. **(C)** $\dfrac{x^2}{4} + \dfrac{y^2}{25} = 1$ and $y = 2$. Substitute 2 for y and then solve for x:

$$\dfrac{x^2}{4} + \dfrac{4}{25} = 1 \implies \dfrac{x^2}{4} = \dfrac{21}{25} \implies \dfrac{x}{2} = \pm\dfrac{\sqrt{21}}{5} \implies x = \pm\dfrac{2\sqrt{21}}{5}.$$

6. **(C)** $a + b = 3$, $a - b = 5$, adding, $2a = 8 \implies a = 4$. You could also use substitution or graphing to solve the system of linear equations.

7. (E) $a^2 - b^2 = 28$ and $a + b = 4$. Use the fact that one expression is a factor of the other to easily solve the problem.

$$\frac{a^2 - b^2}{a + b} = \frac{(a - b)(a + b)}{a + b} = a - b = \frac{28}{4} = 7$$

Now add $a - b = 7$ to $a + b = 4$ to get $2a = 11 \implies a = \frac{11}{2}$.

Another approach would be to solve the linear equation for b and substitute, $b = 4 - a$. Substituting into $a^2 - b^2 = 28$, $a^2 - (4 - a)^2 = 28$. FOILing,

$$a^2 - (a^2 - 8a + 16) = 28 \implies 8a - 16 = 28 \implies 8a = 44 \implies a = \frac{11}{2}.$$

8. (D) It is easiest to square the first equation, which will give a result in terms of m, n and $m^2 + n^2$. Squaring both sides of $m - n = 4$, we get $m^2 - 2mn + n^2 = 16$ (substituting $mn = 10$) $m^2 - 2 \cdot 10 + n^2 = 16$ (solving for $m^2 + n^2$) $m^2 + n^2 = 36$. You could also use substitution and solve for m and n, but that would take much longer.

9. (E) Solve for c in terms of d (or vice versa), substitute into the other equation and find d, then find c and $d - c$.

$$c + d = 8 \text{ and } \frac{c}{d} = \frac{2}{3}. \quad c = \frac{2d}{3} \text{ (substituting) } \frac{2d}{3} + d = 8$$

$$\implies \frac{5d}{3} = 8 \implies d = \frac{24}{5} \text{ (substituting to find } c) \ c = \frac{2d}{3} = \frac{16}{5}$$

(now substitute the values found for each variable to find $d - c$) $d - c = \frac{24}{5} - \frac{16}{5} = \frac{8}{5}.$

10. (A) $y = x^2$ and $y = 2x + 1$. Since both equations are in the form y equals an expression in terms of x, set the two expressions in x equal to each other, and then solve the resulting quadratic. Therefore, $x^2 = 2x + 1$ (get all the terms of the quadratic on one side) $x^2 - 2x - 1 = 0$ (solve using the quadratic formula)

$$x = \frac{2 \pm \sqrt{2^2 - 4(-1)}}{2} = \frac{2 \pm \sqrt{8}}{2} = \frac{2 \pm 2\sqrt{2}}{2} = 1 \pm \sqrt{2}.$$

The larger solution ≈ 2.4.

11. (E) Setting up 2 equations from the description, $a + b = 5$ and $a \cdot b = 3$ (solving the first equation for a) $a = 5 - b$ (substituting) $(5 - b)b = 3 \implies 5b - b^2 = 3$ (getting the terms of the quadratic equation all on one side) $0 = b^2 - 5b + 3$ (now apply the quadratic formula) $b = \frac{5 \pm \sqrt{25 - 12}}{2} = \frac{5 \pm \sqrt{13}}{2}$ (taking the larger solution) $\frac{5 + \sqrt{13}}{2} \approx 4.3$.

12. (E) Multiply the two equations to get $x^2 - y^2$. (Actually solving for x and y would be much more time-consuming.) $x + y = a$ and $x - y = b$. $x^2 - y^2 = (x + y)(x - y) = ab$.

13. (E) Use substitution (you could also use linear combinations) to eliminate y and then solve for x in terms of a.

$2x+3y=a$ and $5x+2y=2a$.

$$3y=a-2x \text{ (divide to solve for } y\text{) } y=\frac{a-2x}{3} \text{ (substituting for } y\text{) } 5x+2\frac{a-2x}{3}=2a$$

$$\implies 5x+\frac{2a}{3}-\frac{4x}{3}=2a \implies \frac{11x}{3}=\frac{4a}{3} \implies x=\frac{4a}{11}.$$

You could also set a equal to 1 or 2 and solve the equations with numbers. Then substitute the value you chose for a into the answer choices and determine which choice matches.

14. (C) $4^a=8$ and $27^{a+b}=9$. Convert the first equation so that the bases are powers of 2 and the second equation to bases which are powers of 3, $2^{2a}=2^3$ and $3^{3(a+b)}=3^2$, take $\log_2$ and $\log_3$ to get 2 linear equations in 2 variables, $2a=3$ and $3a+3b=2$ (get an expression for a by dividing) $a=\frac{3}{2}$ (substitute for a in the second equation)

$$3\cdot\frac{3}{2}+3b=2 \implies 3b=\frac{-5}{2} \implies b=\frac{-5}{6}.$$

15. (E) Convert both equations so that the bases are powers of 2, then take the $\log_2$ of both equations to get 2 equations and 2 variables, and finally solve that system of equations. $(\sqrt{2})^a=32^b$ and $8^a\cdot 4^b=1024$. $2^{\frac{a}{2}}=2^{5b}$ (taking $\log_2$ of both sides) $\frac{a}{2}=5b$ (simplifying and solving for a) $a=10b$ and $2^{3a}\cdot 2^{2b}=2^{10}$ (taking $\log_2$ of both sides) $3a+2b=10$.

(substituting) $3(10b)+2b=10 \implies 32b=10 \implies b=\frac{5}{16}$

(substituting) $a=10b=10\cdot\frac{5}{16}=\frac{50}{16}=\frac{25}{8}$.

16. Quadratic Equations

16.1. Solving Quadratic Equations

You can solve by factoring, the quadratic formula, or completing the square. There are some problems that may ask for factored form and are easier to solve using factoring. However, some equations cannot be factored, and it is surer to just apply a formula. You should memorize the quadratic formula

$$\frac{-b \pm \sqrt{b^2 - 4ac}}{2a}, \quad \text{for } ax^2 + bx + c = 0, a \neq 0.$$

That formula can be derived by completing the square. It is also helpful to know how to solve by completing the square, which might be needed for some difficult circle or conic section problems. An example of completing the square is $x^2 - 4x + 2 = 0$ (completing the square, taking half of the x—coefficient and squaring it, and adding the same number to the other side of the equation) $x^2 - 4x + 4 = 2$ (in squared form) $(x - 2)^2 = 2 \implies x = 2 \pm \sqrt{2}$. Completing the square also works when there are complex solutions. Completing the square is difficult for some more complex equations, and it is difficult to derive the quadratic formula on the fly, so it is better to know the quadratic formula.

1. What is the solution set of $3x^2 - 5 = 0$? ③

   A. $\left\{ \dfrac{\sqrt{15}}{3} \right\}$

   B. $\left\{ \dfrac{-\sqrt{15}}{3} \right\}$

   C. $\left\{ \dfrac{\sqrt{5}}{3}, \dfrac{-\sqrt{5}}{3} \right\}$

   D. $\left\{ \dfrac{\sqrt{15}}{3}, \dfrac{-\sqrt{15}}{3} \right\}$

   E. $\left\{ \dfrac{\sqrt{30}}{3}, \dfrac{-\sqrt{30}}{3} \right\}$

2. What are the solutions of $x^2 - 7x + 12 = 0$? ③

   A. -3 and 4

   B. -2 and 5

   C. 2 and -5

   D. 3 and -4

   E. 3 and 4

3. What are the two solutions of $5x^2+x-4=0$? ③

   A. 1 and $\dfrac{4}{5}$

   B. -1 and $\dfrac{4}{5}$

   C. 1 and $\dfrac{-4}{5}$

   D. $i+2$ and $2-i$

   E. -2 and $\dfrac{4}{5}$

4. Given $f(x)=\dfrac{10}{x+3}$, for what values of t does $f(t)=t$? ④

   A. -5 or 2 *

   B. -4 or 3

   C. -2 or 5

   D. 2

   E. 2 or 5

5. What are the solutions to $x^2-12x+33=0$? ③

   A. $12\pm2\sqrt{3}$

   B. $6\pm\sqrt{3}$

   C. $3\pm\sqrt{3}$

   D. $9\pm\sqrt{3}$

   E. $3\pm2\sqrt{3}$

6. If $px^2+qx+r=0$, what is x? ③

   A. $\dfrac{q\pm\sqrt{q^2-4pr}}{2p}$

   B. $\dfrac{-q\pm\sqrt{q^2-4pr}}{2}$

   C. $\dfrac{-q\pm\sqrt{q^2-4pr}}{2p}$

   D. $\dfrac{-q\pm\sqrt{q^2-pr}}{2p}$

   E. $\dfrac{-2q\pm\sqrt{q^2-4pr}}{2p}$

7. If $x^2+4x+g=0$, what are the solutions for x? ③

   A. $-2\pm\sqrt{8-g}$

   B. $-1\pm\sqrt{4-g}$

   C. $-2\pm\sqrt{2-g}$

   D. $-2\pm\sqrt{4-g}$

   E. $-4\pm\sqrt{4-g}$

16.2. Sum and Product of Solutions to Quadratic Equations

It is helpful to know the sum of solutions of $ax^2+bx+c=0$ is $=\dfrac{-b}{a}$ and product of solutions $=\dfrac{c}{a}$ formulas. Both of these formulas can be derived from the quadratic formula. Their derivations are in the solutions to problems, and it is recommended that you practice deriving these formulas. If you do not know the formula, you can find the solutions to the quadratic equation and then take their sum or product, but that takes significantly longer.

It is also possible to derive those formulas from the quadratic formula or the quadratic formula with values while taking the exam. It is recommended that you both memorize these formulas and practice deriving them.

For example, what is the sum of the solutions of $3x^2 - 8x + 100 = 0$? To find the solutions to the equation, you would need to deal with calculations involving radicals resulting in complex solutions. Using the formula the sum of the solutions $= \dfrac{-b}{a}, \dfrac{-(-8)}{3} = \dfrac{8}{3}$.

8. What is the sum of the two solutions of $5x^2 + 4x + 11 = 0$? ③

   A. $-\dfrac{2}{5}$

   B. $\dfrac{2}{5}$

   C. $-\dfrac{4}{5}$

   D. $-\dfrac{8}{5}$

   E. $-\dfrac{16}{5}$

9. What is the product of the two solutions of $5x^2 + 4x + 11 = 0$? ③

   A. $\dfrac{11}{5}$

   B. $\dfrac{22}{5}$

   C. $-\dfrac{11}{5}$

   D. $-\dfrac{11}{10}$

   E. $\dfrac{11}{10}$

10. What is the sum of the solutions of the equation $3ux^2 + 4vx + 5 = 0$? ③

    A. $-\dfrac{2v}{3u}$

    B. $-\dfrac{4v}{3u}$

    C. $-\dfrac{3u}{4v}$

    D. $\dfrac{5}{3u}$

    E. -4

11. What is the product of the solutions of the equation $3ux^2 + 4vx + 5 = 0$? ③

    A. $\dfrac{5}{3u}$

    B. $\dfrac{3}{5u}$

    C. $\dfrac{10}{3u}$

    D. $\dfrac{5u}{6}$

    E. $\dfrac{10u}{3}$

12. What is the sum of the solutions of $ax^2 + bx + c = 0$? ③

    A. $-\dfrac{b}{2a}$

    B. $-\dfrac{b}{a}$

    C. $\dfrac{b}{a}$

    D. $\dfrac{b}{2a}$

    E. $\dfrac{c}{a}$

16.3. Finding a Quadratic Equation from its Solutions

If the solutions of a quadratic equation are p and q, the equation is $(x - p)(x - q) = x^2 - (p + q)x +$

pq. Therefore, if the solutions are -2 and 5, the equation is $(x+2)(x-5) = x^2 - 3x - 10$. If the solutions are $\frac{1}{2}$ and $\frac{1}{3}$, the equation is

$$\left(x - \frac{1}{2}\right)\left(x - \frac{1}{3}\right) = x^2 - \frac{5x}{6} + \frac{1}{6} = 0;$$

since the equation is set to 0, we can multiply by 6 and clear the denominators, so

$$6x^2 - 5x + 1 = 0.$$

You can also clear the denominators at the beginning and FOIL the expression out with integer coefficients.

Another example involves irrational roots, which come in conjugate pairs, taking the negative of the irrational part of a root to obtain its conjugate (assuming that the equation has rational coefficients). Therefore, if one root is $4 + \sqrt{3}$, the other is $4 - \sqrt{3}$; consequently, taking x minus each root, $(x - 4 - \sqrt{3})(x - 4 + \sqrt{3}) = x^2 - 8x + 16 - 3 = x^2 - 8x + 13$. The irrational terms cancel each other out, and are omitted. Finding the equation from complex roots works similarly and is covered elsewhere.

13. Which of these quadratic equations has solutions 3 and -7? ③
  A. $x^2 - 4x - 28 = 0$
  B. $x^2 - 4x - 21 = 0$
  C. $x^2 - 4x - 14 = 0$
  D. $x^2 + 4x - 28 = 0$
  E. $x^2 + 4x - 21 = 0$

14. Which of these quadratic equations has $\frac{5}{8}$ as its only solution? ③
  A. $64x^2 + 80x + 25 = 0$
  B. $64x^2 - 80x + 25 = 0$
  C. $64x^2 + 84x + 25 = 0$
  D. $64x^2 - 84x + 25 = 0$
  E. $64x^2 - 72x + 25 = 0$

15. Which of these quadratic functions has roots at $x = 2$ and $x = 3$, and $f(0) = 30$? ④
  A. $f(x) = x^2 - 5x + 30$
  B. $f(x) = x^2 - 5x + 6$
  C. $f(x) = 30x^2 - 25x + 30$
  D. $f(x) = 10x^2 - 25x + 30$
  E. $f(x) = 5x^2 - 25x + 30$

16. Which of these quadratic equations has $5 + \sqrt{3}$ as a solution? ④
  A. $x^2 - 10x + 22 = 0$
  B. $x^2 - 10x + 28 = 0$
  C. $x^2 - 10x + 19 = 0$
  D. $x^2 + 10x + 22 = 0$
  E. $x^2 - 10x + 34 = 0$

16.4. Finding a Quadratic Coefficient

substitute in the root and find the missing coefficient. For example, if $x - 3$ is a factor of $5x^2 - 4x + k = 0$, what is k? Take the negative of what is added to x and substitute that in for x and solve. substituting in $-(-3) = 3$ for x,

$$5 \cdot 3^2 - 4 \cdot 3 + k = 0$$
$$\implies 45 - 12 + k = 0 \implies k = -33.$$

If it asks for a coefficient such that the quadratic has exactly one solution, then it needs to be a perfect square trinomial. The easiest way to solve that sort of problem is to set the discriminant in the quadratic formula ($b^2 - 4ac$) equal to zero and solve for the unknown coefficient.

17. $x^2 + bx + c = 0$ and the only possible value of x is 5. What is $b + c$? ③

   A. 10
   B. 12
   C. 15
   D. 20
   E. 25

18. $x^2 + 9x + c = 0$ has exactly one solution for what value of c? ③

   A. $\dfrac{9}{4}$
   B. $\dfrac{27}{4}$
   C. $\dfrac{81}{4}$
   D. 36
   E. 18

19. If $ax^2 + bx + c = 0$ has exactly one solution, what is c in terms of a and b? ④

   A. $\dfrac{b^2}{4a}$
   B. $-\dfrac{b^2}{4a}$
   C. $\dfrac{3b^2}{4a}$
   D. $\dfrac{b^2}{8a}$
   E. $\dfrac{b^2}{2a}$

20. If $x - 5$ is a factor of $3x^2 - 10x + k$, what is k? ④

   A. -30
   B. -25
   C. -20
   D. -15
   E. 25

21. If $x^2 + hx + 10 = 0$ and 3 is a solution, what is h? ④

   A. -6
   B. $\dfrac{-17}{3}$
   C. -5
   D. $\dfrac{-19}{3}$
   E. $\dfrac{-20}{3}$

16.5. Vertex

To find the vertex of $y = ax^2 + bx + c$, use the formula $x = \dfrac{-b}{2a}$, and then substitute in the x-value obtained to get the y-value for the vertex. You can also use completing the square to transform the equation into vertex form.

For example, if $y = x^2 + 6x + 11$, using $\dfrac{-b}{2a}$, $x = \dfrac{-6}{2} = -3$. Then substituting in -3 for x we get $y = (-3)^2 + 6(-3) + 11 = 2$, so the vertex is $(-3, 2)$. Another method is to complete the square, $y = x^2 + 6x + 9 + 2 = (x + 3)^2 + 2$, so the vertex is $(-3, 2)$.

Graphing the equation using a calculator and reading the vertex from the graph is also a possible approach, and it is recommended that you practice it. However, it is important to know the algebraic methods as well, as graphing may be difficult for some problems. For example, if the vertex does not have integer coordinates or the equation includes large numbers which make it difficult to scale correctly, getting the solution by graphing may be difficult.

22. What is the vertex of $y = 2(x-3)^2 + 7$? ③
  - **A.** $(-3, -7)$
  - **B.** $(-3, 7)$
  - **C.** $(3, -7)$
  - **D.** $(3, 7)$
  - **E.** $(7, -3)$

23. What is the vertex of $y = a(x-b)^2 + c$? ③
  - **A.** $(b, -c)$
  - **B.** (b, c)
  - **C.** $(-b, c)$
  - **D.** $\left(b, \dfrac{c}{b}\right)$
  - **E.** $(b, c+b)$

24. What is the axis of symmetry of a parabola where y is a function of x with x−intercepts of -7 and 11? ③
  - **A.** $x = 1$
  - **B.** $x = 2$
  - **C.** $x = 3$
  - **D.** $x = 4$
  - **E.** $x = 5$

25. What is the minimum value of $3x^2 - 2x + 5$? ④
  - **A.** $\dfrac{8}{3}$
  - **B.** $\dfrac{10}{3}$
  - **C.** $\dfrac{11}{3}$
  - **D.** $\dfrac{14}{3}$
  - **E.** $\dfrac{16}{3}$

26. A parabola with y-intercept $(0, 20)$ and vertex $(-4, 2)$ has equation $y - 2 = a(x+4)^2$. What is a? ④
  - **A.** 1
  - **B.** 2
  - **C.** $\dfrac{9}{8}$
  - **D.** $\dfrac{5}{4}$
  - **E.** $\dfrac{3}{2}$

16.6. Factored Form

It is also possible to solve problems like this using the quadratic formula and then transforming the result. Another practical approach (which does not always work) is to substitute a number in for x in the expression given in the problem and the same number into the solutions and see which choice matches the answer from the problem.

For example, what is $3x^2 + 14x + 8$ in factored form? Find two numbers that add to 14 and multiply to 24 ($3 \cdot 8$). Those are 2 and 12. So $3x^2 + 2x + 12x + 8 =$ (factoring by grouping) $x(3x+2) + 4(3x+2) = (x+4)(3x+2)$. Trick approaches are discussed in solution 2 of this section.

27. Which of these is $2x^2 - x - 15$ in factored form? ③
  - **A.** $(2x+3)(x-5)$
  - **B.** $(x+5)(2x-3)$
  - **C.** $(x-5)(2x+3)$
  - **D.** $(2x-5)(x+3)$
  - **E.** $(2x+5)(x-3)$

28. Which of these is $10x^2 + 19x + 6$ in factored form? ③

    A. $(2x+3)(5x+2)$

    B. $(2x+2)(5x+3)$

    C. $(2x+1)(5x+6)$

    D. $(2x+1)(5x-6)$

    E. $(2x-3)(5x-2)$

16.7. Other

29. One square has a side length of $x+3$ cm and another has a side length of $x-2$ cm. What expression represents the difference in the areas of these two squares in square centimeters? ③

    A. $2x+5$

    B. $2x+13$

    C. $7x+13$

    D. $10x+5$

    E. $10x+13$

30. If $3x^2 + a = 0$ has two integer solutions for a, which of these is a possible value of a? ③

    A. -18

    B. -12

    C. -9

    D. 9

    E. 12

1D, 2E, 3B, 4A, 5B, 6C, 7D, 8C, 9A, 10B, 11B, 12D, 13E, 14B, 15E, 16A, 17C, 18C, 19A, 20B, 21D, 22D, 23B, 24B, 25D, 26C, 27E, 28A 29D,30B

16.8. Solutions

1. (D) $x^2 = \dfrac{5}{3} \implies x = \pm\dfrac{\sqrt{5}}{\sqrt{3}} = \pm\dfrac{\sqrt{15}}{3}$.

2. (E) $x^2 - 3x - 4x + 12 = 0 \implies (x-3)(x-4) = 0 \implies x = 3$ or 4. Or use the quadratic formula.

3. (B) $5x^2 + 5x - 4x - 4 = 0$, $5x(x+1) - 4(x+1) = 0$, $(5x-4)(x+1) = 0$, so $x = -1$ or $\dfrac{4}{5}$. It is also possible to solve this problem using the quadratic formula or by back solving.

4. (A) $t = \dfrac{10}{t+3} \implies t^2 + 3t = 10 \implies t^2 + 3t - 10 = 0 \implies (t+5)(t-2) = 0 \implies t = -5$ or 2, by factoring, the quadratic formula, completing the square, or graphing.

5. (B) By the quadratic formula, $\dfrac{12 \pm \sqrt{144 - 132}}{2} = \dfrac{12 \pm 2\sqrt{3}}{2} = 6 \pm \sqrt{3}$.

   Alternative Solution: by completing the square, $x^2 - 12x + 36 = 3$, $(x-6)^2 = 3$, $x = 6 \pm \sqrt{3}$.

6. (C) This is the quadratic formula. Questions will not be asked in that way, but you need to know the formula. That formula can be derived by completing the square, but that is difficult to do, and it is best to memorize it.

7. (D) Applying the quadratic formula and then simplifying,

$$\frac{-4 \pm \sqrt{16 - 4g}}{2} = \frac{-4 \pm 2\sqrt{4-g}}{2} = -2 \pm \sqrt{4-g}.$$

8. (C) Using the sum of the roots formula, $\dfrac{-b}{a} = \dfrac{-4}{5}$. It is also possible to find the 2 solutions and add them.

9. (A) Using the product of the roots formula, $\dfrac{c}{a} = \dfrac{11}{5}$. It is also possible to find the 2 solutions and multiply them.

10. (B) Using the sum of the roots formula, $\dfrac{-b}{a} = \dfrac{-4v}{3u}$. It is also possible to find the 2 solutions and add them.

11. (B) Adding the solutions from the general quadratic formula,

$$\frac{-b + \sqrt{b^2 - 4ac}}{2a} + \frac{-b - \sqrt{b^2 - 4ac}}{2a} = \frac{-2b}{2a} = \frac{-b}{a}.$$

12. (D) Multiplying the solutions from the general quadratic formula,

$$\frac{-b + \sqrt{b^2 - 4ac}}{2a} \cdot \frac{-b - \sqrt{b^2 - 4ac}}{2a} \text{ (since these are conjugates, the radical terms drop out)}$$

$$= \frac{b^2 - (b^2 - 4ac)}{4a^2} = \frac{4ac}{4a^2} = \frac{c}{a}.$$

13. (E) Subtract both solutions from x and multiply. $(x - 3)(x + 7) = x^2 + 4x - 21 = 0$

14. (B) $\left(x - \dfrac{5}{8}\right)^2 = 0$ (multiplying by 8 to clear the denominator and get integer coefficients) $(8x - 5)(8x - 5) = 64x^2 - 80x + 25 = 0$. You could also FOIL out the expression with fractions and then multiply by $8^2 = 64$ to get integer coefficients.

15. (E) First find the equation from the solutions. $(x - 2)(x - 3) = x^2 - 5x + 6$ (We need to multiply by 5 to get a constant term of 30, since the current constant term is 6.)

$$\frac{30}{6} = 5, \quad f(x) = 5 \cdot (x^2 - 5x + 6) = 5x^2 - 25x + 30.$$

16. (A) Since the conjugate must also be a root, subtract the original expression and its conjugate from x and FOIL out (ignoring irrational terms, which cancel each other and drop out),

$$(x - 5 - \sqrt{3})(x - 5 + \sqrt{3}) = x^2 - 10x + 25 - 3 = x^2 - 10x + 22 = 0.$$

17. (C) Since both of the solutions are 5, we have: $(x - 5)(x - 5) = x^2 - 10x + 25$, $b + c = -10 + 25 = 15$.

18. (C) For there to be exactly one double solution the discriminant must be equal to 0, $b^2 - 4ac = 0$ (substituting) $81 = c \implies \dfrac{81}{4} = c.$

19. (A) The discriminant must be equal to 0 for there to be no solutions. Therefore, set $b^2 - 4ac = 0 \implies b^2 = 4ac$ (solving for c) $c = \dfrac{b^2}{4a}.$

20. (B) Substitute 5 for x and then solve for k: $3 \cdot 5^2 - 10 \cdot 5 + k = 0 \implies 25 + k = 0 \implies k = -25$

21. (D) Substitute 3 for x and then solve for h: $3^2 + h \cdot 3 + 10 = 0 \implies 3h = -19 \implies h = \dfrac{-19}{3}.$

22. (D) $(3, 7)$. Take the negative of what is being subtracted from x and squared and leave the constant being added as is.

23. (B) This equation is already in vertex form, so you can read the vertex from the equation.

24. (B) Take the average of the intercepts, $\dfrac{11 - 7}{2}$. $x = 2.$

25. (D) Use the vertex formula to find the x-coordinate of the vertex and then substitute that in to find the y-coordinate. $\dfrac{-b}{2a} = \dfrac{-(-2)}{2 \cdot 3} = \dfrac{1}{3}$. Substituting in $\dfrac{1}{3}$ for x,

$$3\left(\frac{1}{3}\right)^2 - 2 \cdot \frac{1}{3} + 5 = \frac{1}{3} - \frac{2}{3} + 5 = \frac{14}{3}.$$

You can also use completing the square. This problem can probably be solved more easily by graphing with a calculator.

26. (C) $y - 2 = a(x + 4)^2$. Substituting in the x and y-values for y-intercept,

$$20 - 2 = a(0 + 4)^2 \implies 18 = 16a \implies a = \frac{9}{8}$$

27. (E) $2x^2 - x - 15$. We need two numbers that multiply to $2 \cdot (-15) = -30$ and add to -1. Those are 5 and -6. Splitting the x term based on those numbers to factor by grouping, $2x^2 - 6x + 5x - 15$, $2x(x - 3) + 5(x - 3)$, so $(2x + 5)(x - 3)$.

28. (A) $4 \cdot 15 = 6 \cdot 10$ and $4 + 15 = 19$. So

$$10x^2 + 4x + 15x + 6 = 2x(5x + 2) + 3(5x + 2) = (2x + 3)(5x + 2).$$

If you did not know how to do that, you could reverse engineer the solution by setting the expression equal to zero and using the quadratic formula

$$x = \frac{-19 \pm \sqrt{361 - 240}}{20} = \frac{-19 \pm 11}{20} = \frac{-3}{2} \quad \text{or} \quad \frac{-2}{5},$$

$$x = \frac{-3}{2}, \quad x + \frac{3}{2} = 0, \quad 2x + 3 = 0, \quad x = \frac{-2}{5}, \quad x + \frac{2}{5} = 0, \quad 5x + 2 = 0,$$

so $(2x + 3)(5x + 2)$.

Another "trick" approach would be to FOIL out the answer choices

$$(2x + 3)(5x + 2) = 10x^2 + 4x + 15x + 6 = 10x^2 + 19x + 6.$$

If you FOIL out the other answer choices, they will not work.

A fourth approach would be to substitute in a number — let us make that number 2 — for x. Then we have $10(2^2) + 19 \cdot 2 + 6 = 84$. substituting 2 into choice A, you get $(2 \cdot 2 + 3)(5 \cdot 2 + 2) = 7 \cdot 12 = 84$. The values are the same, so choice A is probably the correct answer choice. Normally, when an answer matches, you would assume that is the correct answer and quit. That is generally the best approach considering the time constraints of the test, even though it is not certain it is the correct answer. If we substitute 2 into choice B, $(2x + 2)(5x + 3)$, we get $(2 \cdot 2 + 2)(5 \cdot 2 + 3) = 6 \cdot 13 = 91$. You can continue substituting into all of the answer choices and see that none results in the 84 found from substituting into the problem statement.

29. (D) $(x + 3)^2 = x^2 + 6x + 9$. $(x - 2)^2 = x^2 - 4x + 4$. $x^2 + 6x + 9 - (x^2 - 4x + 4) = 10x + 5$.

30. (B) $3x^2 = -a \implies x^2 = \frac{-a}{3}$, for $= -12$, $\frac{-a}{3} = -\frac{-12}{3} = 4$. $x^2 = 4$ has 2 integer solutions. So -12.

17. Angles

17.1. Angles of a Polygon

The sum of all the angles in a polygon is $180°(n-2)$, where n is the number of sides. Therefore, each angle in a regular polygon is $\dfrac{180(n-2)}{n}$.

It is also possible to solve problems like this using the fact that the sum of the exterior angles adds up to $360°$ and the sum of each interior and exterior angle is $180°$

You can also think of it as the sum of the angles in a triangle is $180°$, a quadrilateral $360°$, and pentagon $540°$, a hexagon $720°$ and so on.

For example, what is the measure of each interior angle in degrees of a regular octagon? Here, $n = 8$, so

$$\frac{(n-2)\cdot 180°}{n} = \frac{6\cdot 180°}{8} = 135°$$

1. What is the degree measure of each angle of a regular pentagon? ③
   A. $72°$
   B. $100°$
   C. $108°$
   D. $120°$
   E. $144°$

2. Which of these is the degree measure of each interior angle in a regular 20-sided polygon? ④
   A. $160°$
   B. $162°$
   C. $165°$
   D. $168°$
   E. $170°$

3. If two interior angles of a hexagon are each $150°$, what is the average value of the other 4 angles? ④
   A. $100°$
   B. $105°$
   C. $110°$
   D. $115°$
   E. $120°$

4. The measure of each of 7 interior angles of an octagon are all $120°$. What is the degree measure of the 8th angle? ④
   A. $120°$
   B. $180°$
   C. $240°$
   D. $270°$
   E. No such octagon

5. The measure of each of 7 interior angles of an octagon are all 100°. What is the degree measure of the 8th angle? ④

    A. 140°

    B. 160°

    C. 270°

    D. 300°

    E. No such octagon

6. A regular polygon has interior angles each measuring 168°. How many sides does it have? ④

    A. 25

    B. 28

    C. 30

    D. 32

    E. 40

7. The interior angles of a pentagon are in the ratio of $3 : 4 : 5 : 6 : 7$. What is the measure of the smallest angle in degrees? ④

    A. 35°

    B. 40°

    C. 50°

    D. 55°

    E. 65°

17.2. Clock Angles

There are $\dfrac{360°}{12} = 30°$ between each number on the clock. The hardest problem likely to appear might ask how many degrees apart are the hands at a particular time. At 5:10, the minute hand is on 2 and the hour hand is $\dfrac{1}{6}$ of the way from 5 to 6. The angle between 2 and 5 is $3 \cdot 30 = 90°$. The angle between 5 and the hour hand is $\dfrac{1}{6} \cdot 30 = 5$.

The answer is $90 + 5 = 95°$.

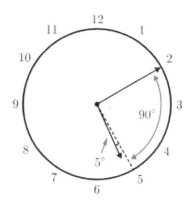

8. How many degrees does the minute hand of a clock travel in 37 minutes? ④

    A. 212°

    B. 217°

    C. 222°

    D. 242°

    E. 252°

9. How many degrees will the hour hand of the clock rotate between 5:45 and 8:35 the same evening? ④

    A. 80°

    B. 85°

    C. 87°

    D. 90°

    E. 95°

10. What is the smaller angle formed by the hands of a clock at 3:30? ⑤

    A. 72°

    B. 75°

    C. 77°

    D. 80°

    E. 82°

11. If the minute hand of a clock has length $\dfrac{10}{\pi}$ cm, how far in cm does the tip of the minute hand travel between 2:50 PM and 6:10 PM on the same afternoon? ④

  A. 66 cm

  B. 67 cm

  C. 68 cm

  D. $\dfrac{202}{3}$ cm

  E. $\dfrac{200}{3}$ cm

12. What is the smaller angle formed by the hands of a clock at 3:40? ⑤

  A. 125°

  B. 128°

  C. 130°

  D. 132°

  E. 135°

17.3. Finding Angles

For this section, it is helpful to know that the sum of the angles in a triangle is 180° and the sum of the angles in a quadrilateral is 360°. By the isosceles triangle theorem, if two sides of a triangle are congruent, their opposite angles are congruent. If two lines are parallel, the corresponding angles and alternate interior angles formed by a traversal are congruent.

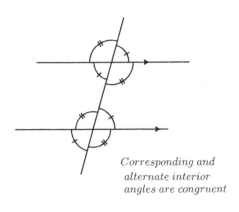

Corresponding and alternate interior angles are congruent

13. What is x? ④

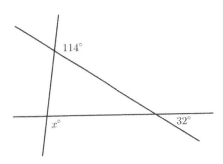

  A. 82°

  B. 86°

  C. 92°

  D. 94°

  E. 98°

14. What is x? ④

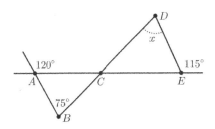

  A. 55°

  B. 60°

  C. 65°

  D. 70°

  E. 75°

15. *ABCD* is a trapezoid. What is *x*? ⑤

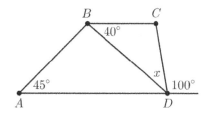

A. 30°

B. 35°

C. 40°

D. 45°

E. 50°

16. What is *x*? ④

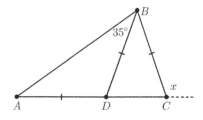

A. 95°

B. 100°

C. 105°

D. 110°

E. 115°

17. If the radius is 10, the length of the minor arc $\overparen{AB}$ is $k\pi$. What is *k*? ④

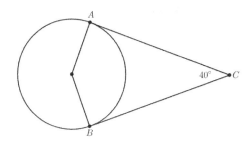

A. $\dfrac{65}{9}$

B. $\dfrac{68}{9}$

C. $\dfrac{64}{9}$

D. $\dfrac{67}{9}$

E. $\dfrac{70}{9}$

18. The minor arc $\overparen{AB}$ is 140°. What is $\angle ABO$? ⑤

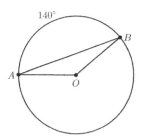

A. 18°

B. 20°

C. 22°

D. 25°

E. 30°

19. Line *m* and *n* are parallel. What is *x*? ⑤

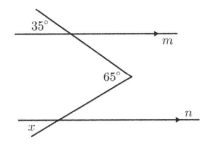

A. 20°

B. 25°

C. 30°

D. 35°

E. 40°

17.4. Solutions

1. (C) Using the formula for the total degrees in a polygon, $180°(n-2) \implies 180°(5-2) = 540°$ in a pentagon. $\frac{540°}{5} = 108°$

2. (B) Taking the sum of the angle measures divided by the number of angles, $\frac{180(n-2)}{n} = \frac{180° \cdot 18}{20} = 162°$.

3. (B) The sum of the angle measures $= 180°(6-2) = 720°$. Now subtract the two known sides: $720° - 300° = 420°$, take the average of the remaining sides: $\frac{420°}{4} = 105°$.

4. (C) The sum of the angle measures $= 180°(n-2) = 180°(8-2) = 1080°$; now set up an equation with the known sides equal to $120°$: $120° \cdot 7 + x = 1080°$,
    $840° + x = 1080°, x = 240°$.

5. (E) The sum of the angle measures $= 180°(n-2) = 180°(8-2) = 1080°$, Now set the total angle measures equal to 1080 $100 \cdot 7 + x = 1080$, $x = 380°$.
    An angle of a polygon cannot be greater than $360°$, so there is no solution.

6. (C) Taking the sum of the angle measures divided by the number of angles, (using the sum of angles formula, where n is the number of sides of the polygon) $\frac{180°(n-2)}{n} = 168°$, $180°n - 360° = 168°n$, $12n = 360°$, $n = 30$, so 30 sides.

7. (E) The sum of the angle measures $= 180°(5-2) = 540°$.
    To find the smallest angle, take its ratio value divided by the sum of the other ratio values,
    $$= 540° \cdot \frac{3}{3+4+5+6+7} = \frac{1620°}{25} = \frac{324°}{5} = 64.8°.$$

8. (C) The minute hand travels once around the circle per hour, which is 360 degrees. Therefore, take the number of minutes divided by 60 minutes in an hour times 360. $\frac{37}{60} \cdot 360° = 222°$.

9. (B) The hour hand travels 30 degrees per hour. Subtracting times, $2\frac{5}{6}$ hours passed. So multiply the time passed times 30.
    $$2\frac{5}{6} \cdot 30° = \frac{17}{6} \cdot 30° = 85°.$$

10. (B) The hour hand is halfway between 3 and 4, and minute hand is at 6, so they are $2\frac{1}{2}$ hours apart (each hour is $30°$) $60 + 15 = 75°$.

11. (E) Take the number of revolution times the circumference of the circle, $3 + \dfrac{1}{3}$ revolutions.

$$2 \cdot \pi \cdot \frac{10}{\pi} \cdot \frac{10}{3} = \frac{200}{3} \text{ cm.}$$

12. (C) The hour hand is $\dfrac{2}{3}$ of the way from 3 to 4 and the minute hand is at 8, so there are $4\dfrac{1}{3}30°$ hour lengths.

$$4 \cdot 30° + 30° \cdot \frac{1}{3} = 130°.$$

13. (E) The angle supplementary to $114°$ is $66°$. The vertical angle to $32°$ is also $32°$. Therefore, by the exterior angle theorem: $x = 32° + 66° = 98°$

14. (D) $\angle BAC$ is $60°$ by supplementary angles. $\angle ACB + 60° + 75° = 180° \implies \angle ACB = 45°$.

$\angle ECD = 45°$ by vertical angles. $\angle CED = 65°$ by supplementary angles.

Therefore, $x + 65° + 45° = 180° \implies x = 70°$.

15. (C) $\angle ADB = 40°$ by alternate interior angles, as $\overline{AD} \parallel \overline{BC}$, since this a trapezoid.

$$40° + x + 100° = 180° \implies x = 40°.$$

16. (D) $\angle A$ is $35°$ degrees by the isosceles triangle theorem.

So, $\angle ADB$ is $110°$, so $\angle CDB$ is $70°$ by supplementary angles. Therefore, $\angle BCD$ is $70°$ by the isosceles triangle theorem. Therefore, x is $110°$.

17. (E) Applying a circle theorem, $\dfrac{\text{major arc } \overset{\frown}{AB} - \text{minor arc } \overset{\frown}{AB}}{2} = 40°$.

major arc $\overset{\frown}{AB}$ − minor arc $\overset{\frown}{AB} = 80°$ and major arc $\overset{\frown}{AB}$ + minor arc $\overset{\frown}{AB} = 360°$

(substituting) $2 \cdot$ major arc $\overset{\frown}{AB} = 440° \implies$ major arc $\overset{\frown}{AB} = 220° \implies$ minor arc $\overset{\frown}{AB} = 140°$

arc length minor $\overset{\frown}{AB} = 10 \cdot 2\pi \left(\dfrac{140}{360}\right) = 20\pi \left(\dfrac{7}{18}\right) = \dfrac{70\pi}{9}$ (simplifying and solving) $k = \dfrac{70}{9}$.

18. (B) $\angle O = 140°$. $\overline{OA} \cong \overline{OB}$, so $\angle A = \angle B$ by the isosceles triangle theorem. So,

$$x + x + 140 = 180 \implies 2x = 40 \quad \text{or} \quad x = 20, \quad \angle A = \angle B = x = 20°.$$

19. (C) If we draw a perpendicular on the left, $90° + 90° + 145° + 65° + (180° - x) = 540°$ (the angles in a pentagon add up to $540°$) $\implies 570° - x = 540° \implies x = 30°$.

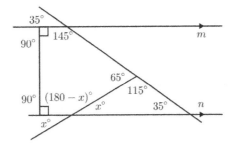

Another solution is to continue the upper diagonal line and form a triangle, $35° + 115° + x = 180° \implies x = 30°$.

18. Area and Volume

18.1. Quadrilaterals

Rectangles and Trapezoids

The perimeter of a rectangle is $2l + 2w$ and its diagonal can be found from the sides using the Pythagorean theorem.

Included is a trapezoid problem which tests 45-45-90 and 30-60-90 triangles.

1. If a rectangular field has area 1000 square meters and its length is twice its width, what is its perimeter to the nearest meter? ③
   A. 128
   B. 130
   C. 132
   D. 134
   E. 136

2. If the diagonal of a rectangle is 7 and one side is 6, what is the area of the rectangle? ③
   A. 18
   B. 27
   C. $6\sqrt{13}$
   D. $12\sqrt{13}$
   E. $\sqrt{13}$

3. What is the area of the trapezoid shown? ⑤

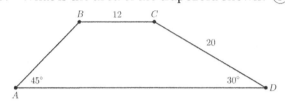

   A. 217
   B. 227
   C. 237
   D. 247
   E. 257

Squares

The problems about squares on the exam are generally fairly easy, but they are common on the exam.

Where s is the side length, he perimeter of a square is $4s$ and the area is s^2

4. What is the perimeter in meters of a square having an area of 76 square meters? ②
   A. $8\sqrt{19}$ m
   B. $19\sqrt{19}$ m
   C. $2\sqrt{19}$ m
   D. $4\sqrt{19}$ m
   E. 361 m

143

5. Baxter has x feet of fencing. How many square feet of a square region could it enclose? ③

    A. $\dfrac{x^2}{4}$

    B. $\dfrac{x^2}{8}$

    C. $\dfrac{x^2}{12}$

    D. $\dfrac{x^2}{16}$

    E. $\dfrac{x^2}{32}$

6. If one side of a square has endpoints $(3, 1)$ and $(1, 8)$, what is the area of the square (in square units)? ③

    A. 49

    B. 53

    C. 55

    D. 57

    E. 64

Rhombus

The rhombus area formula is $\dfrac{d_1 \cdot d_2}{2}$, where d_1 and d_2 are the diagonals. That formula is easy to derive as the sum of right triangles and it also applies to squares (which are special cases of rhombuses).

7. If a rhombus has diagonals 20 and 30, what is its perimeter? ④

    A. $20\sqrt{10}$

    B. $20\sqrt{11}$

    C. $20\sqrt{13}$

    D. $10\sqrt{23}$

    E. $40\sqrt{5}$

8. If a rhombus has diagonals 20 and 30, what is its area? ④

    A. 240

    B. 280

    C. 300

    D. 320

    E. 330

18.2. Triangles

The triangle inequality states that the sum of 2 sides of a triangle is always greater than the other side. The triangle inequality follows from the shortest distance between two points being a straight line. The other two sides are a more indirect path and must be longer. Therefore, if one side is 7 and the other 10, the third side must be between 3 and 17.

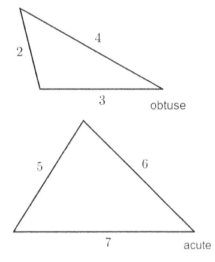

An extension of the Pythagorean Theorem states that if $a^2 + b^2 > c^2$, then the triangle is acute and if $a^2 + b^2 < c^2$, the triangle is obtuse. For example, if a triangle has sides 2, 3, and 4, $2^2 + 3^2$? $4^2 \implies 13 < 16$, so that triangle is obtuse. If a triangle has sides 5, 6, and 7, $5^2 + 6^2$? $7^2 \implies 25 + 36$? $49 \implies 61 > 48$, so this is an acute triangle.

9. If the ratio of the perimeters of two similar triangles is 2:5, what is the ratio of their areas? ④

   A. 2:5

   B. 4:5

   C. 4:25

   D. 4:125

   E. 8:125

10. If one side of a triangle is 11 and another is 17, what is the range for possible values of the third side x? ③

    A. $6 \leq x \leq 28$

    B. $6 < x < 28$

    C. $6 < x$

    D. $\sqrt{67} < x < \sqrt{410}$

    E. $x < 34$

11. Two sides of a triangle are 2 and 3. For what range of values of the third side x is the triangle acute? ④

    A. $\sqrt{5} < x < \sqrt{13}$

    B. $\sqrt{5} < x < \sqrt{15}$

    C. $\sqrt{5} < x < \sqrt{14}$

    D. $5 < x < 13$

    E. $1 < x < 5$

12. What is the area of an equilateral triangle with side a? ⑤

    A. $\dfrac{\sqrt{3}a^2}{2}$

    B. $\dfrac{3\sqrt{3}a^2}{4}$

    C. $\dfrac{a^2}{2}$

    D. $\dfrac{\sqrt{3}a^2}{4}$

    E. $\dfrac{3\sqrt{3}a^2}{8}$

18.3. Area of a Circle

The area of a circle is πr^2. The area of a sector of a circle is $\pi r^2 \dfrac{\theta}{360}$, where θ is the angle of a sector in degrees.

13. If a circle has circumference $10\sqrt{7}\pi$, what is its area? ④

    A. 500

    B. 550

    C. 150π

    D. 175π

    E. 200π

14. If a circle has circumference C, what is its area? ④

    A. $\dfrac{C^2}{4\pi}$

    B. $\dfrac{C^2}{2\pi}$

    C. $\dfrac{3C^2}{8\pi}$

    D. $\dfrac{C}{2\pi}$

    E. $\dfrac{C}{\pi}$

15. In terms of the radius r, what is the ratio of the area to the circumference of a circle? ④

    A. $\dfrac{r}{4}$

    B. $\dfrac{r}{2}$

    C. $\dfrac{r^2}{4}$

    D. r

    E. πr

16. Two concentric circles have radii 70 and 100 meters, respectively. How many square meters is the area inside the larger circle but outside the smaller circle? ④

    A. 5000π

    B. 5100π

    C. 5200π

    D. 5300π

    E. 5400π

17. What is the area inside $x^2 + y^2 = 36$ but outside $x^2 + y^2 = 10$? ④

    A. 24π

    B. 26π

    C. 28π

    D. 30π

    E. 32π

18. If the endpoints of the diameter of a circle are $(-2, -11)$ and $(4, 1)$, what is the area of the circle? ④

    A. 42π

    B. 44π

    C. 45π

    D. 48π

    E. 50π

19. A circle with radius 24 cm is divided into 42 congruent arcs. What is the length in cm of each arc? ③

    A. $\dfrac{7\pi}{8}$

    B. π

    C. $\dfrac{10\pi}{9}$

    D. $\dfrac{9\pi}{8}$

    E. $\dfrac{8\pi}{7}$

18.4. Finding Radius or Circumference of a Circle

The circumference of a circle is $2\pi r$. The arc length of a section of a circle is $2\pi r \dfrac{\theta}{360}$.

For example, if the area of a circle is 200 square cm, what is its radius?

$$A = \pi r^2 \text{ (substituting) } 200 = \pi r^2$$

$$\implies \frac{200}{\pi} = r^2 \implies r = \sqrt{\frac{200}{\pi}} \approx 7.98 \text{ cm.}$$

20. If the area of a circle is $12\pi \ cm^2$, what is its circumference in cm? ④

    A. $2\sqrt{3}\pi$

    B. $\sqrt{3}\pi$

    C. 6π

    D. 8π

    E. $4\sqrt{3}\pi$

21. If the radius of a circle is 10 cm, what is the length to the nearest mm of a $5°$ arc of the circle? ④

    A. 9

    B. 10

    C. 11

    D. 12

    E. 13

22. If a circle with radius a is divided into b congruent arcs, what is the length of each arc? ③

    A. $\dfrac{4a\pi}{b}$

    B. $\dfrac{2a\pi}{b}$

    C. $\dfrac{6a\pi}{b}$

    D. $\dfrac{2a\pi}{3b}$

    E. $\dfrac{6a\pi}{5b}$

23. The area of a pie slice section formed by a 40° angle from the center of a circle is 20π. What is the radius of the circle? ④

  A. $3\sqrt{10}$

  B. $2\sqrt{5}$

  C. $3\sqrt{5}$

  D. $6\sqrt{5}$

  E. $12\sqrt{5}$

18.5. Cubes

The volume of a cube is s^3, its long diagonal is $\sqrt{3}s$, and its surface area is $6s^2$. All of these can be derived from the box formulas (a cube is a special case of a box) by setting $s = l = w = h$, or by basic principles.

24. If the sides of a cube are 5 meters, what is its volume in cubic mm? ③

  A. 3.75×10^{11}

  B. 2.5×10^{11}

  C. 6.25×10^{10}

  D. 1.25×10^{11}

  E. 6.25×10^{11}

25. If the volume of a cube is 27 cubic inches, what is its surface area in square inches? ③

  A. 27

  B. 72

  C. 108

  D. 36

  E. 54

26. If the surface area of a cube is x, what is its volume? ④

  A. $\left(\dfrac{x}{6}\right)^{\frac{2}{3}}$

  B. $\left(\dfrac{x}{6}\right)^{\frac{3}{2}}$

  C. $\left(\dfrac{x}{6}\right)^{3}$

  D. $x^{\frac{3}{2}}$

  E. $x^{\frac{3}{4}}$

18.6. Boxes

The formula for surface area of a box is $2(wl + wh + lh)$. This is the sum of the area on each face, with identical areas on opposite faces. Its volume is lwh and its longest diagonal is $\sqrt{l^2 + w^2 + h^2}$, which can be derived from the Pythagorean theorem.

27. If you triple the length, width, and height of a box, its surface area will be multiplied by what? ③

  A. 3

  B. 6

  C. 8

  D. 9

  E. 27

28. How many $3'' \times 4'' \times 6''$ little boxes can fit into a $2' \times 2' \times 5'$ big box? ④

  A. 240

  B. 360

  C. 420

  D. 480

  E. 540

29. How many cubic feet of mulch would you need to cover an area 20 × 30 yards to a depth of 2 inches? ③

   A. 600

   B. 800

   C. 900

   D. 1200

   E. 5400

30. A rectangular solid has a volume of 300 cubic centimeters. If the length and width are doubled and the height is multiplied by 5, what will the volume of the new solid be? ③

   A. 5400 cm^3

   B. 6000 cm^3

   C. 6200 cm^3

   D. 6400 cm^3

   E. 6600 cm^3

31. What is the surface area of a 2 × 3 × 5 box? ④

   A. 52

   B. 60

   C. 62

   D. 72

   E. 84

32. If all the water in a full pool with a length of 5 meters, a width of 3 meters, and a height of 2 meters is siphoned into an empty pool with a length of 14 meters and a width of 8 meters, how high will the top of the water be to the nearest centimeter? ⑤

   A. 24

   B. 25

   C. 26

   D. 27

   E. 28

18.7. Spheres

The volume of a sphere is $\dfrac{4\pi r^3}{3}$ and its surface area is $4\pi r^2$. The exam will probably provide these formulas or you will only need to know that volume is proportional to the cube of the radius, etc., not the whole formula.

33. Sphere U has a volume of 7 cubic feet. Sphere V has a radius 3 times that Sphere U. What is the volume of sphere V in cubic feet? ③

   A. 21

   B. 63

   C. 112

   D. 189

   E. 252

34. If two spheres have radii $5a$ and $3a$, what is the ratio of the volumes of the spheres? ③

   A. 25:9

   B. 5:1

   C. 125:27

   D. 44:9

   E. 4:1

35. If Jupiter has a radius of 71,492 kilometers, what is its volume in cubic kilometers? ④

   A. 1.5×10^{15}

   B. 2.5×10^{15}

   C. 3.5×10^{15}

   D. 4.5×10^{15}

   E. 7.5×10^{15}

36. If the ratio of the surface areas of two spheres is 2:3, what is the ratio of their volumes? ④

   A. $4 : 9$

   B. $8 : 27$

   C. $2 : 3$

   D. $\sqrt{2} : \sqrt{3}$

   E. $2\sqrt{2} : 3\sqrt{3}$

18.8. Cylinders and Cones

The volume of a cylinder is $\pi r^2 h$ and the volume of a cone is $\dfrac{\pi r^2 h}{3}$. The surface area of a cylinder is $2\pi r^2 + 2\pi rh$. You should not need to know the surface area of a cone.

37. What is the volume in cubic centimeters of a cylinder with diameter 80 cm and height 35 cm? ③
    A. 140π
    B. 5600π
    C. 22400π
    D. 56000π
    E. 224000π

38. Which of these is a formula for the radius of a cylinder in terms of its height and volume? ④
    A. $\sqrt{\dfrac{V}{\pi h^2}}$
    B. $\dfrac{V}{\pi h}$
    C. $\sqrt{\dfrac{V}{\pi}}$
    D. $\sqrt{\dfrac{V}{\pi h}}$
    E. $\sqrt{\dfrac{V}{h}}$

39. The radius of a right circular cylinder is multiplied by a factor of 5 and its height is divided by a factor of 2. What is the ratio of the volume of the old cylinder to the volume of the new one? ④
    A. 2:5
    B. 2:15
    C. 2:25
    D. 5:8
    E. 1:10

40. A cylindrical tank has radius 2 meters and height 3 meters. If it is filled with water and a cubic meter of water weighs 2,205 pounds, about how many pounds does the water in the tank weigh in hundreds of pounds? ④
    A. 415
    B. 622
    C. 831
    D. 1,245
    E. 1,662

41. If a cylinder has height 5 and volume 180π, what is its total surface area? ④
    A. 13π
    B. 124π
    C. 128π
    D. 132π
    E. 136π

42. The region bounded by between $y = 6 - 2x$ and the x and y-axes is rotated about the y-axis. What is the volume of the solid generated? ⑤
    A. 12π
    B. 15π
    C. 18π
    D. 20π
    E. 24π

18.9. Mixed

43. The perimeter of a square is equal to the circumference of a circle. The circle has radius 4 meters. What is the area of the square in square meters? ④
    A. 2π
    B. 4π
    C. $2\pi^2$
    D. $4\pi^2$
    E. $16\pi^2$

— **ANSWER KEY** —————————————————————————————————

1D, 2C, 3E, 4A, 5D, 6B, 7C, 8C, 9C, 10B, 11A, 12D, 13D, 14A, 15B, 16B,17B 18C, 19E, 20E, 21A, 22B, 23D, 24D, 25E, 26B, 27D, 28D, 29C, 30B, 31C, 32D, 33D, 34C, 35A, 36E 37D 38D, 39C, 40C, 41D, 42C, 43D

.

18.10. Solutions

1. (D) $l \cdot w = 1000$ and $l = 2w \implies w \cdot 2w = 1000 \implies w^2 = 500 \implies w = 10\sqrt{5}$ (since the length is twice the width) $l = 20\sqrt{5}$. Perimeter $= 2w + 2l = 60\sqrt{5} \approx 134$.

2. (C) The other side $w = \sqrt{7^2 - 6^2} = \sqrt{13}$ by the Pythagorean Theorem. Therefore, the area $=$ length $\cdot$ width $= 6\sqrt{13}$.

3. (E) By 30-60-90 triangles, the height of the trapezoid is 10 and DE is $10\sqrt{3}$. By 45-45-90 triangles, AF is 10.

   So the height is 10 and the bases are 12 and $22 + 10\sqrt{3}$.

   The area of the trapezoid is: $\dfrac{h(b_1 + b_2)}{2} = \dfrac{10(34 + 10\sqrt{3})}{2} = 170 + 50\sqrt{3} \approx 257$

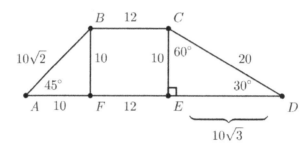

4. (A) The side length is the square root of the area and the perimeter is 4 times the side length. $s = \sqrt{76} = 2\sqrt{19}$, $P = 4s = 8\sqrt{19}$.

5. (D) Each side $= \dfrac{x}{4}$. Area $= \left(\dfrac{x}{4}\right)^2 = \dfrac{x^2}{16}$.

6. (B) The side length of the square $= \sqrt{(8-1)^2 + (1-3)^2} = \sqrt{49 + 4} = \sqrt{53}$. Therefore, the area of the square $= (\sqrt{53})^2 = 53$.

7. (C) Half diagonals are 10 and 15. The diagonals of a rhombus intersect at right angles so you can use the Pythagorean theorem.

   Each side of the rhombus $= \sqrt{10^2 + 15^2} = \sqrt{100 + 225} = \sqrt{325} = 5\sqrt{13}$.   Perimeter $= 20\sqrt{13}$.

8. (C) The rhombus area formula is $\dfrac{d_1 \cdot d_2}{2}$, $\dfrac{20 \cdot 30}{2} = 300$. You can also divide the rhombus into 4 right triangles, $4 \cdot \dfrac{10 \cdot 15}{2} = 300$.

9. (C) Area is proportional to the square of the perimeter. This would not work if the triangles were not similar. $2^2 : 5^2 = 4:25$.

10. (B) By the triangle inequality, and since the shortest distance between two points is a straight line $\implies 17 - 11 < x < 17 + 11 \implies 6 < x < 28$.

11. (A) By an extension of the Pythagorean theorem, a triangle is acute if and only if $a^2 + b^2 < c^2$. Therefore, for the triangle to be acute, $\sqrt{a^2 + b^2}$ must be between the values for either possible right triangle. One triangle is $\sqrt{3^2 - 2^2} = \sqrt{5}$ and the other triangle is $\sqrt{3^2 + 2^2} = \sqrt{13}$, so $\sqrt{5} < x < \sqrt{13}$.

12. (D) Find the altitude by using a right triangle where the altitude is one leg, half of the base is the other leg and a base is the hypotenuse. Let h be the altitude.

$$h^2 + \left(\frac{a}{2}\right)^2 = a^2 \text{ (squaring) } h^2 = \frac{3a^2}{4} \implies h = \frac{\sqrt{3}a}{2}.$$

The area of the triangle

$$= \frac{\text{base} \times \text{height}}{2} = \frac{a \cdot \frac{\sqrt{3}a}{2}}{2} = \frac{\sqrt{3}a^2}{4}.$$

It is also possible to determine the length of the altitudes using 30-60-90 triangles or trigonometry.

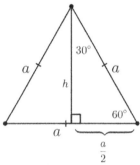

13. (D) Determine the radius from the circumference, and then determine the area from the radius. $C = 2\pi r$, so $10\sqrt{7}\pi = 2\pi r$, $r = 5\sqrt{7}$. Area $= \pi r^2 = (5\sqrt{7})^2\pi = 175\pi$.

14. (A) The area and circumference formulas result in 2 equations in 3 variables. Then eliminate r and solve for A in terms of C.

$$C = 2\pi r, \quad \frac{C}{2\pi} = r, \quad A = \pi r^2 = \pi \left(\frac{C}{2\pi}\right)^2 = \pi \frac{C^2}{4\pi^2} = \frac{C^2}{4\pi}.$$

15. (B) Take the ratio of the area formula to the circumference formula and simplify. $\dfrac{\pi r^2}{2\pi r} = \dfrac{r}{2}$.

16. (B) Subtract the area of the smaller circle from that of the larger circle. $100^2\pi - 70^2\pi = 5100\pi$.

17. (B) Radii are $\sqrt{36} = 6$ and $\sqrt{10}$, so areas $= \pi r^2$ are 36π and 10π. $36\pi - 10\pi = 26\pi$.

18. (C) The distance between the endpoints

$$= \sqrt{(4-(-2))^2 + (1-(-11))^2} = \sqrt{36+144} = \sqrt{180} = 6\sqrt{5}.$$

The distance between the endpoints is the diameter, so the radius is half of that, $3\sqrt{5}$. The area is $\pi r^2 = \pi(3\sqrt{5})^2 = 45\pi$.

19. (E) $\dfrac{2\pi r}{42} = \dfrac{48\pi}{42} = \dfrac{8\pi}{7}$.

20. (E) Find the radius from the area, and then the circumference from the radius. $A = \pi r^2$, $12\pi = \pi r^2$, $r^2 = 12$, $r = 2\sqrt{3}$. $C = 2\pi r = 2\pi \cdot 2\sqrt{3} = 4\sqrt{3}\pi$ cm.

21. (A) Arc length $= 2\pi r \dfrac{\theta}{360} = 2\pi \cdot 10 \cdot \dfrac{5}{360} = \dfrac{100\pi}{360} = \dfrac{5\pi}{18} = 0.873$ cm. Now convert from cm to mm: $0.873 \cdot 10$ mm/cm $= 8.73$ mm.

22. (B) Circumference $= 2\pi r = 2a\pi$. Therefore, the length of each arc $= \dfrac{2a\pi}{b}$.

23. (D) The area of a slice $= \pi r^2 \cdot \dfrac{\theta}{360}$, $20\pi = \pi r^2 \dfrac{40}{360} \implies 180 = r^2 \implies \sqrt{180} = r$, $6\sqrt{5} = r$.

24. (D) Convert to millimeters, and then take the cube of the side length to get the volume: $(5 \cdot 10^3)^3 = 125 \cdot 10^9 = 1.25 \times 10^{11}$.

25. (E) $s^3 =$ volume, $s^3 = 27 \implies s = 3$. Each of 6 sides have area $3 \cdot 3 = 9$. So the surface area is $6 \cdot 9 = 54$ square inches.

26. (B) Find the side length from the surface area, and then the volume from the side length: $x = 6s^2$, $s = \sqrt{\dfrac{x}{6}}$, $V = s^3 = \left(\dfrac{x}{6}\right)^{\frac{3}{2}}$.

27. (D) The area of a box is proportionate to the square of the side lengths, so you can see to just take $3^2 = 9$. Or using the formula is $2(lw+wh+lh)$, $2(3l \cdot 3w + 3w \cdot 3h + 3l \cdot 3h) = 9 \cdot 2(lw+wh+lh)$. So 9.

28. (D) $\dfrac{12}{3} \cdot \dfrac{12}{4} \cdot \dfrac{12}{6} = 4 \cdot 3 \cdot 2 = 24$ small boxes in each cubic foot. The volume of the large box is $2 \cdot 2 \cdot 5 = 20$ cubic feet. Therefore, $24 \cdot 20 = 480$ small boxes can fit into the large box. There are various other methods.

29. (C) Convert yards and inches to feet and multiply. $60 \cdot 90 \cdot \dfrac{1}{6} = 900$ cubic feet.

30. (B) Take the current volume and multiply it by the ratios the sides are increased by: $300 \cdot 2 \cdot 2 \cdot 5 = 6000$.

31. (C) Substitute into the formula for surface area of a box.

$$2(lw + lh + wh) = 2(2 \cdot 3 + 2 \cdot 5 + 3 \cdot 5) = 62.$$

32. (D) Find the volume in the larger pool divided by the area of the smaller pool: $\dfrac{5 \cdot 3 \cdot 2}{14 \cdot 8} = \dfrac{30}{112} = \dfrac{15}{56}$. Now convert from meters to centimeters: $\dfrac{15}{56} \cdot 100 = 26.79$

33. (D) $7 \cdot 3^3 = 7 \cdot 27 = 189$.

34. (C) Just take the ratio of the cubes of the radii. Using the volume of sphere formula is possible, but unnecessary work. $\dfrac{5^3}{3^3} = 125{:}27$.

35. (A) Substitute the radius into the volume of sphere formula to find the volume:

$$\frac{4\pi r^3}{3} = \frac{4\pi \cdot 71492^3}{3} \approx 1.5 \times 10^{15}.$$

36. (E) Surface area is proportional to the square of the radius and volume to the cube of the radius, so $2^{\frac{3}{2}} : 3^{\frac{3}{2}} = 2\sqrt{2} : 3\sqrt{3}$. You could also use the formulas for surface area and volume, but the above approach is easier.

37. (D) Radius is 40. Volume is $\pi r^2 h$. $\pi \cdot 40^2 \cdot 35 = \pi \cdot 1600 \cdot 35 = 56000\pi$ cubic centimeters.

38. (D) Solve for radius in the volume of cylinder formula.

$$V = \pi r^2 h \text{ (isolating } r) \quad \frac{V}{\pi h} = r^2 \implies r = \sqrt{\frac{V}{\pi h}}.$$

39. (C) Square the ratio of the radius, but not the height, because the formula is $\pi r^2 h$: $2 : 5^2 = 2{:}25$.

40. (C) Find the volume and then convert from cubic meters to pounds. $V = \pi r^2 h = \pi 2^2 \cdot 3 = 12\pi$ cubic meters. $12\pi \cdot 2,205 = 83,127$ pounds=831.27 hundreds of pounds.

41. (D) $V = \pi r^2 h$, $180\pi = \pi r^2 \cdot 5$, $36 = r^2$, $r = 6$, total surface area=area of the base+lateral surface area $= 2\pi r^2 + 2\pi r h = 2\pi 6^2 + 2\pi 6 \cdot 5 = 72\pi + 60\pi = 132\pi$.

42. (C) The y-intercept of $y = 6-2x$ is $(0,6)$, and its x-intercept is $(3,0)$. The 3 lines form a triangle. Rotating that triangle about the y-axis generates a cone with $r = 3$, $h = 6$. Using the volume of a cone formula, $\dfrac{\pi r^2 h}{3} = \dfrac{\pi 3^2 \cdot 6}{3} = 18\pi$. You could also use calculus rotation of solids techniques to find the volume.

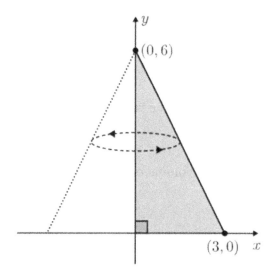

43. (D) Circumference of circle $= 2\pi r = 2\pi 4 = 8\pi$. 8π is then the perimeter of the square. Each side of the square is then 2π meters, so the area of the square is $(2\pi)^2 = 4\pi^2$ square meters.

19. Inscribed Figures

These are fairly difficult problems, which are reasonably common on the test, and not covered in detail in other materials. The key is the diagonal on the rectangle or triangle is the diameter of the circle (which is twice its radius). Similarly with three dimensional figures, the long diagonal of an inscribed cube is the diameter of the circumscribed sphere.

19.1. 2D

If a rectangle is inscribed in a circle, the diameter of the circle equals the diagonal of the rectangle (a square is a rectangle). If a right triangle is inscribed in a circle, the diameter of the circle equals the hypotenuse of the triangle.

For example, a square is inscribed in a circle of area 100π square units. What is the area of the square? $100\pi = \pi r^2 \implies 100 = r^2 \implies r = 10$. The diagonal of the square is the diameter of the circle, so the diagonal is 20. The sides of the square have length $\dfrac{20}{\sqrt{2}} = 10\sqrt{2}$, by 90-45-45 triangles, the Pythagorean Theorem or trigonometry. The area of the square is $\left(10\sqrt{2}\right)^2 = 200$.

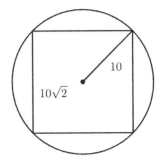

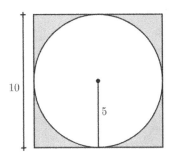

An easier problem is also common on the test, which involves a circle inscribed in a square and may be asked in terms of multiple circles or cylindrical cans in a box.

If a circle of radius 5 is inscribed in a square, what is the area of the region inside the square, but outside the circle. The diameter of the circle is $2 \cdot 5 = 10$. Therefore, the side lengths of the square are 10. The area of the square is $10 \cdot 10 = 100$. The area of the circle is $\pi r^2 = \pi 5^2 = 25\pi$. Therefore, the area between the circle and square is $100 - 25\pi$.

1. If a circle is inscribed in a square, what is the ratio of the area of a circle to the area of the square? ④

   A. $\dfrac{\pi}{5}$

   B. $\dfrac{\pi}{4}$

   C. $\dfrac{\pi}{3}$

   D. $\dfrac{2}{\pi}$

   E. $\dfrac{4}{\pi}$

2. If a square is inscribed in a circle, what is the ratio of the area of the square to the area of the circle? ④

   A. $9 : 4\pi$

   B. $4 : \pi^2$

   C. $2 : \pi$

   D. $10 : 3\pi$

   E. $5 : 6\pi$

3. If a square is inscribed in a circle, what is the ratio of the perimeter of the square to the circumference of the circle? ④

   A. $2 : \pi$

   B. $3 : \pi$

   C. $5 : 2\pi$

   D. $2\sqrt{2} : \pi$

   E. $\sqrt{7} : \pi$

4. What is the largest circle that can be inscribed in the ellipse

$$\frac{(x-4)^2}{9} + \frac{(y-2)^2}{25} = 1?\ ④$$

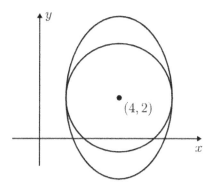

   A. $(x-4)^2 + (y-2)^2 = 9$

   B. $(x-4)^2 + (y-2)^2 = 1$

   C. $(x-4)^2 + (y-2)^2 = 25$

   D. $(x-4)^2 + y^2 = 9$

   E. $(x-4)^2 + y^2 = 1$

5. What is the area in square units of the square inscribed in $(x-4)^2 + (y-2)^2 = 36$? ④

   A. 72

   B. 75

   C. 80

   D. 96

   E. 108

6. A rectangle with sides of length 6 and 10 is inscribed in a circle. What is the area of the region lying inside the circle but outside of the rectangle? ④

   A. $28\pi - 60$
   B. $30\pi - 60$
   C. $32\pi - 60$
   D. $34\pi - 60$
   E. $36\pi - 60$

7. What is the area of the largest rhombus inscribed in $\dfrac{x^2}{4} + \dfrac{y^2}{9} = 1$? ④

   A. 10
   B. 11
   C. 12
   D. $8\sqrt{3}$
   E. $8\sqrt{2}$

8. If a right triangle with legs of length 2 and 3 is inscribed in a circle, what is the area of the circle? ④

   A. 3π
   B. $\dfrac{15\pi}{4}$
   C. $\dfrac{11\pi}{4}$
   D. $\dfrac{13\pi}{4}$
   E. $\dfrac{25\pi}{8}$

19.2. 3D

Suppose a cube is inscribed in a sphere. Since the long diagonal of the cube equals the diameter of the sphere, the sides of a cube are the diameter divided by the ratio of the long diagonal to the sides $= \dfrac{2r}{\sqrt{3}}$. The long diagonal of a cube is $\sqrt{3}\times$ side length, which can be derived using the Pythagorean Theorem twice.

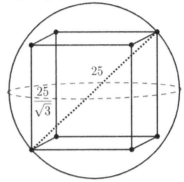

9. If a cube with side length 2 is inscribed in a sphere, what is the surface area of the sphere (surface area of a sphere is $4\pi r^2$)? ④

   A. 8π
   B. 10π
   C. 12π
   D. $\dfrac{32\pi}{3}$
   E. $\dfrac{25\pi}{2}$

10. If a cube is inscribed in a sphere, what is the ratio of the volume of the sphere to the volume of the cube? ⑤

   A. $\pi : 2$
   B. $\sqrt{3}\pi : 2$
   C. $2\pi : 3$
   D. $\sqrt{3}\pi : 3$
   E. $9\pi : 8$

① Easiest

⑤ Most Difficult

19.3. Solutions

1. (B) Let the radius of the circle equal 1. Then the area of the circle is $\pi 1^2 = \pi$. Then the sides of the square are 2, so the area of the square is $2^2 = 4$. So the ratio is $\dfrac{\pi}{4}$. Instead of 1, it is possible to use some other number or x, but 1 is simplest.

2. (C) Assume the circle has radius 1 (you could use a different number or a variable, but 1 makes the calculations simplest). Then the diameter is 2, which is the diagonal of the square. The square's sides are $\sqrt{2}$, by the Pythagorean Theorem, $90-45-45$ triangle ratios or trigonometry. Therefore, the area of the square is $\left(\sqrt{2}\right)^2 = 2$. The area of the circle is $\pi r^2 = \pi$. Therefore, the ratio is $2 : \pi$.

3. (D) Let the radius of the circle be 1 (again, you could assume other values, but 1 is easiest). Then the diagonal of the square is the diameter of the circle $= 2$. Therefore, the sides of the square are $\sqrt{2}$. The perimeter of the square is $4s = 4\sqrt{2}$ and the circumference of the circle is 2π. Hence the ratio is $4\sqrt{2} : 2\pi = 2\sqrt{2} : \pi$.

4. (A) The circle should have the same center, $(4, 2)$, as the ellipse and the circle's radius should be equal to half of the minor axis of the ellipse, which is 3, Therefore, substituting into the circle formula, the equation of the circle is $(x-4)^2 + (y-2)^2 = 9$.

5. (A) The radius is 6, so the diameter is 12. The area of the square is $\dfrac{d_1 \cdot d_2}{2} = \dfrac{12^2}{2} = 72$ by the rhombus formula. You can also determine that the sides are $\dfrac{12}{\sqrt{2}} = 6\sqrt{2}$ by the $90-45-45$ triangle ratios, the Pythagorean Theorem, or trigonometry. Therefore, the area of the square $= (6\sqrt{2})^2 = 72$.

6. (D) The length of the diagonal of the rectangle is $\sqrt{6^2 + 10^2} = \sqrt{136} = 2\sqrt{34}$. Therefore, the radius of the circle is half the diagonal, $\sqrt{34}$, so the area of the circle $= \pi r^2 = 34\pi$. The area of the rectangle is $6 \cdot 10 = 60$, so the area of the region outside the rectangle but inside the circle is $34\pi - 60$.

7. (C) The major axis is $\sqrt{9} \cdot 2 = 6$. The minor axis is $\sqrt{4} \cdot 2 = 4$, so the diagonals are 4 and 6. The diagonals of the rhombus are the vertices and covertices of the ellipse. The area of a rhombus $= \dfrac{d_1 \cdot d_2}{2} = \dfrac{4 \cdot 6}{2} = 12$. You can also find the area of 4 right triangles with legs 2 and 3. $\dfrac{2 \cdot 3}{2} = 3$.

$3 \cdot 4 = 12$ for all 4 triangles.

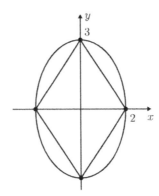

8. (D) The hypotenuse is $\sqrt{2^2 + 3^2} = \sqrt{13}$; therefore the radius is half of that $= \dfrac{\sqrt{13}}{2}$.

   The area of the circle $= \pi r^2 = \left(\dfrac{\sqrt{13}}{2}\right)^2 \cdot \pi = \dfrac{13\pi}{4}$.

9. (C) The long diagonal of the cube is $\sqrt{3}$ times the side length. This can be derived by using the Pythagorean theorem twice or the Pythagorean theorem extended to 3 dimensions. Therefore, the diameter is $2\sqrt{3}$. That is the diameter of the sphere, so the radius of the sphere is $\sqrt{3}$. The surface area of the sphere is $4\pi r^2 = 4\pi(\sqrt{3})^2 = 4\pi \cdot 3 = 12\pi$.

10. (B) Let the sides of the cube be 2; then the volume of the cube $= s^3 = 8$. The long diagonal of the cube is $s \cdot \sqrt{3} = 2\sqrt{3}$, so the radius of the sphere is half that, $\sqrt{3}$. The volume of the sphere is $\dfrac{4\pi r^3}{3} = \dfrac{4\pi(\sqrt{3})^3}{3} = 4\pi\sqrt{3}$. Hence the ratio is $4\pi\sqrt{3} : 8 = \sqrt{3}\pi : 2$.

20. Literal Equations

These problems involve solving for one variable in terms of the others. They are fairly common on both the ACT and SAT and you should master the techniques involved.

20.1. Linear Equations

Isolate the variable you are solving for. Sometimes you need to factor out the variable and divide by what remains.

For example, $a = \dfrac{b+x}{c+x}$, $a \neq 1$, solve for x. $ca+ax = b+x$ (getting the x terms on one side) $ax-x = b-ca$ (factoring out x) $(a-1)x = b-ca$ (dividing to solve for x) $x = \dfrac{b-ca}{a-1}$. The key step is factoring out x.

1. If $5y = 3x + 8$, what is x in terms of y? ③

   A. $x = \dfrac{-8-5y}{3}$

   B. $x = \dfrac{5y-8}{3}$

   C. $x = \dfrac{8-5y}{3}$

   D. $x = \dfrac{8-3y}{5}$

   E. $x = \dfrac{8+5y}{3}$

2. If $F = 32 + \dfrac{9}{5}$, what is C in terms of F? ③

   A. $\dfrac{5}{9}(F-32)$

   B. $\dfrac{9}{5}(F-32)$

   C. $\dfrac{5}{9}(F+32)$

   D. $\dfrac{9}{5}(F+32)$

   E. $\dfrac{5F}{9} - 32$

3. If $A = (b_1 + b_2) \cdot \dfrac{h}{2}$, which of these is b_1 in terms of the other variables? ③

   A. $\dfrac{A}{h} - b_2$

   B. $\dfrac{2A}{h} - b_2$

   C. $2A - b_2$

   D. $\dfrac{2A}{h}$

   E. $\dfrac{2A}{h} + b_2$

4. If $\dfrac{1}{x} + \dfrac{1}{a} = \dfrac{1}{b}$, which of these is x in terms of a and b? ④

   A. $\dfrac{ab}{a^2 - b^2}$

   B. $\dfrac{ab}{b - a}$

   C. $\dfrac{ab}{a - b + 1}$

   D. $\dfrac{ab}{a - b}$

   E. $\dfrac{ab}{a + b}$

5. If $\dfrac{x}{a} + \dfrac{x}{b} = c$, what is x in terms of a, b and c? ③

   A. $\dfrac{abc}{a + b}$

   B. $\dfrac{abc^2}{a + b}$

   C. $\dfrac{abc}{a - b}$

   D. $\dfrac{ab}{a - b}$

   E. $\dfrac{ab}{a + b}$

6. If $ax + b = cx + d$ and $a \neq c$, what is x? ④

   A. $\dfrac{d}{a + c}$

   B. $\dfrac{d}{a - c}$

   C. $\dfrac{d + b}{a - c}$

   D. $\dfrac{b}{a - c}$

   E. $\dfrac{d - b}{a - c}$

7. If $x^{2a} x^{5b} = 1$, what is a in terms of b? ③

   A. $\dfrac{-25b}{2}$

   B. $\dfrac{-5b}{4}$

   C. $\dfrac{-5b}{2}$

   D. $\dfrac{5b}{2}$

   E. $\dfrac{-3b}{2}$

20.2. Nonlinear Equations

You may need to take the square or cube root or the log of both sides. You need to perform the inverse operation of whatever operation occurs in the problem in order to isolate the variable. For example, if $A = \pi r^2$, solve for r.

$$\frac{A}{\pi} = r^2 \implies \sqrt{\frac{A}{\pi}} = r$$

8. If $2^{a+3} = 5b$, what is 2^a in terms of b? ③

   A. $\dfrac{5b}{8}$

   B. $\dfrac{5b}{2}$

   C. $\dfrac{3b}{8}$

   D. $\dfrac{5b}{4}$

   E. $\dfrac{5b}{16}$

9. Which of these is $V = \dfrac{4\pi r^3}{3}$ solved for r? ③

A. $\sqrt[3]{\dfrac{3V}{5\pi}}$

B. $\sqrt[3]{\dfrac{3V}{8\pi}}$

C. $\sqrt[3]{\dfrac{5V}{4\pi}}$

D. $\sqrt[3]{\dfrac{3V}{2\pi}}$

E. $\sqrt[3]{\dfrac{3V}{4\pi}}$

10. If $\log_u\left(v \cdot w^3\right) = t$, what is w in terms of the other variables? ④

A. $\dfrac{u^t}{v}$

B. $\sqrt[3]{\dfrac{u^t}{v}}$

C. $\sqrt[3]{\dfrac{u^t}{v^2}}$

D. $\log_u\left(\dfrac{u^t}{v}\right)$

E. $\sqrt[3]{\dfrac{u}{v}}$

11. Solve $A = P(1+r)^5$ for r. ④

A. $\dfrac{A}{P} - 1$

B. $\sqrt[5]{\dfrac{A}{P}} - 1$

C. $\sqrt[5]{\dfrac{A}{P}}$

D. $\sqrt[5]{AP} - 1$

E. $\sqrt[5]{\dfrac{A}{P} - 1}$

① Easiest

⑤ Most Difficult

— ANSWER KEY

1B, 2A, 3B, 4D, 5A, 6E, 7C, 8A, 9E, 10B, 11B

20.3. Solutions

1. (B) $3x = 5y - 8 \implies x = \dfrac{5y - 8}{3}$

2. (A) $F = 32 + \dfrac{9C}{5}$ (subtract to isolate C) $F - 32 = \dfrac{9C}{5}$ (now multiply to get C by itself) $\dfrac{5}{9}(F - 32) = C$.

3. (B) $A = (b_1 + b_2) \cdot \dfrac{h}{2}$ (dividing is the first step to isolate b_1) $\dfrac{2A}{h} = b_1 + b_2$ (now subtract to isolate b_1) $b_1 = \dfrac{2A}{h} - b_2$.

4. (D) $\dfrac{1}{x} + \dfrac{1}{a} = \dfrac{1}{b}$ (get non-x terms on one side) $\dfrac{1}{x} = \dfrac{1}{b} - \dfrac{1}{a}$ (divide to isolate x) $\dfrac{1}{x} = \dfrac{a - b}{ab}$ (take the reciprocal of both sides to get x) $x = \dfrac{ab}{a - b}$.

5. (A) Find the least common denominator, and then divide to isolate x. $\dfrac{x}{a} + \dfrac{x}{b} = c$ (factoring out x) $\dfrac{(a + b)x}{ab} = c \implies x = \dfrac{abc}{a + b}$.

6. (E) $ax + b = cx + d$ (getting the x terms on one side) $ax - cx = d - b$ (factoring out x) $(a - c)x = d - b$ (dividing to isolate x) $x = \dfrac{d - b}{a - c}$.

7. (C) $2a + 5b = 0 \implies 2a = -5b \implies a = \dfrac{-5b}{2}$.

8. (A) $2^{a+3} = 5b \implies$ (by the laws of exponents) $2^a \cdot 2^3 = 5b$ (simplifying and dividing) $2^a = \dfrac{5b}{8}$.

9. (E) Isolate r^3, then take its cube root to get the radius. $V = \dfrac{4\pi r^3}{3} \implies \dfrac{3V}{4\pi} = r^3$ (taking the cube root) $r = \sqrt[3]{\dfrac{3V}{4\pi}}$.

10. (B) Take both sides u to the power (converting to exponential form), and then solve for w.
$\log_u(v \cdot w^3) = t \implies vw^3 = u^t \implies w^3 = \dfrac{u^t}{v} \implies w = \sqrt[3]{\dfrac{u^t}{v}}$.

11. (B) Divide by P, then take the 5th root to solve for r.

$$\dfrac{A}{P} = (1 + r)^5 \text{ (taking the 5}^{\text{th}}\text{ root) } \sqrt[5]{\dfrac{A}{P}} = 1 + r \text{ (subtracting to solve) } r = \sqrt[5]{\dfrac{A}{P}} - 1.$$

21. Polynomials

21.1. Squaring Expressions

Multiply the binomials, FOIL them out, and combine like terms. It is a trap to square each term individually, rather than FOILing. These problems can generally be solved by making up values for variable.

For example, $(3x + 8y^2)^2 = 9x^2 + 48xy^2 + 64y^4$, FOILing and combining like terms.

1. Which of these is equivalent to $(5x - 4y)^2$?
②
- **A.** $25x^2 + 16y^2$
- **B.** $25x^2 - 40 + 16y^2$
- **C.** $25x^2 - 20xy + 16y^2$
- **D.** $25x^2 - 40xy + 16y^2$
- **E.** $25x^2 - 80xy + 16y^2$

2. $\left(\dfrac{x}{3} + \dfrac{y}{5}\right)^2$ could be rewritten as which of the following? ③
- **A.** $\dfrac{x^2}{3} + \dfrac{xy}{15} + \dfrac{y^2}{25}$
- **B.** $\dfrac{x^2}{9} + \dfrac{2xy}{15} + \dfrac{y^2}{25}$
- **C.** $\dfrac{x^2}{9} + \dfrac{xy}{6} + \dfrac{y^2}{25}$
- **D.** $\dfrac{x^2}{27} + \dfrac{2xy}{6} + \dfrac{y^2}{25}$
- **E.** $\dfrac{x^2}{9} + \dfrac{2xy}{6} + \dfrac{y^2}{75}$

3. Which of these is the xy term of $\left(\dfrac{x}{3} + 4y\right)^2$?
③
- **A.** $\dfrac{8xy}{3}$
- **B.** $\dfrac{10xy}{3}$
- **C.** $\dfrac{8xy}{5}$
- **D.** $8xy$
- **E.** $\dfrac{16xy}{3}$

4. Which of these is $\left(2x + \dfrac{1}{2}\right)^2$ expanded? ③
- **A.** $4x^2 + 2x + 1$
- **B.** $4x^2 + 2x + \dfrac{1}{2}$
- **C.** $4x^2 + 2x + \dfrac{1}{4}$
- **D.** $4x^2 + 4x + \dfrac{1}{4}$
- **E.** $4x^2 + 4x + \dfrac{1}{2}$

21.2. y-intercept

5. What is the y-intercept of $y = (x + 2)(x + 4)(x - 3)$?
    A. -144
    B. -72
    C. -24
    D. -12
    E. 24

21.3. Solving Polynomial Equations

You generally need to factor to reduce the polynomial, and then use the quadratic formula once you reduce it to a quadratic. In some cases, one solution will be given and you will need to use long or synthetic division to reduce the equation and find the other solutions.

For example, solve $x^4 - 13x^2 + 36 = 0$ for x. This is a fourth degree equation in quadratic form, which can be factored as $(x^2 - 9)(x^2 - 4) = 0$. Then set $x^2 - 4 = 0$ and $x^2 - 9 = 0$. Solving both equations, the solutions are ± 2 and ± 3 or $\{-3, -2, 2, 3\}$.

6. What is the solution set of $4x^5 = 30x^4$? ③
    A. $\left\{0, \dfrac{5}{4}\right\}$
    B. $\{0, 15\}$
    C. $\left\{0, \dfrac{15}{2}\right\}$
    D. $\left\{\dfrac{15}{2}\right\}$
    E. $\left\{0, \dfrac{15}{4}\right\}$

7. What is the solution set of $4x^3 = 25x$? ③
    A. $\left\{0, \dfrac{25}{4}\right\}$
    B. $\left\{0, \dfrac{5}{2}, \dfrac{-5}{2}\right\}$
    C. $\left\{0, \dfrac{5}{2}, 5\right\}$
    D. $\left\{0, \dfrac{5}{2}\right\}$
    E. $\left\{0, \dfrac{-5}{2}\right\}$

8. What is the solution set of $x^5 + 5x^4 + 4x^3 = 0$? ③
    A. $\{0, -2, -4\}$
    B. $\{-1, -4\}$
    C. $\{0, -4\}$
    D. $\{0, -3, -4\}$
    E. $\{0, -1, -4\}$

9. Which of these is the smallest solution of $x^4 + 5x^3 + 2x^2 = 0$? ③
    A. $\dfrac{5 + \sqrt{17}}{2}$
    B. $\dfrac{-5 - \sqrt{17}}{2}$
    C. $\dfrac{-5 + \sqrt{21}}{2}$
    D. $\dfrac{5 - \sqrt{17}}{2}$
    E. $\dfrac{-5 + \sqrt{17}}{2}$

10. If 3 is a solution of $x^3 + 8x^2 - 29x - 12 = 0$, what are the other 2 solutions? ③

A. $\dfrac{-11 \pm \sqrt{105}}{2}$

B. $\dfrac{-11 \pm \sqrt{107}}{2}$

C. $\dfrac{-11 \pm \sqrt{111}}{2}$

D. $\dfrac{-11 \pm \sqrt{113}}{2}$

E. $\dfrac{-11 \pm \sqrt{109}}{2}$

11. What is the completely factored form $x^4 - 16$ of over reals? ③

A. $(x^2 + 4)(x + 2)(x - 2)$

B. $(x + 2)^2(x - 2)^2$

C. $(x^2 + 4)(x^2 - 4)$

D. $(x + 2i)(x - 2i)(x + 2)(x - 2)$

E. $(x^2 + 1)(x + 4)(x - 4)$

12. Which of these is the completely factored form of $8x^3 - 27$ over reals? ④

A. $(2x + 3)(4x^2 - 6x + 9)$

B. $(2x - 3)(4x^2 + 6x + 9)$

C. $(2x - 3)(4x^2 - 6x + 9)$

D. $(2x - 3)(4x^2 + 9)$

E. $(2x + 3)(4x^2 + 9)$

21.4. Factoring Polynomials

You should know the difference of squares factorization formula,

$$a^2 - b^2 = (a + b)(a - b).$$

That formula may need to be applied twice when starting with a fourth degree polynomial. It is also useful for understanding problems involving irrational conjugates.

For example,

$$9x^2 - 25 = (3x + 5)(3x - 5),$$
$$x^2 - \frac{25}{49} = (x + 5/7)(x - 5/7),$$
$$x^2 - 5 = x^2 - (\sqrt{5})^2 = (x + \sqrt{5})(x - \sqrt{5}),$$
$$x^2 + 4 = x^2 - (-4) = (x + 2i)(x - 2i).$$

It is helpful to know the sum and difference of cubes factorization formulas, although they may be provided or the problem might be accomplished in other ways:

$$a^3 + b^3 = (a + b)(a^2 - ab + b^2)$$
$$a^3 - b^3 = (a - b)(a^2 + ab + b^2)$$

For example, $(8x^3 + 27) = (2x + 3)(4x^2 - 6x + 9)$.

You can verify that these formulas are correct by FOILing out their right sides.

21.5. Polynomial from Solution Values

We will start with an example with integer solutions to illustrate how a polynomial is found from its solutions. If a fifth degree polynomial has roots 2, 4, 11, 23 and 32, then it must be

$$(x - 2)(x - 4)(x - 11)(x - 23)(x - 32).$$

For example, what is a third degree polynomial with integer coefficients with roots 3 and $5 + \sqrt{2}$? If $5 + \sqrt{2}$ is a root, its conjugate $5 - \sqrt{2}$ must also be a root. Taking x minus each root,

$$\left(x - \left(5 + \sqrt{2}\right)\right)\left(x - \left(5 - \sqrt{2}\right)\right)(x - 3).$$
$$\left(x - 5 - \sqrt{2}\right)\left(x - 5 + \sqrt{2}\right)(x - 3).$$

FOILing the irrational terms first,

$$\left(x^2 - 5x + \sqrt{2}x - 5x + 25 - 5\sqrt{2} - \sqrt{2}x + 5\sqrt{2} - 2\right)$$
$$(x - 3) = (x^2 - 10x + 23)(x - 3)$$

FOILing what remains,

$$x^3 - 3x^2 - 10x^2 + 30x + 23x - 69$$
$$= x^3 - 13x^2 + 53x - 69.$$

13. Which of these is a third degree polynomial with $x = 5$ as its only root? ③

    A. $x^3 - 15x^2 + 90x - 125$

    B. $x^3 - 15x^2 + 75x - 125$

    C. $x^3 - 15x^2 + 80x - 125$

    D. $x^3 - 15x^2 + 70x - 125$

    E. $x^3 - 15x^2 + 100x - 125$

14. Which of these polynomials has roots -2, 1, and 5? ③

    A. $x^3 - 3x^2 - 8x + 10$

    B. $x^3 - 4x^2 - 5x + 10$

    C. $x^3 - 4x^2 - 8x + 10$

    D. $x^3 + 2x^2 - 8x + 10$

    E. $x^3 - 4x^2 - 7x + 10$

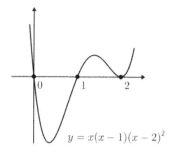

$y = x(x-1)(x-2)^2$

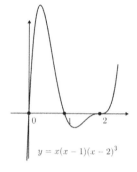

$y = x(x-1)(x-2)^3$

21.6. Polynomial Equations from Graphs

As the figures show, if the graph crosses straight through the x-axis and does not turn or level off, there is a single root at that value. If it turns at the x-axis, there is a double root. If it flattens out as it crosses the x-axis and goes through, there is a triple root.

The degree of the polynomial is the power of its highest degree term if the factors are multiplied out. If the degree of the highest term is even, the end behavior is the same on both sides; if odd, it is different on both sides. If the highest order term has a negative leading coefficient, the end behavior is reversed.

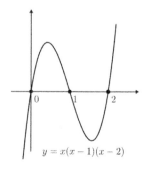

$y = x(x-1)(x-2)$

15. What function is graphed here? ③

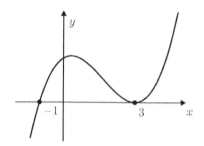

    A. $y = (x+1)(x-3)$

    B. $y = (x+1)(x-3)^2$

    C. $y = x(x+1)(x-3)^2$

    D. $y = (x+1)^2(x-3)$

    E. $y = (x+1)^2(x-3)^2$

16. What function is graphed here? ④

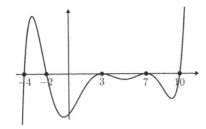

   A. $y = (x+4)(x+2)(x-3)^2(x-7)^2(x-10)^2$
   B. $y = (x+4)(x+2)^2(x-3)^2(x-7)^2(x-10)$
   C. $y = (x+4)^2(x-3)^2(x-7)^2(x-10)$
   D. $y = (x+4)(x+2)(x-3)^2(x-7)^2(x-10)$
   E. $y = (x+4)(x+2)(x-3)(x-7)(x-10)$

17. What could be the equation graphed here? ④

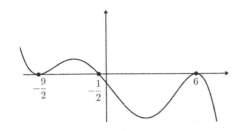

   A. $y = -(2x+9)^2(2x+1)(x-8)^2$
   B. $y = (2x+9)^2(2x+1)(x-6)$
   C. $y = -(2x+9)^2(2x+1)(x-6)^2$
   D. $y = (2x+9)^2(2x+1)(x-6)^2$
   E. $y = -(2x+9)^2(2x+3)(x-6)^2$

18. Which of these is the equation graphed here? ④

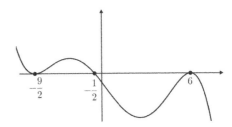

   A. $y = -(x+4)^2(x-3)^3(x-8)^2$
   B. $y = -(x+4)^3(x-3)^2(x-8)^2$
   C. $y = -(x+4)(x-3)^2(x-8)^3$
   D. $y = -(x+4)^3(x-3)^2(x-8)^3$
   E. $y = -(x+4)^2(x-3)^2(x-8)^3$

21.7. Finding Polynomial Coefficients

An example is if $x + 5$ is a factor of $x^3 + 2x^2 + 3x + k$, what is k?

Substitute in the root, -5, as follows:

$$(-5)^3 + 2 \cdot (-5)^2 + 3(-5) + k = 0$$
$$\implies -125 + 50 - 15 + k = 0 \implies k = 90.$$

19. If $x + 2$ is a factor of $x^3 + 2x^2 + 3x + k$, what is k? ④
   A. 4
   B. 8
   C. 10
   D. -4
   E. 6

20. What is the value of v such that $x + 3$ is a factor of $x^3 + 3x^2 + vx - 12$? ④

    A. 4

    B. 2

    C. −4

    D. −2

    E. −1

21. What is the value of v such that $x - 2$ is a factor of $x^3 + vx^2 - 4x - 8$? ④

    A. 8

    B. 6

    C. 4

    D. 3

    E. 2

21.8. Coefficients From Expansion

To find the coefficient in a binomial expansion, you can use the binomial theorem. The binomial theorem is

$$(x + y)^n \sum_{k=0}^{n} {}_nC_k x^k y^{n-k}.$$

Substituting into that formula, $(x+5)^4 = {}_4C_0 x^4 + {}_4C_1 x^3 \cdot 5 + {}_4C_2 x^2 \cdot 5^2 + {}_4C_3 x \cdot 5^3 + {}_4C_4 x^0 \cdot 5^4 = 1 \cdot x^4 + 4 \cdot x^3 \cdot 5 + 6 \cdot x^2 \cdot 5^2 + 4 \cdot x \cdot 5^3 + 5^4 = x^4 + 20x^3 + 150x^2 + 500x + 625$.

It is a good idea to know the binomial theorem if you are going for a perfect score. However, the questions on the exam will probably involve powers small enough that you can multiply the expression out to get the coefficient.

You may be given a problem which does not require the binomial theorem, such as what is the x^5 term is $(2x+7)^5$. Since there is only one combination for the leading term, you can just take $(2x)^5 = 32x^5$, so the answer is 32.

22. What is the coefficient of the x^5 term in $(2x + 5)^5$? ③

    A. 16

    B. 32

    C. 80

    D. 125

    E. 160

23. What is the coefficient of the x^3 term in the expansion of $(x + 1)^6$? ④

    A. 18

    B. 20

    C. 24

    D. 30

    E. 32

24. What is the coefficient of the x^2 term in the expansion of $(2x + 3)^5$? ④

    A. 270

    B. 540

    C. 1,080

    D. 1,440

    E. 1,620

① Easiest

⑤ Most Difficult

— **ANSWER KEY**

1D, 2B, 3A, 4C, 5C, 6C, 7B, 8E, 9B, 10A, 11B, 12A, 13B, 14B, 15E, 16D, 17C, 18D, 19E, 20C, 21E, 22B, 23B, 24C,

21.9. Solutions

1. (D) FOILing, $25x^2 - 40xy + 16y^2$. It would be falling into a trap to square each term rather than FOILing out the identical binomials.

2. (B) FOILing, $\dfrac{x^2}{9} + \dfrac{2xy}{15} + \dfrac{y^2}{25}$. It would be falling into a trap to square each term rather than FOILing out the identical binomials.

3. (A) FOILing, $\dfrac{x^2}{9} + \dfrac{8xy}{3} + 16y^2$. It would be falling into a trap to square each term rather than FOILing out the identical binomials.

4. (C) $\left(2x + \dfrac{1}{2}\right) \cdot \left(2x + \dfrac{1}{2}\right) = 4x^2 + x + x + \dfrac{1}{4} = 4x^2 + 2x + \dfrac{1}{4}$.

5. (C) $2 \cdot 4 \cdot (-3) = -24$. You could also graph it and read the intercept.

6. (C) $4x^5 = 30x^4$ (get everything on one side) $4x^5 - 30x^4 = 0$ (factoring out x^4) $x^4(4x - 30) = 0$ (solve both pieces for x) $x = 0$ or $x = \dfrac{15}{2}$.

7. (B) $4x^3 = 25x$ (get everything on one side) $4x^3 - 25x = 0$ (factoring out x) $x(4x^2 - 25) = 0 \implies x(2x - 5)(2x + 5) = 0$ (finding the zeros of each factor) $x = 0, \dfrac{5}{2}, \dfrac{-5}{2}$.

8. (E) $x^5 + 5x^4 + 4x^3 = 0$, Factor out x^3, and then solve the quadratic part by factoring or another method. $x^3(x^2 + 5x + 4) = x^3(x + 4)(x + 1) = 0$ (finding the zeros of each factor) $x = 0, -1, -4$.

9. (B) $x^4 + 5x^3 + 2x^2 = 0$, Factor out x^2, then solve the quadratic using the quadratic formula. $x^2(x^2 + 5x + 2) = 0$ (using the quadratic formula) $\dfrac{-5 \pm \sqrt{25 - 8}}{2} \implies \dfrac{-5 \pm \sqrt{17}}{2}$, so $(-5 - \sqrt{17})/2$ is the smallest factor.

10. (A)
$$\begin{array}{r|rrrr} 3 & 1 & 8 & -29 & -12 \\ & & 3 & 33 & 12 \\ \hline & 1 & 11 & 4 & 0 \end{array}$$
First, do synthetic division (you could also do long division) to determine what remains after dividing by $x - 3$. We are left with $x^2 + 11x + 4 = 0$, which needs to be solved using the quadratic formula,

$$x = \frac{-11 \pm \sqrt{121 - 16}}{2} = \frac{-11 \pm \sqrt{105}}{2}.$$

11. (B) $y = (x + 1)(x - 3)^2$. Take the negative of each root. Where it just touches is a double root.

12. (A) $x^4 - 16 = (x^2 + 4)(x^2 - 4) = (x^2 + 4)(x + 2)(x - 2)$, using the difference of squares formula twice.

13. (B) $8x^3 - 27$ Substituting $a = 2x$ and $b = 3$ into the difference of cubes formula

$$a^3 - b^3 = (a - b)(a^2 + ab + b^2) \text{ results in } (2x - 3)(4x^2 + 6x + 9).$$

Alternate solution: set $8x^3 - 27$ equal to 0. $\implies 8x^3 = 27 \implies x^3 = \dfrac{27}{8} \implies x = \dfrac{3}{2}$. Then use synthetic or polynomial division to find the quadratic factor.

14. (B) Take x minus each root (which are the same) and multiply out: $(x - 5)(x - 5)(x - 5) = (x^2 - 10x + 25)(x - 5) \implies x^3 - 5x^2 - 10x^2 + 50x + 25x - 125 = x^3 - 15x^2 + 75x - 125$. Another approach is to use the binomial theorem as follows,

$$_3C_0 x^3 + {}_3C_1 x^2(-5) + {}_3C_2 x(-5)^2 + {}_3C_3(-5)^3 = x^3 - 15x^2 + 75x - 125.$$

15. (E) Take x minus each root and multiply out. $(x - 5)(x + 2)(x - 1) = (x^2 - 3x - 10)(x - 1)$ FOILing, $x^3 - 3x^2 - 10x - x^2 + 3x + 10 = x^3 - 4x^2 - 7x + 10$.

16. (D) The polynomial crosses the x-axis at -4, -2, and 10. The graph just touches the x-axis at 3 and 7, so there are double roots at those points. Adding the powers of the roots, it is clear the polynomial is 7th degree; the graph starts at the bottom and ends at the top, so the polynomial must have a positive leading coefficient: $y = (x + 4)(x + 2)(x - 3)^2(x - 7)^2(x - 10)$.

17. (C) The polynomial has double roots at $\dfrac{-9}{2}$ and 6, and a single root at $\dfrac{-1}{2}$. The graph starts positive and ends negative, so the polynomial has a negative leading coefficient. Therefore, the equation is $y = -(2x + 9)^2(2x + 1)(x - 6)^2$.

18. (D) The graph flattens and goes through at -4 and 8, so those are 3rd powers. It touches at 3, so that is second power. Then, adding the degrees of the solution, $2 + 3 + 3 = 8$, the function is of even degree and starts and ends negative, so there needs to be a negative sign in front. $y = -(x + 4)^3(x - 3)^2(x - 8)^3$

19. (E) Since $x + 2$ is a factor, the root is -2. Therefore substitute -2 for x and solve for k. $(-2)^3 + 2 \cdot (-2)^2 + 3 \cdot (-2) + k = 0 \implies -8 + 8 - 6 + k = 0 \implies k = 6$.

20. (C) Substitute -3 for x and solve for v. $(-3)^3 + 3 \cdot (-3)^2 - 3v - 12 = 0 \implies -27 + 27 - 3v - 12 = 0 \implies 3v = -12 \implies v = -4$.

21. (E) Substitute 2 for x and solve for v. $2^3 + v \cdot 2^2 - 4 \cdot 2 - 8 = 0 \implies 8 + 4v - 8 - 8 = 0 \implies v = 2$.

22. (B) $(2x)^5 = 32x^5$, so 32.

23. (B) By the binomial theorem, $_6C_3 \cdot x^3 \cdot 1^3 = 20x^3$. You could also multiply the expression and find the coefficient of the 6th degree polynomial, but that is lengthy.

24. (C) By the binomial theorem, $_5C_3 \cdot (2x)^2 \cdot 3^3 = 10 \cdot 4x^2 \cdot 27 = 1080x^2$.

22. Trigonometry

There are many different approaches to solving problems in the first two sections . You can use different Pythagorean identities, draw a right triangle and find the missing side, or substitute numbers for variables.

22.1. Radians and Degrees

Coterminal

If angles are coterminal, you can add or subtract multiples of 360° degrees and still have the terminal side landing at the same place on the unit circle.To find a coterminal angle between 0° and 360° just add or subtract 360° until you get an angle in that range. Similarly, in radians, add or subtract 2π.

1. What angle between 0° and 360° is coterminal with a 2345° angle? ③
    A. 145°
    B. 85°
    C. 125°
    D. 185°
    E. 65°

Radians to Degrees

It is important to memorize or be able to derive the formulas for conversion between degrees and radians. Problems require these, but the formulas are not given on the exam. For radians to degrees multiply by $\dfrac{180}{\pi}$. For degrees to radians multiply by $\dfrac{\pi}{180}$.

There are 360 degrees in a circle, but 2π radians, so the conversion factor is $\dfrac{360}{2\pi}$ or $\dfrac{180}{\pi}$. Therefore, to convert from radians to degrees, multiply by $\dfrac{180}{\pi}$, so

$$\frac{11\pi}{12} = \frac{11\pi}{12} \cdot \frac{180}{\pi} = 11 \cdot \frac{180}{12} = 165°.$$

2. $\dfrac{5\pi}{24}$ radians is equal to how many degrees? ③
    A. 32.5°
    B. 35°
    C. 37.5°
    D. 42.5°
    E. 47.5°

3. What is $\dfrac{-33\pi}{10}$ radians in degrees between 0° and 360°? ③
    A. 63°
    B. 126°
    C. 202°
    D. 234°
    E. 252°

4. What is $\dfrac{3a\pi}{b}$ radians converted to degrees? ③

   A. $\dfrac{180a}{b}$

   B. $\dfrac{360a}{b}$

   C. $\dfrac{480a}{b}$

   D. $\dfrac{540a}{b}$

   E. $\dfrac{600a}{b}$

Degrees to Radians

To convert from degrees to radians, multiply by $\dfrac{\pi}{180}$; for example,

$$126° = 126 \cdot \frac{\pi}{180} \text{ radians} = \frac{7\pi}{10} \text{ radians.}$$

5. 30° is equivalent to how many radians? ③

   A. $\dfrac{\pi}{12}$

   B. $\dfrac{\pi}{6}$

   C. $\dfrac{\pi}{3}$

   D. $\dfrac{5\pi}{6}$

   E. $\dfrac{-\pi}{6}$

6. 102° is how many radians? ③

   A. $\dfrac{11\pi}{30}$

   B. $\dfrac{17\pi}{30}$

   C. $\dfrac{19\pi}{30}$

   D. $\dfrac{37\pi}{30}$

   E. $\dfrac{39\pi}{30}$

7. What angle (in radians between 0 and 2π) is coterminal with a 23450° angle? ③

   A. $\dfrac{5\pi}{9}$

   B. $\dfrac{23\pi}{18}$

   C. $\dfrac{13\pi}{18}$

   D. $\dfrac{31\pi}{15}$

   E. $\dfrac{5\pi}{18}$

Polar Coordinates

8. Which is NOT equivalent to $(5, 70°)$ in polar coordinates? ③

   A. $(-5, -130°)$

   B. $(-5, 250°)$

   C. $(-5, 710°)$

   D. $(5, 430°)$

   E. $(5, 790°)$

22.2. Range

The range goes up and down by the amplitude from the center line. The range is generally the absolute value of the number in front of cos or sin and the center line is the number added to the trigonometric expression.

$y = a \sin x + b$, the range would be $b \pm a$. Therefore, for $y = 3\cos 8x + 5$, the range is 5 ± 3 or from 2 to 8 or $[2, 8]$ in interval notation.

9. Which of these is the range of
   $y = a\cos(bx + c) + d$? ③

   A. $[d - a, d + a]$
   B. $(d - a, d + a)$
   C. $[d, d + a]$
   D. $[d - 2a, d + 2a]$
   E. $[d - a, d + a + 1]$

10. Which of these is the range of
    $y = 4\sin 3x - 2$? ③

    A. $[-4, 0]$
    B. $[-12, 8]$
    C. $[-6, -2]$
    D. $[-6, 2]$
    E. $[-2, 2]$

22.3. Period

Period is how often the graph of a trigonometric function repeats. It repeats when you go around the unit circle or half the unit circle for tan. The periods of the basic functions for all of $y = \cos x$, $\sin x$, $\sec x$, and $\csc x$ are 2π. The periods of the basic functions for both $y = \tan x$ and $\cot x$ are π. You can verify that tan has a shorter period by graphing or by the unit circle.

For $y = \sin ax$, the period is $\dfrac{2\pi}{a}$; so the period of $y = \sin 4x$ is $\dfrac{2\pi}{4} = \dfrac{\pi}{2}$, and the period of $y = \sin \dfrac{x}{6}$ is $\dfrac{2\pi}{\frac{1}{6}} = 12\pi$. To help understand why this works, if a number greater than 1 is the coefficient of x, that increases the values you are taking sin of and thereby speeds up the function.

11. What is the period of $y = 3\sin\dfrac{x}{4}$? ③

    A. $\dfrac{\pi}{4}$
    B. $\dfrac{\pi}{8}$
    C. 4π
    D. 8π
    E. 16π

12. If $y = \sin ax$ has a period of $\dfrac{5}{2}$, what could the value of a be? ③

    A. $\dfrac{8\pi}{5}$
    B. $\dfrac{2\pi}{5}$
    C. $\dfrac{6\pi}{5}$
    D. $\dfrac{\pi}{5}$
    E. $\dfrac{4\pi}{5}$

13. Which of these is the period of
    $f(x) = a\sin(bx + c) + d$? ③

    A. $\dfrac{\pi}{b}$
    B. $\dfrac{2\pi}{b}$
    C. $\dfrac{\pi}{2b}$
    D. $\dfrac{1}{b}$
    E. $\dfrac{4\pi}{b}$

14. What is the period of $y = \tan 8x$? ③
    A. 2π
    B. 8π
    C. $\dfrac{\pi}{4}$
    D. $\dfrac{\pi}{8}$
    E. $\dfrac{\pi}{16}$

15. Based on the graph below of $y = a \sin bx$, what are a and b? ④

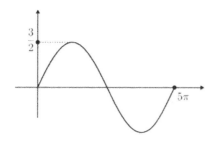

A. $a = \dfrac{3}{2}$; $b = \dfrac{3}{5}$

B. $a = \dfrac{3}{2}$; $b = \dfrac{2}{5}$

C. $a = 3$; $b = \dfrac{2}{5}$

D. $a = \dfrac{5}{2}$; $b = \dfrac{4}{5}$

E. $a = \dfrac{3}{2}$; $b = \dfrac{4}{5}$

16. If the period of $y = 3\cos(ax+2)$ is 10π, what is a? ③

A. $\dfrac{1}{5}$

B. $\dfrac{1}{10}$

C. $\dfrac{2}{5}$

D. $\dfrac{1}{20}$

E. $\dfrac{1}{5\pi}$

17. What is the period of $y = 4\sec(6x + 1) + 3$? ③

A. $\dfrac{2\pi}{3}$

B. $\dfrac{\pi}{6}$

C. $\dfrac{\pi}{3}$

D. $\dfrac{\pi}{9}$

E. $\dfrac{\pi}{12}$

18. What is the smallest positive value of x for which $y = \sin\dfrac{x}{4}$ is a minimum? ④

A. 3π

B. 6π

C. $\dfrac{3\pi}{2}$

D. $\dfrac{\pi}{6}$

E. $\dfrac{\pi}{12}$

19. What is the smallest positive value of x for which $y = 11\sin 10x$ is a maximum? ④

A. 5π

B. $\dfrac{\pi}{2}$

C. $\dfrac{\pi}{5}$

D. $\dfrac{\pi}{10}$

E. $\dfrac{\pi}{20}$

22.4. Finding a Numeric Value

A basic question if is $\sin x = \dfrac{3}{7}$, what is $\cos x$? Observe that

$$\cos x = \pm\sqrt{1 - \sin^2 x} = \pm\sqrt{1 - (3/7)^2}$$

$$= \pm\sqrt{\dfrac{40}{49}} = \pm\dfrac{2\sqrt{10}}{7}.$$

These problems can also be solved by drawing a right triangle and using the Pythagorean theorem, which is similar to using a Pythagorean identity. Not all of the problem solutions explain in detail how to use the diagram.

It is possible to use inverse trig functions to find the angle and them trig functions of that angle. However, there could be issues with the sign of the result, because the calculator gives angles in Quadrants I and IV for sine and tangent and Quadrants I and II for cosine.

There are many different solutions to the problems in this section and the next. All of the solutions do not go over all approaches. You generally can use different Pythagorean identities, as well as draw a triangle and find the missing side.

20. If $\tan x = \sqrt{2}$, $0° < x < 90°$, what is $\cos x$? ④

   A. $\dfrac{\sqrt{5}}{5}$

   B. $\dfrac{2}{5}$

   C. $\dfrac{4}{7}$

   D. $\dfrac{\sqrt{3}}{3}$

   E. $\dfrac{2\sqrt{3}}{3}$

21. If $\tan^2 x = 10$, what is $\sec^2 x$? ④

   A. 9

   B. 11

   C. $8 - \sqrt{10}$

   D. 3

   E. $\sqrt{11}$

22. If $\sin x = \dfrac{2}{3}$, what is $\sec^2 x - \tan^2 x$? ④

   A. $\sin x$

   B. $\cos x$

   C. $\cos 2x$

   D. $-\cos 2x$

   E. 1

23. $0° < x < 90°$ and $\tan x = \dfrac{5}{2}$. What is $\sin x + \cos x$? ④

   A. $\dfrac{7}{\sqrt{29}}$

   B. $\dfrac{2}{\sqrt{29}}$

   C. $\dfrac{5}{\sqrt{29}}$

   D. $\dfrac{-7}{\sqrt{29}}$

   E. $\dfrac{-5}{\sqrt{29}}$

24. If $\sin x = \dfrac{\sqrt{11}}{5}$ and $90° < x < 180°$, what is $\tan x$? ④

   A. $\dfrac{\sqrt{154}}{14}$

   B. $\dfrac{-\sqrt{151}}{14}$

   C. $\dfrac{\sqrt{151}}{14}$

   D. $\dfrac{-\sqrt{155}}{14}$

   E. $\dfrac{-\sqrt{154}}{14}$

25. If $\cos x = \dfrac{3}{4}$, what is $\cos 2x$? ⑤

   A. $\dfrac{-1}{8}$

   B. $\dfrac{1}{4}$

   C. $\dfrac{-1}{4}$

   D. $\dfrac{1}{8}$

   E. $\dfrac{3}{16}$

22.5. Finding a Variable Value

The problems in this section can also be solved using the substituting a made up number for a variable for the angle technique illustrated a solution below and discussed under Trigonometric Expressions and elsewhere. It is recommended that you practice solving these problems using both that method and algebraic techniques.

If $\sin x = a$, what is an expression for $\cos x$? Start with the Pythagorean identity

$$\sin^2 x + \cos^2 x = 1 \text{ (substituting) } a^2 + \cos^2 x = 1$$
$$\implies \cos^2 x = 1 - a^2 \implies \cos x = \pm\sqrt{1-a^2}.$$

This problems and similar ones can also be solved by drawing a right triangle and using techniques similar to those used in trigonometric substitution problems in calculus.

26. Let α be an acute angle of a right triangle. If $\cos\alpha = u$ and $\tan\alpha = v$, what is $\sin\alpha$? ③

    A. $\dfrac{u}{v}$

    B. $\dfrac{v}{u}$

    C. uv

    D. $u^2 v$

    E. uv^2

27. If $\sin x = a$, $0° < x < 90°$, what is $\cos x$? ③

    A. $1 - a^2$

    B. $\sqrt{1-a^2}$

    C. $\dfrac{\sqrt{1-a^2}}{a}$

    D. $\dfrac{1}{\sqrt{1-a^2}}$

    E. $\sqrt{1+a^2}$

28. If $\tan x = \sqrt{a}$ and $0 < x < \dfrac{\pi}{2}$, what is $\cos x$? ④

    A. $\dfrac{1}{\sqrt{a-1}}$

    B. $\dfrac{1}{\sqrt{a^2+1}}$

    C. $\dfrac{1}{\sqrt{a+1}}$

    D. $-\dfrac{1}{\sqrt{a-1}}$

    E. $\dfrac{1}{a-1}$

29. If $\cos x = 3a$ and $0 < x < \dfrac{\pi}{2}$, what is $\tan x$? ④

    A. $\dfrac{1-9a^2}{3a}$

    B. $\dfrac{\sqrt{1-9a^2}}{3a}$

    C. $\dfrac{\sqrt{1-9a^2}}{9a^2}$

    D. $-\dfrac{\sqrt{1-9a^2}}{3a}$

    E. $\dfrac{\sqrt{4-9a^2}}{3a}$

30. If $\sin x = a$ and $0 < x < 2\pi$, which of these expressions is equivalent to $\sin 2x$? ⑤

    A. $4a\sqrt{1-4a^2}$

    B. $4a\sqrt{1-a^2}$

    C. $6a\sqrt{1-a^2}$

    D. $a\sqrt{1-a^2}$

    E. $2a\sqrt{1-a^2}$

22.6. Law of Sines

The law of sines and law of cosines are used to solve (find the sides and angles of) general triangles with no right angle. The law of sines is

$$\frac{a}{\sin \angle A} = \frac{b}{\sin \angle B} = \frac{c}{\sin \angle C},$$

where a is the side opposite $\angle A$, etc. Another form of that law is its reciprocal $\sin\angle A/a = \sin\angle B/b = \sin\angle C/c$. This formula can be used to solve a triangle given an angle and opposite side and one other piece of information. You may be asked to find an expression rather than the answer, so you may not have to memorize the formula or compute the final answer. There are also cases where 2 sides and an angle are given for which using the law of sines results in 2 different triangles or no triangle, but those should not appear on the exam.

It is recommended that you practice and can use these formulas. It is also important to know that you use the law of sines when you have a side and and opposite angle. You use the law of cosines in other cases, with 3 sides given or a side and and included angle. Both formulas are for triangles which are NOT right. You can solve right triangles with simple trigonometry.

31. If in $\triangle ABC$, $\angle A = 2°$, $\angle B = 70°$, $BC = 5$, what is AB? ④

   A. 56
   B. 76
   C. 96
   D. 116
   E. 136

32. The interior angles of a triangle are of the ratio of $2 : 3 : 4$. What is the ratio of the longest side to the shortest side? ④

   A. $1.33 : 1$
   B. $1.43 : 1$
   C. $1.53 : 1$
   D. $1.38 : 1$
   E. $1.48 : 1$

22.7. Law of Cosines

The law of cosines is used to solve a triangle without a right angle when the law of sines does not work, but you have 3 pieces of information — that is, if you have all 3 sides or 2 sides and an included angle. You can use the law of cosines either to solve for an angle or the missing side. The law of cosines is

$$c^2 = a^2 + b^2 - 2ab\cos\angle C.$$

Solved for the angle, it is

$$\angle C = \cos^{-1}\big((a^2 + b^2 - c^2)/2ab\big).$$

Those formulas can be expressed with the variables switched. You will not have to memorize the formula. You will either be given the formula or just need to find the correct expression to solve the problem rather than the answer. In math class, you generally find one angle or side with the law of cosines and then finish solving the triangle with the law of sines, but you should not need to do that for this exam.

33. If in $\triangle ABC$, $\angle A = 60°$, $AB = 4$ and $AC = 5$, what is BC? ④

   A. 4.6
   B. 4.5
   C. 4.4
   D. 4.3
   E. 4.2

34. If it is 11 miles from Chapel Hill to Durham, 31 miles from Chapel Hill to Raleigh, and 37 miles from Durham to Raleigh, which expression gives the angle between the path from Chapel Hill to Durham and the path from Chapel Hill to Raleigh? ④

   A. $\arccos\dfrac{11^2 + 31^2 + 37^2}{2 \cdot 37 \cdot 31}$

   B. $\arccos\dfrac{11^2 + 31^2 - 37^2}{2 \cdot 11 \cdot 31}$

   C. $\arccos\dfrac{31^2 + 37^2 - 11^2}{2 \cdot 11 \cdot 37}$

   D. $\arccos\dfrac{37^2 + 31^2 - 11^2}{2 \cdot 11 \cdot 31}$

   E. $\arccos\dfrac{37^2 + 31^2 - 11^2}{11 \cdot 31}$

35. If the distance from Paris to Berlin is 878 kilometers, from Paris to Vienna is 1034 kilometers, and from Berlin to Vienna is 674 kilometers, what is the angle to the nearest degree at Paris between the direct path to Berlin and the direct path to Vienna? ④

  A. $46°$

  B. $44°$

  C. $42°$

  D. $40°$

  E. $38°$

36. The coordinates of the vertices of $\triangle ABC$, are $A(1,2)$, $B(4,7)$ and $C(3,5)$. What is $\angle C$ to the nearest degree? ⑤

  A. $173°$

  B. $91°$

  C. $93°$

  D. $97°$

  E. $103°$

22.8. Trigonometric Equations

For example, $\sin^2 x = 1/2 \implies \sin x = \pm\dfrac{\sqrt{2}}{2}$ (taking the arcsin and using the unit circle) $x = 45°, 135°, 225°, 325°$.

If going for a top score, it is recommended that you know the unit circle, including the $30°$, $45°$, and $60°$, angles. sin is positive in Quadrants I and II, cos is positive in Quadrants I and IV, and tan is positive in Quadrants I and III. $\sin 30° = \cos 60° = \dfrac{1}{2}$, $\sin 60° = \cos 30° = \sqrt{3}/2$, and $\sin 45° = \cos 45° = \dfrac{\sqrt{2}}{2}$. $\tan 30° = \sqrt{3}/3$ and $\tan 60° = \sqrt{3}$.

Only the basics of trigonometric equations should be covered, NOT the more difficult material in honors precalculus. However, this basic material is not easy, and you should be familiar with the unit circle, etc.

37. What are the values of x, in degrees between $0°$ and $360°$, for which $2\sin x = -1$? ④

  A. $\{330°\}$

  B. $\{210°\}$

  C. $\{30°, 150°\}$

  D. $\{30°, 150°, 210°, 330°\}$

  E. $\{210°, 330°\}$

38. What are all the values of x from $0°$ to $360°$ for which $4\sin^2 x = 3$? ④

  A. $\{60°, 120°\}$

  B. $\{60°, 120°, 240°, 300°\}$

  C. $\{240°, 300°\}$

  D. $\{60°, 300°\}$

  E. $\{120°, 240°\}$

39. What are all the values of x, in degrees between $0°$ and $360°$, for which $\sin^2 x + \cos^2 x = \dfrac{2}{3}$? ③

  A. No solution

  B. $0°$

  C. $50°$

  D. $70°$

  E. $70°, 110°$

40. What are all the solutions between $0°$ and $360°$ of $2\cos^2 x + \sin^2 x = \dfrac{3}{2}$? ④

  A. $\{45°, 135°\}$

  B. $\{225°, 315°\}$

  C. $\{45°, 135°, 225°, 315°\}$

  D. $\{45°, 225°\}$

  E. $\{45°\}$

41. What is the smallest positive value of x in radians for which $\sin 3x = 1$? ④

   A. $\dfrac{\pi}{2}$

   B. $\dfrac{\pi}{3}$

   C. $\dfrac{\pi}{4}$

   D. $\dfrac{\pi}{6}$

   E. $\dfrac{\pi}{12}$

42. If $4\sin^2 x = 3$, what could be the value of $\sec x$? ④

   A. 2

   B. -6 or 6

   C. -2 or 2

   D. $-2\sqrt{2}$ or $2\sqrt{2}$

   E. $-\sqrt{5}$ or $\sqrt{5}$

43. With $0 \le \theta < 2\pi$, $\sin\theta > \dfrac{1}{2}$ on what interval? ④

   A. $(0, \pi)$

   B. $\left(\dfrac{\pi}{3}, \dfrac{2\pi}{3} \right)$

   C. $\left[\dfrac{\pi}{3}, \dfrac{2\pi}{3} \right]$

   D. $\left(\dfrac{\pi}{6}, \dfrac{5\pi}{6} \right)$

22.9. Trigonometric Triangle Area Formula

This formula can be used to find the area of a triangle which is not right. The trigonometric formula for the area of a triangle with two sides and their included angle is given by $\dfrac{1}{2} \cdot AB \cdot AC \cdot \sin(\angle A)$. Therefore, if $AB = 5$, $AC = 8$, and $\angle A = 30°$, then

$$\text{area} = \frac{1}{2} \cdot 5 \cdot 8 \cdot \frac{1}{2} = 10.$$

It is recommended that you memorize this formula, as problems using it will appear on the exam and the formula will usually not be given. Memorizing formulas may not be a good approach to leaning math, but it is important for this exam. If you do not know the formula, the best approach to problems like that will be to estimate, as it is difficult to derive the formula on the fly or find an answer algebraically without it. It usually is possible to estimate the answeer from the diagram or by drawing a diagram, or at least to eliminate answer choices.

44. If in $\triangle ABC$ $\cos\angle A = \dfrac{3}{4}$, $AB = 2$ and $AC = 5$, what is the area of the triangle? ④

   A. $\dfrac{5\sqrt{3}}{2}$

   B. $\dfrac{5\sqrt{5}}{4}$

   C. $\dfrac{5\sqrt{7}}{4}$

   D. $\dfrac{7\sqrt{5}}{4}$

   E. $\dfrac{3\sqrt{11}}{4}$

45. How much larger in square inches is a triangle with sides of lengths 2 inches and 3 inches and an included angle of $60°$ than a triangle with the same sides and an included angle of $30°$? ⑤

   A. 1.1

   B. 1.4

   C. 2.1

   D. 2.2

   E. 2.3

22.10. Trigonometric Expressions

To simplify trigonometric expressions, it is often helpful to convert other trigonometric functions into sines and cosines. The conversion formulas are

$$\tan x = \frac{\sin x}{\cos x}, \quad \cot x = \frac{\cos x}{\sin x},$$

$$\sec x = \frac{1}{\cos x} \quad \text{and} \quad \csc x = \frac{1}{\sin x}.$$

It is also helpful to know the Pythagorean identities. The main identity is $\sin^2 x + \cos^2 x = 1$, which can be expressed as $\sin^2 x = 1 - \cos^2 x$ and $\cos^2 x = 1 - \sin^2 x$. The other forms are less likely to appear, but those are $\tan^2 x + 1 = \sec^2 x$ and $1 + \csc^2 x = \cot^2 x$. Those can be expressed in other forms, such as $\sec^2 x - \tan^2 x = 1$.

If you are going for a top score, it is best to know the double angle identities. $\sin 2x = 2 \sin x \cos x$ is more likely to appear than $\cos 2x = \cos^2 x - \sin^2 x = 2 \cos^2 x - 1 = 1 - 2 \sin^2 x$.

Almost all trigonometric expression problems can be solved by making up a number for the angle, plugging that into the expression in the question and seeing which answer choice that value works for. It is preferable to solve the problems algebraically, but if you do not know how to solve a particular problem algebraically, you should substitute a made up number for a variable. It is recommended to practice solving all types of problems on the exam using the substituting a made up number for a variable technique.

A difficult example is what is $\dfrac{\cos 2x}{\cos x}$ in simplified form? One form of value obtained by the double angle identity for $\cos 2x$ is $2 \cos^2 x - 1$. Using that form and substituting,

$$\frac{2 \cos^2 x - 1}{\cos x} = 2 \cos x - \sec x.$$

That problem could also be solved by substituting a made up number for a variable: set $x = 20°$. Then find $\dfrac{\cos 40°}{\cos 20°} \approx 0.815$, You would substitute $20°$ into the answer choices as follows: $2 \cos x - \sec x = 2 \cos 20° - \sec 20° \approx 0.815$. The other answers should not match. You could also set x to $30°$ or $60°$ (for which you should be

able to find the value of the trigonometric functions for without a calculator), but an uncommon value like $20°$ is safer because with an uncommon value a mock answer is less likely to give the correct value.

46. Which of the following expressions is equal to $(\cos 35°)^2 - (\sin 35°)^2$? ④
    A. $-\cos 70°$
    B. $\cos 105°$
    C. $\cos 70°$
    D. $\sin 70°$
    E. $\cos 70° + \sin 70°$

47. Which of the following is equivalent to $\tan x \cdot \cos x$? ③
    A. $\cot x$
    B. $\sec x \tan x$
    C. $\sec x$
    D. $\sin^2 x$
    E. $\sin x$

48. Which of the following is equivalent to $\sin\left(x + \dfrac{\pi}{2}\right)$? ④
    A. $-\sin x$
    B. $-\cos x$
    C. $\cos x$
    D. $\tan x$
    E. $\cot x$

49. $\sin(x + \pi)$ is equivalent to which? ④
    A. $-\cos x$
    B. $-\sin x$
    C. $\cos x$
    D. $\csc x$
    E. $\tan x$

50. Which of the following is NOT equivalent to $\sin x$? ④

 A. $\cos\left(\dfrac{\pi}{2} - x\right)$

 B. $\tan x \cos x$

 C. $\dfrac{1}{\csc x}$

 D. $\dfrac{\tan x}{\sec x}$

 E. $\cot x \sec x$

51. For $0 < x < \dfrac{\pi}{2}$, the expression $\sqrt{1 - \sin^2 x} \cdot \sqrt{1 - \cos^2 x}$ is equivalent to what? ④

 A. $\sin^2 x$

 B. $\dfrac{\sin 2x}{2}$

 C. $\sin 2x$

 D. $2 \sin 2x$

 E. $\cos 2x$

52. Which of these is equivalent to $\dfrac{\sin^2 x}{\tan^3 x}$? ④

 A. $\cos^2 x \tan x$

 B. $\cos x \cot x$

 C. $\cos^2 x \cot x$

 D. $\cos x \cot^2 x$

 E. $\cos^2 x \cot^2 x$

53. Which of these is $\dfrac{\sin^2 x + \cos^2 x}{\tan^2 x - \sec^2 x}$ in simplified form? ④

 A. -1

 B. 2

 C. $\sin x$

 D. 1

 E. $\cos x$

54. Which of these is equivalent to $\sec x \tan x \cos^2 x$? ④

 A. $\tan x$

 B. $2 \sin x$

 C. $\sin x \cos x$

 D. $\sin x$

 E. $\cos x$

55. Which of these is $\dfrac{\sin 2x}{\cos x}$ in simplified form? ④

 A. $\tan x$

 B. $2 \sin x$

 C. $\cos x$

 D. $\sin 3x$

 E. $2 \tan x$

56. Which of these is equivalent to $10 \sin x \cos x$? ④

 A. $5 \csc 2x$

 B. $5 \tan x$

 C. $5 \cos 2x$

 D. $10 \sin 2x$

 E. $5 \sin 2x$

57. Which of these is equivalent to $\dfrac{\tan^2 x}{\sec^2 x}$? ④

 A. $\cos^2 x$

 B. $1 - \cos^2 x$

 C. $-\cos^2 x$

 D. $\sin x$

 E. $\sin^3 x$

58. Which of these is equivalent to $\dfrac{1 - \sin^2 x}{\cot^2 x}$? ④

 A. $\cos x$

 B. $\sin x$

 C. $\csc^2 x$

 D. $\tan^2 x$

 E. $\sin^2 x$

59. The expression $4 \sin^2 x - 4 \cos^2 x$ is equivalent to which of these? ④

 A. $4 \cos 2x$

 B. $-2 \cos 2x$

 C. $-4 \cos 2x$

 D. $4 \cos 8x$

 E. $2 \cos 2x$

22.11. Word Problems

Included is the fairly difficult height-of-building problem. It is also possible that the height of the building could be provided and you could be asked to find the distance to the building. It is likely that the exam will use angles you should know from the unit circle, 30°, 45°, or 60°.

60. The vertex angle of an isosceles triangle is 50° and the side opposite the vertex has length 10. What is the area of the triangle? ④

   A. 53.6

   B. 59.1

   C. 65.1

   D. 63.1

   E. 57.1

61. Beatrice measures the angle to the top of a building as 45°. After she approaches 200 ft closer to the building along a flat street, the angle increases to 60°. What is the height of the building in feet? ⑤

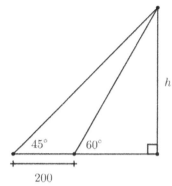

   A. 463

   B. 473

   C. 443

   D. 453

   E. 433

— ANSWER KEY

1D, 2C, 3B, 4D, 5B, 6B, 7E, 8C, 9A, 10D, 11D, 12E, 13B, 14D, 15B, 16A, 17C, 18B, 19E, 20D
21B, 22E, 23A, 24E, 25D, 26C, 27B, 28C, 29B, 30E, 31E, 32C, 33A, 34B, 35D, 36A, 37E, 38B,
39A 40C, 41D, 42C, 43D, 44C, 45A, 46E, 47C, 48C, 49E, 50B 51B, 52C, 53A, 54D, 55B, 56E,
57B 58E, 59C, 60A, 61B.

22.12. Solutions

1. (D) $\dfrac{2345°}{360°} = 6$ remainder 185, so 185° is the answer.

2. (C) Multiply the given angle by the conversion factor $\dfrac{180}{\pi}$ and then simplify:

$$\frac{5\pi}{24} \cdot \frac{180}{\pi} = \frac{75}{2} = 37.5°.$$

3. (B) Find an equivalent value between 0 and 2π.

    Add $4\pi = 40\pi/10$ to get the angle between 0 and 2π,

$$\frac{-33\pi}{10} + \frac{40\pi}{10} = \frac{7\pi}{10} \text{ (converting to degrees) } \frac{7\pi}{10} \cdot \frac{180}{\pi} = 7 \cdot 18 = 126°.$$

4. (B) $30° \cdot \dfrac{\pi}{180} = \dfrac{\pi}{6}$.

5. (D) Multiply the given angle by the conversion factor $\dfrac{180}{\pi}$ and then simplify: $\dfrac{3a\pi}{b} \cdot \dfrac{180}{\pi} = \dfrac{540a}{b}$.

6. (B) Multiply by the conversion factor $\pi/180$ and then simplify: $102 \cdot \dfrac{\pi}{180} = \dfrac{17\pi}{30}$.

7. (E) Find a coterminal angle between 0° and 360° and then convert it to radians. 23450 mod
    $360 = 50$, $50 \cdot \dfrac{\pi}{180} = \dfrac{5\pi}{18}$.

8. (C) $(5, 70 + 360) = (5, 430)$. $(-5, 70 + 180) = (-5, 250)$. $-110° = 250°$. $70 + 720 = 790°$.

9. (A) Go up and down by the amplitude from the center line. $d \pm a$.

10. (D) $\dfrac{2\pi}{\frac{1}{4}} = 2\pi \cdot \dfrac{4}{1} = 8\pi$.

11. (D) Go up and down by the amplitude from the center line. -2 ± 4.

12. (E) $a = \dfrac{2\pi}{\text{period}}$. The period is $\dfrac{5}{2}$, $a = \dfrac{2\pi}{\frac{5}{2}} = \dfrac{4\pi}{5}$.

13. (B) period $= 2\pi$ divided by the coefficient of x, which is b in the equation $f(x) = a\sin(bx+c)+d$, we get $\dfrac{2\pi}{b}$.

14. (D) $\dfrac{\pi}{8}$ because for tan the basic period is π, so we take π divided by the coefficient of x, which is 8.

15. (B) The period is 5π based on the diagram. Therefore, b is $2\pi/5\pi = 2/5$. The amplitude is $3/2$, half the difference from the minimum to the maximum $y-$value, from the diagram.

16. (A) 2π divided by the unknown coefficient of x equals the period, 10π: $\dfrac{2\pi}{a} = 10\pi$, $a = \dfrac{1}{5}$.

17. (C) sec has the same basic period as cos (which is 2π), so divide 2π by the coefficient of x: $\dfrac{2\pi}{6} = \dfrac{\pi}{3}$.

18. (B) The period is $\dfrac{2\pi}{\frac{1}{4}} = 8\pi$; the minimum is at $\dfrac{3}{4}$ of the period, at the point corresponding to $3\pi/2$ on the basic function $y = \sin x$; therefore, the minimum is at $8\pi\dfrac{\frac{3\pi}{2}}{2\pi} = 6\pi$.

19. (E) The period is $\dfrac{2\pi}{10} = \dfrac{\pi}{5}$; the maximum is at $\dfrac{1}{4}$ of the period (which corresponds to $\dfrac{\pi}{2}$ in the basic function). Therefore, the maximum is at $\dfrac{\pi}{5} \cdot \dfrac{1}{4} = \dfrac{\pi}{20}$.

20. (D) Based on the given value of tan, set the opposite side equal to $\sqrt{2}$ and the adjacent side equal to 1, so

$$\text{hypotenuse} = \sqrt{\left(\sqrt{2}\right)^2 + 1^2} = \sqrt{3}, \quad \cos x = \frac{\text{adjacent}}{\text{hypotenuse}} = \frac{1}{\sqrt{3}} = \frac{\sqrt{3}}{3}.$$

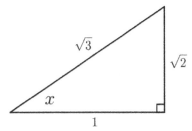

You can also solve using $\sec^2 = \tan^2 + 1$ (substituting the given value, $\sec^2 = 1 + (\sqrt{2})^2 \implies$ $\sec^2 = 1 + 2 \implies \sec^2 = 3 \implies \sec = \sqrt{3} \implies \cos = \dfrac{1}{\sqrt{3}} \implies \cos = \dfrac{\sqrt{3}}{3}$.

It is also possible to find $\tan^{-1}$ with your calculator and then take cos of that angle.

21. (B) $\sec^2 x = \tan^2 x + 1$, $\sec^2 x = 10 + 1 = 11$. You can also find the answer algebraically or using arctan ($\tan^{-1}$) etc. using a calculator.

22. (E) $\sec^2 - \tan^2$ is always 1. That is a Pythagorean identity.

23. (A) Since the tan is 5/2, opposite is 5 and adjacent 2. Therefore, the hypotenuse $= \sqrt{5^2 + 2^2} = \sqrt{29}$. Therefore,

$$\sin x = \frac{5}{\sqrt{29}}, \quad \cos x = \frac{2}{\sqrt{29}}, \quad \sin x + \cos x = \frac{5}{\sqrt{29}} + \frac{2}{\sqrt{29}} = \frac{7}{\sqrt{29}}.$$

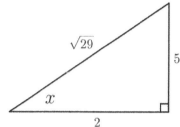

24. (E) Plug the value for $\sin x$ into the Pythagorean identity. We use the negative value of cos since in the 2nd Quadrant. Then find tan using $\tan = \sin / \cos$.

$$\cos^2 x + \sin^2 x = 1 \text{ (substituting) } \cos^2 x + \frac{11}{25} = 1 \implies \cos^2 x = \frac{14}{25} \implies \cos x = \frac{-\sqrt{14}}{5},$$

$$\tan x = \frac{\dfrac{\sqrt{11}}{5}}{\dfrac{-\sqrt{14}}{5}} = \frac{-\sqrt{11}}{\sqrt{14}} = \frac{-\sqrt{154}}{14}.$$

You can also find $\tan\left(180 - \arcsin\left(\dfrac{\sqrt{11}}{5}\right)\right)$ using a calculator.

You can use the diagram to find the adjacent side with the Pythagorean theorem and then cos as adjacent / hypotenuse.

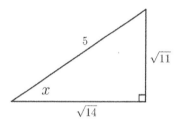

25. (D) $\cos x = \dfrac{3}{4}$, so $(3/4)^2 + \sin^2 x = 1 \implies \sin^2 x = \dfrac{7}{16} \implies \sin x = \pm\dfrac{\sqrt{7}}{4}$, $\cos 2x = \cos^2 x - \sin^2 x =$

$\left(\dfrac{3}{4}\right)^2 - \left(\pm\dfrac{\sqrt{7}}{4}\right)^2 = \dfrac{9}{16} - \dfrac{7}{16} = \dfrac{1}{8}$. You can also use arccos using a calculator, double the value, and then take cos of that. Another approach is

$$\cos 2x = 2\cos^2 x - 1 = 2\left(\dfrac{3}{4}\right)^2 - 1 = 2 \cdot \dfrac{9}{16} - 1 = \dfrac{1}{8}.$$

26. (C) $\tan \alpha = \dfrac{\sin \alpha}{\cos \alpha}$. $v = \dfrac{\sin \alpha}{u} \implies uv = \sin \alpha$. Various other ways to do this, including using opposite, adjacent and hypotenuse or making up a number for angle α.

27. (B) $\sin^2 x + \cos^2 x = 1$. So $a^2 + \cos^2 x = 1 \implies a^2 = 1 - \cos^2 x \implies a = \pm\sqrt{1 - \cos^2 x}$. We are only interested in the positive solution, since the angle is in the 1st quadrant. $\sqrt{1 - a^2}$. You could also solve this by drawing a right triangle and making opposite a and hypotenuse 1. You could make up an angle and check the answer choices with your calculator.

28. (C) Use the identity $\sec^2 x = 1 + \tan^2 x$ (substituting) $\sec^2 x = 1 + (\sqrt{a})^2$ (taking the square root and using the positive solution) $\sec x = \sqrt{1 + a}$ (taking the reciprocal) $\cos x = \dfrac{1}{\sqrt{a + 1}}$. Or draw the right triangle below and use the Pythagorean theorem to determine that the hypotenuse is $\sqrt{a + 1}$. So $\cos x$ is adjacent / hypotenuse $= \dfrac{1}{\sqrt{a + 1}}$.

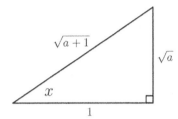

29. (B) Substitute $3a$ for $\cos x$ in the Pythagorean identity, solve for $\sin x$, and then take $\dfrac{\sin x}{\cos x}$ to get $\tan x$. $\cos^2 x + \sin^2 x = 1$, $9a^2 + \sin^2 x = 1$, (choosing the positive solution because of the range of x)

$$\sin x = \sqrt{1 - 9a^2}, \quad \tan x = \frac{\sin x}{\cos x} = \frac{\sqrt{1 - 9a^2}}{3a}.$$

You can also draw a right triangle and make adjacent $3a$ and hypotenuse 1 so that $\cos x$ will be $3a$. Then $3a^2 + \text{opposite}^2 = 1^2 \implies 9a^2 + \text{opposite}^2 = 1 \implies \text{opposite}^2 = 1 - 9a^2 \implies \text{opposite} = \sqrt{1 - 9a^2}$.

$$\tan x = \text{opposite/adjacent} = \sqrt{1 - 9a^2}/3a.$$

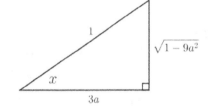

30. (E) Find the value of $\cos x$ from $\sin x$, and then use the double angle formula.

$$\cos x = \pm\sqrt{1 - a^2}, \quad \sin 2x = 2 \sin x \cos x = \pm 2a\sqrt{1 - a^2}.$$

Due to the restrictions on x, we use only the positive solution.

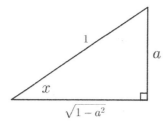

31. (E) Find the other angle and then apply the law of sines.

$$\angle C = 180° - 70° - 2° = 108° \text{ (substituting) } \frac{AB}{\sin 108°} = \frac{5}{\sin 2°} \implies AB \approx 136.3$$

32. (C) The angles are $40°, 60°$, and $80°$. By the law of sines, the sides are proportionate to their opposite angles: $\dfrac{\sin 80°}{\sin 40°} \approx 1.53$

33. (A) Two sides and an included angle are given, so use the law of cosines,

$$c^2 = a^2 + b^2 - 2ab\cos(\angle C) \text{ (substituting) } c^2 = 16 + 25 - 40 \cdot \frac{1}{2} = 21 \implies c = \sqrt{21} \approx 4.58.$$

34. (B) Let the distance from Chapel Hill to Durham $= a = 11$, Chapel Hill to Raleigh $= b = 31$, and Raleigh to Durham $= c = 37$. By the law of cosines,

$$c^2 = a^2 + b^2 - 2ab\cos(\angle C) \text{ (solving for } \cos(\angle C)) \cos(\angle C) = \frac{(a^2 + b^2 - c^2)}{2ab},$$

$$\arccos\left(\frac{11^2 + 31^2 - 37^2}{2 \cdot 11 \cdot 31}\right).$$

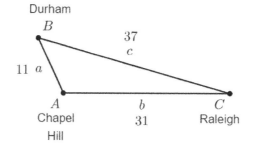

35. (D) Plug the 3 given sides of the triangle into the law of cosines formula and then solve for the cosine of the angle; then take arccos to get the angle. Substituting into the formula,

$$c^2 = a^2 + b^2 - 2ab\cos\angle C \implies 674^2 = 1034^2 + 878^2 - 2 \cdot 1034 \cdot 878\cos x,$$

$$454276 = 1069196 + 770884 - 1815704\cos x, \quad 0.7635 = \cos x, x \approx 40°.$$

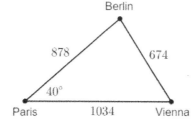

36. (A) Find the 3 sides of the triangle using the distance formula, then use the law of cosines to find the cosine of the angle and arccos to find the angle. Set the angle opposite the largest side as the unknown so as to find the largest angle.

$$AB = \sqrt{(4-1)^2 + (7-2)^2} = \sqrt{34},$$
$$BC = \sqrt{(7-5)^2 + (4-3)^2} = \sqrt{5}, \quad AC = \sqrt{(5-2)^2 + (3-1)^2} = \sqrt{13},$$
$$c^2 = a^2 + b^2 - 2ab\cos\angle C \text{ (substituting the 3 side lengths)}$$
$$(\sqrt{34})^2 = (\sqrt{5})^2 + (\sqrt{13})^2 - 2\cdot\sqrt{5}\cdot\sqrt{13}\cdot\cos\angle C \implies$$
$$\implies 34 = 5 + 13 - 2\sqrt{65}\cos\angle C \implies \quad 16 = -2\sqrt{65}\cos\angle C \implies$$
$$\cos\angle C = \frac{-8}{\sqrt{65}} \implies \quad \arccos\left(\frac{-8}{\sqrt{65}}\right) \approx 173°.$$

37. (E) $2\sin x = -1 \implies \sin x = \frac{-1}{2}$ (take the arcsin to get x) $x = 210°, 330°$. Your calculator would only give you one solution, $-30° = 330°$ The other solution is determined as there is also a value for which $\sin x = \frac{-1}{2}$ in the 3rd Quadrant.

38. (B) $4\sin^2 x = 3$ (isolate $\sin^2 x$) $\sin^2 x = \frac{3}{4}$ (taking the square root of both sides, yielding $\pm$ solutions) $\sin x = \pm\frac{\sqrt{3}}{2}$ (taking the arcsin and using the unit circle) $x = 60°, 120°, 240°, 300°$.

39. (A) $\sin^2 x + \cos^2 x = \frac{2}{3}$. A Pythagorean identity states that $\sin^2 x + \cos^2 x = 1$, and substituting that value into the problem gives $1 = \frac{2}{3}$, which is a contradiction, so there are no solutions.

40. (C) $2\cos^2 x + \sin^2 x = \frac{3}{2}$, $\cos^2 x + (\cos^2 x + \sin^2 x) = \frac{3}{2}$ (since $\sin^2 x + \cos^2 x = 1$ by the identity) $\cos^2 x = \frac{1}{2}$, $\cos x = \pm\frac{\sqrt{2}}{2}$, $x = 45°, 135°, 225°, 325°$.

41. (D) $\sin 3x = 1$, $3x = \arcsin(1) = \frac{\pi}{2}$, $3x = \frac{\pi}{2} \implies x = \frac{\pi}{6}$. Note that the problem asks for the smallest angle. Finding all the solutions is a more difficult problem, and unlikely to be on the exam.

42. (C) $\sin^2 x = \frac{3}{4}, \implies \sin x = \pm\frac{\sqrt{3}}{2}$. It follows that $\cos x = \pm\frac{1}{2}$, which can be found using $\sin^2 + \cos^2 = 1$ or the $30-60-90$ triangle; $\sec x = \frac{1}{\cos x} = \pm 2$.

43. (D) $\sin\left(\frac{\pi}{6}\right) = \sin\left(\frac{5\pi}{6}\right) = \frac{1}{2}$. $\sin(x)$ is larger than that in the interval $\left(\frac{\pi}{6}, \frac{5\pi}{6}\right)$.

44. (C) Find the sin from the cos and then apply the trigonometric area formula. From the Pythagorean identity $\sin = \sqrt{1 - \cos^2}$. Area is the product of 2 side lengths and the sin of their included angle divided by 2.

$$\sin \angle A = \sqrt{1 - \left(\frac{3}{4}\right)^2} = \frac{\sqrt{7}}{4}. \text{ Area } = \frac{2 \cdot 5 \cdot \dfrac{\sqrt{7}}{4}}{2} = \frac{5\sqrt{7}}{4}.$$

45. (A) Apply the area formula for each triangle and subtract. Area is the product of 2 side lengths and the sin of their included angle divided by 2.

$$\frac{2 \cdot 3 \cdot \dfrac{\sqrt{3}}{2}}{2} - \frac{2 \cdot 3 \cdot \dfrac{1}{2}}{2} = \frac{3(\sqrt{3}-1)}{2} \approx 1.1.$$

46. (E) $\dfrac{\sin x}{\cos x} \cdot \cos x = \sin x.$

47. (C) By the double angle formula $\cos 2a = \cos^2 a - \sin^2 a$. You can also determine with your calculator for which answer choice the value matches that in the question.

48. (C) By the angle sum formula, $\sin(a + b) = \sin a \cos b + \cos a \sin b$. So $\sin x \cos \dfrac{\pi}{2} + \cos x \sin \dfrac{\pi}{2} = \sin x \cdot 0 + \cos x \cdot 1 = \cos x$. It is possible to know this fact or to use making up numbers or graphing to solve.

49. (B) The algebraic method requires use of the sum of angles formula, and may not be the easiest. $\sin(x + \pi) = \sin x \cos \pi + \sin \pi \cos x = \sin x \cdot (-1) + \cos x \cdot 0 = -\sin x$. You could also make up an angle for x and test which answer choice works or graph the question and answer choices with your calculator.

50. (E) $\sin x = \cos \left(\dfrac{\pi}{2} - x\right)$ by the cofunction identity. $\tan x \cos x = \dfrac{\sin x}{\cos x} \cdot \cos x = \sin x$. $\dfrac{1}{\csc x} = \dfrac{1}{\dfrac{1}{\sin x}} = \sin x$. $\dfrac{\tan x}{\sec x} = \dfrac{\sin x}{\cos x} \cdot \dfrac{1}{\dfrac{1}{\cos x}} = \sin x$.

51. (B) $\sqrt{\cos^2 x} \cdot \sqrt{\sin^2 x} = \cos x \sin x = \dfrac{2 \cos x \sin x}{2} = \dfrac{\sin 2x}{2}.$

52. (C) Convert to sines and cosines and then simplify.

$$\frac{\sin^2 x}{\dfrac{\sin^3 x}{\cos^3 x}} = \frac{\cos^3 x}{\sin x} = \cos^2 x \cot x.$$

53. (A) $\dfrac{\sin^2 x + \cos^2 x}{\tan^2 x - \sec^2 x}$. By the Pythagorean identities,

$$\sin^2 x + \cos^2 x = 1 \text{ and } \tan^2 x + 1 = \sec^2 x, \quad \frac{1}{-1} = -1.$$

54. (D) $\sec x \tan x \cos^2 x$. Convert to sines and cosines and then simplify.

$$\frac{1}{\cos x} \cdot \frac{\sin x}{\cos x} \cdot \cos^2 x = \sin x.$$

55. (B) $\dfrac{\sin 2x}{\cos x} =$ (by the double angle identity for sine) $\dfrac{2\sin x \cos x}{\cos x} = 2\sin x.$

56. (E) $10\sin x \cos x.$ $\sin 2x = 2\sin x \cos x$ (the double angle identity for sine) (substituting) $10\sin x \cos x = 5\sin 2x.$

57. (B) Convert to sines and cosines and then simplify.

$$\frac{\tan^2 x}{\sec^2 x} = \frac{\dfrac{\sin^2 x}{\cos^2 x}}{\dfrac{1}{\cos^2 x}} = \sin^2 x = 1 - \cos^2 x.$$

58. (E) Simplify the numerator using a version of the Pythagorean identity.

$$\frac{1 - \sin^2 x}{\cot^2 x} = \frac{\cos^2 x}{\dfrac{\cos^2 x}{\sin^2 x}} = \sin^2 x.$$

59. (C) $4\sin^2 x - 4\cos^2 x = -4(\cos^2 x - \sin^2 x) = -4\cos 2x,$ by the cosine double angle identity.

60. (A) $\dfrac{5}{\text{altitude}} = \tan 25° \implies \text{altitude} = \dfrac{5}{\tan 25°} = 10.72$ using the area formula,

$$\text{area} = \frac{\text{base} \times \text{height}}{2}, \quad \text{area} = 10.72 \cdot \frac{10}{2} = 53.6.$$

It is also possible to find the length of the sides adjacent to the vertex using either right angle trigonometry or the law of sines and then find the area of the triangle using either the trigonometric triangle area formula or Heron's rule (which you can look up). However, the method shown above is much quicker and simpler.

61. (B) Let x be the distance to the building when Beatrice gets closer and let h be the height of the building.

Then,

$$\tan 60° = \frac{h}{x} \text{ and } \tan 45° = \frac{h}{x + 200}; \text{ therefore, } h = x\sqrt{3}, \quad 1 = \frac{h}{x + 200}$$

$$\implies x + 200 = h \text{ (substituting) } x + 200 = x\sqrt{3} \implies 200 = x(\sqrt{3} - 1)$$

$$\implies \frac{200}{\sqrt{3} - 1} = x \approx 273.2 \text{ (substituting) } h = 273.2 \cdot \sqrt{3} \approx 473.2.$$

Alternate Solution: We can use the law of sines to find side b, which is also the hypotenuse of $\triangle BDC$. $\angle ADB$ is supplementary to the $60°\angle CDB$, so that angle is $120°$. Therefore, $\angle ABD$ is $15°$. By the law of sines,

$$\frac{b}{\sin 45°} = \frac{200}{\sin 15°} \implies b \approx 546.4.$$

By 30-60-90 triangles or various other methods,

$$h = \frac{b\sqrt{3}}{2} = 546.4 \cdot \sqrt{3}/2 \approx 473.2.$$

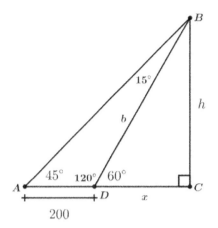

23. Logarithms

While this exam does NOT cover the more difficult logarithm problems in honors math, it can include specific types of tricky problems, and those are covered in this chapter.

23.1. Finding Logarithms

You will need to find logarithms to different bases, using the change of base formula discussed below.

As an example, find the value of $\log_8 32$. In this case, let $\log_8 32 = x$ and convert the expression to the power of the base: $(2^3)^x = 2^5$ (taking $\log_2$ of both sides or equating exponents) $3x = 5 \implies x = \dfrac{5}{3}$.

What is $\log_{128} 64$? Converting 64 and 128 to powers of 2, $\log_{2^7} 2^6$, by the change of base formula that expression equals $(1/7) \log_2 2^6 = (1/7) \cdot 6 = \dfrac{6}{7}$.

You could also use the change of base formula with your calculator and find $\dfrac{\ln 64}{\ln 128} \approx \dfrac{4.159}{4.852} \approx 0.857$. That is $\dfrac{6}{7}$ to 3 decimal places. You can compare your results to the decimal values of the answer choice.

Another example is evaluate $\log_2 \dfrac{\sqrt{32}}{\sqrt[5]{8}}$. Converting to powers of 2, $\log_2 \dfrac{\sqrt{2^5}}{\sqrt[5]{2^3}}$ (converting to fractional exponents) $\log_2 \dfrac{2^{5/2}}{2^{3/5}}$ (now using the laws

of exponents, subtract exponents) $\log_2 2^{5/2-3/5}$ (subtracting fractions) $\log_2 2^{19/10}$; $\log_2$ and 2 to the power are inverse operations, so the answer is $\dfrac{19}{10}$.

Another solution is using a calculator, take $\log_2 \left(\sqrt{32} \cdot 8^{1/5} \right) \approx \log_2(3.732)$ (by the change of base formula) $= \dfrac{\ln(3.732)}{\ln 2} \approx 1.9$ or $\dfrac{19}{10}$.

Calculator methods using the change of base formula etc. work for many of these problems, but are not discussed in all of the solutions.

1. What is $\log 10^{12}$? ②
   - A. 4
   - B. 8
   - C. 10
   - D. 12
   - E. 120

2. What is the value of $\log_2 \sqrt{32}$? ②
   - A. $\dfrac{3}{2}$
   - B. $\dfrac{5}{2}$ *
   - C. $\dfrac{7}{2}$
   - D. $\dfrac{9}{2}$
   - E. 5

3. $\log \dfrac{a^2}{b}$ equals which of the following? ③

    A. $\log a - 2\log b$

    B. $\log a - \log b$

    C. $2\log a - \log b$

    D. $2\log a + \log b$

    E. $4\log a - \log b$

4. Which of these is equivalent to $\log_a b \cdot \log_b a$? ④

    A. a^b

    B. $a + b$

    C. ab

    D. 1

    E. 2

5. What is the value of $\log_3 27 \cdot \log_4 2$? ③

    A. $\dfrac{3}{4}$

    B. 1

    C. $\dfrac{3}{2}$

    D. 2

    E. 6

6. What real value of x satisfies $\log_2\left(32^4\right) = 3x + 5$? ③

    A. 0

    B. $\dfrac{5}{3}$

    C. 5

    D. $\dfrac{35}{3}$

    E. 20

7. Which of these is equivalent to $\log_2 48 - \log_2 6$? ③

    A. 4

    B. 3

    C. $3\log 8$

    D. $3\log 6$

    E. $\log_2 16$

8. Find a numeric value of $\log \dfrac{\sqrt[5]{10^7}}{10^{10}}$. ③

    A. -9.3

    B. -8.6

    C. -7.9

    D. -2.7

    E. -0.7

9. Find the value of $\log \dfrac{100^7}{1000}$. ④

    A. 4

    B. 5.5

    C. 11

    D. 12.5

    E. 17

23.2. Logarithms with Variable Expressions

The following are the laws of logarithms:

$$\log ab = \log a + \log b,$$

$$\log \frac{a}{b} = \log a - \log b, \quad \log a^b = b \log a.$$

These rules apply to logs of any base, not just common logs based 10. For example,

$$\log\left(\frac{a^3 \sqrt{b}}{c^5}\right) = \log a^3 + \log \sqrt{b} - \log(c^5)$$

$$= 3\log a + \frac{1}{2}\log b - 5\log c.$$

10. Which is equivalent to $\log_a \dfrac{a^4}{a^{15}}$? ③

    A. a^{11}

    B. -19

    C. -11

    D. -60

    E. a^{-11}

11. Which is equivalent to $\log_a \sqrt[15]{a^4}$? ③

   A. $\dfrac{4}{5}$

   B. $\dfrac{4}{45}$

   C. $\dfrac{2}{15}$

   D. $\dfrac{2}{5}$

   E. $\dfrac{4}{15}$

12. Find the value of $\log a^b$. ③

   A. ab^2

   B. $b \log a$

   C. $\log a + \log b$

   D. $a \log b$

   E. ab

13. Find the value of $\log_2 \dfrac{8^{3x+3}}{4^{x+5}}$. ④

   A. $7x - 2$

   B. $5x - 2$

   C. $5x + 2$

   D. $7x - 1$

   E. $7x + 2$

14. If $a = 100^{2b+5c}$, find the value of $\log a$. ③

   A. $4b + 10c$

   B. $4b + 12c$

   C. $4b + 15c$

   D. $2b + 5c$

   E. $2b + 10c$

15. Which of these represents $\log_a \dfrac{b^c}{d}$ in terms of natural logarithms? ④

   A. $c \ln b - \ln d$

   B. $\dfrac{c \ln b + \ln d}{\ln a}$

   C. $c \ln b + \ln d$

   D. $\dfrac{\ln b - \ln d}{\ln a}$

   E. $\dfrac{c \ln b - \ln d}{\ln a}$

16. Which of these represents the expanded form of $\log_a(5b^3)$ expressed in terms of natural logarithms? ④

   A. $(\ln 5 + 3 \ln b) \cdot \ln a$

   B. $\ln 5 + 3 \ln b$

   C. $\dfrac{\ln 5 + \ln b}{\ln a}$

   D. $\dfrac{3 \ln b}{\ln a}$

   E. $\dfrac{\ln 5 + 3 \ln b}{\ln a}$

17. Find the simplified value of $\log \dfrac{100^a}{1000^b}$. ④

   A. $2a + 3b$

   B. $a + b$

   C. $3a - 2b$

   D. $a - 3b$

   E. $2a - 3b$

18. If $\log 2 = a$ and $\log 3 = b$, which of these is equal to 288? ④

   A. 6^{5a+2b}

   B. 10^{5a+2b}

   C. e^{5a+2b}

   D. 10^{5a+3b}

   E. 10^{5a-3b}

23.3. Inverse Logarithms

The basic problem is straightforward. In general, you need to raise both sides to the power of the base to eliminate the log, which can also be considered converting to exponential form. From there, it should be easy to solve for what you are taking the log of.

For example, given $\log_3 x = 4$, solve for x. Taking both sides 3 to the power, $x = 3^4 = 81$.

Another example is given $\log x = 3 + \log 7$, solve for x (taking both sides 10 to the power)

$$x = 10^{3+\log 7} = 10^3 \times 10^{\log 7} = 10^3 \times 7 = 7000.$$

19. If $\log_5 x = 3$, what is x? ③

    A. $\dfrac{1}{125}$

    B. 15

    C. 25

    D. 125

    E. 729

20. If $\log_2 x = -5$, find the value of x. ④

    A. $\dfrac{-5}{2}$

    B. $\dfrac{1}{16}$

    C. $\dfrac{1}{32}$

    D. 32

    E. $\dfrac{2}{5}$

21. If $\log x = \dfrac{5}{2}$, find the value of x. ④

    A. 100

    B. $100\sqrt{10}$

    C. 1000

    D. $1000\sqrt{10}$

    E. 250

22. If $\log_2 x = \dfrac{11}{2}$, find the value of x. ④

    A. 32

    B. 48

    C. $16\sqrt{2}$

    D. 64

    E. $32\sqrt{2}$

23. If $\log_2 x = 5a - 2b$, what is x? ④

    A. $\dfrac{32^a}{4^b}$

    B. $\dfrac{64^a}{4^b}$

    C. $\dfrac{16^a}{4^b}$

    D. $\dfrac{8^a}{4^b}$

    E. $\dfrac{32^a}{8^b}$

24. If $\log x = 3a$, what is x? ④

    A. 100^{2+a}

    B. $100 \cdot 10^a$

    C. $1000 \cdot 10^a$

    D. 1000^a

    E. 10000^a

23.4. Finding Bases

Most problems of this type on the exam are relatively easy and can be solved intuitively or by inspection. For example, the exam might ask you to solve $\log_x 36 = 2$ for x. The answer is 6, because $6^2 = 36$. A harder problem would be $\log_x 2 = \dfrac{1}{3}$. The answer is 8 because $8^{\frac{1}{3}} = 2$.

There have been harder problems of this type on the exam, and this book focuses on the most difficult material that might appear.

An example is to solve $\log_a 32 = \dfrac{5}{4}$ for a. You may be able to figure out intuitively that $16^{\frac{5}{4}} = 32$. Another approach is to write the base as

$= 2^x$, since 32 is a power of 2. This is a key step. If it was $\log 27$, you would use 3^x. Then multiply exponents, since you are taking the power of the power. $(2^x)^{\frac{5}{4}} = 2^5$ (taking the $\log_2$ of both sides or equating exponents) $\frac{5x}{4} = 5 \implies x = 4 \implies 2^x = 2^4 = 16$. That is the best way, since 32 is a power of 2, but another approach is $a^{\frac{5}{4}} = 32$ (taking ln of both sides or equating exponents) $\frac{5}{4} \cdot \ln a = \ln 32$ (isolating a) $\ln a = \frac{4}{5} \ln 32$ (simplifying and calculating) $\ln a \approx 2.77$ (taking both sides e to the power to find a) $e^{2.77} \approx 16$. If 32 was not a power of 2, then using logs directly with a calculator would be the best approach. You can also use log base 10 with a calculator rather than ln.

25. If $\log_a 8 = \dfrac{3}{5}$, what is a? ③

    A. 32

    B. $\dfrac{1}{16}$

    C. 128

    D. 16

    E. $\dfrac{1}{32}$

23.5. Log Value Set Equal to a Variable

For example, if $\log 2 = a$, $\log 3 = b$ and $\log 5 = c$ and you are asked to find $\log 22.5$ in terms of a, b, an c. Then

$$\log 22.5 = \log\left(\frac{3^2 \cdot 5}{2}\right)$$

$$= 2\log 3 + \log 5 - \log 2 = 2b + c - a.$$

26. If $\log_7 2 = a$ and $\log_7 3 = b$, which of these is equal to 4.5? ④

    A. 7^{3b-a}

    B. 7^{b+a}

    C. 7^{b-a}

    D. 7^{2b+a}

    E. 7^{2b-a}

27. If $\log 2 = a$ and $\log 5 = b$, which of these is $\log 6.25$ in terms of a and b? ④

    A. $2a - 2b$

    B. $2a + 2b$

    C. $2a - b$

    D. $2b - 2a$

    E. $a - b$

23.6. Logarithmic Equations

Some more difficult problems require exponentiation and solving a quadratic equation. A relatively difficult example which illustrates this approach is $\log_2(x^2 - 3x) = 5$. Taking both sides 2 to the power, we get $x^2 - 3x = 32$. Getting all terms on one side, $x^2 - 3x - 32 = 0$. Now apply the quadratic formula,

$$x = \frac{3 \pm \sqrt{9 + 128}}{2}$$

$$= \frac{3 \pm \sqrt{137}}{2} \approx 7.4 \text{ and } -4.4.$$

Both answers check. The negative answer is possible, because we are not taking the log of the negative quantity.

28. Find all real solutions of $\log_2 48 - \log_2 6 = \log_5 x$? ④

    A. $25\sqrt{5}$

    B. 375

    C. 625

    D. 125

    E. 25

29. What is the exact value of the x-coordinate of the intersection point of $y = \ln(2x+5)+7$ and $y = 10$ in the standard xy-coordinate plane? ④

  A. $\dfrac{e^4 - 5}{2}$

  B. $\dfrac{e^3 - 5}{3}$

  C. $\dfrac{e^3 - 5}{4}$

  D. $\dfrac{e - 5}{2}$

  E. $\dfrac{e^3 - 5}{2}$

30. Find all real solutions of $\log_4(x^2+x-4) = 2$. ④

  A. 4

  B. -5

  C. 2 or -5

  D. 5 or -4

  E. 4 or -5

31. Find all real solutions of $\log(x^2 + 3x) = 1$? ④

  A. -5 or 2

  B. -5 or 4

  C. -5

  D. -5 or 1

  E. 2

23.7. Finding a Value from its Logarithm

Take the power to the base to the logarithm power. For example, if $\log_2 a = 3 - b$, take

$$a = 2^{3-b} = 2^3 \cdot 2^{-b} = \frac{8}{2^b}.$$

32. If $\log a = 3 + b$, which of these is a? ④

  A. $1000b$

  B. $1000\sqrt{b}$

  C. $1000ab$

  D. $100b$

  E. $1000 \cdot 10^b$

33. If $\log a = 4 + \log 4.3$, what is a? ④

  A. 2,150

  B. 4,300

  C. 21,500

  D. 43,000

  E. 430,000

— **ANSWER KEY**

1D, 2B, 3C,4C, 5D, 6C, 7B, 8B, 9C, 10C, 11E, 12B, 13D, 14A, 15E, 16E, 17E, 18B, 19D, 20C, 21B, 22E, 23A, 24D, 25A, 26E, 27D, 28D, 29E, 30E, 31A, 32E, 33D

23.8. Solutions

1. (D) $\log x$ and 10^x are inverse operations, so 12.

2. (B) $\log_2\left(2^5\right)^{1/2} = \log_2 2^{5/2} = \dfrac{5}{2}$.

3. (C) $\log a^2 - \log b = 2\log a - \log b$.

4. (C) $3 \cdot \dfrac{1}{2} = \dfrac{3}{2}$.

5. (D) Using the change of base formula twice, $\log_a b \cdot \log_b a = \dfrac{\ln b}{\ln a} \cdot \dfrac{\ln a}{\ln b} = 1$.

6. (C) $\log_2\left[\left(2^5\right)^4\right] = 3x+5 \implies \log_2 2^{20} = 3x+5 \implies 20 = 3x+5 \implies 15 = 3x \implies x = 5$.

7. (B) Use the property $\log a - \log b = \log \dfrac{a}{b}$: $\log_2 48 - \log_2 6 = \log_2 \dfrac{48}{6} = \log_2 8 = 3$.

8. (B) By the laws of logarithms (log and 10 to the power are inverse operations), $\log 10^{\frac{7}{5}} - \log 10^{10} = 1.4 - 10 = -8.6$.

9. (C) Converting 100 and 1000 to powers of 10, and by the laws of logarithms,

$$\log \frac{(10^2)^7}{10^3} = \log \frac{10^{14}}{10^3} = \log 10^{11} = 11.$$

10. (C) Simplify using the laws of exponents and then use the fact that taking a log and exponentiation of inverse operations $\log_x x^y = y$. $\log_a \dfrac{a^4}{a^{15}} = \log_a a^{-11} = -11$.

11. (E) Convert to fractional exponents and then use the fact that taking a log and exponentiation of inverse operations $\log_x x^y = y$. $\log_a \sqrt[15]{a^4} = \log_a a^{\frac{4}{15}} = \dfrac{4}{15}$.

12. (B) This is one of the laws of logarithms. If you did not know that, you could find $\log 2^4 = \log 16 \approx 1.204$. Then substitute 2 for a and 4 for b in each answer choice and find B is the only one for which you get about 1.204.

13. (D) Convert to powers of 2, simplify, and then take the log.

$$\log_2 \frac{8^{3x+3}}{4^{x+5}} = \log_2 \frac{2^{9x+9}}{2^{2x+10}} = \log_2 2^{7x-1} = 7x - 1.$$

14. (A) $a = 100^{2b+5c}$ Convert the bases to 10 and then take the log.

$$a = 100^{2b+5c} \implies \log a = \log(10^2)^{2b+5c} = \log 10^{4b+10c} = 4b + 10c.$$

15. (E) $\log_a \dfrac{b^c}{d}$. By the laws of logarithms and the change of base formula (divide by ln of the base),

$$\frac{\ln(b^c) - \ln d}{\ln a} = \frac{c \ln b - \ln d}{\ln a}.$$

16. (E) $\log_a(5b^3)$ By the change of base formula (divide by ln of the base) and the laws of logarithms,

$$\frac{\ln(5b^3)}{\ln a} = \frac{\ln 5 + 3 \ln b}{\ln a}.$$

17. (E) Convert to subtraction by the laws of logarithms and then take the log base 10 of powers of 10.

$$\log \frac{100^a}{1000^b} = a \log 100 - b \log 1000 = 2a - 3b.$$

18. (B) $\log 2 = a$ and $\log 3 = b$, which of these is equal to 288? Factor into powers of 2 and 3. $288 = 2^5 \cdot 3^2$ (taking the log of both sides) $\log 288 = \log(2^5 \cdot 3^2) = 5 \log 2 + 2 \log 3$ (substituting) $\log 288 = 5a + 2b$ (taking both sides 10 to the power) $288 = 10^{5a+2b}$.

19. (D) Converting to exponential form, or taking both sides 5 to the power, $5^3 = 125$.

20. (C) $\log_2 x = -5$. Converting to exponential form, $x = 2^{-5} = \dfrac{1}{2^5} = \dfrac{1}{32}$.

21. (B) $\log x = \dfrac{5}{2}$. Taking both sides 10 to the power or converting to exponential form,

$$x = 10^{\frac{5}{2}} = 10^2 \cdot 10^{\frac{1}{2}} = 100\sqrt{10}.$$

22. (E) $\log_2 x = \dfrac{11}{2}$. Take both sides 2 to the power to isolate x or converting to exponential form,

$$x = 2^{\frac{11}{2}} = 2^5 \cdot 2^{\frac{1}{2}} = 32\sqrt{2}.$$

23. (A) $\log_2 x = 5a - 2b$. Taking both sides 2 to the power, $x = 2^{5a-2b} = \dfrac{2^{5a}}{2^{2b}} = \dfrac{32^a}{4^b}$.

24. (D) $\log x = 3a$. Take 10 to the power, then convert 10^3 to 1000. $x = 10^{3a} = (10^3)^a = 1000^a$.

25. (A) Using powers of 2, $a = 8^{\frac{5}{3}} = 32$ or $a^{\frac{3}{5}} = 8$ (converting to powers of 2) $(2^a)^{\frac{3}{5}} = 2^3$ (taking $\log_2$ of both sides or equating exponents) $\dfrac{3a}{5} = 3 \implies a = 5$, so the answer is $2^a = 2^5 = 32$.

Another solution using ln with a calculator is $\dfrac{\ln 8}{\ln a} = \dfrac{3}{5}$ (isolating a) $\ln a = \dfrac{5}{3} \cdot \ln 8 \approx 3.466$ (taking both sides e to the power) $e^{3.466} \approx 32$.

26. (E) Convert 4.5 to an expression involving only powers of 2 and 3, and then express them in terms of a and b,

$$\log_7 4.5 = \log_7 \frac{3^2}{2} = 2\log_7 3 - \log_7 2 = 2b - a.$$

Now take 7 to the power, $4.5 = 7^{2b-a}$.

27. (D) Convert 6.25 to an expression involving only powers of 2 and 5, and then substitute a and b.

$$\log 6.25 = \log \frac{25}{4} = \log \frac{5^2}{2^2} = 2\log 5 - 2\log 2 = 2b - 2a.$$

28. (D) Simplify the logarithmic expression using the laws of logarithms, take the $\log_2$, and then take 5 to the power.

$$\log_2 \frac{48}{6} = \log_5 x \implies \log_2 8 = \log_5 x \implies 3 = \log_5 x, \text{ so } x = 5^3 = 125.$$

29. (E) Set the expressions equal. Then take both sides e to the power to eliminate ln and then solve. $10 = \ln(2x+5) + 7$ (isolating the ln expression) $3 = \ln(2x+5)$ (taking both sides e to the power)

$$e^3 = 2x + 5 \implies \frac{e^3 - 5}{2} = x.$$

30. (E) $\log_4(x^2 + x - 4) = 2$ (taking both sides 4 to the power) $x^2 + x - 4 = 4^2 \implies x^2 + x - 4 = 16$ (getting all terms of the quadratic on one side) $x^2 + x - 20 = 0$ (factoring and solving) $x = 4$ or -5. Both answers check.

31. (A) $\log(x^2 + 3x) = 1$ (taking both sides 10 to the power or converting to exponential form) $x^2 + 3x = 10 \implies x^2 + 3x - 10 = 0$ (factoring) $(x+5)(x-2) = 0 \implies -5$ or 2.

32. (E) Take both sides 10 to the power to isolate a, and then simplify. $\log a = 3 + b$, $a = 10^{3+b} = 10^3 \cdot 10^b = 1000 \cdot 10^b$.

33. (D) Take both sides 10 to the power to isolate a, and then simplify. $\log a = 4 + \log 4.3$ (using the laws of logarithms) $a = 10^{4 + \log 4.3} = 10^4 \cdot 10^{\log 4.3} = 10,000 \times 4.3 = 43,000$.

24. Complex Numbers

This is a topic for which difficult problems intended to test reasoning ability are likely to appear.

24.1. Complex Conjugate

To find the complex conjugate, take the negative of the complex part of a complex number. A complex number times its conjugate is a real number.

For example, the conjugate of 3 - 2i is 3 + 2i. $(3 - 2i)(3 + 2i) = 9 + 6i - 6i - 4i^2 = 9 + 4 = 13$

1. What multiplied by $7 - 4i$ will result in a real number? ②

   A. $-7 - 4i$

   B. $-7 + 4i$

   C. i

   D. $7 - 4i$

   E. $7 + 4i$

2. Which of the following is equal to $\sqrt{(3 + 4i)(3 - 4i)}$? ③

   A. -5

   B. $-\sqrt{7}$

   C. $\sqrt{7}$

   D. 5

   E. $5i$

24.2. Complex Powers

When raising complex numbers to positive integer powers, FOIL everything out and then replace i^2 with -1.

A difficult example is what is $(2 + i)^{-4}$. The easiest approach to that problem is to first square $2 + i$, and then square the result. Finally, take 1 over that result and simplify by multiplying by the conjugate of the denominator,

First find

$$(2 + i)^2 = 2 + 2i + 2i + i^2 = 3 + 4i.$$

Then

$$(2+i)^4 = (3+4i)^2 = 9+12i+12i+16i^2 = -7+24i.$$
$$(2 + i)^{-4} = \frac{1}{(2 + i)^4} = \frac{1}{-7 + 24i}$$

(multiplying by the conjugate of the denominator, as is discussed later in the Complex Division section) $= (-7 - 24i)/((-7 + 24i)(-7 - 24i)) = (-7 - 24i)/625$

3. Assuming $i^2 = -1$, which of these complex numbers is $(3 + 5i)^2$ in simplified form? ③

   A. $30i + 41$

   B. $30i - 20$

   C. $32i - 16$

   D. $30i - 16$

   E. $32i + 41$

4. Assuming $i^2 = -1$, which of these complex numbers is $(\sqrt{5} + i\sqrt{2})^2$ in simplified form? (4)

    A. $3 \pm 2i\sqrt{10}$

    B. $3 + 2i\sqrt{10}$

    C. $6 + 2i\sqrt{10}$

    D. $3 + 4i\sqrt{5}$

    E. $3 + i\sqrt{20}$

24.3. Large Complex Powers

The key to high powers problems is to reduce the power by taking it modula 4. $i^2 = -1$, $i^3 = -i$, $i^4 = 1$, $i^5 = i$. Therefore, powers of i repeat every 4. In fact, that makes sense, because i is a 4th root of 1. Therefore, $i^{337} = i^1 = i$ because 337 mod 4 = 1. You can determine what an integer is mod 4 by dividing by hand and taking the remainder or dividing by the calculator and multiplying the decimal part by 4. You also might be able to get the remainder directly from some calculators.

5. If $i^n = -i$ and $i^2 = -1$, what does i^{n+7} equal? (3)

    A. $-i$

    B. i

    C. -1

    D. 1

    E. 0

6. If k is a positive integer and $i^2 = -1$, which of these equals i^{176k+3} in simplified form? (4)

    A. i

    B. $-i$

    C. 1

    D. -1

    E. 0

7. What is i^{20k-1} in simplified form, where k is a positive integer and $i^2 = -1$? (4)

    A. $-i$

    B. i

    C. 1

    D. -1

    E. 0

8. Assuming $i^2 = -1$, which of these complex numbers is to equivalent to $i^{4k-2} + i^{12k-3}$, where k is a positive integer? (4)

    A. $i + 1$

    B. i

    C. $i - 1$

    D. $-i$

    E. $2 + i$

9. Where $i^2 = -1$, which of these is i^{-11} in simplified form? (4)

    A. -1

    B. $-i$

    C. i

    D. 1

    E. 0

24.4. Complex Multiplication

10. If $i = \sqrt{-1}$, which is equivalent to $(3 + i)(5 + 2i)$? (3)

    A. $17 + 11i$

    B. $17 + 13i$

    C. $17 + 20i$

    D. $13 + 11i$

    E. $13 + 13i$

11. Which of the following is equivalent to $(2x - i)(2x + i)$? (3)

    A. $2x^2 + 1$

    B. $4x^2 - 1$

    C. $4x^2 + 1$

    D. $4x^2 + 2$

    E. $4x^2 + 4$

12. Which of the following is equivalent to $(3x + 2i)^3$? ⑤

  A. $27x^3 - 54ix^2 - 36x - 8i$

  B. $27x^3 - 54ix^2 + 36x - 8i$

  C. $27x^3 + 54ix^2 - 36x - 8i$

  D. $27x^3 + 54ix^2 - 12x - 8i$

  E. $27x^3 + 54ix^2 + 18x - 8i$

24.5. Complex Division

To divide complex numbers, multiply the numerator and denominator by the conjugate of the denominator, which rationalizes the denominator.

$$\frac{2+3i}{5+2i} = \frac{(2+3i)(5-2i)}{(5+2i)(5-2i)}$$
$$= \frac{10 - 4i + 15i - 6i^2}{25 - 10i + 10i - 4i^2} = \frac{16 + 11i}{29}$$

The approach used here is similar to of multiplying by the conjugate if you had a real but irrational denominator such as $1/(5 + \sqrt{3})$.

A complicated case would be

$$\frac{1}{\left(\sqrt{10} + i\sqrt{6}\right)} = \frac{\sqrt{10} - i\sqrt{6}}{\left(\sqrt{10} + i\sqrt{6}\right)\left(\sqrt{10} - i\sqrt{6}\right)}$$
$$= \frac{\left(\sqrt{10} - i\sqrt{6}\right)}{\left(10 - i\sqrt{60} + i\sqrt{60} - 6i^2\right)} = \frac{\sqrt{10} - i\sqrt{6}}{16}.$$

13. Which of the following is equivalent to $\frac{1}{2+i}$? ③

  A. $\frac{2-i}{3}$

  B. $\frac{2-i}{4}$

  C. $\frac{2-i}{5}$

  D. $\frac{2+i}{5}$

  E. $\frac{2+i}{3}$

14. Which of the following is equivalent to $\frac{2+3i}{5+2i}$? ④

  A. $\frac{4+11i}{29}$

  B. $\frac{4+11i}{21}$

  C. $\frac{16+11i}{29}$

  D. $\frac{16+11i}{21}$

  E. $\frac{16+19i}{29}$

15. Where $i^2 = -1$, which of these complex numbers equals $\frac{i}{\sqrt{3}-i}$? ④

  A. $\frac{i\sqrt{3}+1}{4}$

  B. $\frac{i\sqrt{3}-1}{2}$

  C. $\frac{i\sqrt{3}-6}{4}$

  D. $\frac{i\sqrt{3}-1}{4}$

  E. $\frac{i\sqrt{3}-1}{8}$

16. Where $i^2 = -1$, which of these complex numbers equals $\frac{1}{a+bi}$? ④

  A. $\frac{a+bi}{a^2+b^2}$

  B. $\frac{a-bi}{a^2+b^2}$

  C. $\frac{a-bi}{a+b}$

  D. $\frac{-a-bi}{a^2+b^2}$

  E. $\frac{a-b}{a^2+b^2}$

17. If $x \cdot (2+i)^2 = 1$ and $i^2 = -1$, what is x? ④

    A. $\dfrac{3+4i}{25}$

    B. $\dfrac{3+5i}{25}$

    C. $\dfrac{3-4i}{7}$

    D. $\dfrac{3+4i}{7}$

    E. $\dfrac{3-4i}{25}$

18. Assuming that x is real and $i^2 = -1$, which of these complex numbers equals $\dfrac{1}{x^2+i}$? ④

    A. $\dfrac{x^2-i}{x^4+1}$

    B. $\dfrac{x^2-1}{x^4+1}$

    C. $\dfrac{ix^2-1}{x^4+1}$

    D. $\dfrac{ix^2-i}{x^4+1}$

    E. $\dfrac{-x^2-i}{x^4+1}$

24.6. Finding an Equation from its Complex Solutions

You could be given a complex number and be asked to find for which equation it is a solution. You should be aware that if you are given a complex solution (assuming real coefficients), another solution is its conjugate.

For example, if $2-i$ is a solution of a polynomial equation, then another solution is $2+i$. Take x minus each solution and multiply the resulting binomials. This is similar to the approach discussed previously with real but irrational solution. Therefore, a quadratic equation with solution $2-i$ is $(x-2+i)(x-2-i) = x^2-2x+ix-2x+4-2i-ix+2i-i^2 = x^2-4x+5$. The imaginary terms will always drop out when

multiplying binomials formed using conjugate pairs.

If you are asked to find a fourth degree polynomial with integer coefficients and roots $2+i$ and $3+i$, you know the other roots are the conjugates, $2-i$ and $3-i$ respectively. Therefore, $(x-2-i)(x-2+i)(x-3-i)(x-3+i) = (x^2-4x+5)(x^2-6x+10) = x^4-6x^3+10x^2-4x^3+24x^2-40x+5x^2-30x+50 = x^4-10x^3+39x^2-70x+50$ is the polynomial.

19. Which of the following is a quadratic equation with solution $4i$? ③

    A. $x^2-16=0$

    B. $x^2+4=0$

    C. $x^2+8=0$

    D. $x^2+16=0$

    E. $x^2-4=0$

20. Which of the following has a solution $-3\sqrt{2}i$? ③

    A. $x^2-18=0$

    B. $x^2+12=0$

    C. $x^2+18=0$

    D. $x^2+36=0$

    E. $x^2+6=0$

21. Assuming $i^2 = -1$ and x is real, which of these quadratic equations has a solution $8-5i$? ④

    A. $x^2-16x+85=0$

    B. $x^2-16x+87=0$

    C. $x^2-16x+91=0$

    D. $x^2-16x+89=0$

    E. $x^2-16x+93=0$

24.7. Finding Complex Solutions

If the expression is third degree or higher, factor the expression, and once you are left with a quadratic, use the quadratic formula to find the complex solutions. If the expression is quadratic, then use the quadratic formula directly. It is also possible to use completing the square.

When you apply the quadratic formula, you get a negative under the radical, which results in an imaginary number and therefore a complex solution. Similarly, with completing the square, you get a negative on the other side and take the square root of it.

For example, solve $x^2 + 8x + 20 = 0$. Using the quadratic formula, $\dfrac{-8 \pm \sqrt{64-80}}{2} = \dfrac{-8 \pm \sqrt{-16}}{2} = \dfrac{-8 \pm 4i}{2} = -4 \pm 2i$. The same problem by completing the square, $x^2 + 8x + 16 = -4 \implies (x+4)^2 = -4 \implies x+4 = \pm 2i \implies x = -4 \pm 2i$

22. What are the complex solutions of $x^2 + 10 = 0$? ③
    A. $\pm 100i$
    B. $\pm 10i$
    C. $\pm \sqrt{10}i$
    D. $\sqrt{10}i$
    E. $10i$

23. What are the complex solutions of $x^2 - 4x + 13 = 0$? ④
    A. $2 \pm \sqrt{3}$
    B. $-2 \pm 3i$
    C. $-2 \pm 2i\sqrt{3}$
    D. $2 \pm 3i$
    E. $2 \pm 2i\sqrt{3}$

24. What are the complex solutions of $x^2 + 6x + 11 = 0$? ④
    A. $-2 \pm i\sqrt{2}$
    B. $-5 \pm i\sqrt{2}$
    C. $-2 \pm 2i\sqrt{2}$
    D. $-5 \pm 2i\sqrt{2}$
    E. $-3 \pm i\sqrt{2}$

25. Assuming x is real, what are the complex solutions of $5^{x^2+3} = 25$ over complex numbers? ④
    A. $3i$ and $-3i$
    B. $2i$ and $-2i$
    C. i and $-i$
    D. $1+i$ and $1-i$
    E. $4+i$ and $4-i$

26. Assuming x is real, what is the solution set of $x^3 + 25x = 0$ over complex numbers? ④
    A. $\{0, 5i, -5i\}$
    B. $\{0, 5i\}$
    C. $\{5i, -5i\}$
    D. $\{0, -5i\}$
    E. $\{0, 1+2i, 1-2i\}$

27. Assuming x is real, what are the complex solutions of $8x^3 - 27 = 0$? ⑤
    A. $\dfrac{-3 \pm 3\sqrt{3}i}{4}$
    B. $\dfrac{-3 \pm \sqrt{3}i}{4}$
    C. $\dfrac{-3 - \sqrt{3}i}{4}$
    D. $\dfrac{-3 + \sqrt{3}i}{4}$
    E. $\dfrac{3 \pm 3\sqrt{3}i}{4}$

24.8. Factored Form

The exam may ask for an expression in factored form, rather than a high degree polynomial. If given an imaginary or complex root, find the quadratic equation with that root and its conjugate, as discussed above.

28. Which of these is the factored form of a polynomial with roots $\frac{1}{5}$, $-\frac{3}{7}$, $\frac{8}{3}$, and $5i$? ④

    A. $(x^2 + 25)(3x - 8)(5x + 1)(7x - 3)$

    B. $(x^2 + 25)(3x - 8)(5x + 1)(7x + 3)$

    C. $(x^2 + 25)(3x - 8)(5x - 1)(7x + 3)$

    D. $(x^2 + 5)(3x + 8)(5x + 2)(7x + 3)$

    E. $(x^2 - 25)(3x + 8)(5x - 2)(7x + 3)$

24.9. Square Roots of Negative Numbers

Convert the expressions into imaginary numbers and perform complex arithmetic. Generally, the problem which results from that is adding, subtracting or dividing terms with the same number left under the square root sign.

29. Which of these is equivalent to $\sqrt{-50} + \sqrt{-18}$? ③

    A. $4i\sqrt{2}$

    B. $8i\sqrt{2}$

    C. $8\sqrt{2}$

    D. $16i\sqrt{2}$

    E. $12i\sqrt{2}$

30. Using complex arithmetic, what is $\sqrt{-50} \cdot \sqrt{-18}$? ③

    A. -36

    B. -32

    C. -30

    D. -25

    E. -24

31. In complex arithmetic, what is $(\sqrt{-75} - \sqrt{-12})^2$? ③

    A. -36

    B. -27

    C. -18

    D. 18

    E. 27

24.10. Complex Plane

You can plot complex numbers with the real part as the x-coordinate and the imaginary part as the y-coordinate. Some honors precalculus classes cover ways to convert that to polar form and use trigonometry to find roots of complex numbers. However, for this test you should only need to know the distance between numbers in the complex plane. The distance between $a + bi$ and $c + di$ is $\sqrt{(a - c)^2 + (b - d)^2}$ by the distance formula.

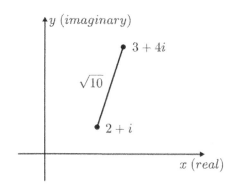

32. What is the distance in the complex plane between $-3 - 7i$ and $2 - i$? ④

    A. $\sqrt{51}$

    B. $\sqrt{47}$

    C. $\sqrt{61}$

    D. $\sqrt{53}$

    E. 7

33. What is the distance in the complex plane between $2 + i$ and $(2 + i)^2$? ④

   A. 3

   B. 4

   C. $\sqrt{11}$

   D. $\sqrt{10}$

   E. $2\sqrt{3}$

24.11. Other Complex

34. Which of the following is NOT equivalent to $2i$? ③

   A. $\dfrac{\sqrt{8}}{\sqrt{-2}}$

   B. $\sqrt{-4}$

   C. $\dfrac{\sqrt{-36}}{3}$

   D. $(3 + i)(-1 + i) + 4$

   E. $(1 + i)^2$

35. Which expression is equivalent to $81x^2 + 49$? ③

   A. $(9x + 7)(9x - 7)$

   B. $(9x + 7)(9x + 7)$

   C. $(9x + 7i)(9x - 7i)$

   D. $(9x + 7i)^2$

   E. $\left(9x + \sqrt{7}i\right)\left(9x - \sqrt{7}i\right)$

36. Which x-value makes y undefined in $y = \dfrac{x - 2}{4x^2 + 9}$? ③

   A. $\dfrac{3}{2}$

   B. $\dfrac{3i}{2}$

   C. 2

   D. $2i$

   E. $3i$

--- **ANSWER KEY** ---

1E,2D 3D, 4B, 5C, 6B 7A, 8C, 9C, 10D, 11C 12C. 13C, 14C 15D, 16B, 17E, 18A, 19D, 20C, 21D, 22C, 23D, 24E, 25C, 26A, 27A, 28C, 29B, 30C, 31B, 32C, 33D, 34A, 35C, 36B

24.12. Solutions

1. (E) The conjugate, taking the negative of the imaginary part, is $7 + 4i$.

2. (D) $\sqrt{9 - 12i + 12i - 16i^2} = \sqrt{9 + 16} = \sqrt{25} = 5$.

3. (D) Expand, FOIL, and then simplify.

$$(3 + 5i)^2 = (3 + 5i)(3 + 5i) = 9 + 15i + 15i + 25i^2 = 30i - 16.$$

4. (B) Expand, FOIL and then simplify.

$$(\sqrt{5} + i\sqrt{2})^2 = 5 + 2i\sqrt{10} + i^2 \cdot 2 = 3 + 2i\sqrt{10}.$$

5. (C) $i^{n+7} = i^n i^7 = i^n i^4 i^3 = (-i) \cdot 1 \cdot (-i) = (-i)^2 = i^2 = -1$.

6. (B) Since i raised to any multiple of 4 is 1 and 176 is a multiple of 4, $i^{176k+3} = i^3 = -i$.

7. (A) Since i raised to any multiple of 4 is 1, $i^{20k-1} = i^{-1} = i^{-1} \cdot i^4 = i^3 = -i$.

8. (C) Simplify both addends, using the fact that i^4 equals 1: $i^{4k-2} + i^{12k-3} = i^{-2} + i^{-3} = i^2 + i = i - 1$.

9. (C) $i^{-11} = \dfrac{1}{i^{11}} = \dfrac{1}{i^3} = \dfrac{1}{(-i)} = \dfrac{1 \cdot i}{(-i) \cdot i} = i$. Alternative solution: $i^{-11} \cdot i^{12} = i^1 = i$ (since $i^{12} = 1$).

10. (D) FOILing, $15 + 6i + 5i + 2i^2 = 15 + 11i - 2 = 13 + 11i$.

11. (C) $4x^2 - i^2 = 4x^2 + 1$.

12. (C) $(3x + 2i)(3x + 2i) = 9x^2 + 6ix + 6ix - 4 = 9x^2 + 12ix - 4$. $(9x^2 + 12ix - 4)(3x + 2i) = 27x^3 + 18ix^2 + 36ix^2 - 24x - 12x - 8i = 27x^3 + 54ix^2 - 36x - 8i$. You could also use the binomial theorem.

13. (C) $\dfrac{2 - i}{(2 + i)(2 - i)} = \dfrac{2 - i}{4 - i^2} = \dfrac{2 - i}{5}$.

14. (C) Multiply the numerator and denominator by the conjugate of the denominator, and then FOIL out both. $\dfrac{(2 + 3i)(5 - 2i)}{(5 + 2i)(5 - 2i)} = \dfrac{10 - 4i + 15i - 6i^2}{25 + 10i - 10i - 4i^2} = \dfrac{16 + 11i}{29}$.

15. (D) To divide, multiply the numerator and denominator by the conjugate of the denominator:

$$\frac{i}{\sqrt{3} - i} \cdot \frac{\sqrt{3} + i}{\sqrt{3} + i} = \frac{i\sqrt{3} - 1}{4}.$$

16. (B) Multiplying by the conjugate,

$$\frac{1}{a+bi} \cdot \frac{a-bi}{a-bi} = \frac{a-bi}{a^2+abi-abi-b^2i^2} = \frac{a-bi}{a^2+b^2}.$$

17. (E) Divide to isolate x, and then perform complex division using the conjugate. $x(3+4i)=1$ (multiplying by the conjugate)

$$x = \frac{1}{3+4i} \cdot \frac{3-4i}{3-4i} = \frac{3-4i}{25}.$$

18. (A) Perform complex division using the conjugate, and then simplify the denominator. Notice that multiplying by the conjugate of a complex number yields the sum of the squares of the coefficients of the real and imaginary parts.

$$\frac{1}{x^2+i} = \frac{x^2-i}{(x^2+i)(x^2-i)} = \frac{x^2-i}{x^4+1}.$$

19. (D) The solutions are $4i$ and its conjugate $-4i$. Taking x minus each, $(x-4i)(x+4i) = x^2-16i^2 = x^2+16$.

20. (C) The other solution is the conjugate $3\sqrt{2}i$.
$$\left(x+3\sqrt{2}i\right)\left(x-3\sqrt{2}i\right) = x^2 - \left(3\sqrt{2}i\right)^2 = x^2 - 9\cdot 2(-1) = x^2+18 \to x^2+18=0.$$

21. (D) The roots must be conjugates. Take x minus each root, FOIL, and then simplify.

$$(x-8+5i)(x-8-5i) = x^2-16x+89 = 0.$$

22. (C) $x^2 = -10 \implies x = \pm\sqrt{-10} \implies x = \pm i\sqrt{10}$

23. (D) Applying the quadratic formula, $\dfrac{-b \pm \sqrt{b^2-4ac}}{2a} \implies \dfrac{4 \pm \sqrt{(4)^2-4\cdot 1\cdot 13}}{2\cdot 1} = $
$\dfrac{4 \pm \sqrt{16-52}}{2} = \dfrac{4 \pm \sqrt{-36}}{2} = \dfrac{4 \pm 6i}{2} = 2 \pm 3i.$

24. (E) Solve using the quadratic formula, which yields complex solutions:

$$\frac{-6 \pm \sqrt{36-44}}{2} = \frac{-6 \pm 2i\sqrt{2}}{2} = -3 \pm i\sqrt{2}.$$

25. (C) Convert to all powers of 5, set the exponents equal, then solve, which results in imaginary solutions. $5^{x^2+3} = 5^2$ (taking $\log_5$ of both sides or equating exponents) $x^2+3=2 \implies x^2 = -1 \implies x = \pm i.$

26. (A) Factor and then solve the resulting quadratic. $x(x^2+25)=0$, setting each factor equal to 0 $\implies x=0$ or $x^2+25=0 \implies x^2=-25 \implies x=\pm 5i.$

27. (A) $(2x-3)(4x^2+6x+9) = 0$ by the cubic factoring formula or by finding one solution and dividing. Solving the quadratic term using the quadratic formula,

$$\frac{-6 \pm \sqrt{36-144}}{8} = \frac{-6 \pm 6\sqrt{3}i}{8} = \frac{-3 \pm 3\sqrt{3}i}{4}.$$

28. (C) $(x - 5i)(x + 5i) = x^2 + 25$. Multiply the other terms by the denominators of the fractions to get integer coefficients. $(x^2 + 25)(3x - 8)(5x - 1)(7x + 3)$.

29. (B) Convert to imaginary numbers and then perform complex arithmetic. $5\sqrt{2}i + 3\sqrt{2}i = 8\sqrt{2}i$.

30. (C) Convert to imaginary numbers and then perform complex arithmetic.

$$5\sqrt{2}i \cdot 3\sqrt{2}i = 15 \cdot 2i^2 = -30.$$

31. (B) Convert to imaginary numbers and then perform complex arithmetic.

$$(5i\sqrt{3} - 2i\sqrt{3})^2 = (3i\sqrt{3})^2 = 27i^2 = -27.$$

32. (C) Applying the distance formula: $\sqrt{(2 - (-3))^2 + (-1 - (-7))^2} = \sqrt{25 + 36} = \sqrt{61}$.

33. (D) Square to find the coordinates: $(2 + i)^2 = 4 + 2i + 2i + i^2 = 3 + 4i$, and now use the distance formula $\sqrt{(3 - 2)^2 + (4 - 1)^2} = \sqrt{10}$.

34. (A) $\dfrac{\sqrt{8}}{\sqrt{-2}} = \dfrac{2\sqrt{2}}{\sqrt{2}i} = \dfrac{2}{i} = -2i$; $\sqrt{-4} = \sqrt{-1}\sqrt{4} = 2i$; $\dfrac{\sqrt{-36}}{3} = \dfrac{6i}{3} = 2i$; $(3 + i)(-1 + i) + 4 = -3 + 3i - i - 1 + 4 = 2i$; $(1 + i)^2 = 1 + i + i + i^2 = 2i$.

35. (C) $81x^2 + 49 = 81x^2 - 49i^2$; this can be expressed as $81x^2 - (-49)$, which is a difference of squares and factors $(9x + 7i)(9x - 7i)$. You may be able to figure out the answer intuitively. You can also multiply the answer choices and see which gets the original.

36. (B) Set the denominator equal to 0: $4x^2 + 9 = 0$, $4x^2 = -9$, $x^2 = -\dfrac{9}{4}$, $x = \pm\dfrac{3i}{2}$

25. Circles Using Analytic Geometry

25.1. Finding the Area of a Circle

The area of a circle with radius r is πr^2. Therefore, given a circle in the form $x^2 + y^2 = r^2$, multiply r^2 by π to get the area.

1. What is the area of the circle
   $(x-3)^2 + (y+5)^2 = 11$? ③
   - **A.** 11
   - **B.** 11π
   - **C.** 22π
   - **D.** 33π
   - **E.** 121π

2. If $a > 0$, what is the area of the circle
   $x^2 + y^2 = a$? ④
   - **A.** $a^2\pi$
   - **B.** $\sqrt{a}\pi$
   - **C.** $a\pi$
   - **D.** $2a\pi$
   - **E.** $\dfrac{a\pi}{2}$

3. What is the area of the circle $x^2 + y^2 = 25\pi$?
   ④
   - **A.** $25\pi^2$
   - **B.** 25π
   - **C.** $15\pi^2$
   - **D.** 625π
   - **E.** $5\pi^2$

4. If two endpoints of a diameter of a circle are
   $(-3, 8)$ and $(7, 2)$, what is the area of the circle? ④
   - **A.** 33π
   - **B.** 34π
   - **C.** 35π
   - **D.** 36π
   - **E.** 37π

5. What is the area of the circle
   $x^2 + y^2 + 4x + 10y = 0$? ⑤
   - **A.** 0
   - **B.** 25π
   - **C.** 29π
   - **D.** 31π
   - **E.** 32π

25.2. Finding the Equation of a Circle

The formula for an equation of a circle is

$$(x-a)^2 + (y-b)^2 = r^2,$$

where the center is (a, b) and the radius is r. You should be able to find the equation from the center and radius and vice versa.

6. What is the equation of a circle with center $(3, -7)$ and radius 4? ③
   A. $(x-3)^2 + (x+7)^2 = 16$
   B. $(x-3)^2 + (x+7)^2 = 4$
   C. $(x+3)^2 + (x-7)^2 = 4$
   D. $(x+3)^2 + (x-7)^2 = 16$
   E. $(x-3)^2 + (x+7)^2 = 64$

7. Which of these is the equation of a circle with center $(\sqrt{2}, \sqrt{3})$ and radius $\sqrt{5}$? ④
   A. $(x-\sqrt{2})^2 + (y-\sqrt{3})^2 = 5$
   B. $(x-\sqrt{2})^2 + (y-\sqrt{3})^2 = \sqrt{5}$
   C. $(x-\sqrt{2})^2 + (y-\sqrt{3})^2 = 25$
   D. $(x-2)^2 + (y-3)^2 = 5$
   E. $(x-2)^2 + (y-3)^2 = 25$

8. Which of these is the equation of a circle with center $(11, 3)$ and area 12π? ④
   A. $(x-11)^2 + (y-3)^2 = 144$
   B. $(x-11)^2 + (y-3)^2 = 12\pi$
   C. $(x-11)^2 + (y-3)^2 = 24$
   D. $(x-11)^2 + (y-3)^2 = 36$
   E. $(x-11)^2 + (y-3)^2 = 12$

9. Which of the following is the equation of a circle with center $(3, -1)$ which goes through $(5, 5)$? ④
   A. $(x-3)^2 + (y+1)^2 = 10$
   B. $(x-3)^2 + (y+1)^2 = 40$
   C. $(x-3)^2 + (y+1)^2 = 1600$
   D. $(x+3)^2 + (y-1)^2 = 10$
   E. $(x+3)^2 + (y-1)^2 = 40$

25.3. Other Circle Problems

To find the x-intercept(s), set $y = 0$ and solve for x and follow a similar procedure to find the y-intercept(s). To find the equation of a tangent line to a circle, determine the slope at the point of tangency by finding the negative reciprocal of the slope of the line from the center to the given point. Using the fact that the tangent line is perpendicular to the radius at the point of tangency, then find the equation of the line using that point and slope. It is also possible to find the slope of the tangent using implicit differentiation in calculus.

10. What is the positive y-coordinate of a point on $x^2 + y^2 = 25$ with an x-coordinate of -2? ③
    A. $\sqrt{23}$
    B. 4
    C. $\dfrac{9}{2}$
    D. $\sqrt{21}$
    E. $2\sqrt{5}$

11. What are the x-intercepts of $(x+2)^2 + (y+3)^2 = 49$? ③
    A. $-2 \pm 2\sqrt{11}$
    B. $-2 \pm 2\sqrt{10}$
    C. $-2 \pm 2\sqrt{13}$
    D. $-2 \pm 2\sqrt{15}$
    E. $-2 \pm 2\sqrt{14}$

12. Which of these is the equation of the tangent to the circle $(x-2)^2 + (y+1)^2 = 26$ at $(3, 4)$? ⑤
    A. $y = \dfrac{-x}{5} + \dfrac{17}{5}$
    B. $y = \dfrac{-x}{5} + \dfrac{19}{5}$
    C. $y = \dfrac{-x}{5} + \dfrac{29}{5}$
    D. $y = \dfrac{-x}{5} + \dfrac{23}{5}$
    E. $y = \dfrac{-x}{50 + \dfrac{21}{5}}$

1B, 2C, 3A, 4B, 5C, 6A, 7A,8E,9B 10D, 11B, 12D

25.4. Solutions

1. (B) Find the radius and then find the area from the radius.

$$r = \sqrt{11}, \quad A = \pi r^2 = \pi(\sqrt{11})^2 = 11\pi.$$

2. (C) Find the radius from the equation and then find the area using the area formula. Radius $= \sqrt{a}$. Area $= \pi r^2 = \pi(\sqrt{a})^2 = a\pi$.

3. (A) Find the radius and then find the area from the radius. $r = 5\sqrt{\pi}, A = \pi r^2 = \pi(5\sqrt{\pi})^2 = 25\pi^2$.

4. (B) The distance between the points is

$$\sqrt{(2-8)^2 + \left(7-(-3)\right)^2} = \sqrt{36+100} = \sqrt{136} = 2\sqrt{34};$$

   that is the diameter, so the radius is half of it, $\sqrt{34}$.
   Then the area of the circle is $\pi r^2 = \pi(\sqrt{34})^2 = 34\pi$.

5. (C) Completing the squares for both x and y (we add 29 to the right because we added $4+25 = 29$ to the left completing the squares. The key is you need to add to the other side what you add to complete the square):

$$x^2 + 4x + 4 + y^2 + 10y + 25 = 29 \implies (x+2)^2 + (y+5)^2 = 29.$$

   The radius is $\sqrt{29}$. The area $= \pi r^2 = 29\pi$.
   This type of problem is more common on the Math SAT, and students going for a top score should be familiar with the techniques involved.

6. (A) Substituting into the general equation of a circle, $(x-h)^2 + (y-k)^2 = r^2$, $(x-3)^2 + (x+7)^2 = 16$.

7. (A) Substituting into the standard form for a circle, $(x - \sqrt{2})^2 + (y - \sqrt{3})^2 = 5$.

8. (E) Find the radius and then determine the equation of the circle from its center and radius. $\pi r^2 = 12\pi$, $r = \sqrt{12}$, so $r^2 = 12$; so the equation of the circle is $(x-11)^2 + (y-3)^2 = 12$.

9. (B) Use the distance formula to obtain the radius, $\sqrt{(5-3)^2 + (5-(-1))^2} = \sqrt{4+36} = \sqrt{40}$ or $2\sqrt{10}$. Equation of circle is $(x-3)^2 + (y+1)^2 = 40$.

10. (D) Substitute -2 for x and solve for y: $(-2)^2 + y^2 = 25$, $y^2 = 21$, $y = \pm\sqrt{21}$.

11. (B) Just as with equations of a line to find the x-intercepts, set $y = 0$ and solve for x: $(x+2)^2 + 3^2 = 49$, $(x+2)^2 = 40$, $x = -2 \pm 2\sqrt{10}$.

12. (D) The center is $(2, -1)$. The slope from the center to the given point is $\dfrac{4-(-1)}{3-2} = 5$. The slope of its tangent line is the negative reciprocal of the slope of the line to the center, $\dfrac{-1}{5}$. Using the slope $-\dfrac{1}{5}$ and the given point $(3, 4)$, the equation of the tangent line is

$$y - 4 = \frac{-1}{5}(x-3), \quad y - 4 = \frac{-x}{5} + \frac{3}{5}, \quad y = \frac{-x}{5} + \frac{23}{5}.$$

You do not need to know this, but you can also find the slope of the tangent line using implicit differentiation from calculus

$$2(x-2) + 2(y+1)\frac{dy}{dx} = 0, \quad \frac{dy}{dx} = \frac{2-x}{y+1} = \frac{2-3}{4+1} = \frac{-1}{5}.$$

26. Conic Sections

26.1. Identifying which Conic Section

Assuming $a > 0$, $b > 0$, and $ax^2 + by^2 = c$ is an ellipse, $ax^2 - by^2 = c$ is a hyperbola, and $ax^2 + by = c$ is a parabola.

1. $x^2 + 6x + 3y + 11 = 0$ is a(n)? ③
   A. circle
   B. ellipse
   C. parabola
   D. hyperbola
   E. line

2. $\dfrac{x+3}{y+4} = \dfrac{y+1}{x-5}$ is a(n)? ③
   A. circle
   B. ellipse
   C. parabola
   D. hyperbola
   E. line

3. The graph of $y^2 = 2x^2 + 3x + 5$ is a(n)? ③
   A. circle
   B. ellipse
   C. parabola
   D. hyperbola
   E. line

4. The graph of $y^2 = -2x^2 + 3x + 5$ is a(n)? ③
   A. circle
   B. ellipse
   C. parabola
   D. hyperbola
   E. line

26.2. Ellipses

The general formula for an ellipse is

$$(x - c)^2/a^2 + (y - d)^2/b^2 = 1,$$

where (c, d) is the center of the ellipse and a and b are the distances from the center to the vertices or covertices. If an ellipse has vertices $(0, 5)$ and $(0, -5)$ and covertices $(3, 0)$ and $(-3, 0)$, the equation of the ellipse is

$$\frac{x^2}{9} + \frac{y^2}{25} = 1.$$

To find its foci, use $c^2 = a^2 - b^2$ (where a is the distance from the center of the ellipse to a vertex, b is the distance from the center to a covertex, and c is the distance from the center to a focus) $\implies c^2 = 25 - 9 \implies c = 4$. Therefore, the foci are along the major axis at $(0, 4)$ and $(0, -4)$.

225

5. Which of these is the equation of an ellipse with vertices $(11,0)$ and $(-11,0)$ and covertices $(0,\sqrt{89})$, $(0,-\sqrt{89})$? ④

   A. $\dfrac{x^2}{121} + \dfrac{y^2}{89} = 1$

   B. $\dfrac{x^2}{210} + \dfrac{y^2}{89} = 1$

   C. $\dfrac{x^2}{211} + \dfrac{y^2}{210} = 1$

   D. $\dfrac{x^2}{32} + \dfrac{y^2}{89} = 1$

   E. $\dfrac{x^2}{89} + \dfrac{y^2}{32} = 1$

6. Which of these can be the equation of the ellipse graphed below? ③

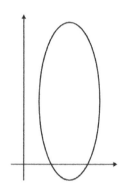

   A. $\dfrac{(x-3)^2}{4} + \dfrac{(y-4)^2}{25} = 1$

   B. $\dfrac{(x-3)^2}{4} + \dfrac{(y-4)^2}{9} = 1$

   C. $\dfrac{(x-3)^2}{16} + \dfrac{(y-4)^2}{25} = 1$

   D. $\dfrac{(x-3)^2}{4} - \dfrac{(y-4)^2}{25} = 1$

   E. $\dfrac{(x-3)^2}{25} + \dfrac{(y-4)^2}{4} = 1$

7. What is the distance between the foci of the ellipse $\dfrac{(x+2)^2}{4} + \dfrac{(y-5)^2}{25} = 1$? ④

   A. 10

   B. $\sqrt{21}$

   C. $2\sqrt{21}$

   D. $\sqrt{29}$

   E. $2\sqrt{29}$

8. $\dfrac{x^2}{152^2} + \dfrac{y^2}{148^2} = 1$ approximates the orbit of the earth in millions of kilometers from the sun. How many kilometers to the nearest million kilometer are the foci of the orbit apart from each other? ④

   A. 34

   B. 43

   C. 58

   D. 69

   E. 74

26.3. Other Conic Section Problems

Conic section problems should be fairly basic, like asking the student to identify the equation of a hyperbola from a graph or vice versa.

9. A parabola can intersect a circle in at most how many points? ③

   A. 1

   B. 2

   C. 3

   D. 4

   E. Infinitely many

10. Which of these is the equation of an upward facing parabola with vertex $(2,1)$ which goes through $(5,7)$?③

   A. $y - 1 = (x - 2)^2$

   B. $y - 1 = \dfrac{2}{3}(x - 2)^2$

   C. $y - 1 = \dfrac{3}{2}(x - 2)^2$

   D. $y - 1 = \dfrac{3}{4}(x - 2)^2$

   E. $y - 1 = \dfrac{7}{10}(x - 2)^2$

11. What could be the equation of the hyperbola graphed below?④

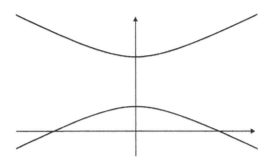

   A. $\dfrac{x^2}{4} - (y - 2)^2 = 1$

   B. $\dfrac{(y + 2)^2}{8} - \dfrac{x^2}{4} = 1$

   C. $\dfrac{(y - 2)^2}{4} - \dfrac{x^2}{4} = 1$

   D. $(y - 2)^2 - \dfrac{x^2}{4} = 1$

   E. $(y + 2)^2 - \dfrac{x^2}{4} = 1$

① Easiest

⑤ Most Difficult

— **ANSWER KEY**

1C, 2D, 3D, 4B, 5A, 6A, 7C, 8D, 9D, 10B, 11D

26.4. Solutions

1. (C) The equation is in the form $ax^2 + by = c$, so it is a parabola.

2. (D) Cross multiplying, $(x+3)(x-5) = (y+1)(y+4)$. This is in the form $ax^2 - by^2 = c$, so it is a hyperbola.

3. (D) The equation is in the form $ax^2 - by^2 = c$, so it is a hyperbola.

4. (B) The equation is in the form $ax^2 + by^2 = c$, so it is an ellipse.

5. (A) Substituting half the distance from the center to the vertices and covertices into the general equation of an ellipse,

$$\frac{x^2}{a^2} + \frac{y^2}{b^2} = 1, \quad \frac{x^2}{11^2} + \frac{y^2}{\sqrt{89}^2} = 1, \quad \frac{x^2}{121} + \frac{y^2}{89} = 1.$$

6. (A) The center is at about $(3,4)$; The vertices are about 5 from the center on y and the covertices are about 2 from the center on x. Therefore,

$$\frac{(x-3)^2}{4} + \frac{(y-4)^2}{25} = 1.$$

   Values of points on the ellipse are omitted because they are omitted in some real exam problems, and you have enough information to eliminate the incorrect answers.

7. (C) Using the formula for the foci of an ellipse: $c^2 = a^2 - b^2$ (substituting) $c^2 = 25 - 4 \implies c = \sqrt{21}$ (so double that to get twice the distance from the center to a focus) $2c = 2\sqrt{21}$.

8. (D) Using the formula for the foci of an ellipse: $c^2 = a^2 - b^2$ (substituting) $c^2 = 152^2 - 148^2 = 1200$ (simplifying and solving) $c = 20\sqrt{3} \approx 34.6$ (double that for twice the focal length) $2c \approx 69$.

9. (D) The diagram shows there can be 4, and it is clear there cannot be more than 4 intersection points.

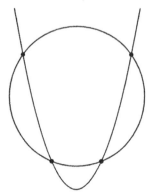

10. (B) Find the equation using the vertex, substitute the values for the other point given into that equation for x and y, and then solve for a.

$$y - 1 = a(x - 2)^2 \text{ (substituting) } 7 - 1 = a(5 - 2)^2 \implies 6 = 3^2 a$$

$$\implies 6 = 9a \text{ (dividing and solving) } a = \frac{2}{3}.$$

11. (D) The center is at about $(0, 2)$; the asymptotes have slopes of $\pm\frac{1}{2}$. $y = \frac{x}{2} + 2$ and $y = \frac{-x}{2} + 2$.

Therefore, the choice must be: $(y - 2)^2 - \frac{x^2}{4} = 1$.

None of the other choices are reasonable. Values of points on the hyperbola are omitted because they are omitted in some real exam problems, and you have enough information to eliminate the incorrect answers.

27. Sequences and Series

A sequence is elements separated by commas and a series is elements added together. In an arithmetic sequence or series the elements go up or down by a fixed amount. In a geometric sequence or series, an element is the previous element multiplied by a fixed number.

You will need to find elements in a sequence and find the sum of series.

A recursive sequence is expressed in terms of its first element and a rule for finding the next element from the current element. More common on the exam are explicitly defined sequences with a formula to determine an element from its element number.

27.1. Arithmetic Sequences

The formula for an element of an arithmetic sequence is $a_n = a_1 + (n-1)d$. Starting from a general element m, it is $a_n = a_m + (n-m)d$.

Find the common difference by subtracting an element from the element after it in the sequence. If the elements are more than one apart, you take the difference between the elements divided by the number of terms they are apart, similarly to the slope formula.

We will start with a relatively easy problem. If the first term in an arithmetic sequence is 10 and the fourth term is 34, what is the 20th term? The common difference

$$d = \frac{34-10}{4-1} = 8.$$

The 20th term is

$$a_1 + (20-1)d = 10 + (20-1) \cdot 8 = 10 + 152 = 162.$$

1. The 1st term in an arithmetic sequence is 8 and the 4th term is 17. What is the 6th term? ③
   - **A.** 20
   - **B.** 22
   - **C.** 23
   - **D.** 24
   - **E.** 26

2. The 1st term in an arithmetic sequence is $\frac{2}{9}$ and the 7th term is $\frac{4}{3}$. What is the 11th term in the sequence? ④
   - **A.** $\frac{14}{9}$
   - **B.** $\frac{56}{27}$
   - **C.** $\frac{224}{81}$
   - **D.** $\frac{5}{2}$
   - **E.** $\frac{8}{3}$

231

3. The 2nd and 5th terms in an arithmetic sequence are 5 and 38, respectively. What is the 100th term? ④

   A. 1068

   B. 1083

   C. 1108

   D. 1121

   E. 1141

27.2. Arithmetic Series

The summation of an arithmetic series is the average of the first and last elements times the number of elements:

$$\frac{a_1 + a_n}{2} \times n.$$

For example, the sum of all the integers from 1 to 100 inclusive is

$$\frac{1 + 100}{2} \times 100 = 5050.$$

What is the sum of $11 + 18 + 25 + \cdots + 319$? First find the number of elements in the series:

$$\frac{319 - 11}{7} = 44,$$

so there are $44 + 1 = 45$ elements in the series (you need to add 1, as there is an extra element, since we are including both ends). Applying the sum of series formula,

$$\frac{(11 + 319) \cdot 45}{2} = \frac{330 \cdot 45}{2} = 7425.$$

4. What is the sum of all the numbers from 1 to 30 inclusive? ③

   A. 450

   B. 465

   C. 480

   D. 510

   E. 930

5. If the sum of all the integers from 1 to x is 105, what is x? ④

   A. 12

   B. 13

   C. 14

   D. 15

   E. 21

6. The sum of 3 consecutive integers is a. Which of these is the first of those integers in terms of a? ④

   A. 400

   B. 472

   C. 488

   D. 492

   E. 500

7. The sum of 3 consecutive integers is a. Which of these is the first of those integers in terms of a? ④

   A. $\dfrac{a-3}{3}$

   B. $\dfrac{a-2}{3}$

   C. $\dfrac{a-1}{3}$

   D. $\dfrac{a-4}{3}$

   E. $\dfrac{a+2}{3}$

8. What is the sum of the odd numbers from 1 to 199 inclusive? ④

   A. 5,000

   B. 9,990

   C. 10,000

   D. 10,100

   E. 10,200

9. What is the sum of the numbers from 101 to 300 inclusive? ④
   A. 40,000
   B. 40,100
   C. 41,000
   D. 42,000
   E. 43,100

27.3. Geometric Sequences

A geometric sequence is a sequence in which each term is a multiple of the previous term.

Exam problems often involve finding the common ratio and then another term. To find the common ratio, take the nth root of terms n apart. In a simpler case, just divide any term by the preceding term. To find a term m elements in the sequence from an existing term, take that term times the ratio to the mth power.

Let us start with an easy problem, but one which might be on the exam. The first four terms in a geometric sequence are 81, -54, 48, and -32. What is the 5th term? The common ratio is $\frac{-54}{81} = \frac{-2}{3}$. The 5th term is then $-32 \cdot \frac{-2}{3} = \frac{64}{3}$

If the first term of a geometric sequence is 8 and the fourth term is 27, what is the 6th term? The common ratio is

$$\left(\frac{27}{8}\right)^{\frac{1}{3}} = \frac{3}{2}.$$

We take the $\frac{1}{3}$ power because there are 3 elements between 8 and 27. We take the common ratio to the power of the difference between the terms, here $6 - 4 = 2$. The 6th term

$$= 4^{th} \text{ term} \times (\text{common ratio})^2 = 27\left(\frac{3}{2}\right)^2 = \frac{243}{4}.$$

10. The 1st term of a geometric sequence is 2 and the 2nd term is 10. What is the 4th term in the sequence? ③
    A. 50
    B. 100
    C. 250
    D. 500
    E. 1250

11. The first and second terms in a geometric sequence are 54 and -18. What is the 6th term? ③
    A. $-\frac{2}{27}$
    B. $-\frac{2}{27}$
    C. $-\frac{2}{9}$
    D. $\frac{2}{9}$
    E. $\frac{2}{3}$

12. The first 3 terms in a geometric sequence are 4, 6, and 9. What is the 6th term? ③
    A. 12
    B. 15
    C. 16
    D. $\frac{81}{4}$
    E. $\frac{243}{8}$

13. What is the 8th term in the geometric sequence $27, -18, 12, -8, \ldots$? ④
    A. $\frac{64}{27}$
    B. $\frac{256}{243}$
    C. $\frac{128}{81}$
    D. $-\frac{128}{81}$
    E. $-\frac{256}{243}$

27.4. Geometric Series

The infinite geometric series formula, which will probably be given, is sum $= \dfrac{a}{1-r}$, where a is the first element and r is the common ratio. You can find the common ratio by divided any term by its preceding term. $|r| < 1$ must be true for the series to converge.

The sum of finite geometric sequence formula is more complicated, and should not be needed for this test. That is there should not be finite series problems which require the use of a formula.

What is the sum $12 + 6 + 3 + \dfrac{3}{2} + \cdots$?

$$\frac{12}{1-\dfrac{1}{2}} = \frac{12}{\dfrac{1}{2}} = 24$$

14. What is the sum of $\dfrac{1}{3} + \dfrac{1}{9} + \dfrac{1}{27} + \ldots$? (4)

    A. $\dfrac{1}{3}$

    B. $\dfrac{2}{3}$

    C. $\dfrac{3}{5}$

    D. $\dfrac{2}{5}$

    E. $\dfrac{1}{2}$

15. Which of these is the sum of the series $5 + 2 + \dfrac{4}{5} + \dfrac{8}{25} + \cdots$? (4)

    A. $\dfrac{25}{3}$

    B. $\dfrac{25}{7}$

    C. $\dfrac{25}{4}$

    D. $\dfrac{26}{3}$

    E. 8

16. Which of these is the sum of the series $5 - 2 + \dfrac{4}{5} - \dfrac{8}{25} + \cdots$? (4)

    A. $\dfrac{25}{3}$

    B. $\dfrac{25}{7}$

    C. $\dfrac{26}{7}$

    D. 6

    E. 8

27.5. Recursive Sequences

17. $a_1 = 1$, $a_n = 3a_{n-1} - 1$. What is a_5? (3)

    A. 14

    B. 32

    C. 37

    D. 41

    E. 122

18. Which of these is an equivalent explicit sequence to the recursive sequence $a_1 = 5$, $a_n = 3a_{n-1}$, $n \geq 2$? (3)

    A. $a_n = 5 \cdot 3^{n-1}$, $n \geq 1$

    B. $a_n = 3 \cdot 5^n$, $n \geq 1$

    C. $a_n = 3 \cdot 5^{n-2}$, $n \geq 1$

    D. $a_n = 5^n$, $n \geq 1$

    E. $a_n = 15^n$, $n \geq 1$

19. What is $a_n = 3\left(\dfrac{3}{4}\right)^n$ for $n >= 1$ expressed as a recursive formula? ④

   A. $a_1 = \dfrac{9}{4}, a_n = a_{n-1} \cdot \dfrac{3}{4}$ *

   B. $a_1 = \dfrac{9}{4}, a_n = a_{n-1} \cdot \dfrac{4}{3}$

   C. $a_1 = 3, a_n = a_{n-1} \cdot \dfrac{3}{4}$

   D. $a_1 = 3, a_n = a_{n-1} \cdot \dfrac{4}{3}$

   E. $a_1 = 4, a_n = a_{n-1} \cdot \dfrac{3}{4}$

20. A recursive formula for a series is $a_1 = 23$, $a_n = a_{n-1} + 14$. Which of the following is an explicit formula for the series?

   A. $a_n = 9 + 14n$

   B. $a_n = 14 + 9n$

   C. $a_n = 19 + 14n$

   D. $a_n = 23 + 14n$

   E. $a_n = 32 + 14n$

① Easiest

⑤ Most Difficult

─ **ANSWER KEY** ──

1C, 2B, 3B, 4E, 5C, 6E, 7A, 8C, 9B, 10C, 11C, 12E, 13D, xxx 15B, 16D, 17D, 18A, 19A, 20A

───

27.6. Solutions

1. (C) Common difference is $\dfrac{17-8}{4-1} = 3$. $a_6 = a_1 + (6-1) \cdot d = 8 + 5 \cdot 3 = 23$.

2. (B) Common difference $= \dfrac{\frac{4}{3} - \frac{2}{9}}{7-1} = \dfrac{\frac{10}{9}}{6} = \dfrac{5}{27}$.

$$a_{11} = a_7 + 4 \times \text{ the common difference } = \frac{4}{3} + 4\left(\frac{5}{27}\right) = \frac{4}{3} + \frac{20}{27} = \frac{36+20}{27} = \frac{56}{27}.$$

3. (B) Common difference $= \dfrac{38-5}{5-2} = 11$.

$$a_{100} = a_5 + d \cdot (100-5) = 38 + 95 \cdot 11 = 38 + 1045 = 1083.$$

4. (E) Common difference $= \dfrac{\frac{13}{6} - \frac{4}{3}}{17-11} = \dfrac{\frac{5}{6}}{6} = \dfrac{5}{36}$.

$$a_{30} = a_{17} + d(30-17) == \frac{13}{6} + 13 \cdot \frac{5}{36} = \frac{13}{6} + \frac{65}{36} = \frac{78+65}{36} = \frac{143}{36}.$$

5. (C) By the sum of an arithmetic series formula, $\dfrac{x(x+1)}{2} = 105$ (distributing and multiplying) $x^2 + x - 210 = 0$ (factoring) $(x+15)(x-14) = 0 \implies x = 14$ or -15. Only the positive solution is relevant to the problem. There are various other ways to solve the quadratic. You could also add the numbers starting at 1 until you get 105 or substitute in the answers.

6. (E) Find the common difference, then use that to find the last element. Then use the first and last elements to find the sum. The common difference $= 4$, $a_1 = 11 - 6 \cdot 4 = -13$,

$$a_{20} = 15 + 4 \cdot 12 = 63, \text{ the sum } = \frac{-13+63}{2} \cdot 20 = 500.$$

7. (A) Let x be the first element, then the others are $x+1$ and $x+2$. Then add and solve.

$$x + x + 1 + x + 2 = a \implies 3x + 3 = a \text{ (solving for } x\text{) } x = \frac{a-3}{3}.$$

8. (C) (Number of elements) $\cdot$ (average of first and last elements) $= \dfrac{(1+199) \cdot 100}{2} = 10,000$ (we multiply by 100 because that is the number of elements; we only count the odd numbers).

9. (B) (Number of elements) $\cdot$ (average of first and last elements) $= \dfrac{200 \cdot (101+300)}{2} = 40,100$.

10. (C) The common ratio is $r = \dfrac{10}{2} = 5$. $a_4 = a_2 \cdot 5^2 = 10 \cdot 25 = 250$.

11. (C) Common ratio $= -\dfrac{18}{54} = -\dfrac{1}{3}$. $a_6 = a_1 \cdot r^5 = 54 \cdot \left(-\dfrac{1}{3}\right)^5 = 54 \cdot -\dfrac{1}{243} = -\dfrac{2}{9}$.

12. (E) Common ratio $= \dfrac{3}{2}$,

$$a_6 = a_3 \cdot r^{6-3} = 9 \cdot \left(\dfrac{3}{2}\right)^3 = 9 \cdot \dfrac{27}{8} = \dfrac{243}{8}.$$

13. (D) Common ratio $= \dfrac{-2}{3}$,

$$a_8 = a_4 \cdot r^{8-4} = a_4 \cdot r^4 = -8 \cdot \left(\dfrac{-2}{3}\right)^4 = -8 \cdot \dfrac{16}{81} = \dfrac{-128}{81}.$$

14. (B) Using the formula for the sum of an infinite series, $\dfrac{a}{1-r} \implies \dfrac{\frac{1}{3}}{1-\frac{1}{3}} = \dfrac{\frac{1}{3}}{\frac{2}{3}} = \dfrac{1}{2}$.

15. (D) Find the first term, and then multiply by the square of the common ratio to obtain the value of the 3rd term. Using $\dfrac{a}{1-r}$:

$$\dfrac{a}{1-\dfrac{3}{4}} = 64 \implies \dfrac{a}{1/4} = 64, \text{ (multiplying) } a = 64 \cdot \dfrac{1}{4}$$

$$\implies a = 16, \quad a_3 = 16 \cdot \left(\dfrac{3}{4}\right)^2 = 16 \cdot \dfrac{9}{16} = 9.$$

16. (D) $a_1 = 1$, $a_2 = 2$, $a_3 = 5$, $a_4 = 14$, $a_5 = 41$.

17. (A) $a_1 = 3\left(\dfrac{3}{4}\right)^1 = \dfrac{9}{4}$. So $a_1 = \dfrac{9}{4}$, $a_n = a_{n-1} \cdot \dfrac{3}{4}$.

18. (A) $5 \cdot 3^{n-1}$. We start with 5 and multiply by 3 each time.

19. (A) $a_n = 9 + 14n$. $a_0 = a_1 - 14 = 23 - 14 = 9$. $14n$ because it increases by 14 every element.

28. Permutations and Combinations

You need to know the basics, but only the basics of permutations and combinations. However, it is important to know when to use combination, when permutations, and when straight exponentiation.

Use combinations when order does not matter and permutations when order does matter. For example, if you need to pick a committee of 3 from 10 people, use combinations:

$$_{10}C_3 = \frac{10!}{7! \cdot 3!} = 120 \text{ ways.}$$

If you need to pick a President, Vice President and Treasurer from 10 people, then use permutations:

$$_{10}P_3 = \frac{10!}{7!} = 720 \text{ ways.}$$

There are 6 ways of arranging the 3 people, so there are 6 times as many permutations as combinations.

28.1. Permutations

Permutations involve selecting items where order matters. The formula is

$$_nP_k = \frac{n!}{(n-k)!}.$$

In addition to the straight permutations problems discussed in this chapter, permutations can also be used in probability ACT problems for selecting in without replacement problems. Additionally, his section discusses the order n items can be arranged, which is $n!$.

Another type of problem, which is best classified as permutation, involves how many ways you can arrange letters some of which are duplicates. An example involves the number of distinct ways aaabbcd can be arranged. The answer is the total number of letters factorial divided by the number of times any letter repeats factorial:

$$\frac{7!}{3! \cdot 2!} = 420.$$

1. In how many distinct ways can 7 people stand in a line with 2 ends? ④
   A. 720
   B. 2,880
   C. 4,000
   D. 5,040
   E. 40,320

2. There are 60 questions each with 5 different answer choices on the math ACT. How many possible combinations of answers are there? ③
   A. 60^5
   B. 5^{60}
   C. $\dfrac{60!}{55!}$
   D. $\dfrac{60!}{5!}$
   E. $\dfrac{60!}{55! \cdot 5!}$

239

3. Of 20 people in a club, how many ways can you pick a President, Vice President, and Treasurer? ④

   A. 1,140
   B. 2,280
   C. 6,840
   D. 4,560
   E. 3,420

4. How many 3-digit orderings with no letter repeated can be made from the letters a–h? ④

   A. 216
   B. 224
   C. 256
   D. 336
   E. 448

5. How many distinct permutations of the letters aabbccc are there? ④

   A. 35
   B. 70
   C. 105
   D. 210
   E. 420

6. What is the number of distinct permutations of the letters in MISSISSIPPI? ④

   A. 3,465
   B. 17,325
   C. 32,400
   D. 34,650
   E. 36,000

28.2. Combinations

The formula for the number of combinations is

$$_nC_k = \frac{n!}{k!(n-k)!},$$

where one is choosing k elements from n total elements. Use combinations when order does not matter. It is likely problems involving combinations will be the relatively easy case, $_nC_2$, which occurs in applications such as matching people problems or diagonals of polygons problems.

When choosing so many in one category and so many in another category, multiply the number of combinations from each category to get the total number of combinations.

7. Calculate $\dfrac{10!}{7! \cdot 3!}$ ③

   A. 120
   B. 126
   C. 210
   D. 240
   E. 720

8. Calculate $\dfrac{8!}{4! \cdot 4! \cdot 2^8}$ ③

   A. $\dfrac{33}{128}$
   B. $\dfrac{1}{4}$
   C. $\dfrac{1}{3}$
   D. $\dfrac{35}{128}$
   E. $\dfrac{5}{16}$

9. Bob has 3 pairs of pants, 7 shirts, and 8 pairs of socks. How many different outfits can he wear? ③

   A. 144
   B. 162
   C. 168
   D. 178
   E. 192

10. In a round-robin chess tournament in Austria in 1903, each player played each other player exactly twice. If there were 12 players, how many games were there? ④
   A. 66
   B. 108
   C. 126
   D. 132
   E. 144

11. How many diagonals does a 10-sided polygon have? ④
   A. 25
   B. 28
   C. 35
   D. 45
   E. 90

12. A dinner at a Spanish restaurant on Route 83 consists of appetizers and entrees. You must pick exactly 2 of 5 appetizers and 2 of 8 entrees. How many possible dinners are there? ④
   A. 126
   B. 140
   C. 240
   D. 280
   E. 560

28.3. Codes

ACT code problems generally involve permutations when characters cannot repeat or straight exponentiation when they can repeat. Often, you will be asked to find an expression for the number of possibilities, rather than actually computing the number.

If a code is 4 digits that can repeat, there are $10^4 = 10,000$ possible codes. If the digits CAN-

NOT repeat, there are $_{10}P_4 = 10 \cdot 9 \cdot 8 \cdot 7 = 5,040$ possible codes.

13. A code consists of two letters a–z followed by two digits 0–9, and the letters and digits CAN be repeated. How many possible codes are there? ④
   A. 63,600
   B. 64,600
   C. 65,600
   D. 66,600
   E. 67,600

14. A code consists of 2 letters a–z followed by 2 digits 0–9 and letters and digits CANNOT be repeated. How many possible codes are there? ④
   A. 58,500
   B. 59,000
   C. 59,500
   D. 60,000
   E. 61,000

15. A license plate number in a certain state consists of 4 of 26 letters that CANNOT repeat, followed by 3 numbers 0–9 that CANNOT repeat. Which of these is an expression for the number of possible license plate numbers? ④
   A. $10^4 \cdot 26^4$
   B. $\dfrac{26! \cdot 10!}{22! \cdot 7!}$
   C. $\dfrac{26! \cdot 10!}{(22! \cdot 6! \cdot 4!)^2}$
   D. $\dfrac{26! \cdot 10!}{22! \cdot 6! \cdot 4!}$
   E. $\dfrac{10^4 \cdot 26^4}{4}$

— ANSWER KEY

1D, 2B, 3C, 4D, 5D, 6D, 7A, 8D, 9C 10D, 11C, 12D, 13E, 14A, 15B,

28.4. Solutions

1. (D) There are $n!$ ways of ordering n events. $7! = 5040$.

2. (B) There are 5 different choices for each problem. Since these are independent events, we multiply to get 5^{60}. This is technically not a permutation problem, but a student might make a mistake and use permutations, and it seems to fit best in the section.

3. (C) Since order matters, use permutations. (If the exam asked for how many committees of 3, you would use combinations.)

$$_{20}P_3 = \frac{20!}{17!} = 20 \cdot 19 \cdot 18 = 6840.$$

4. (D) Since order matters, use permutations. $_8P_3 = 8 \cdot 7 \cdot 6 = 336$.

5. (D) Take the number of elements factorial divided by the number of times each element repeats factorial. $\dfrac{7!}{2! \cdot 2! \cdot 3!} = 210$.

6. (D) Take the number of elements factorial divided by the number of times each element repeats factorial. $\dfrac{11!}{4! \cdot 4! \cdot 2!} = 34650$.

7. (A) $\dfrac{10!}{7! \cdot 3!}$ – cancelling $\dfrac{7!}{7!} - \dfrac{10 \cdot 9 \cdot 8}{3 \cdot 2 \cdot 1} = 120$.

8. (D) $\dfrac{8!}{4! \cdot 4! \cdot 2^8} = \dfrac{8 \cdot 7 \cdot 6 \cdot 5}{4 \cdot 3 \cdot 2 \cdot 2^8} = \dfrac{7 \cdot 5}{2^7} = \dfrac{35}{128}$. Note that this is the probability of 4 heads when flipping 8 coins.

9. (C) $3 \cdot 7 \cdot 8 = 168$.

10. (D) Since the tournament is double round-robin, take the number of combinations times 2, $_{12}C_2 \cdot 2 = 66 \cdot 2 = 132$.

11. (C) $_{10}C_2 - 10 = 45 - 10 = 35$. Take $_{10}C_2$ because there are 10 points and we look and matchings of pairs of those points for diagonals. Subtract 10 for the 10 sides of the polygon, which are not diagonals. You could be asked to find the diagonals of a hexagon or octagon, in which case you could also solve the problem by drawing the diagonals.

12. (D) Since appetizers and entrees are independent events, multiply the combinations of each:

$$_8C_2 \cdot _5C_2 = \frac{8 \cdot 7}{2} \cdot \frac{5 \cdot 4}{2} = 28 \cdot 10 = 280.$$

13. (E) Since the digits can repeat, take the number of elements to the power of the number of characters: $10^2 \cdot 26^2 = 67,600$.

14. (A) Since the digits cannot repeat, use permutations, reducing the number of possibilities by 1 each time a letter or number is selected: $10 \cdot 9 \cdot 26 \cdot 25 = 58,500$.

15. (B) Since the characters cannot repeat, use permutations and multiply the number of arrangements of the letters by the number of arrangements of the numbers,

$$_{26}P_4 \cdot {}_{10}P_3 = \frac{26! \cdot 10!}{22! \cdot 7!}.$$

29. Probability

Probability problems are an increasing and large portion of the problems on current test, and they are an even larger portion of the difficult problems, so this is one of the larger chapters in this book. Some of the problems in this guide are not standard problems in high school textbooks, but may be similar to those that could appear on the exam. This is an area in which difficult problems intended to test reasoning skills are included on the exam. The types of difficult probability problems which may appear on exams are not completely predictable. There will likely be difficult probability problems not covered explicitly in this guide.

29.1. Without Replacement

In without replacement problems, you are looking for the probability that the same color or whatever is drawn repeatedly. The numerator and denominator are both reduced by one each time in repeated trials. For example the probability the first card drawn from a deck is an ace is 4/52. Given the first card is an ace, the probability that the second card is an ace is 3/51, because there is one less card left in the deck and one less ace.

To work an example, if there are 7 red marbles and 7 green marbles and one draws 3 marbles without replacement, what is the probability that all those drawn will all be red?

$$\frac{7}{14} \cdot \frac{6}{13} \cdot \frac{5}{12} = \frac{5}{52}.$$

That problem could also be solved using permutations as follows:

$$\frac{_7P_3}{_{14}P_3} = \frac{7 \cdot 6 \cdot 5}{14 \cdot 13 \cdot 12} = \frac{5}{52}.$$

1. If 3 purple marbles and 2 orange marbles are in a bowl and 2 marbles are taken at random without replacement, what is the probability that both marbles selected will be purple? ④

   A. $\dfrac{9}{25}$

   B. $\dfrac{3}{5}$

   C. $\dfrac{1}{4}$

   D. $\dfrac{3}{10}$

   E. $\dfrac{9}{10}$

2. Pocket aces is the best hand in Texas hol-dem, but it can win or lose large amounts of chips. If Candice is dealt 2 cards from a standard deck, what is the probability that those cards are both aces? ④

   A. $\dfrac{1}{200}$

   B. $\dfrac{1}{26}$

   C. $\dfrac{1}{256}$

   D. $\dfrac{1}{221}$

   E. $\dfrac{1}{169}$

3. There are 7 red and 3 blue marbles in a silver bowl on an ornate carved wooden table and Ingrid takes 2 marbles randomly without re-placement. What is the probability that both marbles will be the same color? ④

   A. $\dfrac{23}{30}$

   B. $\dfrac{8}{15}$

   C. $\dfrac{7}{15}$

   D. $\dfrac{3}{5}$

   E. $\dfrac{2}{3}$

4. If there are 5 red and 4 blue marbles in a bowl, and Sigfried draws 3 marbles without replacement, what is the probability that all the marbles drawn are red? ④

   A. $\dfrac{11}{84}$

   B. $\dfrac{9}{84}$

   C. $\dfrac{5}{42}$

   D. $\dfrac{1}{14}$

   E. $\dfrac{1}{6}$

5. Four balls numbered 1 to 4 are placed in a bin on an ornately carved octagonal table. Emma draws two balls without putting ei-ther ball back into the bin. What is the prob-ability that the sum of the numbers Emma draws is exactly 5? ④

   A. $\dfrac{1}{4}$

   B. $\dfrac{10}{31}$

   C. $\dfrac{3}{10}$

   D. $\dfrac{3}{8}$

   E. $\dfrac{1}{3}$

6. There are 2 red marbles, 2 blue marbles, and 2 green marbles in a bowl. If 3 marbles are drawn at random without replacement, what is the probability they will all be different colors? ⑤

A. $\dfrac{1}{3}$

B. $\dfrac{3}{8}$

C. $\dfrac{2}{5}$

D. $\dfrac{3}{7}$

E. $\dfrac{4}{9}$

7. If there are 6 red marbles, 4 blue marbles, and 2 green marbles in a bowl and 3 marbles are selected at random, what is the probability to the nearest hundredth they will all be of different colors? ⑤

A. 0.22

B. 0.25

C. 0.3

D. 0.33

E. 0.35

29.2. Multiple Events

2 to 4 Times

8. A and B are independent events and $P(A) = 0.8$ and $P(B) = 0.7$. What is $P(A$ and $B)$? ③

A. 0.1

B. 0.28

C. 0.56

D. 0.8

E. 0.94

9. A and B are independent events and $P(A) = 0.8$ and $P(B) = 0.7$. What is $P(A$ or $B)$? ④

A. 0.56

B. 0.8

C. 0.84

D. 0.92

E. 0.94

10. The probability that the Tigers win the first game is 0.8. The probability that they win the second game is 0.6. What is the probability that the Tigers win one and lose one if the games are independent events? ④

A. 0.25

B. 0.40

C. 0.44

D. 0.50

E. 0.56

11. If the probability that the Tigers win each game against the Red Sox is 0.7 and the games are independent events, what is the probability that the Tigers win all 3 games of a 3 game series? ③

A. 0.125

B. 0.25

C. 0.3

D. 0.343

E. 0.512

12. There are 5 multiple choice answer choices to each ACT problem. If Cyrus had only 2 problems left blank at the end of Math ACT and randomly guessed both problems, what is the probability that he got exactly 1 of the 2 questions right? ④

  A. $\dfrac{6}{25}$

  B. $\dfrac{1}{3}$

  C. $\dfrac{2}{5}$

  D. $\dfrac{8}{25}$

  E. $\dfrac{1}{4}$

13. There are 5 multiple choice answer choices to each ACT problem. If Malcolm has one minute left and randomly guesses 3 problems on the math ACT which he was not able to solve, what is the probability that he gets at least 1 of those problems right? ④

  A. $\dfrac{64}{125}$

  B. $\dfrac{2}{5}$

  C. $\dfrac{12}{25}$

  D. $\dfrac{1}{2}$

  E. $\dfrac{61}{125}$

14. If the probability that the Tigers win each game is 60% and the games are independent events, what is the probability that the Tigers win at least one game of a 4-game series? ④

  A. 88%

  B. 90%

  C. 93%

  D. 95%

  E. 97%

15. If the Giants have a 60% chance of winning each of two games. If the games are independent events, what is the chance that the Giants lose both games? ④

  A. 16%

  B. 18%

  C. 20%

  D. 25%

  E. 36%

Many Times

If you are asked for the probability that something happens at least once in so many trials, take 1 minus the probability of 0 occurrences. For example, if a product is defective 0.05 of the time, the probability of at least 1 defective item in a group of 10 is $1 - 0.95^{10} = 0.401$.

The probability that if Sylvester flips 8 coins he gets exactly 4 heads is the number of combinations resulting in 4 heads divided by the total number of combinations.

$$\frac{{}_8C_4}{2^8} = \frac{70}{256} = \frac{35}{128}.$$

16. As part of a game, Attila tosses 7 fair coins simultaneously. In order for Attila to win the game, the coins all must land heads face up. What is the probability that Attila wins? ④

A. $\dfrac{1}{64}$

B. $\dfrac{1}{128}$

C. $\dfrac{1}{256}$

D. $\dfrac{5}{512}$

E. $\dfrac{3}{256}$

29.3. Dice Problems

For two 6-sided dice, there is 1 way to roll a 2 $(1-1)$, so the chance $1/36$, 2 ways to roll a 3 $(1-2, 2-1)$, so $2/36 = 1/8$, 3 ways to roll a 4 $(1-3, 2-2, 3-1)$, so $3/36 = 1/12$, 4 ways to roll a 5 $(1-4, 2-3, 3-2, 4-1)$ $4/36 = 1/9$, 5 ways to roll a 6 $(1-5, 2-4, 3-3, 4-2, 5-1)$ $5/36$, and 6 ways to roll and 7 $(1-6, 2-5, 3-4, 4-3, 5-3, 6-1)$ $6/36 = 1/6$. The probability of a sum of 8 equals that of a sum of 6 and so on. They may also ask about 2 10-sided dice, etc.

	1	2	3	4	5	6
1	2	3	4	⑤	6	7
2	3	4	⑤	6	7	8
3	4	⑤	6	7	8	9
4	⑤	6	7	8	9	10
5	6	7	8	9	10	11
6	7	8	9	10	11	12

The table shows how to find the probability of a total of 5 rolling 2 dice, which is $\dfrac{4}{36} = \dfrac{1}{9}$. The problem solutions do not show tables, but you might find that to be the best approach. You may want to practice solving these problems with tables if you are already at a high score.

17. If Crassius rolls a standard die and flips a coin, what is the probability of heads or a 6? ③

A. $\dfrac{5}{12}$

B. $\dfrac{13}{24}$

C. $\dfrac{7}{12}$

D. $\dfrac{2}{3}$

E. $\dfrac{1}{2}$

18. If Denise rolls two standard dice, what is the probability that the sum is exactly 9? ⑤

A. $\dfrac{1}{9}$

B. $\dfrac{5}{36}$

C. $\dfrac{1}{6}$

D. $\dfrac{1}{12}$

E. $\dfrac{1}{4}$

19. If Alberto rolls two 6-sided dice and wins a prize when the sum is 8 or greater, what is the probability Alberto wins a prize? ⑤

A. $\dfrac{7}{18}$

B. $\dfrac{5}{12}$

C. $\dfrac{4}{9}$

D. $\dfrac{1}{3}$

E. $\dfrac{1}{2}$

29.4. Is the Product Odd or Positive?

For the product of numbers to be odd, then all the number multiplied must be odd. For the product of 2 numbers to be positive, the numbers must be either both positive or both negative.

If there is one set of cards numbered 1-11 and another set numbered 21-35, and Pedro randomly selects a card from each set, what is the probability that the product is odd? For the product to be odd, both cards must be odd. Since these selections are independent, we multiply the probabilities, so the probability both are odd is

$$\frac{6}{11} \cdot \frac{8}{15} = \frac{48}{165}.$$

20. Gertrude randomly selects 3 numbers from slips of paper $\{1, 2, 3, 4, 5\}$. After selecting each slip, she puts it back with the others and thoroughly mixes up the slips. What is the probability that the product of all 3 numbers selected is odd? ⑤

   A. $\dfrac{1}{8}$

   B. $\dfrac{27}{125}$

   C. $\dfrac{1}{4}$

   D. $\dfrac{1}{10}$

   E. $\dfrac{1}{5}$

21. Suppose Samantha randomly selects 2 different numbers (that is after she chooses the first number, she picks from 4 numbers not including the first number) from $\{1, 2, 3, 4, 5\}$. What is the probability that the product of the selected numbers is odd? ⑤

   A. $\dfrac{1}{2}$

   B. $\dfrac{3}{5}$

   C. $\dfrac{3}{10}$

   D. $\dfrac{1}{4}$

   E. $\dfrac{9}{25}$

22. Mary Ann randomly selects one card from cards with $\{1, 2, 3, 4, 5\}$ on them and another card from a pile with $\{6, 7, 8, 9, 10\}$ on them. What is the probability that the product of the numbers on those two cards is odd? ⑤

   A. $\dfrac{2}{9}$

   B. $\dfrac{1}{3}$

   C. $\dfrac{17}{75}$

   D. $\dfrac{6}{25}$

   E. $\dfrac{1}{4}$

23. Betil chooses a card at random from a pile of cards labeled with integers 1 to 5 inclusive and another card at random from a pile of cards labeled with integers 11 to 17 inclusive. What is the probability that the product of the numbers on those two cards is odd? ④

A. $\dfrac{13}{35}$

B. $\dfrac{1}{3}$

C. $\dfrac{12}{35}$

D. $\dfrac{1}{4}$

E. $\dfrac{11}{35}$

24. Celina randomly selects one number from slips of paper labelled $\{-2, -1, 0, 1, 2\}$ and she randomly selects another number from slips of paper labelled $\{-3, -2, -1, 0, 1, 2, 3\}$. What is the probability that the product of those two number will be positive? ⑤

A. $\dfrac{1}{2}$

B. $\dfrac{13}{35}$

C. $\dfrac{12}{35}$

D. $\dfrac{2}{5}$

E. $\dfrac{11}{35}$

29.5. In the Same Group or Next to Each Other

These problems are challenging and designed to test reasoning ability. These are not emphasized in standard textbooks.

For example, what is the probability that Alice and Lisa will be in the same group of 5 out of 10 people? Assume Alice is in one group; then

there are 9 places for Lisa, 4 of which are in Alice's group, so $\dfrac{4}{9}$.

25. Bob and Kevin will be among 10 people randomly seated at a circular table in Chemistry class. What is the probability that they will be seated next to each other? ⑤

A. $\dfrac{2}{9}$

B. $\dfrac{4}{9}$

C. $\dfrac{1}{3}$

D. $\dfrac{1}{4}$

E. $\dfrac{1}{5}$

26. The coach splits 6 team members randomly into groups of 3. If Alvin and Bob are among the 6, what is the probability that they will be in the same group? ⑤

A. $\dfrac{2}{5}$

B. $\dfrac{4}{9}$

C. $\dfrac{3}{7}$

D. $\dfrac{1}{3}$

E. $\dfrac{1}{2}$

27. Jane and Julie are among 8 players in a tennis tournament in June in a park in Santa Monica. If the pairings for each match are random, what is the probability that they will be paired together in the first round? (5)

A. $\dfrac{1}{5}$

B. $\dfrac{3}{14}$

C. $\dfrac{1}{4}$

D. $\dfrac{1}{7}$

E. $\dfrac{3}{16}$

29.6. Draw One Card

The probability of one event or another occurring is the sum of the probabilities of each minus the probability of both, so that you do not double count.

Therefore, the probability of drawing an ace or a spade from a standard deck is

$$\frac{13}{52} + \frac{4}{52} - \frac{1}{52} = \frac{16}{52} = \frac{4}{13}.$$

If it is an and condition, just multiply the probabilities.

(1) Easiest

(5) Most Difficult

28. If Caligula draws a card from a standard deck, what is the probability that the card is a spade and a face card? (4)

A. $\dfrac{11}{26}$

B. $\dfrac{1}{52}$

C. $\dfrac{3}{52}$

D. $\dfrac{1}{13}$

E. $\dfrac{5}{52}$

29. If Benedict draws a card from a standard deck, what is the probability that the card is a spade or a face card? (4)

A. $\dfrac{25}{52}$

B. $\dfrac{5}{13}$

C. $\dfrac{23}{52}$

D. $\dfrac{11}{26}$

E. $\dfrac{6}{13}$

1D, 2D, 3B, 4C, 5C,6C 7A 8E, 9E, 10C,11D, 12D, 13E, 14E, 15A, 16B, 17C, 18A, 19B, 20B, 21C, 22D, 23C, 24C, 25A, 26A, 27D, 28C, 29D

29.7. Solutions

1. (D) $\dfrac{3}{5} \cdot \dfrac{2}{4} = \dfrac{6}{20} = \dfrac{3}{10}$.

2. (D) There are 4 aces out of 52 cards the first time. The second time, there are 3 aces left of 51 cards.
$$\frac{4}{52} \cdot \frac{3}{51} = \frac{1}{221}.$$

3. (B) Add the probability of both red to the probability of both blue:
$$\frac{7}{10} \cdot \frac{6}{9} + \frac{3}{10} \cdot \frac{2}{9} = \frac{42+6}{90} = \frac{48}{90} = \frac{8}{15}.$$

4. (C) The number of red marbles and the number of total marbles are both reduced each time:
$$\frac{5}{9} \cdot \frac{4}{8} \cdot \frac{3}{7} = \frac{5}{42}.$$

5. (E) The possible outcomes whose sum is 5 are $1-4$, $2-3$, $3-2$, $4-1$ out of $4 \cdot 3 = 12$ total possibilities (there are 4 numbers initially, and after 1 number is removed there are only 3 on the second draw), so $\dfrac{4}{12} = \dfrac{1}{3}$.

6. (C) We multiply by 3! because there are 3! arrangements, RBG, RGB, BRG, BGR, GRB, GBR.
$3! \dfrac{2 \cdot 2 \cdot 2}{6 \cdot 5 \cdot 4} = \dfrac{6 \cdot 8}{120} = \dfrac{48}{120} = \dfrac{12}{30} = \dfrac{2}{5}$.

7. (A) We multiply by 3! because there are 3! arrangements, RBG, RGB, BRG, BGR, GRB, GBR.
$3! \dfrac{6 \cdot 4 \cdot 2}{12 \cdot 11 \cdot 10} \approx 0.22$.

8. (C) $P(A) \cdot P(B) = 0.8 \cdot 0.7 = 0.56$.

9. (E) $P(A) + P(B) - P(AB) = 0.8 + 0.7 - 0.8 \cdot 0.7 = 1.5 - 0.56 = 0.94$.

10. (C) Take the probability that the Tigers win the first and lose the second plus the probability that they lose the first and win the second: $0.8 \cdot 0.4 + 0.2 \cdot 0.6 = 0.44$.

    Alternate solution, take 1 minus the probability they win both games minus the probability that they lose both games. $1 - 0.8 \cdot 0.6 - 0.2 \cdot 0.4 = 1 - 0.48 - 0.08 = 0.44$.

11. (D) Multiply the probabilities (since they are all the same, this results in exponentiation), since they all have to be true for the condition to hold: $0.7^3 = 0.343$.

12. (D) Multiply the probabilities of 1 wrong times the probability of 1 right and multiply by 2 because there are 2 possible orders (those orders are right then wrong and wrong then right).

$$2 \cdot \frac{1}{5} \cdot \frac{4}{5} = \frac{8}{25}.$$

Alternate solution: take 1 minus the probability that the problems are both wrong and minus the probability that they are both right:

$$1 - \left(\frac{1}{5}\right)^2 - \left(\frac{4}{5}\right)^2 = 1 - \frac{1}{25} - \frac{16}{25} = \frac{8}{25}.$$

13. (E) Take 1 minus the probability that he misses all of the problems:

$$1 - \left(\frac{4}{5}\right)^3 = 1 - \frac{64}{125} = \frac{61}{125}.$$

14. (E) Take 1 minus the probability that they lose all of the games: $1 - 0.4^4 = 1 - 0.0256 = 0.974$.

15. (A) Take the product of the probabilities that they lose each game: $0.4 \cdot 0.4 = 0.16$.

16. (B) Multiply the probabilities, since they all need to occur. $\left(\frac{1}{2}\right)^7 = \frac{1}{128}.$

17. (C) It is easiest to take 1 minus the probability that neither event occurs:

$$1 - \frac{1}{2} \cdot \frac{5}{6} = 1 - \frac{5}{12} = \frac{7}{12}.$$

18. (A) A sum of 9 can occur in the following ways: $3-6, 4-5, 5-4, 6-3$, so 4 possibilities out of $6 \times 6 = 36$ (there are 6 possibilities for each die, so 6×6 possibilities for 2 dice), so $\frac{4}{36} = \frac{1}{9}$. You can also use a table with the columns the value on one role and the rows the value of the other role.

19. (B) A sum of 8 or greater can occur in the following ways: $2-6, 3-5, 3-6, 4-4, 4-5, 4-6,$ $5-3, 5-4, 5-5, 5-6, 6-2, 6-3, 6-4, 6-5, 6-6 = 15$ possibilities out of 36. Therefore, the probability of a sum of 8 or greater is $\frac{15}{36} = \frac{5}{12}.$

20. (B) the probabilities that each event occurs (since the probabilities are the same, this results in exponentiation): $\left(\frac{3}{5}\right)^3 = \frac{27}{125}.$

21. (C) For the product to be odd, the numbers both must be odd, so we take the product of the probabilities that each will be odd: $\frac{3}{5} \cdot \frac{2}{4} = \frac{3}{10}.$

22. (D) For the product to be odd, the numbers both must be odd, so $\frac{3}{5} \cdot \frac{2}{5} = \frac{6}{25}.$

23. (C) For the product to be odd, the numbers both must be odd, so $\frac{3}{5} \cdot \frac{4}{7} = \frac{12}{35}.$

24. (C) For the product to be positive, the numbers either must be both positive or both negative. There are $5 \cdot 7 = 35$ total possibilities. There are 6 possibilities where both numbers are odd and 6 possibilities where both numbers are even.

$$\text{negative} \cdot \text{negative} = 2 \cdot 3 = 6 \text{ and positive} \cdot \text{positive} = 2 \cdot 3 = 6,$$

$$\text{so } 6 + 6 = 12 \text{ possibilities.} \quad \frac{6+6}{35} = \frac{12}{35}.$$

25. (A) If Bob is in a certain seat, there are 2 seats next to him out of a total of 9 other seats.

26. (A) If Alvin is in one group, there are 2 places for Bob in the same group and 3 places in the other group, so $\frac{2}{5}$.

27. (D) There are 7 people Jane can be paired with, one of whom is Julie.

28. (C) This is an AND condition with independent events, so multiply the probabilities. $\frac{1}{4} \cdot \frac{3}{13} = \frac{3}{52}$.

29. (D) As this is an OR condition, take the probability of each, and subtract from that the probability of both so as not to over count.

$$13 \text{ spades} + 12 \text{ face cards} - 3 \text{ both} = 22 \text{ (dividing by the total number of cards)} \quad \frac{22}{52} = \frac{11}{26}.$$

30. Composition of Functions

30.1. Basic Composition

The basics of composition of function is you substitute one function for x in the other function. For example if f(x) $= 3x + 2$ and g(x) $= 5x - 1$, then f(g(x)) $= 3(5x-1)+2 = 15x-3+2 = 15x-1$. g(f(x) $= 5(3x+2)-1 = 15x+6-1 = 15x+5$.

1. If $f(x) = 3x + 4$ and $g(x) = 2x - 7$, what is $f(g(x))$? ③
   A. $6x + 1$
   B. $6x - 1$
   C. $6x - 7$
   D. $6x - 17$
   E. $6x - 25$

2. If $f(x) = x^2 + 8$ and $g(x) = 3x + 4$, what is $g(f(x))$? ③
   A. $9x^2 + 24x + 24$
   B. $3x^2 + 20$
   C. $3x^2 + 32$
   D. $3x^2 + 12$
   E. $3x^2 + 28$

3. If $f(x) = x^2 + 8$ and $g(x) = 3x + 4$, what is $f(g(x))$? ③
   A. $3x^2 + 28$
   B. $3x^2 + 24$
   C. $9x^2 + 24x + 32$
   D. $9x^2 + 12x + 24$
   E. $9x^2 + 24x + 24$

4. The melting point of zinc is $787°$ Fahrenheit. Fahrenheit to Celsius is related as $F = \dfrac{9C}{5} + 32$ and Kelvin to Celsius as $K = C + 273$. Which is closest to the melting point of zinc in degrees Kelvin? ④
   A. $632°$
   B. $662°$
   C. $692°$
   D. $722°$
   E. $752°$

5. If $f(x) = x^2 - 25$ and $g(x) = x + 4$, which of the following are solutions of $f(g(x)) = 0$? ③
   A. 2 or -2
   B. 5 or -5
   C. 1 or -9
   D. -1 or 9
   E. -1 or 1

30.2. With Value

When you are given the value – for example, if you are asked to find $f(g(3))$ rather than $f(g(x))$ – the easiest way to solve the problem is to substitute that value in at the beginning, rather than determining the composition of functions algebraically.

For example, you might be given $f(x) = \sqrt{x+1}$ and asked to find $f(f(f(5)))$.

$$f(5) = \sqrt{6} = 2.449;$$
$$f(2.449) = \sqrt{3.449} = 1.857;$$
$$f(1.857) = \sqrt{2.857} = 1.690.$$

Finding $f(f(f(x)))$ algebraically would be difficult and time consuming.

Most of the problems where the value of x is not given can also be solved by substituting in numbers for x, as is shown in some of the solutions.

6. If $f(x) = 7 \cdot 2^x$, $g(x) = 2 \cdot 3^x$, and $h(x) = f(x) - g(x)$, what is the value of $h(4)$? ③
   A. −50
   B. −20
   C. 10
   D. 20
   E. 50

7. Let $f(x) = x^2 + 3x - 10$, $g(x) = x^2 + 6x + 8$, and $h(x) = 2g(x) - f(x)$. What is $h(3)$? ③
   A. 34
   B. 44
   C. 52
   D. 54
   E. 62

8. If $f(x) = x + \dfrac{1}{x}$, what is $f(f(2))$? ③
   A. $\dfrac{10}{29}$
   B. $\dfrac{5}{2}$
   C. $\dfrac{29}{10}$
   D. $\dfrac{31}{10}$
   E. 3

9. If $f(x) = x^3 - 3$, what is $f(f(2))$? ④
   A. 5
   B. 72
   C. 122
   D. 125
   E. 128

10. If $f(x) = 3x - 1$ for $x < 3$ and $f(x) = x - 2$ for $x \geq 3$, what is $f(f(f(3)))$? ④
    A. 2
    B. 3
    C. 4
    D. 5
    E. 14

30.3. Complications

There can be some challenging problems in this area on the exam.

For example, given $f(x) = 2x + 5$ and $g(x) = ax - 2$, find a value a for which $f(g(x)) = g(f(x))$. To solve this, substitute each expression in for x in the other equation, set those two equations equal, and then solve for a, as follows:

$$2(ax - 2) + 5 = a(2x + 5) - 2 \text{ (distributing)}$$
$$2ax - 4 + 5 = 2ax + 5a - 2$$
$$\implies 3 = 5a \implies a = \frac{3}{5}.$$

11. If $f(x) = 3x + 2$ and $g(x) = 5x + a$, for what real number a does $f(g(x)) = g(f(x))$? ⑤

    A. 2

    B. 3

    C. 4

    D. 5

    E. 8

12. If $f(x) = 2x + 5$ and $g(x) = ax + 3$, for what real number a does $f(g(x)) = g(f(x))$? ⑤

    A. $\dfrac{5}{3}$

    B. $\dfrac{11}{5}$

    C. $\dfrac{8}{5}$

    D. 2

    E. $\dfrac{4}{5}$

13. If $f(x) = x^2$ and $g(f(x)) = \dfrac{1 + x^2}{x^2}$, what is $f(g(x))$? ④

    A. $\left(\dfrac{1 + x}{x}\right)^3$

    B. $\left(\dfrac{1 + x}{1 - x}\right)^2$

    C. $\dfrac{1 + x}{1 - x}$

    D. $\left(\dfrac{1 + x}{x}\right)^2$

    E. $\dfrac{1 + x}{x}$

14. If $f(x) = x + 4$ and $g(f(x)) = 3x + 7$, what is $f(g(x))$? ④

    A. $3x - 5$

    B. $3x - 1$

    C. $x - 1$

    D. $3x + 2$

    E. $x - 5$

30.4. Finding $f(f(x))$

To find $f(f(x))$, substitute in $f(x)$ for x and simplify.

For example, if $f(x) = 3x + 2$, what is $f(f(x))$?

$$3(3x + 2) + 2 = 9x + 8.$$

Another example is $f(x) = \dfrac{x}{3 + x}$. What is $f(f(x))$?

$$\left(\dfrac{x}{3 + x}\right) \Big/ \left(3 + \dfrac{x}{3 + x}\right)$$
$$= \left(\dfrac{x}{3 + x}\right) \Big/ \left(\dfrac{9 + 3x + x}{3 + x}\right) = \dfrac{x}{9 + 4x}.$$

15. If $f(x) = x^4$, what is $f(f(x))$? ④

    A. x^{16}

    B. $4x^8$

    C. x^8

    D. x^{256}

    E. $4x^{16}$

16. If $f(x) = 4x + 7$, what is $f(f(x))$? ④

    A. $12x + 28$

    B. $16x + 49$

    C. $16x + 28$

    D. $8x + 21$

    E. $16x + 35$

17. If $f(x) = \dfrac{-1}{x^5}$, what is $f(f(x))$? ④

    A. x^{25}

    B. $\dfrac{-1}{x^{25}}$

    C. x^{10}

    D. $\dfrac{1}{x^{10}}$

    E. $\dfrac{1}{x^{25}}$

30.5. Other Composition Problems

If you are asked to find f(3x + 2), then substitute 3x + 2 in for x in f(x).

If you are given functions with fractions, just substitute them in and simplify the complex fraction.

18. If $f(x) = x^2 + 3x + 2$, what is $f(x^5)$? ③

    A. $x^7 + 3x^6 + 2$

    B. $4x^{10} + 6x^5 + 2$

    C. $x^7 + 3x^5 + 2$

    D. $4x^{10} + 3x^5 + 2$

    E. $x^{10} + 3x^5 + 2$

19. If $f(x) = x^2 + 3x + 2$, what is $f(3x^2)$? ③

    A. $9x^4 + 27x^2 + 2$

    B. $9x^4 + 9x^2 + 2$

    C. $3x^4 + 9x^2 + 2$

    D. $27x^4 + 27x^2 + 2$

    E. $9x^4 + 9x^2 + 2x$

20. If $f(x) = x^2 - 25$ and $g(x) = x + 4$, what are the values of x for which $f(g(x)) = 0$? ③

    A. -9 and 1

    B. -9 and 2

    C. -9 and 3

    D. -2 and -1

    E. -2 and 3

21. If $f(g(x)) = \dfrac{x^2 + 3}{x^2 - 1}$ and $g(x) = x^2$, what is $f(x)$? ④

    A. $\dfrac{x}{x-1}$

    B. $\dfrac{x+2}{x-1}$

    C. $\dfrac{x+3}{x-1}$

    D. $\dfrac{x}{1-x}$

    E. $\dfrac{x+3}{1-x}$

① Easiest

⑤ Most Difficult

— ANSWER KEY

1D, 2E,3C 4E, 5E,6A, 7E, 8C, 9C, 10D, 11C, 12C, 13D, 14B, 15A, 16E, 17A, 18E, 19B, 20A, 21C

30.6. Solutions

1. (D) $f(g(x)) = 3(2x - 7) + 4 = 6x - 21 + 4 = 6x - 17$.

2. (E) $3(x^2 + 8) + 4 = 3x^2 + 24 + 4 = 3x^2 + 28$.

3. (C) $787 = \dfrac{9C}{5} + 32 \implies 755 = \dfrac{9C}{5} \implies C \approx 419.4$, $K = C + 273 \implies K = 419.4 + 273 \approx 692$.

4. (E) $(3x + 4)^2 + 8 = 9x^2 + 12x + 12x + 16 + 8 = 9x^2 + 24x + 2$

5. (C) $(x + 4)^2 - 25 = 0 \implies x^2 + 8x + 16 - 25 = 0 \implies x^2 + 8x - 9 = 0 \implies x^2 + 9x - x - 9 = 0 \implies$ $(x + 9)(x - 1) = 0 \implies x = 1$ or -9. You could also use the quadratic formula, completing the square, or graphing. Alternate solution: $x^2 - 25 = 0 \implies x = 5$ or $-5x + 4 = 0 \implies x = -4$ So $5 - 4 = 1$, $-5 - 4 = -9$.

6. (A) $f(4) = 7 \cdot 2^4 = 112$, $g(4) = 2 \cdot 3^4 = 162$. $112 - 162 = -50$.

7. (E) $f(3) = 3^2 + 3 \cdot 3 - 10 = 9 + 9 - 10 = 8$. $g(3) = 3^2 + 6 \cdot 3 + 8 = 9 + 18 + 8 = 35$. $2g(3) - f(3) = 2 \cdot 35 - 8 = 62$.

8. (C) $f(2) = 2 + \dfrac{1}{2} = \dfrac{5}{2}$. $f(f(2)) = \dfrac{5}{2} + \dfrac{2}{5} = \dfrac{29}{10}$.

9. (C) $f(2) = 2^3 - 3 = 5$. $f(f(2)) = 5^3 - 2 = 122$.

10. (D) Substitute 3 for x, then the result of x, and finally that result for x in the given equations. $f(3) = x - 2 = 3 - 2 = 1$, $f(f(3)) = f(1) = 3x - 1 = 3 \cdot 1 - 1 = 2$, $f(f(f(3))) = 3x - 1 = 3 \cdot 2 - 1 = 5$.

11. (C) Find $f(g(x))$ and $g(f(x))$ algebraically, set them equal, and then solve for a.

$$3(5x + a) + 2 = 5(3x + 2) + a \implies 15x + 3a + 2 = 15x + 10 + a \implies 2a = 8 \text{ or } a = 4.$$

12. (C) Find $f(g(x))$ and $g(f(x))$ algebraically, set them equal, and then solve for a.

$$2(ax + 3) + 5 = a(2x + 5) + 3 \implies 2ax + 11 = 2ax + 5a + 3$$
$$\implies 11 = 5a + 3 \implies a = \frac{8}{5}.$$

13. (D) $g(x)$ can be determined by inspection. Then substitute $g(x)$ in for x in $f(x)$.

$$g(x) = \frac{1 + x}{x} \text{ (substituting) } f(g(x)) = \left(\frac{1 + x}{x}\right)^2.$$

14. (B) If $f(x) = x + 4$ and $g(f(x)) = 3x + 7$, what is $f(g(x))$? First, determine $g(x)$ by setting it equal to $ax + b$ and then solve for a and b. Then substitute $g(x)$ in for x in $f(x)$ and finally simplify. Let

$$g(x) = ax + b \text{ (substituting } f(x) \text{ for } x) \ a(x + 4) + b = 3x + 7$$
$$\implies ax + 4a + b = 3x + 7 \implies ax = 3x \implies a = 3.$$

Therefore, $4a + b = 7$ (substituting) $4 \cdot 3 + b = 7 \implies b = -5$.

Therefore, $g(x) = 3x - 5$ (substituting) $f(g(x)) = (3x - 5) + 4 = 3x - 1$.

15. (A) Substitute $f(x)$ for x and then simplify. $f(f(x)) = (x^4)^4 = x^{16}$.

16. (E) Substitute $f(x)$ for x and then simplify.

$$f(f(x)) = 4(4x + 7) + 7 = 16x + 35.$$

Alternative solution: By substituting in numbers, let $x = 2$. Then $f(x) = 15$ and $f(f(x)) = 67$. Substituting 2 into each answer choice, A is 52, B is 61, C is 60, D is 37, and E is 67, so the answer is E.

17. (A) Substitute $f(x)$ for x and then simplify.

$$f(f(x)) = \frac{-1}{\left(\dfrac{-1}{x^5}\right)^5} = \frac{-1}{\dfrac{-1}{x^{25}}} = x^{25}.$$

18. (E) Substitute x^5 for x and then simplify: $(x^5)^2 + 3x^5 + 2 = x^{10} + 3x^5 + 2$.

19. (B) Substitute $3x^2$ for x and then simplify: $(3x^2)^2 + 3 \cdot 3x^2 + 2 = 9x^4 + 9x^2 + 2$.

Alternate Solution: Substitute in 1 for x, which is not ideal, but the easiest choice. Then $3x^2 = 3$ and $f(3) = 20$. substituting 1 into each answer choice, A is 38, B is 20, C is 17, D is 54, and E is 20. Therefore, the substitution did not work perfectly. You could guess between B and E or substitute in another number, say $x = 2$. Then $3x^2 = 12$, $f(12) = 182$. Substituting 2 into B, we get 182. At that point, you should just fill in B. However, if you substitute 2 into E, you get 184.

20. (A) $f(g(x)) = (x + 4)^2 - 25 = x^2 + 8x + 16 - 25 = x^2 + 8x - 9 = x^2 + 9x - x - 9 = x(x + 9) - 1(x + 9) = (x - 1)(x + 9)$, $(x - 1)(x + 9) = 0 \to x = 1$ of $x = -9$. Alternate solution: $x^2 - 25 = 0 \to x = 5$ or $x = -5$. $x + 4 = 5 \to x = 1$, $x + 4 = -5 \to x = -9$.

21. (C) By observation of the pattern.

31. Inverse Functions

To find the inverse of a function, switch x and y and then solve for y. The problem may be given as $f(x)$ instead of y. Then the function after you switch the variables and solve for y is $f^{-1}(x)$.

31.1. Linear Equations

The basic problem is to find the inverse of $y = 3x + 2$:

$$x = 3y + 2 \text{ (isolating } y) \quad x - 2 = 3y$$

$$\text{(dividing to solve for } y) \quad \frac{x-2}{3} = y.$$

1. If $f(x) = 11x - 5$, what is $f^{-1}(x)$? ③

   A. $\dfrac{x+1}{11}$

   B. $\dfrac{x+2}{11}$

   C. $\dfrac{x+3}{11}$

   D. $\dfrac{x+4}{11}$

   E. $\dfrac{x+5}{11}$

2. $f(x) = \dfrac{3x+2}{5x-8}$. Which of these is $f^{-1}(x)$? ④

   A. $y = \dfrac{8x+3}{5x+3}$

   B. $y = \dfrac{8x+2}{5x-4}$

   C. $y = \dfrac{8x-2}{8x-3}$

   D. $y = \dfrac{8x+2}{5x-3}$

   E. $y = \dfrac{8x+2}{8x-3}$

3. If $f(x) = ax + b$, what is $f^{-1}(x)$? ③

   A. $y = \dfrac{x-a}{b}$

   B. $y = \dfrac{x-b}{a}$

   C. $y = \dfrac{b-x}{a}$

   D. $y = \dfrac{x+b}{a}$

   E. $y = \dfrac{x-b}{ab}$

265

31.2. Nonlinear Equations

Switch x and y and then solve for y as discussed previously for linear equations. The following is a really complicated example, but not particularly difficult. If $f(x) = \log(4x^3 + 11) + 5$, what is $f^{-1}(x)$? The key step is taking both sides 10 to the power or converting to exponential form so as to eliminate the logarithm,

$$x = \log(4y^3 + 11) + 5 \implies x - 5$$
$$= \log(4y^3 + 11) \implies 10^{x-5} = 4y^3 + 11 \implies$$
$$\frac{10^{x-5} - 11}{4} = y^3 \implies \sqrt[3]{\frac{10^{x-5} - 11}{4}} = y.$$

In general, isolate the new y, which means undoing what y is inside. Take the log of an exponential, exponentiate a log, take the root of a power, and take a root to a power.

4. What is the inverse function of $f(x) = x^5$? ②

    A. $y = \sqrt[5]{x}$

    B. $y = \sqrt[5]{x^2}$

    C. $y = x^{5/2}$

    D. $y = \sqrt{x^5}$

    E. $y = \sqrt[10]{x}$

5. If $f(x) = \sqrt[3]{3x + 8}$, what is $f^{-1}(x)$? ④

    A. $\dfrac{x^3 - 8}{4}$

    B. $\dfrac{x^3 - 3}{8}$

    C. $\dfrac{x^3 + 8}{3}$

    D. $\dfrac{x^3 - 8}{3}$

    E. $\dfrac{x^3 + 8}{6}$

6. If $f(x) = x^5 + 4$, what is $f^{-1}(x)$? ④

    A. $\sqrt[5]{x + 4}$

    B. $\sqrt[5]{x - 4}$

    C. $\sqrt[5]{x - 16}$

    D. $-\sqrt[5]{x - 4}$

    E. $\sqrt[5]{x - 2}$

7. If $f(x) = \log(3x - 11)$, what is $f^{-1}(x)$? ④

    A. $\dfrac{e^x + 11}{3} = y$

    B. $\dfrac{e^x - 11}{3} = y$

    C. $\dfrac{10^x + 11}{3} = y$

    D. $\dfrac{10^x - 11}{3} = y$

    E. $\dfrac{10^x + 11}{9} = y$

8. If $f(x) = 2^{5x+4}$, about what is $f^{-1}(100)$? ④

    A. 0.53

    B. 0.63

    C. 0.73

    D. 0.83

    E. 0.93

9. If $f(x) = 5^{2x-1}$, what is $f^{-1}(x)$? ④

    A. $\dfrac{\log_5 x + 1}{2}$

    B. $\dfrac{\log_5 x}{2} + 1$

    C. $\dfrac{\log_5 x - 1}{2}$

    D. $\dfrac{\log_5 x}{2} - 1$

    E. $\dfrac{\log_5 x + 3}{2}$

10. If $f(x) = \sqrt[3]{x^5 + 8}$, what is $f^{-1}(x)$? ⑤

    A. $\sqrt[5]{x^3 + 8} = y$

    B. $\sqrt[5]{x^3 - 8} = y$

    C. $\sqrt[3]{x^5 - 8} = y$

    D. $\sqrt[3]{x^5 + 8} = y$

    E. $(x^3 - 8)^5 = y$

1E, 2D, 3B, 4A, 5D, 6B, 7C, 8A, 9A, 10B

31.3. Solutions

1. (E) Switch x and y, and then solve for y.

$$x = 11y - 5 \implies x + 5 = 11y \implies \frac{x+5}{11} = y.$$

2. (D) Switch x and y, multiply both sides by the denominator to eliminate fractions, get the y terms on one side and terms without a y on the other, factor out y, and then divide by the coefficient of y:

$$x = \frac{3y+2}{5y-8} \text{ (multiplying) } 5xy - 8x = 3y + 2 \text{ (getting the } y \text{ terms on one side)}$$

$$5xy - 3y = 8x + 2 \text{ (factoring out } y \text{ and solving) } y = \frac{8x+2}{5x-3}.$$

Alternate solution: by substituting in numbers, let $x = 2$. Then $f(2) = 4$. Substituting 4 into each answer choice, A is 35/23, B is 17/8, C is 30/29, D is 2, and E is 34/29, so D is the answer. By the definition of inverse functions, we need to get the original value back.

3. (B) Switch x and y, and then solve for y. $ay + b = x \implies ay = x - b \implies y = \frac{x-b}{a}$.

4. (A) $x = y^5 \implies y = \sqrt[5]{x}$.

5. (D) Switch x and y, cube both sides to clear the radical, and then solve for y.

$$x = \sqrt[3]{3y+8} \text{ (cubing both sides) } x^3 = 3y + 8 \text{ (isolating } y) \ x^3 - 8 = 3y \implies \frac{x^3-8}{3} = y.$$

6. (B) Switch x and y, solve for y^5, and then take the 5th root of both sides to get y: $x = y^5 + 4$ (isolate y) $x - 4 = y^5$ (taking the 5th root of both sides) $\sqrt[5]{x-4} = y$.

7. (C) Switch x and y, $x = \log(3y-11)$ (taking both sides 10 to the power) $10^x = 3y - 11$ (solving for y)

$$\frac{10^x + 11}{3} = y.$$

8. (A). When taking f^{-1} of a value, substitute that value in for y in the original equation.

$$100 = 2^{5x+4} \text{ (taking ln of both sides) } \ln 100 = (5x+4)\ln 2$$

(taking the logs) $4.605 \approx 0.693(5x + 4) \implies 6.644 \approx 5x + 4 \implies 2.644 \approx 5x, \implies x \approx 0.53$.

Another solution is $x = 2^{5y+4}$ (taking $\log_2$ of both sides or equating exponents) $\log_2 x = 5y + 4$, solving for y,

$$\frac{\log_2 x - 4}{5} = y \text{ (substituting in } x = 100) \ (\log_2 100 - 4)/5 = y \implies \frac{6.44 - 4}{5} = y \implies y \approx 0.53.$$

9. (A) Switch x and y, take $\log_5$ to clear the exponent and then solve for y.

$$x = 5^{2y-1} \text{ (taking } \log_5 \text{ of both sides or equating exponents) } \log_5 x = 2y - 1$$

$$\implies \frac{\log_5 x + 1}{2} = y.$$

10. (B) Switch x and y, cube both sides to clear the radical and then solve for y.

$$x = \sqrt[3]{y^5 + 8} \text{ (cubing both sides) } x^3 = y^5 + 8 \text{ (isolating } y) \; x^3 - 8 = y^5$$

$$\text{(taking the 5}^{\text{th}} \text{ root to solve for } y) \; \sqrt[5]{x^3 - 8} = y.$$

32. Exponential Equations

32.1. Word Problems

These are primarily financial problems involving interest or depreciation. On the SAT, there are exponential growth problems in biology or business, but those are not common on the ACT.

For depreciation, $A = P(1-r)^t$; for interest compounded annually, use $A = P(1+r)^t$; for interest compounded monthly or quarterly, etc. , use

$$A = P\left(1+\frac{r}{n}\right)^{nt};$$

for continuous interest, use $A = Pe^{rt}$ (P is the initial amount, A is the final amount, r is rate, t is time in years, and n is the number of times the money is compounded per year). You might be given the formula or asked to find an expression using the formula, rather than compute the final answer.

1. A group of 15 cells doubles every 24 minutes. At that rate, how many cells will there by after exactly 2 hours? ③
   A. 120
   B. 240
   C. 360
   D. 480
   E. 960

2. Mr. Green invested $10,000 at 8% interest compounded quarterly. Which of these is an expression for how much his investment will be worth after 20 years? ④
   A. $10,000(1+0.08)^{20}$
   B. $10,000\left(1+\dfrac{0.08}{4}\right)^{80}$
   C. $10,000 \cdot e^{1.6}$
   D. $10,000\left(1+\dfrac{0.08}{12}\right)^{240}$
   E. $10,000\left(1+\dfrac{0.08}{4}\right)^{20}$

3. Mr. Verde invested $10,000 at 8% interest compounded continuously. Which of these is an expression for how much his investment will be worth after 20 years? ④
   A. $10,000(1.08)^{20}$
   B. $10,000 \cdot e^{0.8}$
   C. $10,000(1.02)^{80}$
   D. $10,000 \cdot e^{2.4}$
   E. $10,000 \cdot e^{1.6}$

271

4. Bartholomew buys a red Jeep from Sunset Motors for $40,000. That Jeep depreciates at 12% per year, what will it be worth after 10 years? ④
   A. $7,140
   B. $8,140
   C. $9,140
   D. $10,140
   E. $11,140

5. Waylon buys a silver SUV from Good Deal Motors for $50,000. Its value depreciates 25% the first year and 10% per year after that. What will the vehicle be worth after 5 years? ④
   A. $23,600
   B. $24,600
   C. $25,600
   D. $26,600
   E. $27,600

6. Calvin deposited $1,000 at 6% interest compounded annually for 100 years. How much would his investment be worth in thousands of dollars? ④
   A. 219
   B. 227
   C. 282
   D. 327
   E. 339

32.2. Algebraic Equations

These problems are typically solved by getting both sides in terms of powers of 2 or 3 and equating exponents. It is also possible to take the ln or log of both sides with your calculator.

For example, solve the equation $9^{x+3} = 27^{x+5}$ for x. To do so, first express both sides as powers of 3 (since 9 and 27 are powers of 3, and then set the exponents equal. $(3^2)^{x+3} = (3^3)^{x+5}$ (by the laws of exponents) $3^{2x+6} = 3^{3x+15}$ (taking $\log_3$

of both sides) $2x + 6 = 3x + 15$ (simplifying and solving) $x = -9$.

7. If $32^x = 2$, what is x equal to? ③
   A. $\frac{1}{20}$
   B. $\frac{1}{10}$
   C. $\frac{1}{5}$
   D. $\frac{2}{5}$
   E. 5

8. For what real number is $32^{1/3} = 4^x$ true? ③
   A. $\frac{3}{5}$
   B. $\frac{5}{6}$
   C. $\frac{5}{3}$
   D. $\frac{5}{2}$
   E. 10

9. If $2^x = 4^{x+3}$, what is x? ④
   A. −6
   B. −4
   C. −2
   D. 3
   E. 6

10. If $x^{2a} = 5$, what does x^{7a} equal? ④
   A. $5\sqrt{5}$
   B. $25\sqrt{5}$
   C. 125
   D. $125\sqrt{5}$ *
   E. 625

11. For what values of x is the following: equation true: $\dfrac{27^x}{3^4} = 9^5$? ③

   A. $\dfrac{8}{3}$

   B. $\dfrac{11}{3}$

   C. 4

   D. $\dfrac{13}{3}$

   E. $\dfrac{14}{3}$

12. If $2^{\frac{3x+4}{x+8}} = 32$, what is x? ④

   A. -20

   B. -18

   C. -16

   D. -15

   E. -12

13. Which of these is the exact value of the x-coordinate of the intersection point of the graphs of $y = e^{x+5}$ and $y = 100$. ④

   A. $\ln 10 - 5$

   B. $\ln 100 + 5$

   C. $\ln 100 - 5$

   D. $\ln 100 - 8$

   E. $\ln 100 - 12$

14. If $(4\sqrt{2})^a = 128^b$ and $a \neq 0$, $b \neq 0$, what is $\dfrac{a}{b}$? ④

   A. $\dfrac{7}{5}$

   B. $\dfrac{7}{10}$

   C. $\dfrac{16}{5}$

   D. $\dfrac{12}{5}$

   E. $\dfrac{14}{5}$

15. If $16^{x+3} = 8^{2-x}$, what is x? ④

   A. $\dfrac{-5}{7}$

   B. $\dfrac{-6}{7}$

   C. $\dfrac{-8}{7}$

   D. $\dfrac{-9}{7}$

   E. $\dfrac{-10}{7}$

1D, 2B, 3E, 4E, 5B, 6E, 7C 8B 9A 10E 11B,12D 13C, 14E, 15B

32.3. Solutions

1. (D) $2 \cdot \dfrac{60}{24} = 5$, $15 \cdot 2^5 = 480$.

2. (B) Substitute into the compound interest formula $A = P\left(1 + \dfrac{r}{n}\right)^{nt}$.

3. (E) The formula for continuous interest is $A = Pe^{rt}$.

    $$Pe^{rt} = 10,000 \cdot e^{rt} = 10,000 \cdot e^{0.08 \cdot 20} = 10,000 \cdot e^{1.6}.$$

4. (E) Using the formula for depreciation $P(1-r)^t$, $40,000 \cdot 0.88^{10} = 11,140$.

5. (B) Using the depreciation formula with 2 different rates, $50,000 \cdot 0.75 \cdot 0.9^4 = 24603.75$.

6. (E) $1,000 \cdot 1.06^{100} = 339,302$.

7. (C) $32 = 2^5 \implies 32^{1/5} = 2$, so $\dfrac{1}{5}$.

8. (B) $(2^5)^{1/3} = (2^2)^x \implies 2^{5/3} = 2^{2x} \implies \dfrac{5}{3} = 2x \implies x = \dfrac{5}{6}$.

9. (A) $2^x = (2^2)^{x+3} \implies 2^x = 2^{2x+6} \implies x = 2x + 6 \implies x = -6$.

10. (E) $\dfrac{27^x}{3^4} = 9^5 \implies \dfrac{3^{3x}}{3^4} = (3^2)^5 \implies 3^{3x} = 3^4 \cdot 3^{10} \implies 3^{3x} = 3^{14} \implies 3x = 14 \implies x = \dfrac{14}{3}$.

11. (B) Taking the $\log_2$ of both sides or equating exponents,

    $$2^{\frac{3x+4}{x+8}} = 32 \implies \frac{3x+4}{x+8} = 5 \text{ (multiplying) } 3x + 4 = 5x + 40 \implies -36 = 2x \text{ or } x = -18.$$

12. (D). $x^7 a = x^2 a^{7/2}$, $5^{7/2} = 5^3 \cdot 5^{1/2} = 125\sqrt{5}$.

13. (C) Set the two equations equal to each other, and then take ln of both sides to clear the e to the power and then solve for x.

    $$100 = e^{x+5} \text{ (taking ln of both sides) } \ln 100 = x + 5 \implies \ln 100 - 5 = x.$$

14. (E) $(4\sqrt{2})^a = 128^b$ (convert to powers of 2) $\left(2^{\frac{5}{2}}\right)^a = (2^7)^b$,

    $$2^{\frac{5a}{2}} = 2^{7b} \text{ (taking the } \log_2 \text{ of both sides or equating exponents) } \frac{5a}{2} = 7b, \quad \frac{a}{b} = \frac{7}{\frac{5}{2}} = \frac{14}{5}.$$

It is possible to solve these problems by taking the log or ln of both sides using a calculator, but that is not the best approach.

15. (B) $16^{x+3} = 8^{2-x}$ converting to powers of 2,

$$2^{4^{x+3}} = 2^{3^{2-x}} \text{ (multiplying and taking the } \log_2 \text{ of both sides or equating exponents)}$$

$$4x + 12 = 6 - 3x \implies 7x = -6 \implies x = \frac{-6}{7}.$$

You can also use natural logs (this also works using common logs) as follows:

$$(x + 3)\ln 16 = (2 - x)\ln 8;$$

find the values of $\ln 8$ and $\ln 16$ using a calculator, and then solve for x.

33. Reflections, Translations, and Rotations

33.1. Reflections

The exam might ask the student to reflect an equation about the y-axis. That can be accomplished by changing all the x terms to $-x$, which results in negating the coefficients of the odd powered terms. Problems involving reflection about the x-axis are less likely to appear and are easier than about the y-axis. Reflecting about the x-axis, if the equation is solved for y, you would just take the negative of all terms.

For example, to reflect the point $(2, 5)$ about the y-axis, take the negative of the x-term, so the result is $(-2, 5)$. To reflect $(2, 5)$ about the x-axis, take the negative of the y-term, resulting in $(2, -5)$.

Reflecting an equation, $y = x^2 - 2x - 15$ about the y-axis, substitute $-x$ for x, so

$$y = (-x)^2 - 2(-x) - 15, \quad y = x^2 + 2x - 15.$$

To reflect the same equation about the x-axis, take the negative of y, so

$$-y = x^2 - 2x - 15 \implies y = -x^2 + 2x + 15.$$

1. What is the reflection of the point $(3, 5)$ about the x−axis? ③
   A. $(-3, -5)$
   B. $(-3, 5)$
   C. $(3, -5)$
   D. $(5, -3)$
   E. $(5, 3)$

2. What is the point $(3, 5)$ reflected about the y−axis? ③
   A. $(-3, -5)$
   B. $(-3, 5)$ *
   C. $(3, -5)$
   D. $(5, -3)$
   E. $(5, 3)$

3. Which of these is $y = x^2 + 3x + 2$ reflected about the y-axis? ④
   A. $y = -x^2 + 3x - 2$
   B. $y = -x^2 - 3x - 2$
   C. $y = x^2 - 3x + 5$
   D. $y = x^2 - 3x + 2$
   E. $y = x^2 - 3x + 12$

4. Which of these is $y = e^{x+3} + 4$ reflected about the y-axis? ④
   A. $y = e^{x+3} - 4$
   B. $y = e^{x-3} + 4$
   C. $y = -e^{3-x} - 4$
   D. $y = -e^{x+3} - 4$
   E. $y = e^{3-x} + 4$

5. Which of these is $y = x^3 + 3x^2 + 3x + 1$ reflected about the y-axis? ④

   A. $y = -x^3 + 3x^2 - 3x + 1$

   B. $y = -x^3 - 3x^2 - 3x + 1$

   C. $y = x^3 + 3x^2 - 3x + 1$

   D. $y = -x^3 - 3x^2 - 3x - 1$

   E. $y = x^3 + 3x^2 + 3x + 1$

6. Which of these is $y = x^2$ moved down 3 and left 5 and then reflected about the y-axis? ④

   A. $y = (x + 5)^2 - 3$

   B. $y = (x - 5)^2 - 3$

   C. $y = (x - 3)^2 - 5$

   D. $y = (x - 5)^2 - 8$

   E. $y = (x - 5)^2 - 1$

33.2. Translations

If the problem states shift left 3, substitute $x + 3$ for x, and when shifting right 3, substitute $x - 3$ for x. This works the same way for y: $y - a$ is up a if $a > 0$, etc.

7. If $y = \sqrt{x}$ is shifted left 5 and 12 down, what is the new equation? ③

   A. $y = \sqrt{x + 5} - 10$

   B. $y = \sqrt{x + 5} + 12$

   C. $y = \sqrt{x + 5} - 17$

   D. $y = \sqrt{x + 5} - 12$

   E. $y = \sqrt{x + 5} + 10$

8. What transformations of $y = x^3$ results in $y = (x - 3)^3 - 8$? ③

   A. 3 left and 8 down

   B. 3 right and 8 down

   C. 27 right and 8 down

   D. 27 left and 8 down

   E. 3 right and 8 up

9. Which of these is $y = x^2 + 5x + 6$ shifted up 4 and right 3? ④

   A. $y = x^2 + x + 4$

   B. $y = x^2 - 2x + 4$

   C. $y = x^2 - x + 4$

   D. $y = x^2 - 3x + 4$

   E. $y = x^2 - 5x + 4$

10. What equation is graphed here? ④

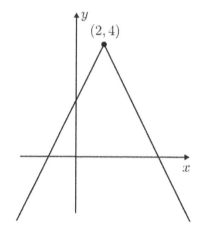

   A. $y = -|x - 2| - 4$

   B. $y = |x + 2| + 4$

   C. $y = -|x - 2| + 4$

   D. $y = -|x + 2| + 4$

   E. $y = |x - 2| + 4$

11. If the circle $(x - 3)^2 + (y + 4)^2 = 17$ is moved up 3 and right 5 and the radius is tripled, what is the equation of the new circle? ⑤

   A. $(x - 8)^2 + (y + 1)^2 = 153$

   B. $(x - 8)^2 + (y + 1)^2 = 51$

   C. $(x - 8)^2 + (y + 7)^2 = 459$

   D. $(x + 8)^2 + (y + 7)^2 = 153$

   E. $(x + 8)^2 + (y - 7)^2 = 153$

33.3. Rotations

Rotation problems have appeared in the exam. These require using the uncommon formulas presented here or reasoning what the formula should be. There are general formulas using trigonometry for say rotating 110°, and those might be helpful for some students to understand the concepts. but rotations like that have never appeared on the exam. The key formulas discussed here are for 90° rotations in either direction. Rotating 90° clockwise:

$$(a, b) \implies (b, -a),$$

rotating 90° counterclockwise:

$$(a, b) \implies (-b, a),$$

rotating 180°:

$$(a, b) \implies (-a, -b).$$

These are special cases of the trigonmetric formula $(x \cos \theta - y \sin \theta, x \sin \theta + y \cos \theta)$, where $\theta = 90°$ or $270°$, which causes one of sin or cos to be 0.

If you do not know the formulas, it is possible to reason what the rotations should be, perhaps by drawing a diagram on the question booklet. For most students, it is better to use reasoning rather than straight memorization of the formulas, but studying the formulas still helps.

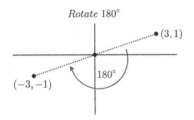

Rotate 180°

Rotate 90° clockwise

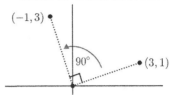

Rotate 90° counterclockwise

12. What are the coordinates of $(2, 5)$ after that point is rotated 180° about the origin? ④

   A. $(-2, 5)$

   B. $(2, -5)$

   C. $(5, 2)$

   D. $(-5, -2)$

   E. $(-2, -5)$

13. What are the coordinates of $(2, 5)$ after that point is rotated 90° clockwise about the origin? ⑤

   A. $(-2, 5)$

   B. $(2, -5)$

   C. $(5, 2)$

   D. $(5, -2)$

   E. $(-5, -2)$

14. What are the coordinates of $(2, 5)$ after that point is rotated 90° counterclockwise about the origin? ④

   A. $(-2, 5)$

   B. $(2, -5)$

   C. $(5, 2)$

   D. $(-5, -2)$

   E. $(-5, 2)$

1C, 2B 3D, 4E, 5A, 6B, 7D, 8B, 9C, 10C, 11A, 12E, 13D, 14E

33.4. Solutions

1. (C) Take the negative of the y–value, $(3, -5)$.

2. (B) Take the negative of the x–value $(-3, 5)$.

3. (D) Replacing x with $-x$ to reflect about the y-axis, $y = (-x)^2 + 3(-x) + 2 = y = x^2 - 3x + 2$.

4. (E) Replacing x with $-x$ to reflect about the y-axis, $e^{3-x} + 4$.

5. (A) Replacing x with $-x$ to reflect about the y-axis, $y = -x^3 + 3x^2 - 3x + 1$.

6. (B) $y + 3 = (x + 5)^2$, performing the shifts. To reflect about the y-axis, replace x with $-x$, $y + 3 = (5 - x)^2$; since the squared value is always positive, this is the same as $y = (x - 5)^2 - 3$.

7. (D) Shift left means add to x. Applying the translations, $y = \sqrt{x + 5} - 12$.

8. (B) 3 right and 8 down. Subtracting from the x term means shifting right.

9. (C) Perform the translations, then FOIL out and then simplify:

$$y - 4 = (x - 3)^2 + 5(x - 3) + 6, \quad y = x^2 - 6x + 9 + 5x - 15 + 6 + 4 = x^2 - x + 4.$$

10. (C) The graph of $y = |x|$ is flipped, so it must be negative; based on the graph, the vertex is at $(2, 4)$, so it is shifted 2 right and 4 up. Implementing the shifts, $y = -|x - 2| + 4$.

11. (A) Since the radius is tripled, r^2 is multiplied by 9, so $r^2 = 17 \cdot 9 = 153$. A longer approach is to say the radius is $\sqrt{17}$, so the tripled radius is $3\sqrt{17}$; $(3\sqrt{17})^2 = 9 \cdot 17 = 153$. Performing the shifts, $(x - 8)^2 + (y + 1)^2 = 153$.

12. (E) (a, b) maps to $(-a, -b)$, so the answer is $(-2, -5)$.

13. (D) (a, b) maps to $(b, -a)$, we get $(5, -2)$. If you do not know the formula, you can figure it out by drawing a sketch.

14. (E) (a, b) maps to $(-b, a)$, so the answer is $(-5, 2)$.

34. Asymptotes, Limits, and Pre-Differentiation

These are calculus related problems, but the exam does not go far in that direction and most of these can be reasoned without even the pre-calculus approach to these topics.

There may be fairly difficult asymptote problems on this exam, for example involving slant asymptotes. As is typical with advanced problems, the limits and differentiation problems tend to be basic.

34.1. Asymptotes

To find the horizontal asymptote of a rational function, set the denominator equal to 0 and solve for x. The reason for this is that when the denomination is equal to 0, the expression will be divided by 0, producing an asymptote.

To find vertical asymptotes of a rational function, set the denominator equal to 0 and then solve for x. To find horizontal asymptotes, if the degree of the numerator and denominator are the same, take the ratio of the coefficients of the highest order terms. If the degree of the denominator is greater than that of the numerator, the horizontal asymptote is $y = 0$. If the degree of the numerator is 1 greater than that of the denominator, there is a slant asymptote, which is a line that can be obtained by dividing the numerator by the denominator. Ideally, you should know how to do simple polynomial division to find the slant asymptotes.

1. What are the vertical and horizontal asymptotes of $y = \dfrac{5x^2 + 2}{4x^2 - 9}$? ④

   A. $y = \dfrac{5}{4}, x = \dfrac{3}{2}, x = \dfrac{-3}{2}$

   B. $y = \dfrac{5}{2}, x = \dfrac{3}{2}, x = \dfrac{-3}{2}$

   C. $y = \dfrac{5}{8}, x = \dfrac{3}{2}, x = \dfrac{-3}{2}$

   D. $y = \dfrac{5}{2}, x = \dfrac{3}{2}$

   E. $y = \dfrac{5}{4}, x = \dfrac{3}{2}$

2. Which of these is the slant asymptote of $y = \dfrac{3x^2 + 2x + 7}{x + 4}$? ④

   A. $y = 3x - 6$

   B. $y = 3x - 8$

   C. $y = 3x - 10$

   D. $y = 4x - 10$

   E. $y = 4x - 6$

3. Which of these is the intersection point of the asymptotes of $y = \dfrac{x^2}{x + 2}$? ④

   A. $(-2, -1)$

   B. $(-2, -2)$

   C. $(-2, -3)$

   D. $(-2, -4)$

   E. $(-2, -5)$

4. Which of these is the intersection point of the asymptotes of $y = \dfrac{51x + 52}{53x + 54}$? ④

A. $\left(\dfrac{54}{53}, \dfrac{51}{53}\right)$

B. $\left(\dfrac{54}{53}, \dfrac{51}{54}\right)$

C. $\left(\dfrac{-54}{53}, \dfrac{26}{27}\right)$

D. $\left(\dfrac{-54}{53}, 1\right)$

E. $\left(\dfrac{-54}{53}, \dfrac{51}{53}\right)$

5. Which of these is the intersection point of the asymptotes of $y = \dfrac{3x^3 + 2x^2 + x + 4}{(2x + 5)(x^2 + 3)}$? ④

A. $\left(\dfrac{-5}{2}, \dfrac{5}{2}\right)$

B. $\left(\dfrac{5}{2}, \dfrac{3}{2}\right)$

C. $\left(\dfrac{-5}{2}, \dfrac{3}{2}\right)$

D. $\left(\dfrac{2}{5}, \dfrac{3}{2}\right)$

E. $\left(\dfrac{5}{2}, \dfrac{-3}{2}\right)$

6. Which of these is the intersection point of the asymptotes of $y = \dfrac{ax + b}{cx + d}$, where $a \neq 0$, $c \neq 0$? ④

A. $\left(\dfrac{-d}{c}, \dfrac{a}{c}\right)$

B. $\left(\dfrac{d}{c}, \dfrac{a}{c}\right)$

C. $\left(\dfrac{-d}{c}, \dfrac{a}{b}\right)$

D. $\left(\dfrac{-d}{c}, \dfrac{c}{d}\right)$

E. $\left(\dfrac{-d}{c}, \dfrac{b}{c}\right)$

34.2. Limits

This exam contains a small amount of material about limits. You do not need to know the calculus or even precalculus version of limits. The questions will probably be phrased "as x increases without bound", and will not use formal limit notation. The limit of a rational function as x approaches ∞ is ∞ or $-\infty$ if the degree of the numerator is greater than the degree of the denominator. If the degrees of the numerator and denominator are the same, the limit as x goes to ∞ is the ratio of the coefficients of the highest order terms. If the degree of the denominator is greater than that of the numerator, the limit as x goes to ∞ is 0. The degree of the numerator or denominator means the degree of the highest order term.

7. As x increases without bound, $\dfrac{3x + 2}{5x^2 - 2}$ approaches what value? ③

A. 1

B. 0

C. $\dfrac{2}{5}$

D. $\dfrac{3}{5}$

E. $\dfrac{\sqrt{10}}{5}$

8. As x increases without bound, $\dfrac{3x + 2}{5x - 2}$ approaches what value? ④

A. 1

B. 0

C. 3

D. $\dfrac{3}{5}$

E. $\dfrac{2}{5}$

34.3. Preparation for Differentiation

The exam probably will ask for $f(x+h)-f(x)$ (an initial step in finding the derivative from the definition of the derivative), and maybe just $f(x+h)$, not the full limit from calculus.

Generally, FOIL out the expression with $x+a$ or similar and then subtract the original polynomial. This is the first step in finding the derivative using the definition of derivative

9. Which of these is $(x+a)^3 - x^3$? ④
    A. $x^2a + xa^2 + a^3$
    B. $x^3 + 3x^2a + 3xa^2 + a^3$
    C. $3x^2a + 3xa^2 + a^3$
    D. $3x^2 + 3xa + a^2$
    E. $3x^2$

10. If $f(x) = x^2 + 3x + 2$, what is $f(x+h) - f(x)$? ④
    A. $2x + 3$
    B. $2x + h + 3$
    C. $2hx + h^2 + 5h$
    D. $2hx + 2h^2 + 3h$
    E. $2hx + h^2 + 3h$

11. If $f(x) = \dfrac{1}{x}$, what is $f(x+h) - f(x)$? ④
    A. $\dfrac{1}{x^2}$
    B. $\dfrac{-h}{(x+h)x}$
    C. $\dfrac{h}{(x+h)x}$
    D. $\dfrac{-1}{(x+h)x}$
    E. $\dfrac{2h}{(x+h)x}$

① Easiest

⑤ Most Difficult

— **ANSWER KEY**

1A, 2C, 3D, 4E, 5C, 6A, 7B, 8D, 9C, 10E, 11B

34.4. Solutions

1. (A) Dividing the highest order terms for the horizontal asymptote, setting the denominator equal to 0, and solving for the vertical asymptote,

$$y = \frac{5x^2}{4x^2} = \frac{5}{4}, \quad 4x^2 - 9 = 0, \quad x^2 = \frac{9}{4}, \quad x = \pm\frac{3}{2}.$$

2. (C) The slant asymptote is the quotient resulting from polynomial division.

$$
\begin{array}{r}
3x - 10 \\
x+4 \overline{\smash{\big)}\ 3x^2 + 2x\ \ + 7} \\
\underline{3x^2 + 12x} \\
0 \ -10x + 7 \\
\underline{-10x - 40} \\
0 \ +47
\end{array}
$$

Then, the dividend is $3x^2 + 2x + 7$, the divisor is $x + 4$, the quotient is $3x - 10$ and the remainder is 47. The slant asymptote is the quotient $3x - 10$. The remainder is ignored when finding the slant asymptote.

3. (D) First, perform long division (or synthetic division) to find the slant asymptote, since the degree of the numerator is one greater than the degree of the denominator.

$$
\begin{array}{r}
x - 2 \\
x+2 \overline{\smash{\big)}\ x^2} \\
\underline{x^2 + 2x} \\
0 \ -2x \\
\underline{-2x - 4} \\
0 \ +4
\end{array}
$$

We need the intersection points of $y = x - 2$ and $x = -2$. Substitute -2 for x in $y = x - 2$, $y = -2 - 2$, $y = -4$, so the intersection point is $(-2, -4)$.

4. (E) Dividing the highest order terms to find the horizontal asymptote and setting the denominator equal to 0 and solving to find the vertical asymptote,

$$y = \frac{51}{53}, \quad 53x + 54 = 0, \quad x = \frac{-54}{53}.$$

5. (C) The horizontal asymptote is the ratio of highest order terms, $y = \frac{3}{2}$; the vertical asymptote occurs when the denominator is 0, $2x + 5 = 0$, $x = \frac{-5}{2}$. There is no real value which makes $x^2 + 3 = 0$, so we ignore that term.

6. (A) To find the horizontal asymptote, take the ratio of highest order terms $= \dfrac{a}{c}$; to find the vertical aymptote, set the denominator $= 0$, $cx + d = 0$, $x = \dfrac{-d}{c}$. Since the asymptotes are vertical and horizontal lines, the intersection point is easy to find once we have the lines.

7. (B) If the denominator is of greater degree than the numerator, the limit approaches 0. You can show this by dividing everything by x^2 or by using L'Hôpital's rule (although calculus is not covered on the exam).

8. (D) Take the ratio of the highest order terms. You can also divide everything by x and get $\dfrac{3 + \dfrac{2}{x}}{5 - \dfrac{2}{x}}$.

As x goes to infinity, this becomes $\dfrac{3}{5}$.

Although calculus is not covered on the exam, you could also use L'Hôpital's rule, taking the derivative of the numerator and denominator and you will then also get $\dfrac{3}{5}$.

You can also graph the expression using a calculator and see what y approaches as x becomes large, or substitute in a large value for x and finding the corresponding y value.

9. (C) $x^3 + 3x^2a + 3xa^2 + a^3 - x^3 = 3x^2a + 3xa^2 + a^3$.

10. (E) $f(x+h) - f(x) = (x+h)^2 + 3(x+h) + 2 - (x^2 + 3x + 2) = x^2 + 2hx + h^2 + 3x + 3h + 2 - x^2 - 3x - 2 = 2hx + h^2 + 3h$.

11. (B) $f(x+h) - f(x) = \dfrac{1}{x+h} - \dfrac{1}{x} = \dfrac{x - x - h}{(x+h)x} = \dfrac{-h}{(x+h)x}$.

35. Other Advanced Topics

35.1. Domain

There are certain things that cause restrictions on the domain, and these are the keys to solving ACT domain problems. You cannot divide by 0, cannot take the square root of a negative number and cannot take the log of a negative number or 0. To find the domain of a problem involving a square root, set what is under the square root ≥ 0 and then solve. For a log, including $\ln$, $\log_2$, etc., set what you are taking the log of > 0. For fractional expressions, set what is in the denominator equal to 0 and the solutions are NOT in the domain.

1. Which of these is the domain of $\dfrac{\sqrt{2-3x}}{\sqrt{x+4}}$? ④

   A. $\left(-4, \dfrac{-2}{3}\right)$

   B. $\left[-4, \dfrac{2}{3}\right]$

   C. $\left(-4, \dfrac{2}{3}\right]$

   D. $\left(-4, \dfrac{3}{2}\right)$

   E. $\left(-4, \dfrac{2}{3}\right)$

2. Which of these is the domain of $y = \sqrt{25 - x^2}$? ④

   A. $(-\infty, -5] \cup [5, \infty)$

   B. $(-\infty, -10] \cup [10, \infty)$

   C. $(-\infty, -25] \cup [25, \infty)$

   D. $(-5, 5)$

   E. $[-5, 5]$

3. Which of these is all the real numbers NOT in the domain of $f(x) = \dfrac{1}{|2x+3|}$? ④

   A. $\left\{\dfrac{-3}{2}\right\}$

   B. $\left\{\dfrac{-3}{2}, \dfrac{3}{2}\right\}$

   C. $\left\{\dfrac{-3}{2}, \dfrac{1}{2}\right\}$

   D. $\left\{\dfrac{-3}{2}, 0, \dfrac{3}{2}\right\}$

   E. $\left\{\dfrac{3}{2}\right\}$

287

4. Which of these is all the real numbers NOT in the domain of $f(x) = \dfrac{17}{|3x+4|-2}$? ④

   A. $\left\{\dfrac{-8}{3}, -2\right\}$

   B. $\left\{\dfrac{-2}{3}, -4\right\}$

   C. $\left\{\dfrac{2}{3}, -2\right\}$

   D. $\left\{\dfrac{-4}{3}, -2\right\}$

   E. $\left\{\dfrac{-2}{3}, -2\right\}$

5. Which of these is the domain of $f(x) = \sqrt{x+5} + \sqrt{3-x}$? ④
   A. $[-5, \infty)$
   B. $(-5, 3]$
   C. $[5, 5]$
   D. $(-5, 3)$
   E. $[-5, 3]$

6. If a and b are real, what value(s) are all the real numbers NOT in the domain of $y = \dfrac{x+a}{x-b^2}$? ④
   A. $\{b\}$
   B. $\{b, -b, -a\}$
   C. $\{b, -b\}$
   D. $\{-b, 0\}$
   E. $\{-a, -b\}$

7. Which of these is the domain of $\log(x^2 + 2x - 15)$? ④
   A. $-3 < x < 5$
   B. $x \le -3$ or $x \ge 5$
   C. $x < -3$ or $x > 5$
   D. $-3 \le x \le 5$
   E. $x < -5$ or $x > 3$

8. Assuming that a, b, and c are real, for what values is $\dfrac{(x+a)(x^2-b)}{x^2-c}$ undefined?
   A. $\pm\sqrt{c}$ and $-a$
   B. $\pm\sqrt{c}$ and $\pm\sqrt{b}$ and $-a$
   C. $\sqrt{c}$
   D. $\pm\sqrt{c}$
   E. It is defined everywhere

9. If $f(x) = \dfrac{x+3}{(x+1)(x+6)}$, what are the real numbers NOT in the domain of $f(x-4)$? ④
   A. -1 and -6
   B. $-3, -1$ and -6
   C. 1 and 6
   D. -2 and 3
   E. 2 and -3

10. Which of these is the domain of $\sqrt{(x-5)^7}$ ④?
    A. $[5, \infty)$
    B. $[125, \infty)$
    C. $(5, \infty)$
    D. $(-\infty, 5]$
    E. $[25, \infty)$

11. Which of these is the domain of $\sqrt{x^3 - 8}$? ④
    A. $(-\infty, \infty)$
    B. $(2, \infty)$
    C. $[2, 4]$
    D. $[2, \infty)$
    E. $(-\infty, -2] \cup [2, \infty)$

35.2. Matrices

A common type of problem asks which matrices can be multiplied by which other matrices. The number of columns in the first matrix must be equal of the number of rows in the second one so that the matrices will match when you turn the rows in the first one on their sides. There are also problems for which you need to multiply the correct way to determine if the result is a 1×1 or a 3×3 matrix

It is important that you understand the concepts involved in matrix multiplication. It would be too lengthy to teach it here, but if you do not know matrix multiplication, you should study and practice it.

It is important to know how to find the determinant of a 2×2 matrix as follows:

$$\begin{vmatrix} a & b \\ c & d \end{vmatrix} = ad - bc.$$

12. What is the matrix product $\begin{bmatrix} 1 & 2 \\ 3 & 4 \end{bmatrix} \cdot \begin{bmatrix} a \\ b \end{bmatrix}$? ③

  A. $\begin{bmatrix} a + 2b \\ 3 + 4b \end{bmatrix}$

  B. $\begin{bmatrix} 1 + 2b \\ 3 + 4b \end{bmatrix}$

  C. $\begin{bmatrix} a + 2b \\ 3a + 4b \end{bmatrix}$

  D. $\begin{bmatrix} a + 3b & 2a + 4b \end{bmatrix}$

  E. $\begin{bmatrix} 1 & 2b \\ 3a & 4b \end{bmatrix}$

13. If $\begin{vmatrix} a & 2 \\ b & 5 \end{vmatrix} = 4$ and $a = 2b$, what is a? ④

  A. 0
  B. 1
  C. 2
  D. 3
  E. 4

14. What is the matrix product $\begin{bmatrix} 1 \end{bmatrix} \cdot \begin{bmatrix} 4 & 5 & 6 \end{bmatrix}$? ④

  A. $\begin{bmatrix} 4 & 5 & 6 \\ 8 & 10 & 12 \\ 12 & 15 & 18 \end{bmatrix}$

  B. $\begin{bmatrix} 15 \end{bmatrix}$

  C. It is not possible to multiply these.

  D. $\begin{bmatrix} 4 \\ 5 \\ 6 \end{bmatrix}$

  E. $\begin{bmatrix} 4 & 5 & 6 \end{bmatrix}$

15. What is the matrix product $\begin{bmatrix} 1 & 2 & 3 \end{bmatrix} \cdot \begin{bmatrix} 4 \\ 5 \\ 6 \end{bmatrix}$? ④

  A. $\begin{bmatrix} 4 \\ 10 \\ 18 \end{bmatrix}$

  B. $\begin{bmatrix} 12 \end{bmatrix}$

  C. $\begin{bmatrix} 4 & 10 & 18 \end{bmatrix}$

  D. $\begin{bmatrix} 32 \end{bmatrix}$

  E. $\begin{bmatrix} 4 & 5 & 6 \\ 8 & 10 & 12 \\ 2 & 15 & 18 \end{bmatrix}$

16. If $\begin{vmatrix} x & 3 \\ x & x \end{vmatrix} = 10$, what are the possible values of x? ④

  A. 2
  B. 2 or 5
  C. 2 or -3
  D. 2 or -6
  E. -2 or 5

17. What is the matrix product $\begin{bmatrix} 1 & 2 \\ 3 & 4 \end{bmatrix} \cdot \begin{bmatrix} 4 & 2 \\ a & b \end{bmatrix}$?

④

A. $\begin{bmatrix} 4+a & 4+2b \\ 12+3a & 8+4b \end{bmatrix}$

B. $\begin{bmatrix} 4+2a & 2+2b \\ 12+4a & 6+4b \end{bmatrix}$

C. $\begin{bmatrix} 4+2a & 2+2b \end{bmatrix}$

D. $\begin{bmatrix} 4+2a \\ 12+4a \end{bmatrix}$

E. $\begin{bmatrix} 10+5a & 6+3b \\ 28+7a & 20+5b \end{bmatrix}$

35.3. Solving for a Constant

In most of the problems, you just need to find the constant, and not find other values of the equation, but this book emphasizes problems in the most difficult form they may be given. For example, $f(x) = ax^3 - 3$ and $f(3) = 5$. What is $f(4)$?

Substitute in the x and y-values and then solve for a. $5 = a \cdot 3^3 - 3$ (cubing)

$$5 = 27a - 3 \implies a = \frac{8}{27}.$$

(now substitute the a value into the equation)

$$f(x) = \frac{8x^3}{27} - 3;$$

(finally, substitute in 4 for x)

$$f(4) = \frac{8 \cdot 4^3}{27} - 3 = \frac{512}{27} - 3 = \frac{431}{27}.$$

18. If the graph of $f(x) = ax + 7$ goes through $(4, 8)$, what is $f(1)$? ③

A. 7

B. $\dfrac{15}{2}$

C. $\dfrac{29}{4}$

D. 6

E. 8

19. If the point $(4, 1000)$ is on the graph of $y = ax^2$, what is a? ④

A. 62.5

B. 64

C. 64.5

D. 66

E. 70.5

20. If $f(x) = x^2 - 3x + a$ passes through the point $(5, 7)$, what is $f(8)$? ④

A. 33

B. 34

C. 35

D. 36

E. 37

21. If the point $\left(5, \dfrac{4}{7}\right)$ is on the graph of $f(x) = \dfrac{x}{x+a}$, what is $f(8)$? ④

A. $\dfrac{3}{4}$

B. $\dfrac{32}{47}$

C. $\dfrac{9}{13}$

D. $\dfrac{8}{11}$

E. $\dfrac{4}{5}$

35.4. Mixture

The basic difficult mixture problem might state that there are 10 liters of 10% acid solution. How much 90% acid solution would you need to add to make a mixture that is 25% acid. Set the total acid over the total liquid equal to the new percentage. Applying that method,

$$\frac{10 \cdot 0.1 + 0.9x}{10 + x} = 0.25 \implies$$
$$1 + 0.9x = 2.5 + 0.25x$$
$$\implies 0.65x = 1.5, \quad x \approx 2.31.$$

Easier mixture problems may appear on the exam, and those are also covered in the exercises.

22. 10 liters of 20% acid solution are mixed with 15 liters of pure acid. What is the percentage acid of the resulting mixture? ③

  A. 68
  B. 70
  C. 72
  D. 74
  E. 76

23. A 120 liter solution that is 5% salt is mixed with an 80 liter solution that is x% salt. The combined solution is 10% salt. What is the value of x? ④

  A. 16
  B. 17.5
  C. 18.75
  D. 20
  E. 22

24. The Tigers have won 12 games and lost 8. How many straight games do the Tigers need to win to increase their winning percentage to 80%? ④

  A. 18
  B. 20
  C. 21
  D. 22
  E. 24

25. How many liters of an 80% salt solution would you need to add to 3 liters of 10% salt solution to obtain a 30% salt solution? ⑤

  A. 1
  B. 1.2
  C. 1.5
  D. 1.8
  E. 2.4

35.5. Inequalities

For what range of values is $\frac{x+3}{x+1} > 0$? To find the critical points, solve $x + 3 = 0$ and $x + 1 = 0$ (subtracting to solve) $x = -3$ and $x = -1$. We can use $-4, -2$, and 0 as test points in each interval. -4 and 0 yield a positive result, but -2 does not. Therefore, the solution is $(-\infty, -3) \cup (-1, \infty)$. This particular problem can be solved more easily by graphing with your calculator.

26. Which of these inequalities represent the shaded region? (4)

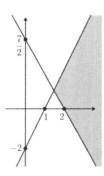

A. $y \leq 2x - 2$ and $y \leq \dfrac{-7x}{4} + \dfrac{7}{2}$

B. $y \geq 2x - 2$ and $y \geq \dfrac{-7x}{4} + \dfrac{7}{2}$

C. $y \leq 2x - 2$ and $y \geq \dfrac{-7x}{4} + \dfrac{7}{2}$

D. $y \leq 2x - 2$ and $y \geq \dfrac{-5x}{4} + \dfrac{7}{2}$

E. $y \geq 2x - 2$ and $y \leq \dfrac{-7x}{4} + \dfrac{7}{2}$

27. Which of these inequalities represent the shaded region? (4)

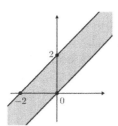

A. $y \geq x$ and $y \leq x - 2$
B. $y \geq x - 2$ and $y \leq x + 2$
C. $y \geq x$ and $y \leq x + 2$
D. $y \leq x$ and $y \leq x + 2$
E. $y \geq x$ and $y \geq x + 2$

28. Which of these is the range of x-values for which $x^2 > 4x$? (4)
A. $x > 0$ and $x < 4$
B. $x \leq 0$ or $x > 4$
C. $x < 0$ or $x > 4$
D. $x \leq 0$ or $x \geq 4$
E. $x > 4$

29. For what values of x is $x^2 + 3x \geq 10$? (4)
A. $(-\infty, -5] \cup [2, \infty)$
B. $(-\infty, -5) \cup (2, \infty)$
C. $[-5, 2]$
D. $(-\infty, -5]$
E. $[2, \infty)$

35.6. Finding Area

Area Bounded By

Determine the triangle, trapezoid, etc. that makes up the described region and then use area formulas.

30. Which of these is the area of the region in the first quadrant bounded by $y = \dfrac{-5x}{4} + 6$ and the x and y-axes? (5)
A. 15
B. $\dfrac{31}{2}$
C. $\dfrac{29}{2}$
D. 14
E. $\dfrac{72}{5}$

31. Which of these is the area bounded by the x and y-axes and the lines $y = \dfrac{x}{2} + 2$ and $x = 6$? (5)
A. 18
B. 19
C. 20
D. 21
E. 22

Shaded Area

Find the shaded area divided by the total area. Often you will need to find areas of triangles, as in these problems.

Sometimes it is easier to find the area not shaded and subtract that from the whole.

32. What fraction of square $ABCD$ is shaded? ④

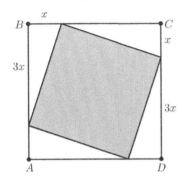

A. $\dfrac{5}{8}$

B. $\dfrac{5}{9}$

C. $\dfrac{4}{7}$

D. $\dfrac{1}{2}$

E. $\dfrac{2}{3}$

33. What fraction of the entire figure is shaded? ④

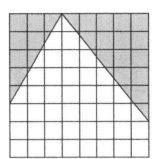

A. $\dfrac{3}{8}$

B. $\dfrac{23}{64}$

C. $\dfrac{5}{16}$

D. $\dfrac{21}{64}$

E. $\dfrac{45}{128}$

35.7. Circle Theorems

The following diagrams show the main circle theorems which are likely to appear on the test. Usually, a diagram like one of these showing the relevant theorem will be given, but it is best to know them. The diagram on the right, showing the inscribed angle theorem, should be understood and/or memorized.

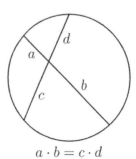

$$a \cdot b = c \cdot d$$

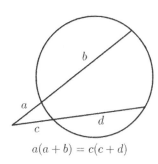

$$a(a + b) = c(c + d)$$

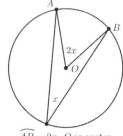

$\overset{\frown}{AB} = 2x$, O is center.

34. If the diameter of the circle is 24, what is the length of the minor arc $\overset{\frown}{AB}$? ④

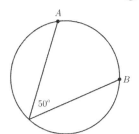

A. 7π

B. $\dfrac{10\pi}{3}$

C. 6π

D. $\dfrac{13\pi}{2}$

E. $\dfrac{20\pi}{3}$

35. If the radius of the circle is 8, what is the length of the major arc $\overset{\frown}{ACB}$? ④

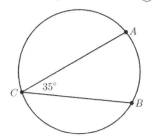

A. 39.5

B. 40.5

C. 41.5

D. 42.5

E. 43.5

36. What is x? ⑤

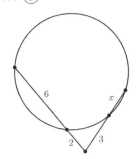

A. $\dfrac{11}{5}$

B. 2

C. $\dfrac{5}{2}$

D. $\dfrac{7}{3}$

E. $\dfrac{8}{3}$

37. Which of these is closest to x? ④

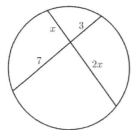

A. 2.8

B. 3.0

C. 3.2

D. 3.4

E. 3.6

38. Assuming that O is the center of the circle, what is the measure of $\angle ACO$ in degrees? ⑤

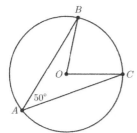

A. 20°

B. 25°

C. 30°

D. 35°

E. 40°

35.8. Equations and Values

For example, if $2^x = a$, what is an expression for 8^{x+2} in terms of a? $8^x = (2^x)^3$ (substituting a for 2^x) $= a^3$, $8^2 = 64$, so

$$8^{x+2} = 8^x 8^2 = 64a^3.$$

A common problem on the exam asks for $f(-3)$ or f() some other negative number. This is a trap, because you can get the wrong answer computing something like $f(x) = x^2$ with a calculator, which could give you -9 rather than 9 if you do not use parentheses correctly. It is generally best

to do calculations like that by hand rather than with a calculator.

39. If $a = b^2$, to what is ab equal in terms of b? ④

A. $8b^4$

B. $2b^2$

C. b^2

D. b^3

E. b^4

40. If $3^{x+3} = a$, what does 3^x equal? ④

A. $\dfrac{a}{27}$

B. $\dfrac{a}{9}$

C. $\dfrac{a}{81}$

D. $\dfrac{a^2}{27}$

E. $\dfrac{a^2}{9}$

41. If $2^{x-1} = b$, what is an expression for 2^{x+4} in terms of b? ④

A. $16b$

B. $8b$

C. $32b$

D. $16b^2$

E. $8b^4$

42. If $(x-2)^3 = 10$, what is x to the nearest tenth? ④

A. 4.1

B. 4.2

C. 4.3

D. 4.4

E. 4.5

43. Which of these is the value of $f(-4)$ if $f(x) = \dfrac{x^2 + 3x + 2}{x^2 - 2x - 15}$? ③

    A. $\dfrac{2}{3}$

    B. $\dfrac{8}{5}$

    C. $\dfrac{7}{5}$

    D. $\dfrac{6}{5}$

    E. $\dfrac{4}{5}$

35.9. Range of Values for Variables

You need to determine what maximizes or minimizes the expression. In order to do that, examine the end points of the inequalities.

44. If $3 \le x \le 8$ and $10 \le y \le 20$, what is the largest value of $\dfrac{x + y}{y}$? ⑤

    A. $\dfrac{7}{5}$

    B. $\dfrac{8}{5}$

    C. $\dfrac{9}{5}$

    D. $\dfrac{11}{5}$

    E. $\dfrac{12}{5}$

45. If $3x + 5y = 20$ and $x \le 4$, what is the range of values for y? ⑤

    A. $y \ge \dfrac{8}{5}$

    B. $y \ge \dfrac{9}{5}$

    C. $y \ge \dfrac{7}{5}$

    D. $y \ge \dfrac{6}{5}$

    E. $y \ge \dfrac{4}{5}$

46. If $-3 \le x \le 2$ and $-4 < y < 7$, what is the maximum value of $|y - 3x|$? ④

    A. 5

    B. 10

    C. 14

    D. 16

    E. 20

47. If $-3 \le x \le 2$ and $-4 < y < 7$, what is the maximum value of $|y - 5x|$? ⑤

    A. 11

    B. 14

    C. 21

    D. 22

    E. 27

35.10. Variation

These problems are solved by finding the constant k in an equation like $y = kx$. For direct variation, use $y = kx$, for varying as the square $y = kx^2$, for inverse variation, $y = k/x$, for varying inversely as the square $y = k/x^2$, and so on.

For example, y is directly proportional to x and $y = 8$ when $x = 3$. What does y equal when x is 4?

$y = kx$ (substituting in the values for x and y)

$$8 = k \cdot 3 \implies k = \frac{8}{3}$$

(substituting in the k-value) $y = \dfrac{8x}{3}$

(substituting in the given x-value) $y = \dfrac{32}{3}$.

Another example is y is directly proportional to the cube of x and $y = 8$ when $x = 3$. What does y equal when x is 4?

$y = kx^3$ (substituting in x and y-values

to find k) $8 = k \cdot 3^3 \implies k = \dfrac{8}{27}$

(substituting the k-value in) $y = \dfrac{8x^3}{27}$

(substituting the given x-value in)

$$y = 8 \cdot \dfrac{64}{27} = \dfrac{512}{27}.$$

48. If y is directly proportional to x and $y = 5$ when $x = 2$, what does y equal when $x = 5$? ④

  A. 10
  B. 12
  C. 12.5
  D. 15
  E. 17.5

49. Suppose y varies inversely as x. When $x = 2$, $y = 5$. What does y equal when $x = 5$? ④

  A. 1.5
  B. 1.7
  C. 1.8
  D. 2
  E. 2.5

50. Suppose y varies directly as the square of x. When $x = 2$, $y = 5$. what does y equal when $x = 5$? ④

  A. 30.25
  B. 31.25
  C. 34.25
  D. 32.25
  E. 33.25

51. Suppose y is inversely proportional to the square of x. If $y = 5$ when $x = 2$, what does y equal when x is 5? ④

  A. $\dfrac{3}{125}$

  B. $\dfrac{6}{125}$

  C. $\dfrac{4}{5}$

  D. $\dfrac{4}{25}$

  E. $\dfrac{1}{25}$

52. Which of these is an equation in which y varies directly with the square of x, inversely with the square root of v and inversely with the cube of w? ③

  A. $y = k\dfrac{x^2 w^3}{\sqrt{v}}$

  B. $y = k\dfrac{x^2}{v w^3}$

  C. $y = k\dfrac{x^2}{\sqrt{v} w^2}$

  D. $y = k\dfrac{x^2}{\sqrt{v} w^3}$

  E. $y = k\dfrac{x^2}{\sqrt{v^3} w^3}$

35.11. Other Problems

If you switch the order of a logical statement and take the negative of both, the new statement is called the contrapositive and has the same truth value as the orginal. For example, the contrapositive of all poodles are dogs is if it is not a dog, it is not a poodle. They could also ask about the converse, which is just switching the two conditions. The inverse or negation involves just taking the negative of both conditions.

53. If $x^3 = 300$ and x is real, then x is between which of the following integers? ③

A. 4 and 5

B. 5 and 6

C. 6 and 7

D. 7 and 8

E. 8 and 9

54. What is the sum of the y-intercepts of the functions $f(x) = (x+3)(x-5)$ and $g(x) = 2^x + 4$? ③

A. -20

B. -15

C. -10

D. 5

E. 10

55. If $a = b + \dfrac{2}{3}$, what does $(a-b)^5$ equal? ④

A. $\dfrac{8}{27}$

B. $\dfrac{32}{243}$

C. $\dfrac{-32}{243}$

D. $\dfrac{32}{81}$

E. $\dfrac{64}{243}$

56. If $(x+y)^2 = 20$ and $xy = 3$, what does $(x-y)^2$ equal? ④

A. 4

B. 5

C. 6

D. 8

E. 12

57. If $x = 3t + 5$, $y = 2t - 3$, what is y in terms of x? ④

A. $y = \dfrac{2x}{3} - \dfrac{10}{3}$

B. $y = \dfrac{2x}{3} - \dfrac{11}{3}$

C. $y = \dfrac{2x}{3} - \dfrac{13}{3}$

D. $y = \dfrac{2x}{3} - \dfrac{19}{3}$

E. $y = \dfrac{2x}{3} - \dfrac{16}{3}$

58. Which of these is logically equivalent to "All tables are flat"? ④

A. "If it's not flat, it's a table"

B. "If it's not a table, it's not flat"

C. "If it's flat, it's a table"

D. "If it's not flat, it isn't a table"

E. "If it's a table, it might be flat"

59. If $a > 0$ and $b > 0$, what does $3 \cdot (a^0 + b^0)^4$ equal? ④

A. 96

B. 64

C. 48

D. 54

E. 192

60. Simplify $\dfrac{300x^7 + 108x^5}{12x^3}$. ③

A. $25x^4 + 12x^2$

B. $25x^4 + 6x^2$

C. $25x^4 + 16x^2$

D. $25x^4 + 9x^2$

E. $25x^4 + 18x^2$

1C, 2E, 3A, 4E, 5E, 6C, 7E, 8D, 9D, 10A, 11D, 12C, 13B, 14E, 15D, 16E, 17B, 18C 19A, 20E, 21B, 22A, 23B, 24B, 25B, 26C, 27C, 28C, 29A, 30E, 31D, 32A, 33E, 34E, 35B, 36D, 37C, 38B, 39D, 40A, 41C, 42B, 43A, 44C, 45A, 46D, 47D, 48C, 49D, 50B, 51C, 52D, 53C 54B 55B, 56D, 57D, 58D, 59C, 60D

35.12. Solutions

1. (C) Set up inequalities for both terms under the square roots,

$$2 - 3x \geq 0 \implies \frac{2}{3} \geq x \text{ and } x + 4 > 0 \implies x \geq -4 \text{ (in interval notation) } \left(-4, \frac{2}{3}\right].$$

Note that the second inequality is a > rather than ≥ condition in the denominator because you cannot divide by 0.

2. (E) Setting what is under the radical equal to 0, $25 - x^2 = 0 \implies x = \pm 5$. That expression is nonnegative for $x \geq -5$ or $x \leq 5$.

3. (A) $|2x + 3| = 0$ (splitting into two equations) $2x + 3 = 0$ or $-2x - 3 = 0$ (since both equations are essentially the same) $x = \frac{-3}{2}$ (Note there is only one solution).

4. (E) Setting the denominator equal to 0 and splitting into two cases based on the absolute value,

$$3x + 4 - 2 = 0 \text{ and } -3x - 4 - 2 = 0, \text{ so } 3x = -2 \implies x = \frac{-2}{3} \text{ and } 3x = -6 \implies x = -2.$$

5. (E) What is under each square root must be ≥ 0: $x + 5 \geq 0 \implies x \geq -5$ and $3 - x \geq 0 \implies 3 \geq x$, so the domain is $[-5, 3]$.

6. (C) Set the denominator equal to 0, and then solve for x:

$$x - b^2 = 0 \implies x = b^2 \implies x = \pm b.$$

7. (E) The expression we are taking a log of must be greater than 0. Factor that expression, and then solve the inequality. $x^2 + 2x - 15 > 0$ (factoring) $(x + 5)(x - 3) > 0$ (by checking intervals) $x < -5$ or $x > 3$. You could also graph the inequality and see for what intervals it is greater than zero.

8. (D) Set the denominator equal to 0, then take the square root, resulting in two solutions.

$$x^2 - c = 0 \implies x = \pm\sqrt{c}.$$

9. (D) We need to shift and then take the values in the denominator minus 4.

$$f(x - 4) = \frac{x - 1}{(x - 3)(x + 2)} \implies x - 3 \neq 0 \text{ and } x + 2 \neq 0 \implies x \neq 3 \text{ or } -2.$$

Therefore, in interval notation, the domain is $(-\infty, -2) \cup (-2, 3) \cup (3, \infty)$.

10. (A) Since $x - 5$ is taken to an odd power, for the purpose of finding the domain, this is the same as $\sqrt{x - 5}$. $x - 5 \geq 0 \implies x \geq 5$.

11. (D) Set what is under the square root ≥ 0. $x^3 - 8 \geq 0 \implies x^3 \geq 8$ (taking the cube root) $x \geq 2$.

12. (C) By matrix multiplication, $\begin{bmatrix} a + 2b \\ 3a + 4b \end{bmatrix}$.

13. (B) Take the determinant which results in two equations in two variables, and then solve that resulting system. Those equations are

$$5a - 2b = 4 \text{ and } a = 2b \text{ (substituting) } 5 \cdot 2b - 2b = 4$$

$$\implies 8b = 4 \implies b = \frac{1}{2}, \text{ since } a = 2b, \quad a = 1.$$

14. (E) These are each 1-element multiplications, 91×1 element multiplications.

15. (D) This results in a 1-element matrix and is sort of like vector multiplication. When you turn the first element on its side, there is only one multiplication. $[1 \cdot 4 + 2 \cdot 5 + 3 \cdot 6] = [32]$.

16. (E) Using the determinant formula, $x^2 - 3x = 10 \implies x^2 - 3x - 10 = 0$ (by factoring and solving or the quadratic formula) $x = -2$ or 5.

17. (B) By matrix multiplication,

$$\begin{bmatrix} 1 \cdot 4 + 2 \cdot a & 1 \cdot 2 + 2 \cdot b \\ 3 \cdot 4 + 4 \cdot a & 3 \cdot 2 + 4 \cdot b \end{bmatrix} = \begin{bmatrix} 4 + 2a & 2 + 2b \\ 12 + 4a & 6 + 4b \end{bmatrix}.$$

18. (C) $8 = a \cdot 4 + 7 \implies 1 = 4a \implies a = \frac{1}{4}$. So $f(x) = \frac{x}{4} + 7$. $f(1) = \frac{1}{4} + 7 = \frac{29}{4}$.

19. (A) Substituting (4, 1000) for x and y into $y - ax^2$, $1000 = 4^2 a \implies a = \frac{1000}{16} = 62.5$.

20. (E) $7 = 5^2 - 3 \cdot 5 + a \implies 7 = 25 - 15 + a \implies -3 = a$ (substitute that constant into the equation) $f(x) = x^2 - 3x - 3$ (now substitute 8 for x) $f(8) = 8^2 - 3 \cdot 8 - 3 = 37$.

21. (B) $\dfrac{4}{7} = \dfrac{5}{5 + a} \implies (5 + a) \cdot 4 = 7 \cdot 5 \implies 20 + 4a = 35 \implies a = \dfrac{15}{4}$.

$f(x) = \dfrac{x}{\left(x + \dfrac{15}{4} \right)}$ (substituting the given second x-value into the new general equation)

$$f(8) = \frac{8}{8 + \dfrac{15}{4}} = \frac{8}{\dfrac{47}{4}} = \frac{32}{47}.$$

22. (A) $\dfrac{10 \cdot 0.2 + 15}{25} = \dfrac{17}{25} = 68\%$, taking total acid divided by total liquid. This is similar to a weighted average problem.

23. (B) $\dfrac{120 \cdot 0.05 + 80x}{120 + 80} = 0.1 \implies 6 + 80x = 20 \implies 80x = 14$ (dividing and simplifying) $x = \dfrac{7}{40}$.

As a percentage, $\dfrac{7}{40} \cdot 100 = 17.5\%$.

24. (B) Set games won divided by total games equal to the winning proportion (x is the unknown number of games needed to win):

$$\frac{12 + x}{20 + x} = 0.8 \implies 12 + x = 16 + 0.8x \implies 0.2x = 4 \implies x = 20.$$

25. (B) Take total salt divided by total liquid and set that equal to the desired salt proportion (x is the amount needed to be added):

$$\frac{x \cdot 0.8 + 3 \cdot 0.1}{3 + x} = 0.3 \implies 0.8x + 0.3 = 0.9 + 0.3x \implies 0.5x = 0.6 \implies x = 1.2.$$

26. (C) $y = 2x - 2$ and $y = \dfrac{-7x}{4} + \dfrac{7}{2}$. Using test points, $y \le 2x - 2$ and $y \ge \dfrac{-7x}{4} + \dfrac{7}{2}$.

27. (C) From the graph, $y \ge x$ and $y \le x + 2$. It is possible to test a point in the region, such as $(0, 1)$ and check for which answer choices it works for both equations. However, you should be able to determine the answer quicker intuitively and logically.

28. (C) $x^2 - 4x > 0$, $x(x - 4) > 0$; therefore, there are critical points at 0 and 4; checking intervals, use test points -1, 2, and 5. The condition is true for -1 and 5, but not 2, so $x < 0$ or $x > 4$.

29. (A) $x^2 + 3x - 10 \ge 0 \implies (x + 5)(x - 2) \ge 0$, so the critical points are 2 and -5. Using test points-6, 0, and 3, (checking intervals) $(-\infty, -5] \cup [2, \infty)$.

30. (E) The y-intercept can be read from the equation as $(0,6)$. To find the x-intercept, set $y = 0$,

$$0 = \frac{-5x}{4} + 6 \implies \frac{5x}{4} = 6 \implies x = \frac{24}{5} \text{ (as an intercept, it is expressed as)}$$

$\left(\dfrac{24}{5}, 0\right)$ now find the area of the triangle as $\dfrac{bh}{2} = \dfrac{\frac{24}{5} \cdot 6}{2} = \dfrac{72}{5}$.

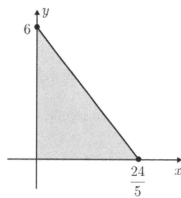

31. (D) To find the y-intercept, setting $x = 0$ in $y = \dfrac{x}{2} + 2$, $y = \dfrac{0}{2} + 2 \implies y = 2$ (as an intercept, it is expressed as $(0, 2)$). Since $x = 6$, Substituting 6 for x in $y = \dfrac{x}{2} + 2$, we find that the lines intersect at $y = \dfrac{6}{2} + 2 = 5$, so the intersection point is $(6, 5)$.

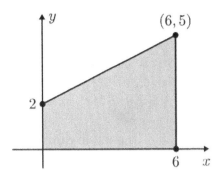

By the trapezoid area formula,

$$\frac{(b_1 + b_2)h}{2}, \quad \left(\frac{5+2}{2}\right) \cdot 6 = 21.$$

32. (A) From the diagram, each side of the square $ABCD$ is $3x + x = 4x$.

Since the area of a square is $(\text{side})^2$, the area of this square is $(4x)^2 = 16x^2$ (That will be the denominator, the area of the big square).

Now use the Pythagorean theorem to find one side of the shaded square.

$$(3x)^2 + x^2 = c^2 \implies (9x)^2 + x^2 = c^2 \implies 10x^2 = c^2,$$

which is also the area of the shaded square (This is now your numerator).

Thus, taking shaded area divided by total area: $\dfrac{10x^2}{16x^2}$ which reduces to $\dfrac{5}{8}$.

Alternative solution: Let the side length equal 4 (you could use x or some other number but 4 or a multiple of 4 makes the calculations easiest). The area not shaded is $4 \cdot \dfrac{3 \cdot 1}{2} = 6$.

The total area is 16, so the portion shaded is

$$\frac{(\text{total area - area not shaded})}{\text{total area}} = \frac{16 - 6}{16} = \frac{5}{8}.$$

33. (E) Take the area of the two shaded triangles divided by the area of the square:

$$\frac{3 \cdot \dfrac{5}{2} + 5 \cdot \dfrac{6}{2}}{8 \cdot 8} = \frac{\dfrac{45}{2}}{64} = \frac{45}{128}.$$

Alternative solution: On the triangle to the left, count shaded boxes vertically (5) and then horizontally (3) and then multiple $5 \cdot 3 = 15$ and then divide by $2 = 7.5$.

Do the same for the other shaded triangle on the right $(6 \cdot 5) = 30$ then divide by $2 = 15$. Add $7.5 + 15 = 22.5$. Then divide by $8 \cdot 8 = 64$ square boxes.

$\dfrac{22.5}{64}$, but that is not one of the answer choices, so double it to get it as a fraction with integer terms, $\dfrac{45}{128}$.

34. (E) $\overset{\frown}{AB} = 2 \cdot 50 = 100$ by the inscribed angle theorem.

$$\text{Arc length} = 2\pi r \frac{\theta}{360} = 2\pi \cdot 12 \frac{100}{360} = \frac{2400\pi}{360} = \frac{20\pi}{3}.$$

35. (B) The minor arc $\overset{\frown}{AB}$ is $2 \cdot 35 = 70°$ by the inscribed angle theorem, so the major arc $\overset{\frown}{ACB}$ is $360° - 70° = 290°$. The length of the major arc $\overset{\frown}{ACB}$ is:

$$8 \cdot 2\pi \cdot \left(\frac{290}{360}\right) = 16\pi \cdot \frac{29}{36} = \frac{116\pi}{9} \approx 40.5.$$

36. (D) $3(3+x) = 2(2+6) \implies 9 + 3x = 16$ (simplifying and solving) $x = \frac{7}{3}$.

37. (C) By the theorem for lengths of intersecting chords, $7 \cdot 3 = x \cdot 2x \implies \frac{21}{2} = x^2 \implies x \approx 3.2$.

38. (B) $\angle BOC = 100°$ by the inscribed angle theorem; therefore, $\angle BAC = 260°$, since the angles in a circle add up to $360°$. The angles in the quadrilateral also have to add up to $360°$, so:

$$\angle ACO + \angle ABO + 50° + 260° = 360° \implies \angle ACO + \angle ABO = 50°.$$

You can determine that $\angle ACO \equiv \angle ABO$ by solving or by corresponding parts of congruent triangles.

Since those angles are equal and their sum is $50°$, each of those angles is $25°$.

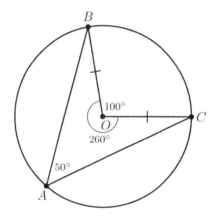

39. (D) Substituting b^2 for a, $ab = b^2 \cdot b = b^3$.

40. (A) $3^{x+3} = a$ (by the laws of exponents) $3^x \cdot 3^3 = a \implies 27 \cdot 3^x = a$ (dividing to solve) $3^x = \frac{a}{27}$.

41. (C) $2^{x+4} = 2^{x-1} \cdot 2^5 = 32b$ (since $2^{x-1} = b$).

42. (B) $x - 2 = 10^{\frac{1}{3}} \implies x = 10^{\frac{1}{3}} + 2 \approx 4.2$. This problem can also be solved by backsolving.

43. (A) $f(x) = \dfrac{x^2 + 3x + 2}{x^2 - 2x - 15}$. Substitute in -4 (this tests your ability to compute negative numbers raised to powers correctly, with which you can make errors using a calculator)

$$f(-4) = \frac{(-4)^2 + 3(-4) + 2}{(-4)^2 - 2(-4) - 15} = \frac{16 - 12 + 2}{16 + 8 - 15} = \frac{6}{9} = \frac{2}{3}.$$

It is also possible to graph the function using a calculator and find the approximate y-value when x equals -4.

44. (C) $\dfrac{x+y}{y} = \dfrac{x}{y} + 1$, which is maximized when x is maximized and y is minimized. Therefore,

$$\frac{8+10}{10} = \frac{18}{10} = \frac{9}{5}.$$

45. (A) $3 \cdot 4 + 5y = 20$ (simplifying and solving) $y = \dfrac{8}{5}$.

46. (D) Consider all the extremes, $|7 - 3(-3)| = |16| = 16$,

$$|7 - 3 \cdot 2| = |1| = 1, \quad |-4 - 3 \cdot (-3)| = |5| = 5, \quad |(-4) - 3 \cdot 2| = |-10| = 10.$$

47. (D) Consider all the extremes,

$$|7 - 5(-3)| = |22| = 22, \quad |7 - 5 \cdot 2| = |-3| = 3,$$
$$|-4 - 5 \cdot (-3)| = |11| = 11, \quad |(-4) - 5 \cdot 2| = |-14| = 14.$$

Therefore, the maximum is 22.

48. (C) $y = kx$ (substituting) $5 = k \cdot 2$ (solving for k) $k = 2.5$ (substitute the value of k to find the general equation) $y = 2.5x$ (substitute x into the general equation to find y) $y = 2.5 \cdot 5 = 12.5$.

49. (D) $y = \dfrac{k}{x}$ (substituting) $5 = \dfrac{k}{2}$ (solving for k) $k = 10$ (substitute the value of k to find the general equation) $y = \dfrac{10}{x}$ (substitute x into the general equation to find y) $y = \dfrac{10}{5}$ $y = 2$.

50. (B) $y = kx^2$ (substituting) $5 = k \cdot 2^2$ (solving for k) $k = \dfrac{5}{4}$ (substitute the value of k to find the general equation) $y = \dfrac{5x^2}{4}$ (substitute x into the general equation to find y) $y = \dfrac{5 \cdot 5^2}{4} = \dfrac{125}{4} = 31.25$.

51. (C) $y = \dfrac{k}{x^2}$ (substituting) $5 = \dfrac{k}{4}$ (solving for k) $k = 20$ (substitute the value of k to find the general equation) $y = \dfrac{20}{x^2}$ (substitute x into the general equation to find y) $y = \dfrac{20}{25} = \dfrac{4}{5}$.

52. (D) $y = k\dfrac{x^2}{\sqrt{v} \cdot w^3}$ (terms for which y varies directly with x go into the numerator and those for which it varies inversely go into the denominator).

53. (C) 6 and 7. With your calculator, $\sqrt[3]{300} = 300^{1/3} \approx 6.693$. Or take third powers, $5^3 = 125$, $6^3 = 216$, $7^3 = 343$.

54. (B) $3x^2 = -a \implies x^2 = \dfrac{-a}{3}$, for $=-12$, $\dfrac{-a}{3} = -\dfrac{-12}{3} = 4$. $x^2 = 4$ has 2 integer solutions. So -12.

55. (B) If $a = b + \dfrac{2}{3}$, what does $(a-b)^5$ equal? $a - b = \dfrac{2}{3}$. $(a-b)^5 = (b + \dfrac{2}{3} - b)^5 = (2/3)^5 = \dfrac{32}{243}$.

56. (D) $(x-y)^2 = x^2 - 2xy + y^2 = (x+y)^2 - 4xy = 20 - 3 \cdot 4 = 8$.

57. (D) $x = 3t + 5$, $y = 2t - 3$ (solve for t in terms of x) $t = \dfrac{x-5}{3}$ (substitute the expression in terms of x for t) $y = \dfrac{2(x-5)}{3} - 3$, $y = \dfrac{2x}{3} - \dfrac{19}{3}$.

58. (D) The contrapositive has the same truth value as the original statement. To obtain the contrapositive, take the negation and converse; that is, take the negative of each statement and switch them.

59. (C) Any number except 0 raised to the 0 power is 1, so $3 \cdot (1 + 1)^4 = 48$.

60. (D) Factor and then simplify.

$$\frac{300x^7 + 108x^5}{12x^3} = 12x^5 \cdot \frac{25x^2 + 9}{12x^3} = x^2 \cdot (25x^2 + 9) = 25x^4 + 9x^2.$$

36. Comprehensive Study Guide

This study guide covers almost everything likely to be on the exam. If you study this guide thoroughly, you should be will prepared for the ACT Math exam. It is accessible to a wider range of students than the problems, which are generally extremely challenging. It is recommended that students at more of an average level, do the common problems first, and then this study guide. The difficulty level of the problems is indicated, as well as particularly common problems and trap problems.

Key:

① Easiest

⑤ Most Difficult

© Common

©© Very Common

Ⓕ Helpful to Know Formula

Ⓣ Trap

36.1. Factoring

③ What is the factorization of $x^2 - 3x - 28$?
$x^2 + 4x - 7x - 28 \implies$
$x(x+4) - 7(x+4) = (x+4)(x-7)$.
You could also use the quadratic formula and reverse engineer the factorization.

④ If $x - 3$ is a factor or $3x^2 - 4x + k$, what is k? Substitute in 3, set equal to 0 and solve.
$3 \cdot 3^2 - 4 \cdot 3 + k = 0 \implies$
$27 - 12 + k = 0 \implies k = -15$.

④ What is the factorization of $3x^3 + 2x^2 - 5x$?
$x(3x^2 + 2x - 5) \implies x(3x^2 - 3x + 5x - 5) \implies$
$x(3x(x-1) + 5(x-1)) \implies x(x-1)(3x+5)$. It might be possible to use the quadratic formula or plug in answer choices.

36.2. Average

Mean

The simple version of a mean problem involves adding all the values and dividing by the number of values.

② What is the mean of 17, 11, 23, 8, 18, 21, 24, and 14?

$$\frac{17 + 11 + 23 + 8 + 18 + 21 + 24 + 14}{8} =$$

$$\frac{136}{8} = 17.$$

Median

The median is the middle value when the values are in sorted order. It is falling into a trap to take the middle without first sorting the values. If there are an even number of values, the median is the average of the two middle values. If the data is in intervals, you need to add the number of values in the intervals from either direction and determine in which interval the median must be.

③ The median of 11 numbers is 17 and no two numbers are the same. How many of the number are greater than 17?
$\frac{10}{2} = 5$.

④ ⓒ What is the median of 17, 11, 23, 8, 18, 21, 24, and 14?
First sort the numbers: 8, 11, 14, 17, 18, 21, 23, and 24.
Since there is an even number of numbers, the median is the average of the two middle number, 17 and 18: $\frac{17 + 18}{2} = 17.5$.

Weighted Average

To find the weighted average, take each value times the number of element in that value, then add all those products, and divide that by the sum of the number of elements in all values.

④ A restaurant had the following ratings 37 5s, 17 4s, 8 3s, 5 2s, and 11 1s. What was the weighted average?

$$\frac{37 \cdot 5 + 17 \cdot 4 + 8 \cdot 3 + 5 \cdot 2 + 11 \cdot 1}{37 + 17 + 8 + 5 + 11} =$$

$$\frac{185 + 68 + 24 + 10 + 11}{78} = \frac{298}{78} \approx 3.82.$$

Need on Test

For need on test problems you take the sum of your current test scores (or the average of your current test scores times the number of current tests) and that to the unknown x divide by the number of tests including the one with the unknown score, set that equal to the desired score, and solve for x. There could be fairly difficult problems in which the current average or desired score is unknown, and you need to get an expression in terms of variables.

④ Bob has a 78, 83, 86, 90, and 92 on 5 equally weighted tests. What is the minimum score he needs on the 6th test to raise his average by 3 points?
Current average $= \frac{78 + 83 + 86 + 90 + 92}{5} = \frac{429}{5} = 85.8$. Therefore, he needs an 88.8.
$\frac{429 + x}{6} = 88.8 \implies 429 + x = 532.8 \implies x = 103.8$ or 104.

④ The average of 5 numbers is 76. A new list of numbers has all the same numbers except the 5th number is changed from 67 to 82. What is the average of the new list?
$\frac{82 - 67}{5} = 3$, $76 + 3 = 79$.

④ⓒ A student has a 78, 74, and 82 on 3 tests. What is the minimum he needs on the 4th equally weighted test to average 80 for all 4 tests?

$\frac{78 + 74 + 82 + x}{4} = 80 \implies \frac{234 + x}{4} = 80 \implies 234 + x = 320 \implies x = 86$.

④ A student has an average of 78 on 6 equally weighted tests. What does he need on the 7th test to average 80 for all 7?
$\frac{78 \cdot 6 + x}{7} = 80 \implies 468 + x = 560 \implies x = 92$.

⑤ A student has an average of x on 8 equally weighted tests. If the lowest grade is removed, his average is y. What was the lowest grade?
$8x$ on the 8 tests.
$\frac{8x - w}{7} = y$.
Now solve for w, the lowest score.
$8x - w = 7y \implies w = 8x - 7y$.

Mean and Median

④ⓒ What is the difference between the mean and the median of the squares of the integers from 1 to 4?

The squares of those integers are 1, 4, 9, 16. Since there are an even number of elements and the data is sorted, the median is the average of the two middle elements: $\frac{4+9}{2} = 6.5$.

The mean is the average of all the elements: $\frac{1+4+9+16}{4} = 7.5$.

Therefore, the difference is 1.0.

④ What is the product of the mean and median of the first 7 prime numbers?

2, 3, 5, 7, 11, 13, 17. Median is the middle value in sorted order, 7. Mean is

$$\frac{2+3+5+7+11+13+17}{7} = \frac{58}{7},$$

$7 \cdot \frac{58}{7} = 58$

36.3. Percent

Percent of

Divide the percent by 100 to convert it to a decimal, and then multiply that decimal by the number you are taking a percent of.

② What is 150% of 236? $236 \cdot 1.5 = 354$.

② What is a 15% tip on a $65 restaurant bill? $65 \cdot 0.15 = \$9.75$.

③ⓒ What is 6% of 2.52×10^5?

Multiplying, $0.06 \cdot 2.52 \cdot 10^5 = 0.1512 \cdot 10^5 = 1.512 \cdot 10^4$.

You can also enter the whole thing with your calculator.

A key step is converting 6% to 0.06.

Percent of Percent

For percent of percent, multiply by each percentage converted to a decimal.

③ What is 30% of 40% of 90?

$0.3 \cdot 0.4 \cdot 90 = 10.8$.

Percent Change

Take the difference divided by the original value and then multiply by 100.

③ The price of a motel room was decreased for $80 night to $70 night . What was the percent decrease?

$80 - 70 = 10$. $\frac{10}{80} \cdot 100 = 12.5\%$.

③ A motel room costs $80 night, but its price was increased by 35% on high demand weekend. What was the higher price?

$80 \cdot 1.35 = \$108$.

③ A shirt was originally priced at $30, but is sold at 30% off, but with 7% sales tax on the sale price. How much did the customer pay including tax?

$30 \cdot 0.7 = 21$ (0.7 because $1 - 0.3$ for 30%). $21 \cdot 1.07 = \$22.47$.

Compound Percent

For compound percent (one percent change followed by another), add or subtract each percentage change as a decimal from 1, depending if it is an increase or decrease. Then multiply the resulting decimal. Finally, subtract 1 from the result, and multiply by 100 to convert back to a percentage.

⑤ If the price of a stock goes up 10% in 2022 and 30% in 2023, what is the total percent increase in the stock price?

$1.1 \cdot 1.3 = 1.43$. $(1.43 - 1) \cdot 100 = 43\%$.

⑤ If the length, width, and height of a box are each increased by 20%, what is the percent increase in its volume?

$1.2^3 = 1.728$, so approximately 73%.

⑤ The length of a rectangle is increased by 40% and its width is decreased by 20%. By what percent is the area of the new rectangle larger than the original one?

$1.4 \cdot 0.8 = 1.12$. $(1.12 - 1) \cdot 100 = 12\%$.

④ The price of an item was reduced by 20% then by 30%. The fully discounted price is what of the original price?

$0.8 \cdot 0.7 = 0.56$ or 56%.

36.4. Midpoint

It is a good idea to know the midpoint formula $\left(\dfrac{x_1 + x_2}{2}, \dfrac{y_1 + y_2}{2}\right)$. You can also understand the concept, which is the average of the xs and the average of the ys. These problems should be solvable without the formula.

① What is the midpoint on the number line between 7 and 23?

Just average the numbers: $\dfrac{7 + 23}{2} = 15$.

②Ⓕ©© What is the midpoint between point $A(2, -5)$ and $B(10, 7)$?

Applying the midpoint formula,
$\left(\dfrac{2 + 10}{2}, \dfrac{-5 + 7}{2}\right) = (6, 1)$.

③Ⓕ©© M is the midpoint of AB. A is $(2, 1)$ and M is $(5, 9)$. What is B?

There are various ways to reason this, but the algebraic approach is to substitute in the answer M and the endpoint A and then solve for B.

$5 = \dfrac{2 + x}{2} \implies 10 = 2 + x \implies$
$x = 8$.
$9 = \dfrac{1 + y}{2} \implies 18 = 1 + y \implies$
$y = 17$.
Therefore, the answer is $(8, 17)$.

36.5. Distance

For distance problems, the main thing is to know the distance formula. If you do not know the formula, then you can also use the Pythagorean theorem directly, and the formula can be derived from that theorem. The distance formula is $d = \sqrt{(x_2 - x_1)^2 + (y_2 - y_1)^2}$.

②Ⓕ© A common problem all students should know is what is the distance between $(-2, 5)$ and $(-7, -6)$?

Applying the distance formula,
$d = \sqrt{(-2 - (-7))^2 + (5 - (-6))^2} =$
$\sqrt{5^2 + 11^2} = \sqrt{25 + 121} = \sqrt{146}$.

②Ⓕ Another problem is about what is the distance between $(0, 30)$ and $(30, 0)$?

$\sqrt{(30 - 0)^2 + (0 - 30)^2} = \sqrt{900 + 900} = \sqrt{1800} \approx 42$. You could also use that the ratios of a $45 - 45 - 90$ triangle are $1 - 1 - \sqrt{2}$ or use trigonometry with your calculator.

36.6. Wages and Charges

Wages

②© Carlos gets $18/hour plus time and a half for overtime. If he worked 54 hours last week, how much did he get paid?

$18 \cdot 40 + 27 \cdot 14 = 720 + 378 = \$1098$.

③ Abdul earns $28 for the first 40 hours a week and time and a half for overtime. If he earned $1540 for the week, how many hours did he work?

Full-time pay is $28 \cdot 40 = 1120$. Overtime pay is $1540 - 1120 = 420$. $\dfrac{420}{28 \cdot 1.5} = 10$. $40 + 10 = 50$ hours.

Charge

③ A rental car company charges $60/day plus 45 cents per mile. What would the charge for 5 days and 400 miles be?

$60 \cdot 5 + 0.45 \cdot 400 = 300 + 180 = \$480$.

36.7. Fractions

Just Fractions

③ⓒ Abdul and Julio were painting a house. They started with 6 gallons of paint. The first day Abdul used $1\frac{5}{8}$ gallons and Julio used $2\frac{1}{4}$ gallons. How many gallons were left?

$6 - 1\frac{5}{8} - 2\frac{1}{4} = 6 - \frac{13}{8} - \frac{9}{4} = \frac{48 - 13 - 18}{8} = \frac{17}{8} = 2\frac{1}{8}.$

③ If $x + 2\frac{1}{4} = 4\frac{5}{8}$? $x = 4\frac{5}{8} - 2\frac{1}{4} = 2\frac{3}{8}.$

④ For what integers does $\frac{5}{x}$ lie between $\frac{1}{4}$ and $\frac{1}{3}$? 16, 17, 18, 19. By your calculator or other methods.

Complex Fractions

④ Which of the following is equivalent to

$\dfrac{\frac{a}{b} + 1}{\frac{1}{a} + \frac{1}{b}}$? $\dfrac{\frac{a+b}{b}}{\frac{b+a}{ab}} \implies \dfrac{(a+b)ab}{(a+b)b} = a.$

④ Which of the following is equivalent to

$\dfrac{\frac{x}{3} + \frac{2}{5}}{\frac{1}{4} + \frac{1}{3}}$?

$\dfrac{\frac{5x+6}{15}}{\frac{7}{12}} \implies \dfrac{(5x+6)12}{15 \cdot 7} = \dfrac{4(5x+6)}{35}.$

Rational Expressions

③ Which of the following is equivalent to $\frac{2}{x} + \frac{3}{5}$? The least common denominator is $5x$.

$\dfrac{2}{x} \cdot \dfrac{5}{5} + \dfrac{3}{5} \cdot \dfrac{x}{x} = \dfrac{10 + 3x}{5x}.$

③ Which of the following is equivalent to

$\dfrac{1}{x-2} + \dfrac{1}{x+2}$? $\dfrac{x+2+x-2}{(x-2)(x+2)} \implies \dfrac{2x}{x^2 - 4}.$

③ Which of the following is equivalent to

$\dfrac{1}{x} + \dfrac{5}{x^3}$? $\dfrac{x^2 + 5}{x^3}.$

Rational Functions

Generally, factor the numerator and denominator. Then cancel like terms.

④ Which is equivalent to

$\dfrac{x^2 - 2x - 35}{x^2 - 25}$? $\dfrac{(x-7)(x+5)}{(x+5)(x-5)} = \dfrac{x-7}{x-5}.$

This also can be solved by substituting a number for x in the problem and in the answer choices.

36.8. Least Common Multiple

③ⓒ What is the least common denominator of $\frac{3}{8}, \frac{5}{12}$, and $\frac{11}{28}$?
$8 = 2 \cdot 2 \cdot 2$, $12 = 2 \cdot 2 \cdot 3$, $28 = 2 \cdot 2 \cdot 7$. The least common denominator is $2 \cdot 2 \cdot 2 \cdot 3 \cdot 7 = 168$

③ⓒ One sign flashes every 6 seconds and another every 8 seconds. At a certain instant, they flash at the same time. How many seconds until they flash at the same time again?
This is asking for the least common multiple. Take $6 = 2 \cdot 3$ and $8 = 2 \cdot 2 \cdot 2$. Take all factors in either: $2 \cdot 2 \cdot 2 \cdot 3 = 24$.

③ⓒⓒ What is the least common multiple of 50, 60, and 90?
$50 = 2 \cdot 5 \cdot 5$, $60 = 2 \cdot 2 \cdot 3 \cdot 5$, $90 = 3 \cdot 3 \cdot 2 \cdot 5$. Therefore, the least common multiple is $2 \cdot 2 \cdot 3 \cdot 3 \cdot 5 \cdot 5 = 900$.

36.9. Binomial Multiplication

②ⓒ What is $(4x + 7)(4x - 7)$?
$16x^2 - 28x + 28x - 49 = 16x^2 - 49.$

②ⓒ What is the area of a rectangle with length $2x + 3$ and width $x + 5$?

$(2x + 3)(x + 5) = 2x^2 + 10x + 3x + 15 = 2x^2 + 13x + 15.$

③ Which is equivalent to $\left(\dfrac{x}{2} - 4\right)^2$?

$\dfrac{x^2}{4} - 2x - 2x + 16 = \dfrac{x^2}{4} - 4x + 16.$

③ Which is equivalent to $\left(a + \sqrt{b}\right)\left(a + 3\sqrt{b}\right)$?

$a^2 + 3a\sqrt{b} + a\sqrt{b} + 3b = a^2 + 4a\sqrt{b} + 3b.$

36.10. Pythagorean Theorem

$a^2 + b^2 = c^2$, where a and b are legs of a right triangle and c is the hypotenuse.

② A rectangle is 24 feet long and 10 feet wide. What is the length of its diagonal?
$10^2 + 24^2 = d^2 \rightarrow 100 + 576 = d^2 \rightarrow 676 = d^2 \rightarrow d = 26$ feet.

③ If one leg of a right triangle is $\sqrt{7}$ and the hypotenuse is 4, what is the length of the other leg?
$\left(\sqrt{7}\right)^2 + b^2 = 4^2 \rightarrow 7 + b^2 = 16 \rightarrow b^2 = 9 \rightarrow b = 3.$

36.11. Simplification

① What is $7 - 3(x - 5)$?
$7 - 3x + 15 = 22 - 3x.$

① What is $(3a - 3b + 7c) - (2a + 4b - 6c)$?
$3a - 3b + 7c - 2a - 4b + 6c = a - 7b + 13c.$

②Ⓒ Which of the following expressions is equivalent to $5(x + 4) - 2(2x - 3)$?
$5x + 20 - 4x + 6 = x + 26$

④ Which of the following expressions is equivalent to $\dfrac{x^2 + 8x + 15}{x + 3} + 2x + 4$?
$\dfrac{(x + 5)(x + 3)}{x + 3} + 2x + 4 = x + 5 + 2x + 4 = 3x + 9.$

36.12. Closest to

①Ⓒ What is the smallest positive integer greater than $\sqrt{130}$?
12. With your calculator $\sqrt{130} \approx 11.4$, so 12. Rounding down to 11 would be falling into a trap. It is possible to do this problem if you know the perfect squares without using your calculator.

36.13. Exponentiation

This is a fairly common type of relatively easy problems on the exam.
$x^a \cdot x^b = x^{a+b}$, $(x^a)^b = x^{ab}$, $(2x^4)^3 = 8x^{12}.$

②Ⓒ Which of the following expressions is equivalent to $(3x^5 y^3)(8x^3 y^2)$?
Grouping like terms, $(3 \cdot 8)(x^5 \cdot x^3)(y^3 \cdot y^2) = 24x^8 y^5.$
When multiplying variables raised to exponents, add the exponents.

②Ⓒ Which of the following is equal to $\left(x^4\right)^{24}$?
x^{96} When taking the power of the power, you multiply the exponents.

②Ⓒ Which of the following is equivalent to $(2x^2)^4$?
$2^4 \cdot (x^2)^4 = 16x^8$. When taking the power of the power, multiply exponents.

②ⒸⒸ Which of the following is equivalent to $(5x^3) \cdot (4x^8)$?
$20x^{11}.$

Fractions

③Ⓒ The expression $\dfrac{4a^3 b^5 c^2}{10a^4 b^3 c^5}$ is equivalent to what?
$\dfrac{4}{10} \cdot \dfrac{a^3}{a^4} \cdot \dfrac{b^5}{b^3} \cdot \dfrac{c^2}{c^5} = \dfrac{2b^2}{5ac^3}.$

③ $\dfrac{\dfrac{x^5}{x^8}}{\dfrac{x^7}{x^2}} = ?$

Flip the fraction you are dividing by: $\dfrac{x^5 \cdot x^2}{x^8 \cdot x^7} = \dfrac{x^7}{x^{15}} = \dfrac{1}{x^8}$.

Other

③ $(2x^4)^3(3x^2)^2 = ?$ $8x^{12} \cdot 9x^4 = 72x^{16}$.

③ $2^4 x^5 y^{-3} 3^{-2} = ?$ $\dfrac{16x^5}{9y^3}$.

36.14. Converting Units

③ How many seconds would it take to travel 30 miles at 50 miles per hour?
$\dfrac{30}{50} = \dfrac{3}{5}$ hour $\implies \dfrac{3}{5} \cdot 60 \cdot 60 = 2160$ seconds.

③ 540 square feet is how many square yards? Each square yard is $3 \times 3 = 9$ square feet. Therefore, $\dfrac{540}{9} = 60$ square yards.

③ A 120 feet by 210 feet field is how many square yards? That is 40 yards by 70 yards, so 2800 square yards. You could also take $\dfrac{120 \cdot 210}{9} = 2800$.

③ What is the minimum number of 6-inch by 9-inch tiles needed to cover a 12 feet by 15 feet floor?
The area of the floor is $12 \times 15 = 180$ square feet.
Each tile is $\dfrac{1}{2} \cdot \dfrac{3}{4} = \dfrac{3}{8}$ square feet.
Therefore, $\dfrac{180}{\frac{3}{8}} = 480$ tiles.
You could also calculate each tile is 54 square inches and find the area of the floor in square inches, but that is more time consuming.

③Ⓒ A board which is 11 feet 2 inches long is cut into two equal parts. How long is each part in feet and inches?
Half of 11 feet is 5 feet 6 inches. Half of 2 inches is 1 inch, so 5 feet 7 inches.
Or convert to inches: $11 \cdot 12 + 2 = 134$. Half of 134 is 67.
$\dfrac{67}{12} = 5$ with remainder 7, so 5 feet 7 inches.

36.15. Scientific Notation

In Scientific Notation

③ What is 38 million in scientific notation? One million is 10^6. 38 is 3.8×10. Therefore, $3.8 \times 10 \cdot 10^6 = 3.8 \times 10^7$.

③Ⓒ What is 0.00000456 in scientific notation? The 4 is the 6th digit after the decimal point, so 4.56×10^{-6}.

Equations

④ $5.5 \times 10^{3x+2} \cdot 4 \cdot 10^{-5} = 220$. What is x?
$22 \cdot 10^{3x+2} \cdot 10^{-5} = 220 \implies$
$2.2 \times 10 \cdot 10^{3x-3} = 2.2 \cdot 10^2 \implies$
$2.2 \times 10^{3x-2} = 2.2 \cdot 10^2 \implies$
$3x - 2 = 2 \implies 3x = 4 \implies x = \dfrac{4}{3}$.

Add, Subtract, and Divide

③ There are 3×10^{16} molecules in an 8×10^{10} cubic cm box, how many molecules are there per cubic cm?
$\dfrac{3 \times 10^{16}}{8 \times 10^{10}} = \dfrac{3}{8} \times 10^6 = 0.375 \times 10^6 = 3.75 \times 10^3$.

③ What is sum of $45,000 + 78,000$ in scientific notation?
$123,000 = 1.23 \times 10^5$.

③ What is the sum of 7.3×10^3 and 2.1×10^4?
$7.3 \times 10^3 = 0.73 \times 10^4$. $2.1 \times 10^4 + 0.73 \times 10^4 = 2.83 \times 10^4$.

How Many Zeros

③ 3.74×10^{-23} would have how many zeros after the decimal if expressed as $0.0\ldots374$? The 3 starts at the 22nd place, so 21 zeros.

36.16. Linear Equations and Inequalities One Variable

①ⓒ If $7x - 11 = 4x + 7$, then $x =$?
$3x = 18 \implies x = 6$.

②ⓒ If $\dfrac{4x}{5} - 3 = 17$, what does x equal?
$\dfrac{4x}{5} = 20 \implies x = 20 \cdot \dfrac{5}{4} = 25$.

②ⓒ Which of the following is inequalities is equivalent to $5x - 3 > 2x + 4$?
$3x > 7,\ x > \dfrac{7}{3}$.

② $\dfrac{5x}{3} + 8 = 20 \implies \dfrac{5x}{3} = 12 \implies$
$x = 12 \cdot \dfrac{3}{5} \implies x = \dfrac{36}{5}$.

③ For what value of x is $\dfrac{5+x}{2+x} = \dfrac{3}{5}$?
$(5+x)5 = (2+x)3 \cdot 25 + 5x = 6 + 3x \implies 2x = -19 \implies x = \dfrac{-19}{2}$.

③ For what value of x does $4.2x + 2.4 = 1.7x + 5.9$? $2.5x = 3.5 \implies x = 1.4$.

③ $\dfrac{2x}{3} + \dfrac{3}{4} = \dfrac{5}{2}$. What is x?
$\dfrac{2x}{3} = \dfrac{7}{4} \implies x = \dfrac{7}{4} \cdot \dfrac{3}{2} \implies x = \dfrac{21}{8}$.

36.17. Difference in Time and Distance

③ A flight was scheduled to depart at 9:37 AM but was 476 minutes late. When did it depart?
7 hours 56 minutes or 8 hours minus 4 minutes 5:33 PM.

③ 17 ft 3 inches is how much longer than 12 ft 8 inches?
5 feet minus 5 inches or 4 feet 7 inches.

④ⓒ A train left Atlanta at 7:46 PM and arrived in Baltimore at 3:12 AM the next day. How many hours and minutes did the trip take?
7 hours to 2:46 AM and another 26 minutes to 3:12 AM, so 7 hours and 26 minutes.

36.18. Triangular Inequalities

The sum of 2 sides of a triangle is always greater than the third side.

③ If two sides of a triangle have length 7 and 10, what range must the third side be in?
$10 - 7 < x < 10 + 7 \implies 3 < x < 17$.

In a triangle the larger side is opposite the larger angle.

36.19. Number Theory

There are many different types of number theory problems on the exam. They tend to be fairly difficult and intended to test reasoning ability.

Units Digit

The units digits of powers of numbers ending in 2, 3, 7 and 8 repeat every 4. Therefore, determine the pattern and take the exponent modula 4.

④ If the units digit of 73^{235} is 7, what is the units digit of 73^{238}?
$7 \cdot 3^3 = 7 \cdot 27 = 189$, so 9.

⑤ What is the units digit of 78^{138}?
$8^1 = 8$, $8^2 = 4$, $8^3 = 2$, $8^4 = 6$, all mod 10. Now 138 mod 4 = 2, so we use 8^2, which is 4.

Other Number Theory

④ If x is a positive integer, the sum of $8x$ and $9x$ is always divisible by what number? $8x + 9x = 17x$, so 17.

④ What is the least positive number which has remainder 5 when divided by 7 and remainder 7 when divided by 11?
Numbers with remainder 5 when divided by 7: 5, 12, 19, 26, 33, 40;
numbers with remainder 7 when divided by 11: 7, 18, 29, 40.
Therefore, the answer is 40.

⑤ What is the 573rd digit to the right of the decimal in $\overline{.3756}$?

573 mod 4 = 1, so take the first digit in the sequence, 3.

You can accomplish modula arithmetic by dividing like in elementary school and taking the remainder or dividing by 4 with your calculator and then multiplying the decimal part by 4.

⑤ How many numbers between 1 and 200 are divisible by 2, 3, and 7.

They must be divisible by $2 \cdot 3 \cdot 7 = 42$. 42, 84, 126, 168. Therefore, 4 numbers.

⑤ What percent of even numbers between 2 and 40, inclusive, have units digits twice the tens digit?

12 24 36, so 3 out of 20, so 15%.

⑤ What is the largest 3-digit number divisible by 7 and 11.

It needs to be divisible by 77. $77 \cdot 12 = 924$.

⑤ How many prime numbers between 50 and 80.

Taking odd numbers 51 53 55 57 59 61 63 65 67 69 71 73 75 77 79.

Remove numbers divisible by 3 (sum of digits divisible by 3) and numbers divisible by 5 (if the last digit is 5). 53 59 61 67 71 73 77 79. Remove numbers divisible by 7: 53 59 61 67 71 73 79, so 7 prime numbers.

36.20. Line

Slope

②ⒸⒻ In the standard xy-coordinate plane, what is the slope of a line containing $(5,7)$ with y-intercept of -2?

The points are $(5,7)$ and $(0,-2)$.

The slope formula is $\dfrac{y_2 - y_1}{x_2 - x_1}$.

Therefore, $\dfrac{7-(-2)}{5-0} = \dfrac{9}{5}$ is the slope.

②ⒸⒸ In the standard xy-coordinate plane, what is the slope of the line $5x - 11y = 17$?

Convert to slope-intercept form:

$$11y = 5x - 17 \implies y = \frac{5x}{11} - \frac{17}{11},$$

so the slope is the x-coefficient, $\dfrac{5}{11}$.

②ⒸⒸⒻ What is the slope of a line through $(-5,7)$ and $(4,1)$ in the standard xy-coordinate plane?

Using the slope formula

$$\frac{y_2 - y_1}{x_2 - x_1} \cdot \frac{7-1}{-5-4} = \frac{6}{-9} = \frac{-2}{3}.$$

②Ⓒ What is the slope of

$$y - 17 = \frac{3}{4}(2x + 5)?$$

Distributing, $y - 17 = \dfrac{3x}{2} + \dfrac{15}{4}$.

The slope is the coefficient of x, so it is $\dfrac{3}{2}$.

Intercept

To find the x-intercept, set y equal to 0 and solve for x. To find the y-intercept, set x equal to 0 and solve for y. If an equation is in slope-intercept form, that is solved for y, the y-intercept is the constant term.

② What is the x-intercept of $3x + 5y = 11$?

$$3x + 5 \cdot 0 = 11 \implies 3x = 11 \implies x = \frac{11}{3}.$$

④ What is the x-intercept of the line through $(2, 5)$ and $(4, 8)$?

Slope $= \frac{8-5}{4-2} = \frac{3}{2}$.

$5 = 2 \cdot \frac{3}{2} + b \implies b = 2$.

Therefore, $y = \frac{3x}{2} + 2$. $0 = \frac{3x}{2} + 2 \implies$

$-2 = \frac{3x}{2} \implies x = \frac{-4}{3}$.

④ What is the x-intercept of the line through $(3, 8)$ with slope of 2?

$y = mx + b \implies 8 = 2 \cdot 3 + b \implies b = 2$. Therefore, $y = 2x + 2$. Setting $y = 0$, $0 = 2x + 2 \implies$ $x = -1$.

Equation of Line

③ What is the equation of the line through $(3, 5)$ with slope of $\frac{1}{2}$?

$y = mx + b$. $5 = 3 \cdot \frac{1}{2} + b \implies 5 = \frac{3}{2} + b \implies$

$b = \frac{7}{2}$. $y = \frac{x}{2} + \frac{7}{2}$.

④Ⓕ What is the equation of line through $(3, 1)$ and $(6, 5)$?

Slope $= \frac{5-1}{6-3} = \frac{4}{3}$

$y = mx + b$. $1 = 3 \cdot \frac{4}{3} + b \implies$

$1 = 4 + b \implies b = -3$. $y = \frac{4x}{3} - 3$.

36.21. Rates

Same Person, Different Rates

④ Bob drove 500 miles in 10 hours. By averaging 10 mph faster, how many minutes would he save?

$\frac{500}{10} = 50$ mph. 10 mph faster is 60 mph. $\frac{500}{60} = \frac{25}{3}$. $10 - \frac{25}{3} = \frac{5}{3}$ hours. $\frac{5}{3} \cdot 60 = 100$ minutes.

④ Steve drove at 40 mph for 10 minutes and 60 mph for 15 minutes. What was his average speed for the 25 minutes?

Distance traveled $= 40 \cdot \frac{1}{6} + 60 \cdot \frac{1}{4} = \frac{20}{3} + 15 = \frac{65}{3}$ miles.

Time spent traveling $= 25$ minutes $= \frac{25}{60}$ hours $= \frac{5}{12}$ hours.

Therefore, the rate or speed is

$\frac{D}{T} = \frac{\frac{65}{3}}{\frac{5}{12}} = \frac{780}{15} = 52$ mph.

④ Sally travels for 5 hours at 50 mph to get there. Due to heavy traffic, for the first 2 hours of her return trip, she averages 20 mph. What must her average speed for the rest of her return trip be for her to finish the return trip in 6 hours total?

$5 \cdot 50 = 250$, so the one-way trip is 250 miles. She has traveled $20 \cdot 2 = 40$ miles so far. Therefore, she has $250 - 40 = 210$ miles to go. She has $6 - 2 = 4$ hours left.

Therefore, the average speed must be $\frac{210}{4} = 52.5$ mph.

Distance and Time

③ A 5.3 kilometer cab ride took 12 minutes. What was the average speed in mph (1 mile $= 1.6$ kilometers)? 12 minutes $= \frac{12}{60}$ hours $= \frac{1}{5}$ hours. $\frac{5.3}{\frac{1}{5}} = 26.5$ kilometers/hour. $\frac{26.5}{1.6} \approx$ 16.6 mph.

④ An object traveled 300 feet in 2.5 seconds. What was its average speed in mph (1 mile $= 5,280$ feet)?

$\frac{300}{2.5} = 120$ feet/second. $120 \cdot 60 \cdot \frac{60}{5280} \approx 81.8$ mph.

④ Darrel ran 20 miles in $2\frac{1}{2}$ hours. What is the average number of minutes it took him to run

one mile?
$\dfrac{20}{\frac{5}{2}} = 8$ mph. Since one hour is 60 minutes, the time in minutes is
$\dfrac{60 \text{ minutes}}{8 \text{ mph}} = 7.5$ minutes.

Two Different Runners

④ Vehicle X gets 20 mpg and Vehicle Y gets 32 mpg. How many more gallons will vehicle X consume than vehicle Y. both traveling 2000 miles?
$\dfrac{2000}{20} = 100$ gallons. $\dfrac{2000}{32} = 62.5$ gallons.
$100 - 62.5 = 37.5$ gallons.

④ Robert ran a 6-mile cross country course in 35 minutes; Willie ran the same course in 40 minutes. What is the difference in their speeds in mph? $\dfrac{6}{\frac{40}{60}} = 9$ mph. $\dfrac{6}{\frac{35}{60}} \approx 10.28$ mph. Therefore, the difference is 1.28 mph.

36.22. Portions of

④ The marbles in a bowl are $\dfrac{1}{3}$ red, $\dfrac{1}{4}$ blue, $\dfrac{1}{5}$ yellow, and the other 26 green. How many marbles in the bowl?
The portion that are green are
$1 - \dfrac{1}{3} - \dfrac{1}{4} - \dfrac{1}{5} = \dfrac{60}{60} - \dfrac{20}{60} - \dfrac{15}{60} - \dfrac{12}{60} = \dfrac{13}{60} = \dfrac{26}{120},$
so there are 120 marbles in the bowl.

④ Bob did $\dfrac{1}{3}$ of a job and Steve did $\dfrac{1}{4}$ of the job. Then Robert completed the job in 10 hours. If they all worked at the same rate, how many hours did the job take?
The portion remaining after Bob and Steve's initial work is
$1 - \dfrac{1}{3} - \dfrac{1}{4} = \dfrac{12}{12} - \dfrac{4}{12} - \dfrac{3}{12} = \dfrac{5}{12}.$
If x represents the total time to finish the job,
$\dfrac{5}{12} x = 10 \implies x = 24.$

36.23. Proportions

④ A container is $\dfrac{1}{4}$ full of water. After 12 cups of water are added, it is $\dfrac{5}{8}$ full. How much water does the container hold?
The portion of the container that 12 cups of water contributes is
$\dfrac{5}{8} - \dfrac{1}{4} = \dfrac{3}{8}. \quad \dfrac{3}{8} \cdot x = 12 \implies$
$x = 8 \cdot \dfrac{12}{3} = 32$ cups.

36.24. Vectors

④ Sally is driving directly southeast at 30 mph. Which vector is closest to representing her travel?
$\left\langle \dfrac{30}{\sqrt{2}}, \dfrac{-30}{\sqrt{2}} \right\rangle \implies 21\hat{\imath} - 21\hat{\jmath}$

36.25. Absolute Value

Absolute Value Expressions

Find the total of what is inside the absolute value bars. If that is negative take the positive or absolute value of it. Then simplify further.

① ⓒ What is $|5 - x|$ when $x = 17$?
Substituting, $|5 - 17| = |-12| = 12$.

① ⓒ What is $|-27| - |12 - 44|$?
$27 - |-32| = 27 - 32 = -5$

① ⓒ ⓒ What is $|11 - 4| - |3 - 8|$?
$|7| - |-5| = 7 - 5 = 2$.

Absolute Value Equations and Inequalities

These are fairly rare on the exam and reasonably difficult. They key is to split them into 2 equations.

Equations

② ⓒ What are the solutions to $|3x - 5| = 2$?
Split the absolute value portion in 2.

$3x - 5 = 2$ or $3x - 5 = -2 \implies 3x = 7$ or $3x = 3 \implies x = \dfrac{7}{3}$ or $x = 1$.

⑤ A difficult problem, which is generally not covered in school is what are the solutions to $|x|^2 + 3|x| - 10 = 0$?

If you can graph it with your calculator with the absolute value and read the solutions, that may be the best approach.

It does not matter whether the x^2 term has an absolute value around it or not, as it is positive anyway.

You split this into 2 equations, $x^2 + 3x - 10 = 0$ and $x^2 - 3x - 10 = 0$.

The solutions to the first equation are -5 and 2 and to the second equation -2 and 5.

These can be obtained using the quadratic formula, factoring, by completing the square, or by graphing the expressions on your calculator. Only 2 and -2 check.

You can also see that the first equation applies only for positive x and the second one for negative values of x, so the -5 and 5 are extraneous. (Obtained values of x not satisfying the equation are called extraneous roots)

Inequalities

There are some important issues with absolute value inequalities. You need to split them up, taking the negative of what is inside the absolute value. If you take the negative of what the absolute value is greater than or less than, you will get a wrong answer. Also, when multiplying by a negative, you need to switch the direction of the inequality. However, it is usually possible to avoid multiplying by a negative.

③ What is the solution to $|x - 5| < 2$?

$x - 5 < 2$ and $5 - x < 2 \implies x < 7$ and $x > 3$, so solution is the interval $(3, 7)$.

③Ⓣ What is the solution to $|x - 5| < -2$?

Absolute value can never be negative, so there are no solutions. If you work it algebraically, you will get answers, but they do not check.

④ The solution for $|3x - a| < 2$ is $\dfrac{11}{3} < x < 5$.

What is a?

$3x - a < 2$ and $a - 3x < 2 \implies$
$3x < 2 + a$ and $a - 2 < 3x \implies$
$x < \dfrac{2 + a}{3}$ and $\dfrac{a - 2}{3} < x$.

Therefore, $\dfrac{2 + a}{3} = 5 \implies$
$2 + a = 15 \implies a = 13$.

13 checks in the other equation.

36.26. Radicals

Simplify

$\sqrt{x^2} = x$, $\sqrt[3]{x^3} = x$, etc. Use that to simplify roots of variables and of constants in factored form.

④ What is $\sqrt[3]{80}$ simplified?

$\sqrt[3]{2^4 \cdot 5} = \sqrt[3]{2^3 \cdot 2 \cdot 5} = 2\sqrt[3]{10}$.

④ What is $5\sqrt[3]{3x^2}\sqrt[3]{2x^2}$? $5\sqrt[3]{6x^4} = 5x\sqrt[3]{6x}$.

④ What is $\sqrt[3]{\sqrt[5]{x^4}}$? $\sqrt[15]{x^4}$ or $x^{4/15}$.

Fractional Exponents

④ What is $\left(\dfrac{9}{7}\right)^{-5/2}$?

$\left(\dfrac{7}{9}\right)^{5/2} = \dfrac{7^{5/2}}{9^{5/2}} = \dfrac{49\sqrt{7}}{3^5} = \dfrac{49\sqrt{7}}{243}$.

④ What is $\left(\dfrac{8}{125}\right)^{-2/3}$? $\left(\dfrac{125}{8}\right)^{2/3} = \dfrac{5^2}{2^2} = \dfrac{25}{4}$.

Adding

Generally, simplify each term first. They will have the same squareroot term and can then be added.

④Ⓒ What is $\sqrt{12} + \sqrt{75} - \sqrt{27}$?

$2\sqrt{3} + 5\sqrt{3} - 3\sqrt{3} = 4\sqrt{3}$ or $\sqrt{48}$.

④ What is $\dfrac{12\sqrt{45}}{2\sqrt{5}}$? $\dfrac{36\sqrt{5}}{2\sqrt{5}} = 18$.

Converting Fractional Exponents to Radical Form

Take the expression to the power of the numerator and the root of the denominator.

④ What is $a^{1/2}b^{1/4}c^{5/8}$ in simplest radical form?

$a^{4/8}b^{2/8}c^{5/8} = (a^4b^2c^5)^{1/8} = \sqrt[8]{a^4b^2c^5}$.

④ What is $x^{1/2}x^{1/6}$ is simplest radical form?

$x^{3/6}x^{1/6} = x^{4/6} = x^{2/3} = \sqrt[3]{x^2}$.

Radical Equations

Generally, isolate the radical and then take both sides to the power of the radical to clear the radical.

Some problems can be solved by backsolving (plugging in and checking the answer choices). That is the preferred method for the SAT where some solutions generally do not check, so working the problem algebraically is a waste of time. However, for the ACT it is generally fine to work the problem algebraically.

③ $\sqrt{x} + \sqrt{4} = \sqrt{49}$. What is x?

$\sqrt{x} + 2 = 7 \implies \sqrt{x} = 5 \implies x = 25$.

④ $\sqrt[3]{x+3} + 3 = 7$. What is x?

$\sqrt[3]{x+3} = 4 \implies x + 3 = 64 \implies x = 61$.

④ Solve $\sqrt{x+4} - 3 > 4$.

$\sqrt{x+4} > 7 \implies x + 4 > 49 \implies x > 45$.

36.27. Systems of Equations

Straight Solving

Problems on the exam are generally best solved by solving for one of the variables in an equation and then substituting into the other equation. In some cases, you can add the equations and one of the variables will drop out. A more sophisticated approach involves linear combinations, but that is not needed for this exam. You can also graph the equations with your calculator and find the intersection point. There are programs for the calculator which will solve these problems. These problems can usually also be solved by plugging in answer choices.

③ⓒ If $x + y = 17$ and $x - y = 9$, what does x equal?

Adding the equations, $2x = 26 \implies x = 13$.

④ What is the solution of $2x - 3y = 2$ and $x + 5y = 14$?

The easiest approach is to use substitution and solve the second equation for x. $x = 14 - 5y$. $2(14 - 5y) - 3y = 2 \implies 28 - 10y - 3y = 2 \implies 13y = 26 \implies y = 2$. $x + 5 \cdot 2 = 14 \implies x = 4$, so $(4, 2)$.

Other Methods

If two lines have different slopes, then they intersect at one point. If the slopes are the same, they are usually parallel lines. If they are multiples of each other, they are the same line, and have an infinite number of points in common.

④ $2x + 3y = 7$ and $5x + 2y = 23$. What does $8x + y$ equal?

One way is take two the second equation and subtract the first one from it. $10x + 4y = 46$. Subtracting, $8x + y = 39$. Therefore, the answer is 39.

You can also solve the system by substitution or linear combinations and then plug the solutions into $8x + y$.

Word Problems

④ Apples and pears have constant prices. The combination of 3 apples and 5 pears costs $5.66, while 6 pears costs $4.02. How much does each apple cost?

Each pear costs $\frac{4.02}{6} = 0.67$. $3A + 5 \cdot 0.67 = 5.66 \implies 3A + 3.35 = 5.66 \implies 3A = 2.31 \implies A = 0.77$ or 77 cents.

④ Sally has 101 marbles, all of which are red, blue, or green. She has 10 more blue marbles than red marbles, and 6 more green marbles than blue marbles. How many green marbles does she have?

$R + B + G = 101$, $B = R + 10$, $G = B + 6$. Therefore, $G = R + 16$. $R + R + 10 + R + 16 = 101$. $3R = 75 \implies R = 25 \implies G = 25 + 15 = 40$

36.28. Quadratic Equations

Sum of the Solutions

It is easiest to do these problems using the formula $\frac{-b}{a}$.

③ⒻⒸ What is the sum of the solutions of $2x^2 - 10x + 17 = 0$?

You could find the solutions and add them, but it is easier to use the formula $\frac{-b}{a}$: $\frac{-(-10)}{2} = 5$.

Nature of Solutions

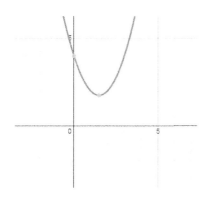

③ What is the nature of the solutions of the equation graphed?

Two complex solutions, because the parabola does not cross the x-axis. If it crossed in two places, there would be two real solutions. If it just touched the x-axis, there would be exactly one real solution.

④ What is the nature of the solutions of $2x^2 + 11x + 15 = 0$?

Two real solutions. This can be determined by solving the equation by factoring. Also, if you use the quadratic formula, the discriminant (what is under the radical) is positive: $b^2 - 4ac = 11^2 - 4 \cdot 2 \cdot 15 = 121 - 120 = 1$. If the discriminant was negative, there would be two complex solutions. If the discriminant was zero, there would be one real solution.

③ For what value of k does $x^2 - 12x + k = 0$ have exactly one solution?

Completing the square, $\left(\frac{-12}{2}\right)^2 = 36$. Or set the discriminant equal to 0, $b^2 - 4ac = 0 \implies (-12)^2 - 4 \cdot 1 \cdot k = 0 \implies 144 = 4k \implies k = 36$.

Equation From Roots

Take x minus each solution, FOIL out, and set equal to 0.

③ Which of the following is an equation with solutions -5 and 8?

$(x + 5)(x - 8) = x^2 - 3x - 40$.

④ Which of the following is an equation with solutions $\frac{2}{3}$ and $\frac{1}{5}$?

$$\left(x - \frac{2}{3}\right)\left(x - \frac{1}{5}\right) = 0 \implies$$
$$x^2 - \frac{2x}{3} - \frac{x}{5} + \frac{2}{15} = 0 \implies$$
$$x^2 - \frac{13x}{15} + \frac{2}{15} = 15x^2 - 13x + 2 = 0.$$

Or (first multiplying by constants to clear the fractions) $(3x - 2)(5x - 1) = 15x^2 - 3x - 10x + 2 = 15x^2 - 13x + 2 = 0$.

Solving Quadratics

The quadratic formula will usually not be given, so it helps to memorize it: $\dfrac{-b \pm \sqrt{b^2 - 4ac}}{2a}$

③ⒸⒻ What are the solutions of $x^2 + 5x = 14$? Get all the terms on one side, $x^2 + 5x - 14 = 0$. Now by factoring or the quadratic formula, the solutions are -7 and 2.
It is also possible to plug the solution choices in and see which works.

36.29. Angles

In a Polygon

The sum of the angles in a triangle is $180°$, in a quadrilateral $360°$.

③ In a quadrilateral the interior angles are $80°$, $120°$, $100°$ and $x°$. What is x?
$x° = 360° - 100° - 120° - 80° = 60°$

Isosceles Triangles

If two sides of a triangle are congruent, their opposite angles are also congruent.

③ In $\triangle ABC$, $AB = AC$ and $\angle A = 36°$.
What is $\angle B$?
$\angle B = \angle C$. $\angle B + \angle C = 180° - 36° = 144°$. Therefore, $\angle B = \dfrac{144°}{2} = 72°$.

Clock

④ How many degrees does the hour hand of a clock move between 4:20 and 5:40 PM?
The time elapsed is 1:20. $\dfrac{360°}{12} = 30°$ / hour.
$30° \cdot \dfrac{4}{3} = 40°$.

⑤ What is the angle between the hour and minute hands of a clock at 3:30?
$\dfrac{360}{12} = 30°$ per hour. $60°$ between 4 and 6.
$\dfrac{30}{2} = 15°$ between the hour hand's position at 3:30 and 4. $60° + 15° = 75°$.

Exterior Angles

An exterior angle of a triangle is equal to the sum of the opposite interior angles.

36.30. Circumference and Area

Circumference $= 2\pi r$ Area $= \pi r^2$, where r is the radius. These formulas are generally not given, so it is best to know or memorize them.

③ⒻⒸ The diameter of a circle is 10, what is its area?
$r = \dfrac{10}{2} = 5$. Area $= \pi r^2 = \pi 5^2 = 25\pi$ square units.

④ The circumference of a certain circle is 50 meters. What is its radius?
$C = 2\pi r$, $50 = 2\pi r \implies r = \dfrac{50}{2\pi} \implies r = \dfrac{25}{\pi}$ meters.

④Ⓕ The circumference of a certain circle is 30π. What is the area of that circle?
$C = 2\pi r \implies 30\pi = 2\pi r \implies r = 15$. Area $= \pi r^2 = \pi 15^2 = 225\pi$ square units.

36.31. Area

Circles

④Ⓕ What is the area in square coordinate units of a circle with center $(5, 7)$ which is tangent to the y-axis?
The radius must be 5, so $\pi r^2 = 25\pi$ square units.

④Ⓕ A circle with radius 5 is inside a circle with radius 6. What is the area inside the larger circle, but outside the smaller circle?
Area $= \pi r^2$. $\pi 6^2 - \pi 5^2 = 36\pi - 25\pi = 11\pi$ square units.

Rectangles

④ What is the minimum number of 6-inch by 6-inch tiles needed to cover an 8 feet 6 inches by 11 feet 6 inches floor?

17 by 23 tiles = 391 tiles.

Alternative solution: each tile is $\frac{1}{2} \times \frac{1}{2}$ feet, so $\frac{1}{4}$ square feet each. $8.5 \cdot 11.5 = 97.75$. $\dfrac{97.75}{\frac{1}{4}} =$ 391 tiles.

④ Sally has a 6 foot by 8 foot rectangular deck. She wants to add the same amount to the length and width so as to double the area. How much should she add?

$(6+x)(8+x) = 2 \cdot 48 \implies$
$x^2 + 14x + 48 = 96 \implies x^2 + 14x - 48 = 0.$
$\dfrac{-14 \pm \sqrt{14^2 - 4 \cdot 1 \cdot (-48)}}{2} =$
$\dfrac{-14 \pm \sqrt{196 + 192}}{2} \approx \dfrac{-14 \pm 19.7}{2}.$
The positive solution is $\dfrac{5.7}{2} \approx 2.9$ feet.

Triangles

③ⓒⒻ What is the area of a right triangle with sides 5, 12, and 13?

Since this is a right triangle, the two shorter sides are the legs or the base and height: $5 \cdot \dfrac{12}{2} = 30.$

Rhombus

④Ⓕ One diagonal of a rhombus is of length 10 and the other of length 6. What is the area of the rhombus?

$\dfrac{d_1 \cdot d_2}{2} = \dfrac{10 \cdot 6}{2} = 30.$

You could also find the area of each of 4 triangles (which are right and the same, since the diagonals of a rhombus are perpendicular) and multiply by 4.

⑤ What is the area of a rhombus with side lengths 6 and 2 angles measuring 60°?

It can be divided into two equilateral triangles with sides 6. The area of an equilateral triangle is $\dfrac{s^2\sqrt{3}}{4} = \dfrac{6^2\sqrt{3}}{4} = 9\sqrt{3}$, so both together are $18\sqrt{3}$. You can also find the height by the Pythagorean Theorem or $30-60-90$ triangles. Alternative Solution: one diagonal of the rhombus is 6. The other is $3\sqrt{3} \cdot 2 = 6\sqrt{3}$. The area of a rhombus is $\dfrac{d_1 \cdot d_2}{2} = \dfrac{6 \cdot 6\sqrt{3}}{2} = 18\sqrt{3}.$

36.32. Volume

Cube

④ A large cube has side lengths 5 times those of a small cube. The volume of the large cube is how many times the volume of the small cube?

$5^3 = 125.$

④ A cube has surface area 294 square inches. What is the surface area of one face of the cube?

$\dfrac{294}{6} = 49$ square inches.

Box

The formula for the volume of a box is length × width × height.

③ A rectangular solid is $\frac{1}{3}$ foot by 12 feet by 8 feet. How many cubic feet is its volume?

$\dfrac{1}{3} \cdot 12 \cdot 8 = 4 \cdot 8 = 32$ cubic feet.

③ A rectangular box has sides 12 times that of a scale model of it. What is the ratio of the volume of the box to the volume of the model?

$12^3 = 1728.$

④ A box has length 8 cm, width 6 cm and height 20 cm. If 384 cubic cm of sand are poured into the box, how deep will the sand be? $\dfrac{384}{6 \cdot 8} = 8$ cm.

④ A box is 12 meters by 6 meters by 10 meters. If it is filled to 75% capacity, how many cubic meters of material does it contain? $12 \cdot 6 \cdot 10 = 720$. $720 \cdot .75 = 540$ cubic meters.

④ How many 4-inch by 6-inch by 8-inch boxes will fit into a 2 feet by 3 feet by 4 feet large box?
The small box is $\dfrac{1}{3} \cdot \dfrac{1}{2} \cdot \dfrac{2}{3}$ cubic feet $= \dfrac{1}{9}$ cubic feet.
The large box has volume $2 \cdot 3 \cdot 4 = 24$ cubic feet.
$\dfrac{24}{\frac{1}{9}} = 216$.
You could also use cubic inches, but the numbers would be larger.

④ An inflatable bed has dimensions 50 inches by 80 inches by 8 inches. If it is inflated at the rate of 50 cubic inches per minute, how many minutes will it take to inflate?
$50 \cdot 80 \cdot 8 = 32,000$ cubic inches.
$\dfrac{32,000}{50} = 640$ minutes.

Cylinder

The volume of a cylinder is $\pi r^2 h$.

④ A cylinder has height 12 and diameter 12. What is its volume?
Radius $= \dfrac{12}{2} = 6$.
Volume $= \pi \cdot 6^2 \cdot 12 = 432\pi$ cubic units.

⑤ A cylindrical can has height 8 inches and inside diameter 6 inches. If the contents of that can is poured into a cylinder with diameter 10 inches, how high will it be?
Volume $= \pi r^2 h = \pi 3^2 \cdot 8 = 72\pi$.
The larger container was
$V = \pi r^2 h \implies 72\pi = \pi 5^2 h \implies h = \dfrac{72}{25}$.

Sphere

The formula for the volume of a sphere is $\dfrac{4\pi r^3}{3}$.

④ If the radius of a sphere is 5 cm, which is closest to its volume?
$\dfrac{4\pi 5^3}{3} = \dfrac{500\pi}{3} \approx 524$ cubic cm.

36.33. Inscribed

If a square, rectangle, or right triangle is inscribed in a circle, the diagonal or hypotenuse is the diameter of the circle. The radius is half the diameter. From that, you can find the area or circumference of the circle. That will allow you to determine the area inside the circle and outside the rectangle, etc.

③Ⓕ A 5 by 12 rectangle is inscribed in a circle. What is the area of the circle?
The diagonal of the rectangle is $\sqrt{5^2 + 12^2} = 13$. The radius of the circle is therefore $\dfrac{13}{2}$. The area of a circle is
$\pi r^2 = \pi \left(\dfrac{13}{2}\right)^2 = \dfrac{169\pi}{4}$.

⑤Ⓕ A square is inscribed in a circle of area 64π. What is the area of the square? $\pi r^2 = 64\pi \implies r^2 = 64 \implies r = 8$.
The diagonal of the square is therefore 16. Therefore, the sides of the square are $8\sqrt{2}$.
The area of a square is $\left(8\sqrt{2}\right)^2 = 128$.

36.34. Trigonometry

Trigonometric Area Formula

The general formula will find the area of any triangle given 2 sides and their included angle. It is area $= \dfrac{\sin A \cdot AB \cdot AC}{2}$. For a right triangle, it reduces to $\dfrac{\text{base} \cdot \text{height}}{2}$, as the sin 90° is 1.

④ Ⓕ Ⓣ In triangle ABC, angle A is 30°, AB is 3 and AC is 5. What is the area of the triangle?

$\sin 30° \cdot 3 \cdot \dfrac{5}{2} = \dfrac{1}{2} \cdot 3 \cdot \dfrac{5}{2} = \dfrac{15}{4}$. Treating it as a $30-60-90$ triangle or $3-4-5$ right triangle would be falling into a trap.

Amplitude and Period

To find the period, take 2π divided by the constant in front of x. The amplitude is the absolute value or the constant before the trigonometric function.

④Ⓒ What is the amplitude and period of $y = 5\sin(4x + \pi)$?

Amplitude is 5; the period is $\dfrac{2\pi}{4} = \dfrac{\pi}{2}$.

Trigonometric Function from Another

④Ⓒ For an angle with a measure of θ in a right triangle, $\sin \theta = \dfrac{2}{5}$. What is $\tan \theta$?

$\text{adjacent}^2 + 2^2 = 5^2 \implies$
$\text{adjacent}^2 = 21 \implies \text{adjacent} = \sqrt{21}$.
$\tan \theta = \dfrac{\text{opposite}}{\text{adjacent}} = \dfrac{2}{\sqrt{21}}$.

Alternate solution: $\sin^2 \theta + \cos^2 \theta = 1 \implies$
$\left(\dfrac{2}{5}\right)^2 + \cos^2 \theta = 1 \implies \dfrac{4}{25} + \cos^2 \theta = 1 \implies$
$\cos^2 \theta = \dfrac{21}{25} \implies \cos \theta = \dfrac{\sqrt{21}}{5}$.

$\tan \theta = \dfrac{\sin \theta}{\cos \theta} = \dfrac{\frac{2}{5}}{\frac{\sqrt{21}}{5}} = \dfrac{2}{\sqrt{21}}$.

You can also use $1 + \cot^2 = \csc^2$ or take $\sin^{-1}$ with your calculator and then take tan of that angle.

③Ⓒ If $\sin x = \dfrac{24}{25}$ and $\tan x = \dfrac{24}{7}$, what is $\cos x$?

$\tan x = \dfrac{\sin x}{\cos x} \implies \cos x = \dfrac{\sin x}{\tan x}$,

Therefore, $\cos x = \dfrac{\frac{24}{25}}{\frac{24}{7}} = \dfrac{7}{25}$.

Trigonometric Function from Sides

③Ⓒ In triangle ABC, angle A is a right angle, $AB = 4$ and $AC = 5$. What is $\sin B$?

$BC^2 = 4^2 + 5^2$ by the Pythagorean theorem
$\implies BC^2 = 16 + 25 = 41 \implies BC = \sqrt{41}$.

$\sin B = \dfrac{\text{opposite}}{\text{hypotenuse}} = \dfrac{AC}{BC} = \dfrac{5}{\sqrt{41}}$.

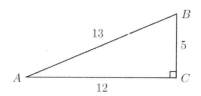

In $\triangle ABC$, what is $\cos A$?

$\cos A = \dfrac{\text{adjacent}}{\text{hypotenuse}} = \dfrac{12}{13}$.

Find Side of Triangle Using Trigonometry

This involves basic right triangle trigonometry, which is often taught in Geometry as well as Algebra II.

$\sin = \dfrac{\text{opposite}}{\text{hypotenuse}}, \cos = \dfrac{\text{adjacent}}{\text{hypotenuse}}$,

$\tan = \dfrac{\text{opposite}}{\text{adjacent}}$.

The hypotenuse is opposite the right angle and is also technically adjacent to the angle in question.

④ In triangle ABC, angle C is a right angle, angle A is $25°$ and $AC = 20$, what is BC?

$\tan 25° = \dfrac{x}{20} \implies x = 20\tan 25° \implies$
$x = 20 \cdot 0.466 \implies x = 9.32$.

Sum and Double Angle Formulas

Memorizing these formulas should NOT be a high priority. Questions on this are rare, and knowing the formulas is generally helpful but not absolutely necessary. $\sin(2\theta) = 2\sin \theta \cos \theta$;

$\cos(2\theta) = \cos^2\theta - \sin^2\theta = 2\cos^2\theta - 1 = 1 - 2\sin^2\theta$; $\sin(\alpha + \beta) = \sin\alpha\cos\beta + \sin\beta\cos\alpha$; $\sin(\alpha - \beta) = \sin\alpha\cos\beta - \sin\beta\cos\alpha$; $\cos(\alpha + \beta) = \cos\alpha\cos\beta - \sin\alpha\sin\beta$; $\cos(\alpha - \beta) = \cos\alpha\cos\beta + \sin\alpha\sin\beta$.

④Ⓕ If $\sin x = v$, what is equal to $\cos 2x$?
$\cos 2x = 1 - 2\sin^2 x = 1 - 2v^2$.
They may give the basic form of the formula $\cos^2 - \sin^2$, and you would need to derive the needed form if you didn't know it. This problem could also be solved by substituting a number for the angle.

Laws of Sines and Cosines

You need to know how to apply these and which one to use for a particular problem. You may or may not be given the formulas. Often you will need to find an expression using one of the laws rather than a numerical answer. Therefore, me law of sines problems result in no solutions or two solutions, but those should NOT be on the exam. These formulas are for solving general triangles, which do not have right angles.

The law of sines is $\dfrac{\sin A}{a} = \dfrac{\sin B}{b} = \dfrac{\sin C}{c}$ or $\dfrac{a}{\sin A} = \dfrac{b}{\sin B} = \dfrac{c}{\sin C}$. This is a more precise formulation of the larger side is opposite the larger angle. Use the law of sines when you have a side and an opposite angle and one other piece of information.

The law of cosines is $c^2 = a^2 + b^2 - 2ab\cos C$. a, b, and c are interchangeable. This is a generalization of the Pythagorean theorem. Use the law of cosines when you have 2 sides and an included angle or 3 sides. Another form of this formula is angle $C = \arccos\dfrac{a^2 + b^2 - c^2}{2ab}$.

④Ⓒ In $\triangle ABC$, $\angle A = 40°$, $\angle B = 60°$ and $AB = 20$. What is BC?
Since the angles in a triangle add to $180°$, $\angle C = 80°$.
$\dfrac{BC}{\sin A} = \dfrac{AB}{\sin C} \implies \dfrac{BC}{\sin 40°} = \dfrac{20}{\sin 80°} \implies$

$\dfrac{BC}{0.64} = \dfrac{20}{0.98} \implies BC = 20 \cdot \dfrac{0.64}{0.98} = 13.1$.

④Ⓒ What is the smallest angle in a triangle with sides 2, 3, and 4?
$2^2 = 3^2 + 4^2 - 2 \cdot 3 \cdot 4\cos C \implies$
$4 = 25 - 24\cos C \implies \cos C = \dfrac{21}{24} \implies$
$C = \arccos\dfrac{21}{24} \approx 29°$.

36.35. Logarithms

Expressions

$\log xy = \log + \log y$, $\log\dfrac{x}{y} = \log x - \log y$,
$\log x^y = y\log x$, $\log_a a^b = b$

③ What is $\log_x \dfrac{x^7}{x^{22}}$?
$\log_x \dfrac{1}{x^{15}} = \log_x x^{-15} = -15$.

③ Which is equivalent to $\log\left(\dfrac{a^2}{b}\right)$?
$\log(a^2) - \log b = 2\log a - \log b$.

③ What is the value of $(\log_3 27)(\log_2 64)$?
$3 \cdot 6 = 18$.

④ For $x > -1$, what is $\log(x + 1) + \log(x + 3)$?
$\log((x + 1)(x + 3)) = \log(x^2 + 4x + 3)$.

④ If $\log x = c$ and $\log y = d$, what is $\log(x^2 y^5)$?
$2\log x + 5\log y = 2c + 5d$.

Equations

These are general solved by taking both sides to the base of the log to eliminate the log expression. This is also called converting to exponential form.

③ What value satisfies $\log_x 81 = 4$?
This can be solved intuitively or by reasoning. Algebraically, $x^4 = 81 \implies x = \sqrt[4]{81} \implies x = 3$.

③ If $\log_3 x = -4$, what is x?
Taking both sides 3 to the power or converting to exponential form, $x = 3^{-4} = \frac{1}{81}$.

③ If $\log_x \frac{1}{8} = -3$, what is x?
$\frac{1}{8} = x^{-3} \implies \frac{1}{8} = \frac{1}{x^3} \implies x^3 = 8 \implies x = 2$.

④ For what value of x is $\log_3 9^5 = 3x$?
$\implies$ (taking both sides 3 to the power or converting to exponential form) $9^5 = 3^{3x} \implies 3^{10} = 3^{3x} \implies 10 = 3x \implies x = \frac{10}{3}$.

⑤ For what real value of x, if any, does $\log_{x+2}(x^2 + 2) = 2$?
$x^2 + 2 = (x+2)^2 \implies x^2 + 2 = x^2 + 4x + 4 \implies 4x = -2 \implies x = \frac{-1}{2}$.
Checking, $\log_{3/2}\left(\frac{9}{4}\right) = 2 \implies 2 = 2$.
For many students, this problem can best be solved by plugging in the answer choices.

⑤ What is the solution of $\log_2 \frac{\sqrt{4x-1}}{x-1} = 1$?
Taking both sides 2 to the power or converting to exponential form, $\frac{\sqrt{4x-1}}{x-1} = 2 \implies$
$\sqrt{4x-1} = 2x - 2 \implies 4x - 1 = 4x^2 - 8x + 4 \implies 4x^2 - 12x + 5 = 0 \implies$
$\frac{12 \pm \sqrt{144-80}}{8} \implies \frac{12 \pm 8}{8} = \frac{20}{8}$ or
$\frac{4}{8} = \frac{5}{2}$ or $\frac{1}{2}$. For $\frac{5}{2}$, $\log_2 \frac{\sqrt{4 \cdot \frac{5}{2} - 1}}{\frac{5}{2} - 1} = 1 \implies$
$\frac{\sqrt{10-1}}{\frac{3}{2}} = 2 \implies \frac{3}{\frac{3}{2}} = 2$, which checks.
For $\frac{1}{2}$, $\log_2 \frac{\sqrt{4 \cdot \frac{1}{2} - 1}}{\frac{1}{2} - 1} = 2 \implies \frac{\sqrt{1}}{\frac{-1}{2}} = 2$

$\implies -2 = 2$, which does not check. Therefore, the only solution is $\frac{5}{2}$.

Other

④ If $\log 8 = 0.9$, what does $\log(8 \times 10^{143})$ equal?
$\log 8 + \log 10^{143} = 0.9 + 143 = 143.9$.

④ The number of decibals, d, is given by $d = 10\log\left(\frac{I}{10^{-12}}\right)$, where I is sound intensity. What sound intensity produces 80 decibals?
$80 = 10\log\left(\frac{I}{10^{-12}}\right) \implies$
$8 = \log\left(\frac{I}{10^{-12}}\right) \implies$
$10^8 = \frac{I}{10^{-12}} \implies I = 10^8 \cdot 10^{-12} = 10^{-4}$.

36.36. Complex Numbers

The key thing to use is $i^2 = -1$.

Ⓒ② A common problem is to expand and simplify $(5 + 2i)^2$. FOIL it out $(5 + 2i)(5 + 2i) = 25 + 10i + 10i + 4i^2 = 25 + 20i - 4 = 21 + 20i$.

②Ⓒ Another common problem is what multiplied by a nonzero complex number $a + 8i$ gives a rational number?
You need to multiply by the complex conjugate, which is the same thing but with the imaginary part made negative, so $a - 8i$.
If it asked for what times $c - di$ gives a rational number, the answer would be $c + di$.

② You could be asked to solve $x(4 + 5i) = 1$. Then $x = \frac{1}{4 + 5i}$. Now multiply the numerator and denominator by the conjugate of the denominator.
$x = \frac{4 - 5i}{(4 + 5i)(4 - 5i)} = \frac{4 - 5i}{16 - 20i + 20i - 25i^2} = \frac{4 - 5i}{41}$.

④ Another type of division problem is which is equivalent to $\frac{i^4 + i^3}{i + 1}$?

This is $\dfrac{1-i}{1+i}$. Now multiply the numerator and denominator by the conjugate of the denominator,

$$1-i: \frac{(1-i)(1-i)}{(1+i)(1-i)} = \frac{1-i-i+i^2}{1-i+i-i^2} =$$
$$\frac{1-2i-1}{2} = \frac{-2i}{2} = -i.$$

③ What is $\sqrt{-12} + \sqrt{-75}$?

$2i\sqrt{3} + 5i\sqrt{3} = 7i\sqrt{3} = \sqrt{-1} \cdot \sqrt{3} \cdot \sqrt{7^2} = \sqrt{-1 \cdot 3 \cdot 49} = \sqrt{-147}$.

⑤ A difficult problem is what quadratic equation has $3 + 2i$ as a solution?

It might be possible to solve each of the choices with the quadratic formula, but that is a time trap.

The other solution must be the conjugate, $3 - 2i$. Therefore, take $(x - (3 + 2i))(x - (3 - 2i)) = (x - 3 - 2i)(x - 3 + 2i)$.

Now FOIL out and the imaginary terms cancel each other:
$x^2 - 3x + 2ix - 3x + 9 - 6i - 2ix + 6i - 4i^2 = x^2 - 6x + 9 + 4 = x^2 - 6x + 13 = 0$.

If you were asked to find an equation with solution $7 + \sqrt{3}$ (with an irrational but real number), you would use a similar approach.

36.37. Circles Using Analytic Geometry

④ Ⓒ Ⓕ What is the equation of a circle with center $(2, 5)$ going through $(-1, -1)$? By the distance formula, the radius of the circle is $\sqrt{(2+1)^2 + (5+1)^2} = \sqrt{3^2 + 6^2} = \sqrt{45}$.

Therefore, the equation of the circle is $(x-2)^2 + (y-5)^2 = 45$.

36.38. Conic Sections

Ellipses

⑤ What are the foci of $\dfrac{(x-6)^2}{25} + \dfrac{(y+2)^2}{9} = 1$?

$c^2 = a^2 - b^2 \implies c^2 = 25 - 9 = 16 \implies c = 4$.

The center of the ellipse is $(6, -2)$, based on what is subtracted from x and y.

You go 4 from the center in either direction along the major axis.

The major axis is the x-values, since $25 > 9$.

Therefore, the foci are $(6 - 4, -2)$ and $(6 + 4, -2) \implies$
$(2, -2)$ and $(10, -2)$ are the foci.

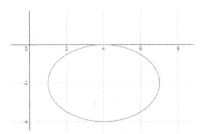

④ What is the equation of this ellipse?

The center is $(4, -2)$. It extends 3 in the x directions and 2 in the y directions.

Therefore, $\dfrac{(x-4)^2}{9} + \dfrac{(y+2)^2}{4} = 1$.

Hyperbolas

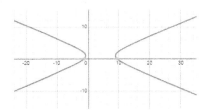

⑤ What is the equation of this hyperbola?

The center is at $(4, 1)$, by taking the average of the coordinates of the vertices. It opens in the x direction, so the x term is positive.

The slope of the asymptotes are about $\pm\dfrac{2}{5}$, so divide the y-term by $2^2 = 4$ and the x-term by $5^2 = 25$.

The exact amount is hard to determine, but the various answer choices should be very different.

Therefore, $\dfrac{(x-4)^2}{25} - \dfrac{(y-1)^2}{4} = 1$.

36.39. Sequences and Series

Sequences

Arithmetic

③ What two terms can be placed in the blanks to make it an arithmetic sequence? 15, _____, _____, 51?
$\frac{51-15}{3} = 12$. Therefore, the terms are 27 and 39.

③ The 8th term a_8 in an arithmetic sequence is 40 and the common difference is 3. What is the 1st term?
$a_1 = a_8 - 7 \cdot d = 40 - 7 \cdot 3 = 19$.

④ If the 3rd term in an arithmetic sequence is $\frac{1}{2}$ and the 6th term is $\frac{9}{8}$, what is the 10th term? Common difference $= \dfrac{\frac{9}{8} - \frac{1}{2}}{6-3} = \dfrac{\frac{5}{8}}{3} = \dfrac{5}{24}$.
Therefore, $a_{10} = a_6 + 4\left(\dfrac{5}{24}\right) = \dfrac{9}{8} + \dfrac{5}{6} = \dfrac{54}{48} + \dfrac{40}{48} = \dfrac{94}{48} = \dfrac{47}{24}$.

Geometric

③ⓒⓒ The first 5 terms of a geometric sequence are -7, 14, -28, 56, and -112. What is the 6th term?
The common ratio is -2.
So the 6th term is $-2 \cdot (-112) = 224$.

Series

The formula for the sum of a geometric series is $\dfrac{a}{1-r}$, where a is the first term and r is the common ratio.

④ If the sum of a series is 100 and the common ratio is $\dfrac{2}{3}$, what is the 3rd term in the series?
$100 = \dfrac{a}{1 - \frac{2}{3}} \implies 100 = \dfrac{a}{\frac{1}{3}} \implies a = \dfrac{100}{3}$.
$a_3 = \dfrac{100}{3} \cdot \left(\dfrac{2}{3}\right)^2 = \dfrac{100}{3} \cdot \dfrac{4}{9} = \dfrac{400}{27}$.

36.40. Permutations and Combinations

With permutations order matters; while with combinations order does not matter. Therefore, there are more permutations than combinations. The formula for permutations is $\dfrac{n!}{(n-k)!}$. The formula for combinations is $\dfrac{n!}{n! \cdot (n-k)!}$, where you are choosing k out of n elements.

Permutations

④ⓒ There are 9 players in a baseball starting lineup. The second baseman will bat first and the catcher will bat last. How many different possible lineups of those 9 players are there?
2 players are fixed, so we have 7 to arrange. $7! = 5040$.

④ How many ways can you arrange different 7 letters in 3 places?
$_7P_3 = \dfrac{7!}{(7-3)!} = 7 \cdot 6 \cdot 5 = 210$.

Combinations

④ How many diagonals does an octagon have? The number of line segments connecting the 8 vertices is $_8C_2 = \dfrac{8 \cdot 7}{2} = 28$.
Subtract the 8 sides, so 20 diagonals.

One From Each

③ⓒ Karen has 5 dresses, 4 blouses, and 10 pairs of shoes. How many outfits can she pick out?
$5 \cdot 4 \cdot 10 = 200$ outfits

36.41. Probability

NOT

These problems are generally easy.

①ⓒ Suppose there are 5 red, 7 blue, and 9 green marbles in a bowl. If a marble is drawn

at random, what is the probability it is not red?
$$\frac{7+9}{7+9+5} = \frac{16}{21}.$$

OR

OR condition probability problems on this exam are generally easy and should just require adding the probabilities. They assume mutually exclusive events. Or conditions with independent events are more complicated, but should not appear, and it is a trap to do complicated math.

②ⓒ The probability of Event A occurring is .3 and the probability of Event B occurring is .2. Those events are mutually exclusive. What is the probability that Event A or Event B occurs?
$.3 + .2 = .5$

Dice and Sum of Values

Take all the combinations that will give the requested value divided by the number of total combinations. For two dice, the number of total combinations is the number of faces on a single die squared.

④ If you roll two standard 6-sided dice, what is the probability that the total will be 4?
This occurs with outcomes $1-3, 3-1$, and $2-2$, so 3 possibilities out of $6^2 = 36$ total. Therefore,
$$\frac{3}{36} = \frac{1}{12}.$$

④ If you roll two 8-sided dice numbered $1-8$, what is the probability that the total will be 10?
This occurs with outcomes $2-8, 8-2, 3-7, 7-3, 4-6, 6-4$ and $5-5$,
so 8 possibilities out of $7^2 = 64$ total. Therefore,
$$\frac{7}{64}$$

Without Replacement

In without replacement problems, you reduce the number of the item drawn by one on the next draw and also reduce the number of total items by one.

③ For example, suppose there are 7 red marbles and 3 blue marbles in a bowl. If you draw two marbles without replacement, what is the probability they will both be red?
$$\frac{7}{10} \cdot \frac{6}{9} = \frac{42}{90} = \frac{7}{15}.$$

④ Suppose there are 7 red marbles and 3 blue marbles in a bowl. If you draw two marbles without replacement, what is the probability one will be red and the other blue?
$$\frac{7}{10} \cdot \frac{3}{9} + \frac{3}{10} \cdot \frac{7}{9} = \frac{42}{90} = \frac{7}{15}.$$
Here the number of possibilities of the other marble type is not reduced.

④ Suppose there are 6 red, 4 blue, and 2 yellow marbles in a bowl. If you draw two marbles without replacement, what is the probability both marbles will be of the same color?
$$\frac{6}{12} \cdot \frac{5}{11} + \frac{4}{12} \cdot \frac{3}{11} + \frac{2}{12} \cdot \frac{1}{11} = \frac{30+12+2}{132} = \frac{44}{132} = \frac{1}{3}.$$

④ Two slips of papers with numbers $1-7$ are placed in a bowl and drawn without replacement. What is the probability that the sum of the number will be 8?
The possibilities are $1-7, 7-1, 2-6, 6-2, 3-5$ and $5-3$.
The total possibilities are $7 \cdot 6 = 42$.
Therefore, $\frac{6}{42} = \frac{1}{7}.$
Note that $4-4$ is not a possibility, as the numbers cannot repeat. Also note that the number of possibilities on the second draw is reduced by one.

⑤ Suppose there are 6 red, 4 blue, and 2 yellow marbles in a bowl. If you draw three marbles without replacement, what is the probability they will all be of different colors?
$$3! \cdot \frac{6 \cdot 4 \cdot 2}{12 \cdot 11 \cdot 10} = 6 \cdot \frac{48}{1320} = \frac{12}{55}.$$
We multiply by 3! because there are 3! arrangements of the 3 marbles.
The number in the numerator is not reduced because the marbles are different colors.

Conditional Probability

Conditional probability is the probability of an event given another event occurs.

④ 40% of the balls in a bowl are red. 8% of the balls in that bowl are red and have a square on them. If a randomly drawn ball is red, what is the probability it has a square on it? $\dfrac{0.08}{0.4} = \dfrac{1}{5}$ or 0.2.

Product or Sum

④ One bowl contains slips of paper numbered $1-5$ and another contains slips of paper numbered $11-17$. If one slip of paper is taken at random from each bowl, what is the probability that the product of the numbers is odd? For the product to be odd, both numbers must be odd, so we multiply probabilities. $\dfrac{3}{5} \cdot \dfrac{4}{7} = \dfrac{12}{35}$.

④ In one bowl are slips of paper numbered $1-5$ and another slips of paper numbered $11-17$. If one slip of paper is taken at random from each bowl, what is the probability that the sum of the numbers is odd? For the sum to be odd, one must be odd and the other even. Therefore, $\dfrac{3}{5} \cdot \dfrac{3}{7} + \dfrac{2}{5} \cdot \dfrac{4}{7} = \dfrac{17}{35}$.

36.42. Composition of Functions

This is generally a precalculus topic. You need to know the basics.

③ⓒ Given the functions $f(x) = 7x + 2$ and $g(x) = x^2 - 4$, what is $f(g(-3))$?
$g(-3) = (-2)^2 4 = 5$.
$f(5) = 7 \cdot 5 + 2 = 37$.
This is the easiest approach. You could also find $f(g(x))$ and then substitute -3 for x.

③ⓒ $f(x) = 3x + 5$ and $g(x) = x^2 - 3$. What is $f(g(4))$?
It is better to substitute the constant 4 in first.
$g(4) = 4^2 - 3 = 13$. $f(g(4)) = f(13) = 3 \cdot 13 + 5 = 44$.

Alternate solution $f(g(x)) = 3(x^2 - 3) + 5 = 3x^2 - 4 \implies f(g(4)) = 3 \cdot 4^2 - 4 = 48 - 4 = 44$.

③ⓒ If $f(x) = 2x - 5$ and $g(x) = x^2 + 3$, what is $f(g(x))$?
$f(g(x)) = 2(x^2 + 3) - 5 = 2x^2 + 6 - 5 = 2x^2 + 1$.

③ $f(x) = 2x - 5$ and $g(x) = 3x + 2$. What is $f(g(x))$? $2(3x + 2) - 5 = 6x + 4 - 5 = 6x - 1$.

④ $f(x) = x^2 - 25$ and $g(x) = x + 2$. What are the solutions of $f(g(x)) = 0$?
$(x + 2)^2 - 25 = 0 \implies x^2 + 4x - 21 = 0 \implies x = -7$ or 3.
Alternative solution: $f(x) = 0 \implies x^2 - 25 = 0 \implies x = -5$ or 5. Substitute $x + 2$ for x and get -7 or 3.

②ⓒ $f(x) = \dfrac{1}{x - 4}$ and $g(x) = x^3$.
What is $f(g(x))$? $\dfrac{1}{x^3 - 4}$

④ $f(x) = x^2 + 3x + 2$ and $g(x) = x + 4$. What is $f(g(x))$?
$(x + 4)^2 + 3(x + 4) + 2 = x^2 + 8x + 16 + 3x + 12 + 2 = x^2 + 11x + 30$.

④ If $f(x) = 2x + a$ and $g(x) = 3x + 5$, for what value of a is $f(g(x)) = g(f(x))$? $2(3x + 5) + a = 3(2x + a) + 5 \implies 6x + 10 + a = 6x + 3a + 5 \implies 5 = 2a \implies a = \dfrac{5}{2}$.

36.43. Inverse Functions

These problems are not common and generally involve solving for a variable and do not explicitly request to find the inverse function, Usually, they will be given with odd powers to avoid domain issues.

② $y = 4x + 11$. What is x in terms of y?

Solve for x. $4x = y - 11 \implies x = \dfrac{y - 11}{4}$.

② What is the inverse function of $f(x) = x^5$?
Switch x and y and then solve for y.
$x = y^5 \implies \sqrt[5]{x} = y = f^{-1}(x)$

③ $y = 8x^3 - 15$. Which is equivalent to x. Again, solve for x.

$$y + 15 = 8x^3 \implies \frac{y+15}{8} = x^3 \implies$$

$$\sqrt[3]{\frac{y+15}{8}} = x \implies x = \frac{\sqrt[3]{y+15}}{2}$$

36.44. Exponential Equations

Variable Equations

③ $\frac{-1}{32} = -2^x$. What is x?

$2^x = \frac{1}{32} \implies 2^x = 2^{-5} \implies x = -5.$

③ If $2^x \cdot \frac{2^3}{(2^5)^6} = \frac{1}{16}$, what is x?

$2^x \cdot \frac{2^3}{2^{30}} = \frac{1}{2^4} \implies$

$\frac{2^x}{2^{27}} = \frac{1}{2^4} \implies 2^x = 2^{23} \implies x = 23.$

③ If $2^x \cdot 8 = 2^5$, what is x?

$2^x \cdot 2^3 = 2^5 \implies 2^x = 2^2 \implies x = 2.$

④ $8^{x-3} = 2$. What is x?

$2^{3(x-3)} = 2^1 \implies 3x - 9 = 1 \implies$

$3x = 10 \implies x = \frac{10}{3}.$

④Ⓒ If $4^{5x+3} = 8^{2x+7}$, what is x?

$2^{2(5x+3)} = 2^{3(2x+7)} \implies$

$2^{10x+6} = 2^{6x+21} \implies 10x + 6 = 6x + 21 \implies$

$4x = 15 \implies x = \frac{15}{4}$. Alternate solution: $(5x+3)\log 4 = (2x+7)\log 8$ (you could also use natural logarithms) $\implies$ $(5x+3)0.6 = (2x+7)0.9 \implies 3x + 1.8 = 1.8x + 6.3 \implies$ $1.2x = 4.5 \implies x = 3.75.$

④ What real numbers satisfy $5^{x^2+3x-10} = 1$?

$5^{x^2+3x-10} = 5^0 \implies x^2 + 3x - 10 = 0 \implies x = -5$ or 2 (by the quadratic formula or factoring).

④ If $8^{x^2} = 4^{x+8}$, what could x be?

$(2^3)^{x^2} = 2^{2(x+8)} \implies 3x^2 = 2x + 16 \implies$

$3x^2 - 2x - 16 = 0. \quad \frac{2 \pm \sqrt{4 + 3\cdot 16 \cdot 4}}{2 \cdot 3} \implies$

$\frac{2 \pm \sqrt{196}}{6} \implies \frac{2 \pm 14}{6} \implies \frac{8}{3}$ or $-2.$

It is also possible to solve the quadratic equation by factoring. It is possible to use logarithms initially, but that is not the best approach.

Word Problems

③Ⓒ The mass of a certain type of bacteria doubles every 15 minutes. How much will an initial sample of 5 mg be after 2 hours? There are 8 15-minute periods in 2 hours, so $5 \cdot 2^8 = 5 \cdot 256 = 1280$ mg.

④ How much will $7000 invested at 5% interest compounded annually be after 20 years? $\$7000 \cdot 1.05^{20} = \$18,573$

36.45. Reflection, Rotation, and Translation

Reflection

To reflect about the y-axis, take the negative of the x-value; to reflect about the x-axis, take the negative of the y-value. Most reflection problems on this exam involve reflecting about the y-axis.

②Ⓒ What is the point $(-2, -4)$ reflected about the y-axis?
Take the negative of the x-value, so $(2, -4)$.

② What is the point $(-2, -4)$ reflected about the x-axis?
Take the negative of the y-value, so $(-2, 4)$.

④ What is the point $(-2, -4)$ reflected about the line $y = 3$?
The y-value is 7 below the line, so take 7 above the line, which is $3 + 7 = 10$. Therefore, $(-2, 10)$.

Translation

④Ⓒ What is the equation of $y = x^2$ shifted 5 left and 7 up?
$y = (x+5)^2 + 7.$

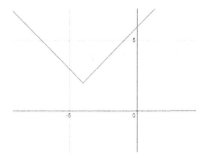

④ What is the equation graphed above?

The vertex is at $(-4, 2)$, so $y = |x + 4| + 2$.

Rotation

180° rotation: $(-x, -y)$; 90° clockwise: $(y, -x)$; 90° counterclockwise: $(-y, x)$. General trigonometric formula $(x \cos \theta - y \sin \theta, x \cos \theta + y \sin \theta)$. These problems can also be solved by reasoning without knowing formulas.

④Ⓕ What is the point $(5, 2)$ rotated 180°?
$(-5, -2)$

⑤Ⓕ What is the point $(5, 2)$ rotated 90° counterclockwise?
$(-2, 5)$

36.46. Asymptotes

To find the vertical asymptote of a rational function, set the denominator equal to 0 and solve for x. To find the horizontal asymptote, if the numerator and denominator have the same degree, take the ratio of the highest order terms in the numerator and denominator. There are other rules for horizontal aymptotes, but all problems on the exam should have numerators and denominators of the same degree.

③ What is the vertical asymptote of
$f(x) = \dfrac{3x + 4}{2x + 5}$?
Set $2x + 5 = 0 \implies x = \dfrac{-5}{2}$.

③Ⓒ What is the horizontal asymptote of
$f(x) = \dfrac{3x + 4}{2x + 5}$?

Since the degrees of the highest terms in the numerator and denominator are the same, take the ratio of the highest order terms:
$\dfrac{3}{2}$, so $y = \dfrac{3}{2}$.

36.47. $f()$

These are problems that require evaluating an expression for a particular value of a variable.

①Ⓒ If $f(x) = (5x + 7)^2$, what is $f(1)$?
Substituting 1 for x, $(5 + 7)^2 = 12^2 = 144$.

①Ⓒ If $a = 4$, $b = 3$, and $c = 5$, what is $(a + b - c)(b + c)$?
Substituting for each variable, $(4 + 3 - 5)(3 + 5) = 2 \cdot 8 = 16$.

②Ⓒ If $f(x, y) = 3xy^2 - x^2$, what is $f(5, 4)$?
Substituting for x and y,
$3 \cdot 5 \cdot 4^2 - 5^2 = 15 \cdot 16 - 25 = 215$.

② What is the value of $x^2 + xy + y^2 - 5$ when $x = 2$ and $y = 4$?

$2^2 + 2 \cdot 4 + 4^2 - 5 = 4 + 8 + 16 - 5 = 23$.

② What is $2x^2 y + 3y^2 z$ when $x = 3$, $y = -2$ and $z = 5$?
$2 \cdot 3^2 \cdot (-2) + 3 \cdot (-2)^2 \cdot 5 = 2 \cdot 9 \cdot (-2) + 3 \cdot 5 \cdot 4 = -36 + 60 = 24$.

② What is the value of $\sqrt{\dfrac{b}{a - 5}}$ when $b = -10$ and $a = 3$?
$\sqrt{\dfrac{-10}{-2}} = \sqrt{5}$

36.48. Domain and Range

Domain

Domain problems may explicitly ask for the domain, ask for the possible x-values, or ask for the x-values for which the expression is undefined. The key to domain problems is to set the denominator equal to 0, and then any solution to that equation is not in the domain.

② For what values is $f(x) = \dfrac{(x+1)(x+2)}{(x+3)(x+4)(x+5)}$ undefined?

Set the denominator equal to 0.

$(x+3)(x+4)(x+5) = 0$.

Therefore, $x = -3$, -4, and -5 are values for which the expression is undefined.

② For what values is $f(x) = \dfrac{1}{x^3 - 64x}$ undefined?

Set the denominator equal to 0.

$x^3 - 64x = 0 \implies x(x^2 - 64) = 0$ (since this is a difference of squares) $\implies$ $x(x-8)(x+8) = 0$.

Therefore, it is undefined for 0, 8, and -8.

② For what values is $f(x) = \dfrac{1}{|x| - 7}$ undefined?

Set $|x| - 7 = 0$. Therefore, $x - 7 = 0$ or $-x - 7 = 0 \implies x = 7$ or -7.

Range

Range problems are rare, and are relatively difficult. They are usually best approached by graphing the function or expression and determining the possible y-values from the graph.

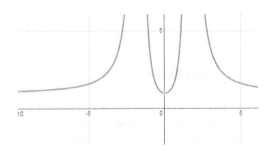

③ What is the range of $f(x) = \left(\dfrac{x^2 + 3}{x^2 - 3}\right)^2$?

Determining what the graph looks like algebraically is too time consuming. One approach is to graph the expression, and see the y-values appear to be $[1, \infty)$. Another is to see that it is square, so the values must be positive.

③ What are possible y-values for $y = \dfrac{x}{x-3}$ for $x > 3$?

Graph it and verify that it appears to go from 1 to infinity for that domain.

Or plug in answer choices for y and see if the equation works.

Also, you can see that y goes to infinity as x goes to 3 from above and y goes to 1 as x goes to infinity.

36.49. Mixture

③ⓒ A bag contains 6 red marbles, 7 yellow marbles, and 9 blue marbles. How many additional red marbles must be added to the bag for the probability of drawing a red marble to be $\dfrac{3}{5}$?

$\dfrac{6+x}{22+x} = \dfrac{3}{5} \implies$
$5(6+x) = 3(22+x) \implies$
$30 + 5x = 66 + 3x \implies$
$2x = 36 \implies x = 18$.

③ⓒ If 500 ml 10% alcohol solution is mixed with 300 ml 40% alcohol solution, what percent alcohol is the resulting mixture?

$\dfrac{500 \cdot 0.1 + 300 \cdot 0.4}{800} = \dfrac{50 + 120}{800} = \dfrac{170}{800} = 0.2125$ or $\approx 21.3\%$.

⑤ How much 80% salt solution would you need to add to 8 liters 10% salt solution to make the mixture 30% salt?

Set salt over liquid equal to 30%.

$\dfrac{8 \cdot 0.1 + x \cdot 0.8}{8 + x} = 0.3 \implies$
$0.8 + 0.8x = 2.4 + 0.3x \implies$
$0.5x = 1.6 \implies x = 3.2$ liters.

③ The Tigers have won 40% of their first 30 games. How many games in a row would they need to win to increase their win percentage to 60%?

$\dfrac{12 + x}{30 + x} = 0.6 \implies 12 + x = 18 + 0.6x \implies$
$0.4x = 6 \implies x = \dfrac{6}{0.4} = 15$.

36.50. Matrices

Adding and Subtracting

This is simple. Just add the corresponding elements. To multiply by a scalar, multiply each element by that scalar.

②Ⓒ Which of the following matrices is equal to $\begin{bmatrix} 2 & -5 \\ 4 & 8 \end{bmatrix} + \begin{bmatrix} 7 & 11 \\ -4 & -2 \end{bmatrix}$?

$$\begin{bmatrix} 2+7 & -5+11 \\ 4+(-4) & 8+(-2) \end{bmatrix} = \begin{bmatrix} 9 & 6 \\ 0 & 6 \end{bmatrix}$$

③ Which of the following is equivalent to $2\begin{bmatrix} 3 & 6 \\ -5 & 3 \end{bmatrix} + 5\begin{bmatrix} -5 & -2 \\ 2 & 3 \end{bmatrix}$?

First multiply

$$\begin{bmatrix} 6 & 12 \\ -10 & 6 \end{bmatrix} + \begin{bmatrix} -25 & -10 \\ 10 & 15 \end{bmatrix} =$$

$$\begin{bmatrix} -19 & 2 \\ 0 & 21 \end{bmatrix}$$

Multiplication

It is important to understand how to do matrix multiplication. You also should know that the number of columns in the first matrix being multiplied has to equal the number of rows in the second one for the matrices to be multiplied. This is because you turn the rows of this first one on their side and multiply them by the columns of the second one.

④ $A = \begin{bmatrix} 1 \\ 3 \end{bmatrix}$ and $B = \begin{bmatrix} 5 & 4 \end{bmatrix}$, what is AB?

Turning A's rows on their sides, $\begin{bmatrix} 5 & 4 \\ 15 & 12 \end{bmatrix}$.

④ $A = \begin{bmatrix} 1 \\ 3 \end{bmatrix}$ and $B = \begin{bmatrix} 5 & 4 \end{bmatrix}$, what is BA?

Turning B on its side, this is just one multiplication $\begin{bmatrix} 1\cdot5+3\cdot4 \end{bmatrix} = \begin{bmatrix} 17 \end{bmatrix}$.

④ $A = \begin{bmatrix} 1 & 2 & 5 \\ 4 & 3 & 2 \end{bmatrix}$ $B = \begin{bmatrix} 5 & 4 & 1 \\ 3 & 1 & 2 \\ 1 & 2 & 3 \end{bmatrix}$ What is AB?

$$\begin{bmatrix} 1\cdot5+2\cdot3+5\cdot1 & 1\cdot4+2\cdot1+5\cdot2 & 1\cdot1+2\cdot2+5\cdot3 \\ 4\cdot5+3\cdot3+2\cdot1 & 4\cdot4+3\cdot1+2\cdot2 & 4\cdot1+3\cdot2+2\cdot3 \end{bmatrix}$$

$$= \begin{bmatrix} 16 & 16 & 20 \\ 31 & 23 & 16 \end{bmatrix}.$$

④ $A = \begin{bmatrix} 1 & 2 & 5 \\ 4 & 3 & 2 \end{bmatrix}$ $B = \begin{bmatrix} 5 & 4 & 1 \\ 3 & 1 & 2 \\ 1 & 2 & 3 \end{bmatrix}$

What is BA?

The number of columns in B does not equal the number of rows in A, so this multiplication is impossible.

Determinants

The determinant of the matrix $\begin{bmatrix} a & b \\ c & d \end{bmatrix}$ is $ad - bc$. They will typically not provide that formula.

③Ⓕ What is the determinant of $\begin{bmatrix} 3 & 2 \\ 4 & 5 \end{bmatrix}$?

$3\cdot5 - 2\cdot4 = 7$.

④Ⓕ For what value of x does the determinant of $\begin{bmatrix} 2 & 5 \\ x & 4 \end{bmatrix}$ equal 3?

$2\cdot4 - 5x = 3 \implies 8 - 5x = 3 \implies$
$5 = 5x \implies x = 1$.

36.51. Variation

③ y varies directly as x. If when $x = 3$ $y = 10$, then when $x = 4$ what does y equal?

$y = kx$, $10 = k3 \implies k = \dfrac{10}{3}$. $y = \dfrac{10x}{3}$.

$y = 10\cdot\dfrac{4}{3} = \dfrac{40}{3}$.

④ y varies directly as the square of x. When $x = 3$ $y = 20$. When x equals 5, what does y equal?

$y = kx^2$, plugging in values, $20 = k3^2 \implies k = \dfrac{20}{9}$.

Substituting in for k, $y = \dfrac{20x^2}{9}$,

substituting in $x = 5$. $y = \dfrac{20 \cdot 5^2}{9} = 20 \cdot \dfrac{25}{9} = \dfrac{500}{9}$.

④ How would you express algebraically that x varies directly with a, inversely with the square of b, and directly with the cube of c? $x = \dfrac{kac^3}{b^2}$.

⑤ If force varies inversely with the square of distance, how far away would an object need to be for force to be twice as much as when it is 6 cm away?

Let $F = 24$. $F = \dfrac{k}{d^2} \implies 24 = \dfrac{k}{6^2} \implies k = 864$, so $F = \dfrac{864}{d^2}$.

Twice 24 is 48, substituting, $48 = \dfrac{864}{d^2} \implies d^2 = 18 \implies d = 3\sqrt{2} \approx 4.2$.

It is also possible to solve this by reasoning and intuition. The distance would need to be reduced by $\sqrt{2}$, since $\sqrt{2^2} = 2$.

36.52. Logic

Which of the following statements is equivalent to "If it is a table, then it is flat"? "If it is not flat, then it is not a table" The contrapositive has the same truth value as the original. To get the contrapositive, take the negation of both portions and switch their order.

36.53. Statistics

Mean and Standard Deviation

68% of data is within 1 standard deviation of the mean; 95% is within 2 standard deviations; and 99% is within 3 standard deviations.

④ If the mean age of 10 children is m and the standard deviation is s, 8 years later what will the mean and standard deviation be? Mean $m + 8$, standard deviation s.

Mean, Median, Mode, Range

④ The highest temperature recorded on the top of Mount Washington is 76° Fahrenheit. The lowest is 108° below zero. What is the range, median, and mean temperatures there?
The range is $76 - (-108) = 186°$.
There is not enough information to determine the median or mean.

④ Set A includes 10 numbers. Set B includes 9 of the same numbers as A, but the largest number in Set B is smaller than in A. Which measure must be less for B than for A?
The mean, range, and standard deviation must be less.
The median will be the same.

④ There are 5 values in a data set. The largest value is greatly increased. What happens to the median and mean?
The mean will be significantly increased.
The median will be uneffected.

36.54. Venn Diagram and Similar

④ⓒ Of 40 people, 18 have only dogs, 12 have only cats and 4 have both. How many have neither?
$40 - 18 - 12 - 4 = 6.$

36.55. Term in Expansion

③ What is the coefficient of the x^4 term in

$(2x - 5)^4$?
$(2x)^4 = 16x^4$, so 16.

④ What is the coefficient of the x^3 term in $(x + 1)^5$?
$_5C_3 = \dfrac{5!}{3! \cdot 2!} = \dfrac{5 \cdot 4}{2} = 10.$

Key:

① Easiest

⑤ Most Difficult

ⓒ Common

ⓒⓒ Very Common

Ⓕ Helpful to Know Formula

Ⓣ Trap

37. Common Problems

These are problems which are likely to often appear on the exam. They are mostly relatively easy problems, but it is important that the student be able to do them. Students who find some of the other material in this book difficult should start with these problems, and then proceed to the study guide.

1. What is the difference between the mean and the median of the squares of the integers from 3 to 6? ③
   A. 0
   B. 0.5
   C. 0.75
   D. 1
   E. 1.5

2. What is 8% of 3.46×10^6? ③
   A. 276
   B. 2,768
   C. 27,680
   D. 276,800
   E. 2,768,000

3. What number is halfway between $\frac{3}{5}$ and $\frac{2}{3}$? ③
   A. $\frac{5}{16}$
   B. $\frac{19}{30}$
   C. $\frac{5}{8}$
   D. $\frac{7}{10}$
   E. $\frac{19}{15}$

4. Point M is the midpoint of AB. A is $(4, -2)$ and M is $(-3, -4)$. What are the coordinates of point B? ③
   A. $\left(\frac{1}{2}, -3\right)$
   B. $(11, 0)$
   C. $(-9, -7)$
   D. $(-10, -6)$
   E. $(-12, -8)$

5. In the standard xy-coordinate plane, what is the midpoint of the line segment between $(-5,-2)$ and $(-1,7)$? ③

  A. $(-9,-3)$

  B. $(3,16)$

  C. $\left(\dfrac{5}{2},2\right)$

  D. $\left(-3,\dfrac{5}{2}\right)$

  E. $\left(2,\dfrac{-9}{2}\right)$

6. What is the distance between $(-2,3)$ and $(4,10)$? ③

  A. 9

  B. $\dfrac{25}{3}$

  C. $\sqrt{85}$

  D. $\sqrt{87}$

  E. $\sqrt{53}$

7. Bob and Kevin were painting a house. They started with 8 gallons of paint. The first day Bob used $1\dfrac{7}{8}$ gallons and Julio used $1\dfrac{3}{4}$ gallons. How many gallons were left? ③

  A. $3\dfrac{3}{8}$

  B. $4\dfrac{3}{8}$

  C. $5\dfrac{3}{8}$

  D. $4\dfrac{5}{8}$

  E. $3\dfrac{5}{8}$

8. If $f(x) = (3x+4)^2$, what is $f(1)$? ②

  A. 7

  B. 14

  C. 16

  D. 49

  E. 100

9. If $a = 6$, $b = 2$, and $c = 5$, what is $(a+b-c)(b-c)$? ②

  A. -39

  B. -9

  C. 0

  D. 21

  E. 30

10. If $f(x,y) = 4xy^2 - x^2$, what is $f(2,5)$? ②

  A. 36

  B. 76

  C. 196

  D. 200

  E. 396

11. What is the least common denominator of $\dfrac{5}{8}$, $\dfrac{1}{12}$, and $\dfrac{3}{10}$? ③

  A. 24

  B. 60

  C. 120

  D. 240

  E. 960

12. One sign flashes every 9 seconds and another every 12 seconds. At a certain instant, they flash at the same time. How many seconds until they flash at the same time again? ③

  A. 24

  B. 36

  C. 48

  D. 72

  E. 108

13. What is the least common multiple of 40, 60, and 80? ③

  A. 120

  B. 240

  C. 720

  D. 1440

  E. 14400

14. Which of these expressions is equivalent to $(2x + 7)(5x - 2)$? ②

  A. $2x^2 + 31x - 14$

  B. $5x^2 + 31x - 14$

  C. $10x^2 + 31x - 14$

  D. $10x^2 + 31x + 14$

  E. $10x^2 + 39x - 14$

15. Which of the following expressions is equivalent to $6(x + 3) - 4(2x - 5)$? ①

  A. $-22x + 28$

  B. $-2x + 38$

  C. $2x - 2$

  D. $10x - 2$

  E. $20x + 38$

16. Which of the following expressions is equivalent to $(2x^4 y^5)(4x^2 y^3)$? ②

  A. $4x^4 y^5$

  B. $6x^6 y^8$

  C. $6x^8 y^{15}$

  D. $8x^6 y^8$

  E. $8x^8 y^{15}$

17. Which of the following is equivalent to $(x^3)^{18}$? ②

  A. x^{21}

  B. x^{24}

  C. x^{36}

  D. x^{54}

  E. x^{108}

18. Which of the following is equivalent to $(3x^2)^3$? ②

  A. $6x^6$

  B. $9x^6$

  C. $9x^5$

  D. $27x^5$

  E. $27x^6$

19. Which of the following is equivalent to $(5x^3) \cdot (4x^8)$? ②

  A. $5x^{11/4}$

  B. $20x^{11}$

  C. $20x^{24}$

  D. $100x^{11}$

  E. $625x^{11}$

20. A train left Atlanta at 8:54 PM and arrived in New York at 10:12 AM the next day in the same time zone. How many hours and minutes did the trip take? ④

  A. 12 tasks and 18 minutes

  B. 13 hours and 18 minutes

  C. 13 hours and 22 minutes

  D. 13 hours and 28 minutes

  E. 14 hours and 18 minutes

21. What is the smallest positive integer greater than $\sqrt{210}$? ②

  A. 13

  B. 14

  C. 15

  D. 16

  E. 17

22. If $8x - 7 = 3x + 8$, then $x =$? ①

    A. $\dfrac{1}{11}$

    B. $\dfrac{1}{5}$

    C. $\dfrac{15}{11}$

    D. $\dfrac{8}{5}$

    E. 3

23. If $\dfrac{3x}{4} - 2 = 13$, then $x =$? ③

    A. $\dfrac{-45}{4}$

    B. $\dfrac{33}{4}$

    C. $\dfrac{45}{4}$

    D. $\dfrac{44}{3}$

    E. 20

24. Which of the following inequalities is equivalent to $6x - 5 > 2x + 7$? ③

    A. $x > \dfrac{1}{4}$

    B. $x > \dfrac{1}{2}$

    C. $x > \dfrac{3}{2}$

    D. $x < 3$

    E. $x > 3$

25. A board which is 9 feet 4 inches long is cut into two equal parts. How long is each part in feet and inches? ③

    A. 4 feet 2 inches

    B. 4 feet 4 inches

    C. 4 feet 8 inches

    D. 4 feet 9 inches

    E. 5 feet 2 inches

26. In the standard xy-coordinate plane, what is the slope of a line containing $(3, 2)$ with y-intercept of 4? ③

    A. -2

    B. $\dfrac{-3}{2}$

    C. $\dfrac{-2}{3}$

    D. $\dfrac{2}{3}$

    E. $\dfrac{3}{2}$

27. In the standard xy-coordinate plane, what is the slope of the line $4x + 7y = -11$? ③

    A. $\dfrac{-7}{4}$

    B. $\dfrac{-11}{7}$

    C. $\dfrac{-4}{7}$

    D. $\dfrac{4}{7}$

    E. $\dfrac{7}{4}$

28. What is the slope of a line through $(-4, -2)$ and $(-1, 5)$ in the standard xy-coordinate plane? ③

    A. $\dfrac{3}{7}$

    B. 1

    C. $\dfrac{3}{2}$

    D. $\dfrac{7}{3}$

    E. $\dfrac{7}{2}$

29. What is the slope of $y - 11 = \frac{2}{3}(5x + 4)$? ③

    A. $\frac{3}{10}$

    B. $\frac{8}{3}$

    C. $\frac{10}{3}$

    D. 10

    E. 11

30. Which of the following lines is perpendicular to $5x + 4y = 7$? ③

    A. $-5x - 4y = 3$

    B. $-5x + 4y = 3$

    C. $4x - 5y = 9$

    D. $4x + 5y = 12$

    E. $5x - 4y = 23$

31. What is the 342rd digit to the right of the decimal point in $.8\overline{245}$? ④

    A. 2

    B. 3

    C. 4

    D. 5

    E. 8

32. If $\frac{2x - y}{x + y} = \frac{3}{5}$, what does $\frac{x}{y}$ equal? ④

    A. $\frac{-7}{8}$

    B. $\frac{-1}{2}$

    C. $\frac{1}{2}$

    D. $\frac{7}{8}$

    E. $\frac{8}{7}$

33. If $\frac{1}{4}$ inch represents 30 miles, how far apart are two towns which are $\frac{7}{8}$ inch apart on the map? ③

    A. 35

    B. 100

    C. 105

    D. 210

    E. 420

34. What is $|3 - x|$ when $x = 11$? ②

    A. -8

    B. 7

    C. 8

    D. 14

    E. 33

35. What is $|-18| - |17 - 33|$? ②

    A. -2

    B. 2

    C. 18

    D. 34

    E. 35

36. What is $|15 - 3| - |2 - 9|$? ②

    A. -1

    B. 1

    C. 5

    D. 15

    E. 22

37. What is the sum of the solutions of $x^2 - 5x - 18 = 0$? ③

    A. -5

    B. $\frac{5}{2}$

    C. $\frac{18}{5}$

    D. 5

    E. 10

38. Which of the following is a factor of $x^2 + 4x - 21$? ③

 A. $x - 7$

 B. $x - 4$

 C. $x - 3$

 D. $x + 3$

 E. $x + 4$

39. What is the area of a circle with circumference $8\sqrt{5}\pi$? ③

 A. 40π

 B. 60π

 C. 72π

 D. 80π

 E. 90π

40. A square has sides 24. A rectangle has the same area has width 8. What is the length of that rectangle? ②

 A. 24

 B. 48

 C. 72

 D. 81

 E. 108

41. Two adjacent sides of a rectangle have lengths $2x - 5$ and $x + 3$. What is the area of that rectangle? ②

 A. $x^2 - 9x - 15$

 B. $x^2 + x + 15$

 C. $x^2 + 9x - 15$

 D. $x^2 + 9x + 15$

 E. $2x^2 + x - 15$

42. A square and a rectangle have the same area. The length of the rectangle is 75 and its width is 12. What is the side length of the square? ③

 A. 24

 B. 30

 C. 32

 D. 36

 E. 40

43. A triangle has sides of length x, $2x - 1$, and $3x - 7$ and perimeter 34. What is its longest side length? ③

 A. 7

 B. 13

 C. 14

 D. 15

 E. 17

44. In triangle ABC, angle A is a right angle, $AB = 3$ and $AC = 2$. What is $\sin \angle B$? ③

 A. $\dfrac{2}{5}$

 B. $\dfrac{2}{\sqrt{13}}$

 C. $\dfrac{3}{\sqrt{13}}$

 D. $\dfrac{2}{3}$

 E. $\dfrac{2}{\sqrt{5}}$

45. For an angle with measure θ in a right triangle, $\sin \theta = \dfrac{5}{7}$. What is $\tan \theta$? ③

 A. $\dfrac{5}{4\sqrt{6}}$

 B. $\dfrac{5}{\sqrt{74}}$

 C. $\dfrac{7}{\sqrt{74}}$

 D. $\dfrac{7}{5}$

 E. $\dfrac{4\sqrt{6}}{5}$

46. If $\sin x = \dfrac{7}{25}$ and $\tan x = \dfrac{7}{24}$, what is $\cos x$? ③

 A. $\dfrac{7}{26}$

 B. $\dfrac{17}{24}$

 C. $\dfrac{18}{25}$

 D. $\dfrac{24}{25}$

 E. $\dfrac{12}{13}$

47. What is the amplitude of $y = 3\sin\left(\dfrac{x}{2} + \dfrac{\pi}{8}\right)$? ③

 A. -3

 B. $\dfrac{1}{2}$

 C. $\dfrac{3}{2}$

 D. 3

 E. 6

48. In triangle ABC, what is $\cos \angle A$? ③

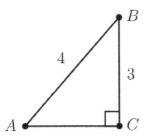

 A. $\dfrac{3}{5}$

 B. $\dfrac{\sqrt{7}}{4}$

 C. $\dfrac{3}{4}$

 D. $\dfrac{4}{5}$

 E. $\dfrac{4}{\sqrt{23}}$

49. For $i = \sqrt{-1}$, $(2 + 5i)^2$ equals which of these? ③

 A. -1

 B. $4 + 45i$

 C. $20i - 21$

 D. $20i - 29$

 E. 29

50. When a is rational and $i = \sqrt{-1}$, the product of $3a - 2i$ and which of the following numbers must be a rational number? ②

 A. i

 B. $3a - 2i$

 C. $3a + 2i$

 D. $3a - i$

 E. $3a + i$

51. The first 5 terms of a geometric sequence are 6, -12, 24, -48 and 96. What is the 6th term? ③

 A. -192

 B. -144

 C. -96

 D. 192

 E. 384

52. There are 9 players in a baseball starting lineup. The center fielder will bat first, the shortstop will bat 8th, and the catcher will bat last. How many different possible line-ups of those 9 players are there? ③

 A. 21

 B. 120

 C. 720

 D. 2520

 E. 5040

53. Given the functions $f(x) = 5x + 3$ and $g(x) = x^2 - 7$, what is $f(g(-3))$? ③

 A. -77

 B. -12

 C. 3

 D. 13

 E. 137

54. If $f(x) = 3x - 2$ and $g(x) = x^2 + 5$, what is $f(g(x))$? ③

- **A.** $x^2 - 3$
- **B.** $3x^2 - 13$
- **C.** $3x^2 + 3$
- **D.** $3x^2 + 17$
- **E.** $9x^2 - 12x + 9$

55. Which of the following matrices is equivalent to $\begin{bmatrix} -3 & 2 \\ 5 & -4 \end{bmatrix} + \begin{bmatrix} 3 & 5 \\ 6 & -7 \end{bmatrix}$?

- **A.** $\begin{bmatrix} -9 & 10 \\ 30 & 28 \end{bmatrix}$
- **B.** $\begin{bmatrix} -6 & -3 \\ -1 & 3 \end{bmatrix}$
- **C.** $\begin{bmatrix} 0 & 7 \\ 11 & -11 \end{bmatrix}$
- **D.** $\begin{bmatrix} 0 & 7 \\ 16 & -14 \end{bmatrix}$
- **E.** $\begin{bmatrix} 11 & 13 \\ -53 & 40 \end{bmatrix}$

56. Which of the following is the result of reflecting the point $(-7, 3)$ about the y-axis? ③

- **A.** $(-14, 3)$
- **B.** $(-14, 6)$
- **C.** $(-7, -3)$
- **D.** $(-7, 3)$
- **E.** $(7, 3)$

57. The point $(7, -5)$ is translated right 3 units and down 8 units. What are the coordinates of the new point? ③

- **A.** $(-1, -2)$
- **B.** $(-1, 2)$
- **C.** $(7, -13)$
- **D.** $(10, -13)$
- **E.** $(10, -2)$

58. Which of the following statements is equivalent to "All cats have fur"?

- **A.** "If it does not have fur, then it is not a cat"
- **B.** "If it does not have fur, then it is a cat"
- **C.** "If it has fur, then it is not a cat"
- **D.** "If it has fur, then it is a cat"
- **E.** "If it is not a cat, then it does not have fur"

— ANSWER KEY

1D, 2D, 3B, 4D, 5D, 6C, 7B, 8D, 9B, 10C, 11C, 12B, 13B, 14C, 15B, 16D, 17D, 18E, 19B, 20B, 21C, 22E, 23E, 24E, 25C, 26C, 27C, 28D, 29C, 30C, 31A, 32E, 33C, 34C, 35B, 36C, 37D, 38C, 39D, 40C, 41E, 42B, 43C, 44B, 45A, 46D, 47D, 48B, 49C, 50C, 51A, 52C, 53D, 54B, 55C, 56C, 57D, 58A.

37.1. Solutions

1. (D) The squares are 9, 16, 25, and 36. The mean is $\dfrac{9+16+25+36}{4} = \dfrac{86}{4} = 21.5$. The median is the average of the two middle terms, $\dfrac{16+25}{2} = 20.5$. The difference is $21.5 - 20.5 = 1$.

2. (D) $.08 \cdot 3.46 \times 10^6 = 0.2768 \times 10^6 = 2.768 \times 10^5 = 276,800$.

3. (B) $\dfrac{\frac{3}{5}+\frac{2}{3}}{2} = \dfrac{\frac{19}{15}}{2} = \dfrac{19}{30}$.

4. (D) Algebraically, substitute in one endpoint and the result into the midpoint formula $\left(\dfrac{x_1+x_2}{2}, \dfrac{y_1+y_2}{2}\right)$. $-3 = \dfrac{4+x}{2} \implies -6 = 4+x \implies x = -10$. $\dfrac{-2+y}{2} = -4 \implies -2+y = -8 \implies y = -6$, so B has coordinates $(-10, -6)$.

   There are various ways to reason this without knowing the midpoint formula. For example, you go -7 in x-values from A to M and -2 in y-values. So you need to go another -7 in x and -2 in y from M to B. So $B = (-3-7, -4-2) = (-10, -6)$.

5. (D) The midpoint formula is $\left(\dfrac{x_1+x_2}{2}, \dfrac{y_1+y_2}{2}\right)$. So $\left(\dfrac{-5+-1}{2}, \dfrac{-2+7}{2}\right) = \left(\dfrac{-6}{2}, \dfrac{5}{2}\right) = \left(-3, \dfrac{5}{2}\right)$.

   If you do not know the midpoint formula, you can understand or derive it as taking the average of the x-coordinates and the average of the y-coordinates.

6. (C) Apply the distance formula, distance $= \sqrt{(x_2-x_1)^2 + (y_1-y_2)^2}$ So distance is $\sqrt{(4-2)^2 + (10-3)^2} = \sqrt{(6^2+7^2)} = \sqrt{85}$.

   The formula can be derived from the Pythagorean theorem. If you do not remember the formula, you can also use the Pythagorean theorem directly, finding one leg as the difference in x-coordinates and the other as the difference in y-coordinates. Many ACT problems are like this. They are easiest if you memorized a formula, but you can also reason the answer or derive the formula on the fly.

7. (B) $1+1 = 2$, $\dfrac{7}{8} + \dfrac{3}{4} = \dfrac{7}{8} + \dfrac{6}{8} = \dfrac{13}{8} = 1\dfrac{5}{8}$. So total gallons used $= 2 + 1\dfrac{5}{8} = 3\dfrac{5}{8}$. $8 - 3\dfrac{5}{8} = 4 + 1 - \dfrac{5}{8} = 4 + \dfrac{8}{8} - \dfrac{5}{8} = 4 + \dfrac{3}{8}$, so the answer is $4\dfrac{3}{8}$.

8. (D) $(3 \cdot 1 + 4)^2 = 7^2 = 49$

9. (B) $(6+2-5)(2-5) = 3(-3) = -9$

10. (C) $4 \cdot 2 \cdot 5^2 - 2^2 = 8 \cdot 25 - 4 = 196$.

11. (C) This requires finding the least common multiple of the denominators. $8 = 2^3$, $12 = 3 \cdot 2^2$, $10 = 5 \cdot 2$. We take the highest power of any factor which occurs: $2^3 \cdot 3 \cdot 5 = 120$.

12. (B) This is just a least common multiple problem. $9 = 3^2$, $12 = 2^2 \cdot 3$. Taking the highest powers of 2 and 3, $2^2 \cdot 3^2 = 36$.

13. (B) $40 = 2^3 \cdot 5$, $60 = 2^2 \cdot 3 \cdot 5$, $80 = 2^4 \cdot 5$. So $2^4 \cdot 3 \cdot 5 = 240$. You could also find the least common multiple of 4, 6, and 8, which is 24, and then multiply to 10.

14. (C) $10x^2 - 4x + 35x - 14 = 10x^2 + 31x - 14$.

15. (B) $6x + 18 - 8x + 20 = -2x + 38$.

16. (D) $2 \cdot 4 \cdot x^4 \cdot x^2 \cdot y^5 \cdot y^3 = 8x^6 y^8$

17. (D) x^{54}. When taking the power of the power, you multiply the exponents.

18. (E) $3^3 (x^2)^3 = 27x^6$. When taking the power of the power, multiply exponents.

19. (B) $5 \cdot 4 \cdot x^3 \cdot x^8 = 20x^{11}$.

20. (B) 13 hours from 8:54 PM to 9:54 AM. 18 minutes from 9:54 AM to 10:12 AM. Therefore, 13 hours and 18 minutes.

21. (C) $\sqrt{210} \approx 14.5$, so the smallest integer greater is 15. It is a trap to round down to 14. You can do this by knowing or determining the perfect squares, but finding $\sqrt{210}$ with your calculator is easiest.

22. (E) $5x = 15 \implies x = 3$.

23. (E) $\dfrac{3x}{4} = 15 \implies x = 15 \cdot \dfrac{4}{3} = 20$.

24. (E) $4x > 12 \implies x > 3$.

25. (C) One-half of 9 feet is 4 feet 6 inches. One-half of 4 inches is 2 inches. 4 feet 6 inches plus 2 inches is 4 feet 8 inches. Alternative solution: 9 feet 4 inches is $9 \cdot 12 + 4 = 112$ inches. One-half of that is 56 inches or 4 feet 8 inches.

26. (C) Find the slope between $(3, 2)$ and $(0, 4)$: $\dfrac{y_2 - y_1}{x_2 - x_1} \implies \dfrac{4-2}{0-3} = \dfrac{2}{-3} = \dfrac{-2}{3}$.

27. (C) Solve for y to get the equation into slope-intercept form, $7y = -4x - 11 \implies y = \dfrac{-4x}{7} - \dfrac{11}{7}$. The slope is the number in front of x, $\dfrac{-4}{7}$.

28. (D) Use the slope formula, $\dfrac{y_2 - y_1}{x_2 - x_1}$, $\dfrac{5 - (-2)}{-1 - (-4)} = \dfrac{7}{3}$.

29. (C) Distributing, $y - 11 = \dfrac{10x}{3} + \dfrac{8}{3}$. The slope is the constant in front of x, $\dfrac{10}{3}$.

30. (C) $4x - 5y = 24$. Solving for y, $4y = -5x + 7 \implies y = \dfrac{-5x}{4} + \dfrac{7}{4}$, so the slope is the x-coefficient, $\dfrac{-5}{4}$. Any line perpendicular to the original has a slope that is the negative reciprocal of $\dfrac{-5}{4}$, which is $\dfrac{4}{5}$, so $4x - 5y = 9$.

31. (A) The digits repeat every 4. So take 342 modula 4 (this is the remainder when dividing by 4), which is 2, so take the 2nd digit in the repetition, which is 2.

32. (E) Cross multiplying, $5(2x - y) = 3(x + y) \implies 10x - 5y = 3x + 3y \implies 7x = 8y \implies \dfrac{x}{y} = \dfrac{8}{7}$.

33. (C) $\dfrac{\frac{7}{8}}{\frac{1}{4}} = \dfrac{x}{30} \implies x = 30 \cdot \dfrac{\frac{7}{8}}{\frac{1}{4}} \implies x = \dfrac{\frac{210}{8}}{\frac{1}{4}} \implies x = \dfrac{210}{8} \cdot 4 \implies x = \dfrac{210}{2} = 105$ miles.

34. (C) $|3 - 11| = |-8| = 8$.

35. (B) $18 - |-16| = 18 - 16 = 2$.

36. (C) $|12| - |-7| = 12 - 7 = 5$.

37. (D) The formula for the sum of the solutions is $\dfrac{-b}{a} = \dfrac{-(-5)}{1} = 5$. You can also find the solutions with the quadratic formula and add them.

38. (C) $x^2 + 7x - 3x - 21 = x(x + 7) - 3(x + 7) = (x - 3)(x + 7)$. So $x - 3$. It is also possible to use the quadratic formula to find the solutions and then subtract them from x to find the factors. You can also determine the roots from the answer choices and plug them into the original expression and see which give zero.

39. (D) The circumference is $2\pi r$, so $2\pi r = 8\sqrt{5}\pi \implies r = 4\sqrt{5}$. The area is $\pi r^2 = (4\sqrt{5})^2 \pi = 80\pi$.

40. (C) The area of the square is $24^2 = 576$. $A = lw$ for a rectangle: $576 = l \cdot 8 \implies l = \dfrac{576}{8} = 72$.

41. (E) Area = length · width, so $(2x - 5)(x + 3) = 2x^2 + 6x - 5x - 15 = 2x^2 + x - 15$.

42. (B) The area of the rectangle is $l \cdot w = 75 \cdot 12 = 900$. The side length of the square is $\sqrt{900} = 30$.

43. (C) $x + 2x - 1 + 3x - 7 = 34 \implies 6x - 8 = 34 \implies 6x = 42 \implies x = 7$. The longest side is $3x - 7 = 3 \cdot 7 - 7 = 14$.

44. (B) $BC = \sqrt{2^2 + 3^2} = \sqrt{13}$, by the Pythagorean theorem. $\sin \angle B = \dfrac{\text{opposite}}{\text{hypotenuse}} = \dfrac{AC}{BC} = \dfrac{2}{\sqrt{13}}$.

45. (A) Opposite is 5 and hypotenuse is 7 from the sin function. So $\text{adjacent}^2 + 5^2 = 7^2 \implies \text{adjacent}^2 + 25 = 49 \implies \text{adjacent}^2 = 24 \implies \text{adjacent} = 2\sqrt{6}$. So $\tan \theta = \dfrac{\text{opposite}}{\text{adjacent}} = \dfrac{5}{2\sqrt{6}}$. You can also take $\sin^{-1}\left(\dfrac{7}{25}\right)$ with your calculator and take the tan of that angle. Another approach would be to use one of the Pythagorean identities. For example $1 + \cot^2 = \csc^2$. $\csc \theta = \dfrac{1}{\sin \theta} = \dfrac{7}{5}$. So $1 + \cot^2 \theta = \left(\dfrac{7}{5}\right)^2 \implies 1 + \cot^2 \theta = \dfrac{49}{25} \implies \cot^2 \theta = \dfrac{24}{25} \implies \cot \theta = \dfrac{4\sqrt{6}}{5} \implies \tan \theta = \dfrac{5}{2\sqrt{6}}$.

46. (D) $\dfrac{24}{25}$. Using $\sin^2 + \cos^2 = 1$, $\left(\dfrac{7}{25}\right)^2 + \cos^2 x = 1 \implies \dfrac{49}{625} + \cos^2 x = 1 \implies \cos^2 x = \dfrac{576}{625} \implies \cos x = \dfrac{24}{25}$. You can also take $\sin^{-1}\left(\dfrac{7}{25}\right)$ or $\tan^{-1}\left(\dfrac{7}{24}\right)$ with your calculator and take the cos of that angle. Another approach would be to draw the right triangle and determine the adjacent side with the Pythagorean theorem.

47. (D) The amplitude is the absolute value of the number in front of sin, so 3.

48. (B) $AC^2 + 3^2 = 4^2 \implies AC^2 + 9 = 16 \implies AC^2 = 7 \implies AC = \sqrt{7}$. $\cos \angle A = \dfrac{\text{adj}}{\text{hyp}} = \dfrac{AC}{AB} = \dfrac{\sqrt{7}}{4}$.

49. (C) $4 + 10i + 10i + 25i^2 = 20i - 21$.

50. (C) $3a + 2i$. Take the negative of the imaginary part. That gives the conjugate, which multiplied by the original yields a real number.

51. (A) The common ratio is -2. $96 \cdot (-2) = -192$.

52. (C) 720. 3 players are fixed, so there are $6! = 720$ ways of arranging the remaining players.

53. (D) $g(-3) = (-3)^2 - 7 = 9 - 7 = 2$. $f(2) = 5 \cdot 2 + 3 = 13$. You could also find $f(g(x))$ and then substitute -3 for x, but that would be more work.

54. (B) $3(x^2 + 5) - 2 = 3x^2 + 15 - 2 = 3x^2 + 13$.

55. (C) Add corresponding terms $\begin{bmatrix} 0 & 7 \\ 16 & -14 \end{bmatrix}$.

56. (C) Take the negative of the x-value, so $(7, 3)$.

57. (D) $(7 + 3, -5 - 8) = (10, -13)$.

58. (A) "If it does not have fur, then it is not a cat". The contrapositive has the same truth value as the original. To get the contrapositive, take the negation of both portions and switch their order.

38. Multiple Solutions to Real Problems

Chapter 5 Midpoint and distance formula Pythagorean theorem

13. In the isosceles right triangle below, $AB = 10$ feet. What is the length, in feet, of $\overline{AC}$?

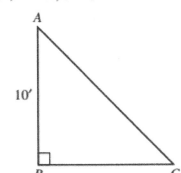

A. 5
B. 10
C. 20
D. $\sqrt{20}$
E. $10\sqrt{2}$

The hypotenuse must be the longest side, which eliminates all choices except $10\sqrt{2}$ and 20. By the triangle inequality, the sum of the 2 shorter sides needs to be greater than the longer side, so 20 is also impossible. Therefore, the solution must be $10\sqrt{2}$.

By the Pythagorean Theorem,

$$10^2 + 10^2 = x^2 \rightarrow 100 + 100 = x^2 \rightarrow 200 = x^2 \rightarrow x = 10\sqrt{2}.$$

It is also possible to use the ratio of an isosceles right triangle or $90 - 45 - 45$ triangle $1 - 1 - \sqrt{2}$. Therefore the hypotenuse is $10 \cdot \sqrt{2}$.

You could also use trigonometry,

$$\sin 45° = \frac{10}{x} \rightarrow x = \frac{10}{\sin 45°} = \frac{10}{.707} \cong 14.3 \cong 10\sqrt{2}.$$

Chapter 6 Midpoint and distance formula Pythagorean theorem

20. If a rectangle measures 54 meters by 72 meters, what
is the length, in meters, of the diagonal of the rectangle?

    F.   48
    G.   63
    H.   90
    J. 126
    K. 252

A and B are impossible because the hypotenuse of a right triangle must be longer than either leg. D
and E are impossible by the triangle inequality, the sum of the 2 shorter sides must be greater than
the longer side. Therefore, the answer in C.

This is a $3-4-5$ right triangle, so the hypotenuse must be 90.

By the Pythagorean theorem,

$$54^2 + 72^2 = c^2 \rightarrow 8100 = c^2 \rightarrow c = 90.$$

For all these solutions, it is important to recognize that the diagonal is the hypotenuse of a right
triangle.

Chapter 7 Rational expressions

38. For all x in the domain of the function $\frac{x+1}{x^3-x}$, this function is equivalent to:

F. $\frac{1}{x^2} - \frac{1}{x^3}$

G. $\frac{1}{x^3} - \frac{1}{x}$

H. $\frac{1}{x^2-1}$

J. $\frac{1}{x^2-x}$

K. $\frac{1}{x^3}$

It is possible to graph the expression in the problem and those in each of the answer choices and see which match (setting y equal to each expression). This might be useful to do when studying, but it is too time consuming to be a good approach for this problem on the exam.

A good non algebraic approach would be to substitute a number for x. If $x = 2$, the expression in the problem is

$$\frac{2+1}{2^3-2} = \frac{3}{6} = \frac{1}{2}.$$

F is $\frac{1}{4} - \frac{1}{8} = \frac{1}{8}$. G is $\frac{1}{8} - \frac{1}{2} = \frac{-3}{8}$. H is $\frac{1}{2^2-1} = \frac{1}{3}$. J is $\frac{1}{2^2-2} = \frac{1}{2}$. K is $\frac{1}{2^3} = \frac{1}{8}$. J is the only one that matches, so that is the answer.

Algebraically,

$$\frac{x+1}{x^3-x} = \frac{x+1}{x(x^2-1)} = \frac{x+1}{x(x+1)(x-1)} = \frac{1}{x(x-1)} = \frac{1}{x^2-x},$$

which is J.

Chapter 7 Rational expressions

36. For all $x > 21$, $\dfrac{(x^2 + 8x + 7)(x - 3)}{(x^2 + 4x - 21)(x + 1)} = ?$

F. 1

G. $\dfrac{9}{7}$

H. $\dfrac{x-3}{x+3}$

J. $\dfrac{2(x-3)}{x+1}$

K. $-\dfrac{4(x-3)}{x+1}$

Ignore the "for all $x > 21$". That is just to ensure you are not dividing by 0 and appears intended to confuse and discourage students considering using graphing or making up numbers. It is a trap that you might try to substitute in 22 for x and have to deal with difficult large numbers.

If you set y equal to the expression in the statement of the problem and graph it, you will see it is the line $y = 1$, so F. If it was a more complicated curve, you might need to also graph the last 3 choices.

I would start by substituting $x = 1$ for x,

$$\frac{(1^2 + 8 \cdot 1 + 7)(1 - 3)}{(1^2 + 4 \cdot 1 - 21)(1 + 1)} = \frac{16 \cdot (-2)}{(-16) \cdot 2} = \frac{-32}{-32} = 1,$$

so F. If you instead substituted 2, you would get

$$\frac{(2^2 + 8 \cdot 2 + 7)(2 - 3)}{(2^2 + 4 \cdot 2 - 21)(2 + 1)} = \frac{27 \cdot (-1)}{(-9) \cdot 3} = \frac{-27}{-27} = 1.$$

Factoring,

$$\frac{(x + 7)(x + 1)(x - 3)}{(x + 7)(x - 3)(x + 1)}.$$

All factors cancel out, so we have 1, which is F.

If you do not know how to factor, you could use the quadratic formula,

$$\frac{-b \pm \sqrt{b^2 - 4ac}}{2a}.$$

For $x^2 + 8x + 7$, we have

$$\frac{-8 \pm \sqrt{8^2 - 4 \cdot 1 \cdot 7}}{2} = \frac{-8 \pm \sqrt{36}}{2} = \frac{-8 \pm 6}{2} = -7$$

or -1, $x + 7 = 0$ or $x + 1 = 0$, so $(x + 7)(x + 1)$. You could factor $x^2 + 4x - 21$ similarly. This approach is not ideal, but could be useful if you have extra time at the end.

Technically, you could also use completing the square. $x^2 + 8x + 7 = 0 \rightarrow x^2 + 8x + 16 = 9 \rightarrow (x + 4)^2 = 9 \rightarrow x + 4 = \pm 3 \rightarrow x = -4 \pm 3 = -7$ or -1 and you could proceed to the factorization as with the quadratic formula.

Chapter 7 Rational Expressions

45. For all $x \neq \pm y$, $\dfrac{x}{x+y} + \dfrac{y}{x-y} = ?$

   A. $\dfrac{1}{x-y}$

   B. $\dfrac{x+y}{x-y}$

   C. $\dfrac{x+y}{2x}$

   D. $x^2 + y^2$

   E. $\dfrac{x^2+y^2}{x^2-y^2}$

Making up numbers, set $x = 5$ and $y = 2$ (it is better to use $x > y > 0$ to avoid dealing with negative numbers). Then the expression in the problem is

$$\frac{5}{5+2} + \frac{2}{5-2} = \frac{5}{7} + \frac{2}{3} = \frac{29}{21}.$$

A would be $\dfrac{1}{5-3} = \dfrac{1}{2}$. B is $\dfrac{5+2}{5-2} = \dfrac{7}{3}$. C is $\dfrac{5+2}{2 \cdot 5} = \dfrac{7}{10}$. D is $5^2 + 2^2 = 29$. E is $\dfrac{5^2 + 2^2}{5^2 - 2^2} = \dfrac{29}{21}$, so E is the answer.

Algebraically,

$$\frac{x(x-y) + y(x+y)}{(x+y)(x-y)} = \frac{x^2 - xy + xy + y^2}{x^2 - y^2} = \frac{x^2 + y^2}{x^2 - y^2}.$$

Which is E.

Chapter 8 Fundamental Topics: Exponents

4. Which of the following is equivalent to $(4x^2)^3$?

    F. $64x^8$

    G. $64x^6$

    H. $12x^6$

    J. $12x^5$

    K. $4x^6$

You can plug in 1 for x, giving 64 in the expression in the problem. Only F and G give 64, so you could guess between them. You could also now plug in 2 for x and check F and G. If $x = 2$, the expression in the problem is 4,096. F would be 16,384, but G would be 4,096, so G is the answer.

If you did not know how to do the exponentiation, you could write it as $4x^2 \cdot 4x^2 \cdot 4x^2 = 64x^6$, which would not be practical with higher exponents.

$$(4x^2)^3 = 4^3 \cdot (x^2)^3 = 64x^6.$$

Note that the problem tests the laws of exponents, $(x^2)^3 = x^6$, not x^5. Also, you need to cube the 4, as well as the variable expression.

Chapter 10 Lines

35. Which of the following is the graph of the equation $2x + y = 4$ in the standard (x,y) coordinate plane?

A. 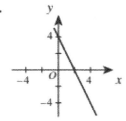   **B.** 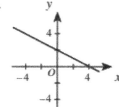   **C.**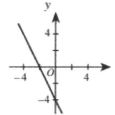

D. 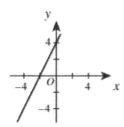   **E.**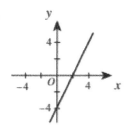

You can convert the equation to slope-intercept form $y = -2x + 4$, graph with your calculator, and determine that the answer is Choice A.

With the equation in slope-intercept form $y = -2x + 4$, the slope is -2 and the y-intercept is 4, so Choice A.

You could also find the $x-$ and y-intercepts, $2x + y = 4$, $2 \cdot 0 + y = 4 \rightarrow y = 4$ or $(0, 4)$. $2x + 0 = 4 \rightarrow 2x = 4 \rightarrow x = 2$ or $(2, 0)$. These results also match Choice A only.

Chapter 14 Radicals

48. $\dfrac{4}{\sqrt{2}} + \dfrac{2}{\sqrt{3}} = ?$

    F. $\dfrac{4\sqrt{3}+2\sqrt{2}}{\sqrt{5}}$

    G. $\dfrac{4\sqrt{3}+2\sqrt{2}}{\sqrt{6}}$

    H. $\dfrac{6}{\sqrt{2}+\sqrt{3}}$

    J. $\dfrac{6}{\sqrt{5}}$

    K. $\dfrac{8}{\sqrt{6}}$

This problem is nasty, because if you rationalize the denominators as you presumably have been taught to do, you get

$$2\sqrt{2} + 2\frac{\sqrt{3}}{3} = \frac{6\sqrt{2}+2\sqrt{3}}{3},$$

which is not obviously any of the answer choices. You might be able to guess from there that the answer is F or G, and that G makes more sense than F.

Crunching with your calculator, the expression at the top is about 3.98. F is about 4.36. G is about 3.98, so that is the answer.

The trick is to use the least common denominator $\sqrt{6}$,

$$\frac{4}{\sqrt{2}} \cdot \frac{\sqrt{3}}{\sqrt{3}} + \frac{2}{\sqrt{3}} \cdot \frac{\sqrt{2}}{\sqrt{2}} = \frac{4\sqrt{3}+2\sqrt{2}}{\sqrt{6}}.$$

So the answer is G.

---

22. If $x + y = 32$, and $x - y = 12$, then $y = ?$

    F. 6
    G. 10
    H. 20
    J. 22
    K. 44

Backsolving, substituting $y = 6$, then $x + 6 = 32 \rightarrow x = 26$, $26 - 6 = 12 \rightarrow 20 = 12$, which is false. Substituting $y = 10$, $x + 10 = 32 \rightarrow x = 22$, $22 - 10 = 12 \rightarrow 12 = 12$, which works, so G is the answer. This approach is time consuming and should only be used if the student has time and does not know algebraic approaches.

Adding the equations, we get $2x = 44 \rightarrow x = 22$, $22 + y = 32 \rightarrow y = 10$, so G.

Solving by substitution, $x = 12 + y$, $12 + y + y = 32 \rightarrow 2y = 20 \rightarrow y = 10$, so G.

Chapter 16 Quadratic Equations

28. If $2x^2 + 6x = 36$, what are the possible values of x ?

    F.   −12 and 3
    G.   −6 and 3
    H.   −3 and 6
    J.   −3 and 12
    K.   12 and 15

It is easier to simplify $2x^2 + 6x = 36$ to $x^2 + 3x = 18$. It is also possible, but harder, to work with the problem in its original form.

If you do not know how to approach the problem otherwise and have plenty of time, you can plug in the answer choices. This approach is not generally recommended, and is sort of a time trap, but does work. The choices are -12, -6, -3, 3, 6, 12, and 15.

$$(-12)^2 + 3(-12) = 18 \rightarrow 144 - 36 = 18, \quad 108 = 18, \qquad \text{which is false.}$$

$$(-6)^2 + 3 \cdot (-6) = 18 \rightarrow 36 - 18 = 18, \quad 18 = 18, \qquad \text{which works.}$$

$$(-3)^2 + 3(-3) = 18 \rightarrow 9 - 9 = 18 \rightarrow 0 = 18, \qquad \text{which is false.}$$

$$3^2 + 3 \cdot 3 = 18 \rightarrow 9 + 9 = 18 \rightarrow 18 = 18, \qquad \text{which works.}$$

There cannot be more than 2 solutions to a quadratic, so we have our answers, -6 and 3.

A more effective approach would be to graph $y = x^2 + 3x - 18$ with your calculator and find the point where the parabola intersects the x-axis. You could also graph $y = x^2 + 3x$ and $y = 18$ and find the intersection points.

Since this is a quadratic, get all the terms on one side. $x^2 + 3x - 18 = 0$. This can be factored

$$x^2 + 6x - 3x - 18 = 0 \rightarrow x(x+6) - 3(x+6) = 0 \rightarrow (x-3)(x+6) = 0 \rightarrow x - 3 = 0$$

or $x + 6 = 0 \rightarrow x = 3$ or $x = -6$.

You can also use the quadratic formula,

$$\frac{-b \pm \sqrt{b^2 - 4ac}}{2a} \quad \text{for an equation in the form of } ax^2 + bx + c = 0.$$

$$\frac{-3 \pm \sqrt{3^2 - 4 \cdot 1 \cdot (-18)}}{2} = \frac{-3 \pm \sqrt{9 + 72}}{2} = \frac{-3 \pm \sqrt{81}}{2} = \frac{-3 \pm 9}{2} = \frac{-12}{2} \text{ or } \frac{6}{2} = -6 \text{ or } 3.$$

Chapter 16 Quadratic Equations

23. Which of the following is a factored form of the expression $5x^2 - 13x - 6$?

    A. $(x - 3)(5x + 2)$
    B. $(x - 2)(5x - 3)$
    C. $(x - 2)(5x + 3)$
    D. $(x + 2)(5x - 3)$
    E. $(x + 3)(5x - 2)$

We can plug in a number, 4, for x. Then the expression in the problem is $5 \cdot 4^2 - 13 \cdot 4 - 6 = 80 - 52 - 6 = 22$. Substituting 4 into Choice A, we get 22. Therefore A is probably the answer, so in practice we could stop at that point. Into B, we get 34; into C, we get 46; into D, we get 102; into E, we get 126. So A is the answer.

You could also FOIL out each answer choice and see which gives the expression in the problem. In general, this could be a time trap. However, in this case, if you did A first, you would see it is correct and that is the answer.

Factor $5x^2 - 13x - 6$. We need two numbers which add to -13 and multiply to $-30 = (5 \cdot (-6))$. 2 and -15.

$$5x^2 - 15x + 2x - 6 \rightarrow 5x(x - 3) + 2(x - 3) \rightarrow (5x + 2)(x - 3).$$

With the quadratic formula,

$$\frac{-b \pm \sqrt{b^2 - 4ac}}{2a}, \quad \frac{13 \pm \sqrt{(-13)^2 - 4 \cdot 5 \cdot (-6)}}{2 \cdot 5} = \frac{13 \pm \sqrt{169 + 120}}{10} = \frac{13 \pm \sqrt{289}}{10} = \frac{13 \pm 17}{10},$$

so

$$\frac{30}{10} \quad \text{or} \quad \frac{-4}{10} \rightarrow 3 \quad \text{or} \quad \frac{-2}{5} \rightarrow x = 3 \quad \text{or} \quad x = \frac{-2}{5} \rightarrow (x - 3)\left(x + \frac{2}{5}\right) \rightarrow (x - 3)(5x + 2).$$

We can multiply by 5 as the equation is set to 0.

Chapter 16 Quadratic Equations

42. What are the real solutions to the equation
$|x|^2 + 2|x| - 3 = 0$?

   F. ± 1
   G. ± 3
   H. 1 and 3
   J. -1 and -3
   K. ± 1 and ± 3

The best way to do this problem is backsolving, plugging in the answer choices. 1 and -1 work, but 3 and -3 do not work.

You should also be able to graph $y =$ the expression and find the x-intercept.

You can split it into 2 problems, $x^2 + 2x - 3 = 0$ for $x > 0$ and $x^2 - 2x - 3 = 0$ for $x < 0$. I will show solving by factoring, but you could also use the quadratic formula and you could theoretically use completing the square. $x^2 + 2x - 3 = 0 \to x^2 + 3x - x - 3 = 0 \to x(x+3) - 1(x+3) = 0 \to (x-1)(x+3) = 0 \to x = 1$ or $x = -3$. Only 1 is in the range and only 1 checks in the original equation. $x^2 + -2x - 3 = 0 \to x^2 + x - 3x - 3 = 0 \to x(x+1) - 3(x+1) = 0 \to (x-3)(x+1) = 0 \to x = 3$ or $x = -1$. Only -1 is in the range and only -1 checks in the original equation. Therefore the solutions are ± 1.

Chapter 20 Solving for a Variable

32. For all pairs of real numbers M and V where $M = 3V + 6$, $V = ?$

    F. $\dfrac{M}{3} - 6$

    G. $\dfrac{M}{3} + 6$

    H. $3M - 6$

    J. $\dfrac{M - 6}{3}$

    K. $\dfrac{M + 6}{3}$

In the expression at the top, let $V = 4$. Then $M = 3 \cdot 4 + 6 = 18$. Substituting 18 for M in F, we get 0. In G, we get 12, in H 48, but in J 4, so J is the right answer.

Algebraically, $M = 3V + 6 \rightarrow M - 6 = 3V \rightarrow \dfrac{M - 6}{3} = V$, which is J.

Chapter 21 Polynomials

27. Which of the following expressions is a factor of $x^3 - 64$?

    A. $x - 4$
    B. $x + 4$
    C. $x + 64$
    D. $x^2 + 16$
    E. $x^2 - 4x + 16$

This is an interesting problem. You sort of need to know the difference of cubes formula, but there is an interesting way to do it by substituting in numbers.

Letting $x = 1$, the expression in the problem is -63. A is -3, B is 5, C is 65, D is 17, E is 13. Only A$= -3$ is a factor of -63.

The difference of cubes formula is $a^3 - b^3 = (a - b)(a^2 + ab + b^2)$. In $x^3 - 64$, $a = x$ and $b = 4$, $(x - 4)(x^2 + 4x + 16)$. Therefore $x - 4$ is a factor.

Chapter 22 Trigonometry

49. If $\tan A = \frac{a}{b}$, $a > 0$, $b > 0$, and $0 < A < \frac{\pi}{2}$, then what is $\cos A$?

A. $\frac{a}{b}$

B. $\frac{b}{a}$

C. $\dfrac{a}{\sqrt{a^2 + b^2}}$

D. $\dfrac{b}{\sqrt{a^2 + b^2}}$

E. $\dfrac{\sqrt{a^2 + b^2}}{b}$

Let $a = 3$ and $b = 4$. Then draw a right triangle and the hypotenuse $= 5$ by the Pythagorean theorem or $3 - 4 - 5$ triangles. So

$$\cos x = \frac{\text{adjacent}}{\text{hypotenuse}} = \frac{4}{5}.$$

Plugging in 3 for a and 4 for b in each answer choice, $A = \frac{3}{4}$, $B = \frac{4}{3}$, $C = \frac{3}{5}$, $D = \frac{4}{5}$, which is the answer, so D.

Draw a right triangle. Let opposite $= a$ and adjacent $= b$. So hypotenuse is $\sqrt{a^2 + b^2}$. Therefore

$$\cos x = \frac{\text{adjacent}}{\text{hypotenuse}} = \frac{b}{\sqrt{a^2 + b^2}},$$

which is D.

Using the identity

$$\sec^2 = 1 + \tan^2,$$

$$\sec^2 x = 1 + \left(\frac{a}{b}\right)^2 \rightarrow \sec^2 x = 1 + \frac{a^2}{b^2} \rightarrow \sec^2 x = \frac{b^2 + a^2}{b^2} \rightarrow \sec x = \frac{\sqrt{b^2 + a^2}}{b}$$

(we are only interested in the positive value since the angle is in the 1st quadrant.

$$\cos x = \frac{1}{\sec x} = \frac{b}{\sqrt{b^2 + a^2}},$$

which is D.

Chapter 23 Logarithms

60. What is the real value of x in the equation
$\log_2 24 - \log_2 3 = \log_5 x$?

    F.   3
    G. 21
    H. 72
    J. 125
    K. 243

You could guess J, because it asks for $\log_5 x$. 125 is the only answer which is a multiple of 5, so it is the only answer possible if the log is an integer.

You can also use the change of base formula

$$\frac{\ln 24}{\ln 2} - \frac{\ln 3}{\ln 2} = 3 \quad \text{and} \quad \frac{\log 24}{\log 2} - \frac{\log 3}{\log 2} = 3.$$

Then take $5^3 = 125$.

Algebraically,

$$\log_2 24 - \log_2 3 = \log_2 \frac{24}{3}$$

by the laws of logarithms $\log_2 8 = 3$. Then $5^3 = 125$.

Chapter 23 Logarithms

49. The value of $\log_5\left(5^{\frac{13}{2}}\right)$ is between which of the following pairs of consecutive integers?

    A. 0 and 1
    B. 4 and 5
    C. 5 and 6
    D. 6 and 7
    E. 9 and 10

$$5^{\left(\frac{13}{2}\right)} \cong 34,939. \quad \frac{\log 34,939}{\log 5} \cong 6.5 \quad \text{and} \quad \frac{\ln 34,939}{\ln 5} \cong 6.5,$$

both by the change of base formula. It is worthwhile to practice this problem with the change of base formula even if you know the easier solution.

By the definition of logarithms, $\log_a a^b = b$ and $a^{\log_a b} = b$. Therefore

$$\log_5 5^{\left(\frac{13}{2}\right)} = \frac{13}{2}$$

or 6.5

Chapter 23 Logarithms

49. What is the value of $\log_2 8$?

    A. 3
    B. 4
    C. 6
    D. 10
    E. 16

If you notice that $2^3 = 8$, then by the definition of logarithms, you can find the answer is 3.

If you do not know that, you can take $\ln 8 \cong 2.07$ with your calculator, which is closest to 3 of all the choices. You could assume than $\ln 8$ is close to $\log_2$ of 8, since $e \cong 2.718\ldots$ is close to 2.

If you know the change of base formula, you can take $\dfrac{\ln 8}{\ln 2}$ or $\dfrac{\log 8}{\log 2}$, both of which are approximately equal t3 2.

Chapter 24 Complex numbers

46. For $i^2 = -1$, $(4 + i)^2 = ?$

    F. 15
    G. 17
    H. $15 + 4i$
    J. $15 + 8i$
    K. $16 + 4i$

$(4+i)^2 = (4+i)(4+i) = 16 + 4i + 4i + i^2 = 16 + 8i + i^2 = 15 + 8i$. Since they tell you that $i^2 = -1$, you could do the problem correctly knowing nothing about complex numbers.

It is a trap to not FOIL it out and take $4^2 + i^2 = 16 - 1 = 15$.

Note that only the correct answer choice contains $8i$, so you should be able to immediately determine that is the answer after FOILing, even without understanding complex multiplication.

This is not a recommended approach, but it useful for understanding the problem and checking that your answer is correct. Some honors precalculus classes teach about complex numbers in polar form. I am not going explain this in detail. However, in polar form, $4 + i$ is

$$\left(\sqrt{4^2 + 1^2}, \tan^{-1} \frac{1}{4} \right) = \left(\sqrt{17}, 14° \right).$$

Therefore, $(4 + i)^2 = (17, 28°)$. Choice G is $(17, 0°)$, but Choice J is $(17, 28°)$.

Chapter 28 Combinations and Permutations

37. What is the maximum number of distinct diagonals that can be drawn in the hexagon shown below?

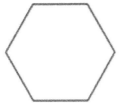

A. 4
B. 5
C. 6
D. 9
E. 12

You could eliminate choices A, B, and C as obviously too small and guess between D and E.

It is possible to draw and count the diagonals. It is best to do that methodically, but I will not get into systems for that.

You can also use combinations as follows: $_6C_2$ is the number of ways of connecting two points from that you substract 6 for the 6 edges, which are not considered diagonals.

$$_6C_2 = \frac{6!}{(6-2)! \cdot 2!} = \frac{6!}{(4! \cdot 2!)} = \frac{6 \cdot 5}{2} = 15.$$

You should also be to get combinations with your calculator without using the formula.

$$\text{Number of connections} - \text{number of edges} = 15 - 6 = 9,$$

which is the answer.

Note that they could ask for the number of diagonals for an 8 or more sided polygon, in which cases drawing the diagonals could be difficult. I recommend practicing this problem with larger number of sides polygons both by drawing the diagonals and with combinations. I also recommend practicing calculating combinations and permutations both using the formula with and without a calculator and by using the combinations key on your calculator. It is possible you will need to find combinations without a calculator on the no calculator portion of the math SAT. Usually, combinations problems on the math ACT are $_xC_2$, involving matching pairs of items as here.

Chapter 30 Composition of Functions

32. Given $f(x) = 4x + 1$ and $g(x) = x^2 - 2$, which of the following is an expression for $f(g(x))$?

F. $-x^2 + 4x + 1$

G. $x^2 + 4x - 1$

H. $4x^2 - 7$

J. $4x^2 - 1$

K. $16x^2 + 8x - 1$

Most books recommend that you not substitute 1 for a variable, but for this problem, 1 makes it easiest. Then $g(1) = 1^2 - 2 = -1$ and $f(g(1)) = 4 \cdot (-1) + 1 = -3$. It is clear looking at the answer choices that substituting 1 gives -3 for H and no other choice.

If you substituted 4 for x, $g(4) = 4^2 - 2 = 14$ and $f(g(4)) = 4 \cdot 14 + 1 = 57$. In H, we have $4x^2 - 7 \rightarrow 4 \cdot 4^2 - 7 = 64 - 7 = 57$. You can verify that the other answer choices do not yield 57.

Algebraically, $f(g(x)) = 4(x^2 - 2) + 1 = 4x^2 - 8 + 1 = 4x^2 - 7$.

Chapter 30 Composition of Functions

53. Given that $f(x) = x^2 - 4$ and $g(x) = x + 3$, what are all the values of x for which $f(g(x)) = 0$?

A. -5 and -1

B. $-3, -2,$ and 2

C. -1 and 1

D. 1 and 5

E. $-\sqrt{5}$ and $\sqrt{5}$

Backsolving does not look like a good idea, as there are 9 possible answers included in the answer choices. However, if we try that starting at the top, we get $g(-5) = -2$ and $f(-2) = 0$; $g(-1) = 2$ and $f(2) = 0$. Therefore A is the answer.

If we work backwards, setting $f(x) = 0$, then $x^2 - 4 = 0 \rightarrow x = 2$ or $x = -2$. Set

$$g(x) = x + 3 = 2 \rightarrow x = -1;$$

setting $x + 3 = -2 \rightarrow x = -5$.

Working algebraically,

$$f(g(x)) = (x + 3)^2 - 4 = x^2 + 6x + 9 - 4 = x^2 + 6x + 5 = (x + 5)(x + 1).$$

The solutions to $(x + 5)(x + 1) = 0$ are -1 and -5. You could also solve the quadratic equation by the quadratic formula or completing the squares.

Chapter 32 Exponential Equations

49. In the real numbers, what is the solution of the equation $8^{2x+1} = 4^{1-x}$?

A. $-\dfrac{1}{3}$

B. $-\dfrac{1}{4}$

C. $-\dfrac{1}{8}$

D. 0

E. $\dfrac{1}{7}$

Backsolving is a reasonable approach to this problem. For A,

$$8^{2\frac{-1}{3}+1} = 4^{1-\frac{-1}{3}} \rightarrow 8^{\frac{1}{3}} = 4^{\frac{4}{3}} \rightarrow 2 = 4 \cdot \sqrt[3]{4},$$

which is clearly wrong.

$$8^{2\frac{-1}{4}+1} = 4^{1-\frac{-1}{4}} \rightarrow 8^{\frac{1}{2}} = 4^{\frac{5}{4}} \rightarrow 2^{\frac{3}{2}} = 2^{\frac{5}{2}}$$

or $\approx 4.76 = 5.66$, which is wrong. For C,

$$8^{2\frac{-1}{8}+1} = 4^{1-\frac{-1}{8}} \rightarrow 8^{\frac{3}{4}} = 4^{\frac{9}{8}} \rightarrow 2^{\frac{9}{4}} = 2^{\frac{9}{4}}$$

or $4.76 = 4.76$, so C is the answer.

$$(2x+1)\ln 8 = (1-x)\ln 4 \rightarrow (2x+1)$$

$$2.08 = (1-x) \quad 1.39 \rightarrow 4.16x + 2.08 = 1.39 - 1.39x \rightarrow 5.55x = -.69 \rightarrow x = -0.124 \cong \frac{-1}{8}.$$

The most elegant solution is

$$8^{2x+1} = 4^{1-x} \rightarrow 2^{3^{2x+1}} = 2^{2^{1-x}} \rightarrow 2^{6x+3} = 2^{2-2x}$$

(equating exponents or taking the $\log_2$ of both sides) $6x + 3 = 2 - 2x \rightarrow 8x = -1 \rightarrow x = \dfrac{-1}{8}.$

Chapter 32 Exponential Equations

33. For a population that grows at a constant rate of $r\%$ per year, the formula $P(t) = p_o\left(1 + \dfrac{r}{100}\right)^t$ models the population t years after an initial population of p_o people is counted.

The population of the city of San Jose was 782,000 in 1990. Assume the population grows at a constant rate of 5% per year. According to this formula, which of the following is an expression for the population of San Jose in the year 2000 ?

A. $782,000(6)^{10}$

B. $782,000(1.5)^{10}$

C. $782,000(1.05)^{10}$

D. $(782,000 \times 1.5)^{10}$

E. $(782,000 \times 1.05)^{10}$

If you try the choices out with your calculator, all yield huge numbers, except for Choice C. If you apply the formula,

$$782,000\left(1 + \frac{5}{100}\right)^{10} = 782,000 \; (1.05)^{10},$$

which is C. Note this formula is the same as the simple interest formula.

Chapter 35 Other Advanced: Area of Region

33. In the figure below, *ABCD* is a square. Points are chosen on each pair of adjacent sides of *ABCD* to form 4 congruent right triangles, as shown below. Each of these has one leg that is twice as long as the other leg. What fraction of the area of square *ABCD* is shaded?

A. $\frac{1}{9}$

B. $\frac{2}{9}$

C. $\frac{4}{9}$

D. $\frac{5}{9}$

E. $\frac{8}{9}$

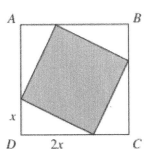

The diagram is drawn to scale, and it is obvious looking at it that the shaded region is about half of the total region, so $\frac{5}{9}$ and $\frac{4}{9}$ are the only possible answers. The shaded region appears to be more than half of the total, so $\frac{5}{9}$ is the likely answer.

You can do the computation with x, but it is easier to set the sides of the triangle to 1 and 2 and the side of the square to 3. Then the area of each white triangle is

$$\frac{b \cdot h}{2} = \frac{1 \cdot 2}{2} = 1.$$

There are 4 such triangles, so the total white area is $1 \cdot 4 = 4$. The area of the square is $3 \cdot 3 = 9$. Therefore, the area of the shaded region is $9 - 4 = 5$. The shaded region is $\frac{5}{9}$ of the triangle.

Another approach, which is more difficult, is to find the sides of the shaded square. Using the Pythagorean Theorem, $1^2 + 2^2 = y^2 \rightarrow 1 + 4 = y^2 \rightarrow 5 = y^2 \rightarrow y = \sqrt{5}$. The area of the shaded square is then $(\sqrt{5})^2 = 5$. The area of the larger square is $3^2 = 9$. Therefore the shaded square is $\frac{5}{9}$ of the larger square.

Chapter 35 Other Advanced

34. If $a = b + 2$, then $(b - a)^4 = ?$

    F. −16

    G. −8

    H.   1

    J.   8

    K. 16

Let $b = 5$, so $a = 7$. Then $(b - a)^4$ is $(-2)^4 = 16$, so K.

Algebraically, $a = b + 2 \rightarrow b - a = -2$. Therefore $(b - a)^4 = (-2)^4 = 16$, so K.

Note this is a calculator trap. You can incorrectly compute $(-2)^4$ as -2^4 with a calculator and get -16.

Chapter 35 Other Advanced: Parametric Equations

59. If $x = 2t - 9$ and $y = 5 - t$, which of the following
expresses y in terms of x ?

A. $y = \dfrac{1 - x}{2}$

B. $y = \dfrac{19 - x}{2}$

C. $y = 14 - 2x$

D. $y = 5 - x$

E. $y = 1 - x$

Using the nature of parametric equations, set $t = 2$: then $x = -5$ and $y = 3$. Substituting into a

$$3 = \frac{1 - (-5)}{2} \rightarrow 3 = 3,$$

so A works. The other choices do not work. A will work for any t value you pick.

Algebraically, $t = 5 - y$, (substituting)

$$x = 2(5 - y) - 9 \rightarrow x = 10 - 2y - 9 \rightarrow x = 1 - 2y \rightarrow 2y = 1 - x \rightarrow y = \frac{1 - x}{2}.$$

Solving first for t in terms of x,

$$2t = x + 9 \rightarrow t = \frac{x + 9}{2} \rightarrow \text{(substituting)} \ y = 5 - \frac{x + 9}{2} \rightarrow y = \frac{10 - x - 9}{2} \rightarrow y = \frac{1 - x}{2}.$$

Chapter 35 Other Advanced: Equations and Values

25. The expression $-8x^3(7x^6 - 3x^5)$ is equivalent to:

    A. $-56x^9 + 24x^8$

    B. $-56x^9 - 24x^8$

    C. $-56x^{18} + 24x^{15}$

    D. $-56x^{18} - 24x^{15}$

    E. $-32x^4$

This is an interesting problem in that nonalgebraic approaches do not work well. You could graph $y = $ the expression and $y = $ each answer choice. However, that involves 6 graphs and the high degrees and high coefficients will make it difficult to read the graphs.

If you plug in 1 for x, the expression in the problem is -32 and A, C, and E are all also -32. Now you could guess after narrowing it down. You could also maybe eliminate E, which is 1 term. You could plug in 2 for x or maybe 1.1 or 0.5, but the calculations will be difficult, and that is much harder than just solving this relatively easy problem algebraically.

The problem tests multiplication of negative numbers and use of the laws of exponents. Distributing gives $-56x^9 + 24x^8$.

Other Topics

19. For the function $h(x) = 4x^2 - 5x$, what is the value of $h(-3)$?

    A. -93
    B. -9
    C. 21
    D. 51
    E. 159

You can graph $y = $ the expression and find the y-value for $x = -3$. You would need to set the screen parameters for fairly large y-value.

It is best to do the math on paper for this

$$4 \cdot (-3)^2 - 5(-3) = 4 \cdot 9 + 15 = 51.$$

You can do it with a calculator, but that can introduce errors with the negative value, such as you can do $-3^2 = -9$ rather than the correct $(-3)^2 = 9$.

Made in the USA
Monee, IL
11 April 2025